英語版
アジア太平洋地域におけるロッテルダム・ルールズ

The Rotterdam Rules in the Asia-Pacific Region

Edited by Tomotaka Fujita

商事法務

Preface

On December 11, 2008, during its 63rd session, the UN General Assembly adopted the "United Nations Convention on Contracts for the International Carriage of Goods Wholly or Partly by Sea." The draft Convention had been discussed by the United Nations Commission on International Trade Law (UNCITRAL) since 2002 as the new rule that would replace the existing international conventions on the carriage of goods by sea, such as the Hague-Visby Rules or the Hamburg Rules. The Convention was opened for signatures at the signing ceremony in Rotterdam on September 23, 2009. To date, twenty-five states have signed, and three have ratified the Convention[1]. Several countries are reported to be preparing their own ratifications.

The Convention known as the "Rotterdam Rules" is a large code consisting of 96 articles, and it includes noteworthy provisions regarding e-commerce, right of control, delivery of goods, and special rules for volume contracts (an exception to the mandatory regulations). Industry groups are interested in the new rules and have actively expressed their views. Many symposia, seminars, and colloquia on the Rotterdam Rules have been organized around the world. Unfortunately, the Rotterdam Rules have not yet been fully recognized by governments, industries, or academia in the Asian region, including Japan. Hence, the Japanese Maritime Law Association, in cooperation with the University of Tokyo's Global COE Program, organized an international symposium featuring the experts who contributed to the drafting of the Convention, prominent lawyers from the Asian region, and people from the industry. The symposium was held on November 21 and 22, 2011 at Kaiun-kaikan Tokyo. The symposium was intended to enhance the understanding of the Rotterdam Rules by the people involved in the carriage of goods by sea. This book is the comprehensive record of the symposium.

This book consists of three parts. **Part I** is divided into five chapters that comprise the presentations at the symposium. **Chapter 1: Introduction to the Rotterdam Rules** explains the features of the Convention, how it evolved, and the interested parties' involve-

---

[1] Signatories as of March 2014 are as follows: Armenia (29 Sep. 2009), Cameroon (29 Sep. 2009), Congo (23 Sep. 2009, ratified 28 Jan. 2014), Democratic Republic of the Congo (23 Sep. 2010), Denmark (23 Sep. 2009), France (23 Sep. 2009), Gabon (23 Sep. 2009), Ghana (23 Sep. 2009), Greece (23 Sep. 2009), Guinea (23 Sep. 2009), Guinea-Bissau (24 Sep. 2013), Luxembourg (31 Aug. 2010), Madagascar (25 Sep. 2009), Mali (26 Oct. 2009), Netherlands (23 Sep. 2009), Niger (22 Oct. 2009), Nigeria (23 Sep. 2009), Norway (23 Sep. 2009), Poland (23 Sep. 2009), Senegal (23 Sep. 2009), Spain (23 Sep. 2009, ratified 19 Jan 2011), Sweden (20 Jul. 2011), Switzerland (23 Sep. 2009), Togo (23 Sep. 2009, ratified 17 Jul. 2012),United States of America (23 Sep. 2009).

ment in the negotiation. **Chapter 2: Coverage and the Parties' Liabilities under the Rotterdam Rules** examines the liability regime under the Convention. The obligations and liabilities of the carrier and the shipper, carrier's period of responsibility, the Convention's scope of application and the mandatory nature of the rules are discussed in the chapter. **Chapter 3: Aspects of Transport Regulated by the Rotterdam Rules** deals with aspects, other than the liability regime, that are governed by the Convention, i.e., transport documents and electronic transport records, right of control, transfer of rights, and delivery of goods. These issues are not fully addressed by the existing conventions on the carriage of goods by sea. Based on the examination provided in the preceding three chapters, **Chapter 4: Rotterdam Rules and Industries** evaluates the Convention from the viewpoints of relevant industries, i.e., carriers, cargo interests, freight forwarders, and insurers. Finally, **Chapter 5: The Rotterdam Rules and Asia-Pacific States** provides the latest information[2] about the acceptance of the Convention in Asia-Pacific countries.

Part II is devoted to **"Workshop on the Rotterdam Rules."** The panelists discussed the fourteen cases distributed in the symposium. The workshop, which extended for more than four hours, focused on how the Rotterdam Rules worked under specific situations and examined the practical difference between the Hague-Visby Rules and the Rotterdam Rules. The questions prepared by the practitioners and academics in Japan included issues of practical and theoretical importance. The panelists in this workshop provided analyses that clarify for the reader how the Rotterdam Rules work in practical contexts.

Part III comprises the text of the Rotterdam Rules. Because some errors were found in the original text of the Rotterdam Rules, the Secretary General of the United Nations, in its capacity as the depositary, commenced the correction procedure on October 11, 2012. The corrections took effect on January 9, 2013[3]. The text in this book includes these corrections.

I wish to express my sincere gratitude to UNCITRAL, Comité Maritime International (CMI), the Ministry of Foreign Affairs, the Ministry of Justice, the Ministry of Land, Infrastructure, Transport and Tourism, and the Institute of Maritime Law (Waseda University) for their sponsorship of the symposium. I also thank the Japanese Institute of International Business Law, Inc., the Egusa Foundation for International Cooperation in the Social Sciences, the Commercial Law Centre, Inc., the Japan International Freight Forwarders Association, Inc., the Japan Shipping Exchange, Inc., the Japan Maritime Center, the Japanese Shipowners' Association, the Japan Ship Owners' Mutual Protection & Indemnity Associa-

---

[2] This chapter includes information that was updated after the symposium.
[3] For the procedure to correct errors in the texts of international treaties, *see* Article 79(2) of the Vienna Convention on the Law of Treaties, 1969.

tion, and the Nomura Foundation for their financial support of the symposium. I owe many thanks to Mr. Mitsuo Matsuzawa and Mr. Yasushi Kanno who took charge of the organization of the symposium. Finally, I am grateful to Mr. Hidetoshi Onodera and Mr. Yoshiyuki Shibuya (Shojihomu Co., Ltd.) for their efforts in publishing this book.

March 2014

Tomotaka Fujita

Contents

Preface i
About authors xi

Part I, Chapter 1
Introduction to the Rotterdam Rules 1

  1 The Role of UNCITRAL and the Current Status of the Rotterdam Rules 3
  2 The Need for Change and the Role of the CMI 9
  3 Basic elements and features of the Rotterdam Rules: Five Words on the
      Rules 16
      I. Introduction 16
      II. Modernization 17
      III. Flexibility 19
      IV. Freedom 20
      V. Comprehensivity 21
      VI. Balance 21

Part I, Chapter 2
Coverage and the Parties Liabilities under the Rotterdam Rules 29

  4 Scope of Application and Freedom of Contract 31
      I. Scope of Application 32
      II. Freedom of Contract 49
      III. Conclusion 64
  5 Period of Responsibility and Multimodal Aspects 66
      I. Introduction 66
      II. The Carrier's Period of Responsibility: "Door-to-door" Application of
          the Convention 67
      III. Multimodal Aspects 70
      IV. The Regulation of "Performing Parties" 74
      V. Conclusions 78
  6 The Obligations and Liability Of The Carrier 79
      I. Background 79
      II. The carrier's obligations concerning carriage of goods 80
      III. The carrier's liability for loss of or damage to the goods 81

  IV. The carrier's liability for delay in the delivery of the goods and certain other matters 86
  V. Conclusions 87
 7 Shipper's Obligation 88
  I. Introduction 88
  II. Various Cargo Interests 89
  III. Shipper's Obligation Subject to Fault Liability 90
  IV. Shipper's Obligation Subject to Strict Liability 97
  V. Freedom of Contract and its Limitation 101
  VI. Shipper's Vicarious Liability 103
  VII. Other Issues 104
  VIII. Conclusion 105

Part I, Chapter 3
Aspects of Transport Regulated by the Rotterdam Rules 107

 8 Transport Documents and Electronic Transport Records 109
  I. Introduction 109
  II. Electronic Transport Records 110
  III. Transport Documents 112
  IV. Excluded Documents 113
  V. Issuing Transport Documents 114
  VI. Information Contained in the Transport Document 115
  VII. Requirement for a Signature 121
  VIII. Qualifications of the Information Provided 122
  IX. Effect of Deficiencies 124
  X. Evidentiary Effect 124
  XI. Other Matters: Who Is the Carrier? 126
  XII. Conclusion 127
 9 Right of Control and Transfer of Rights 129
  I. Introduction 129
  II. Why Right of Control is Necessary under Rotterdam Rules 130
  III. Who is Controlling Party 134
  IV. Exercise and execution of right of control 135
  V. Transfer of right under Rotterdam Rules 136
  VI. Impact on Laws in Peoples Republic of China (PRC) 137
 10 DELIVERY OF THE GOODS 141

I. Preliminary Remarks 141
  II. What is Delivery? 143
  III. The nature of the contract of carriage 145
  IV. Article 43 – Whether, When and Where the Consignee Must Accept Delivery 146
  V. To Whom the Goods Must Be Delivered – The Structure of the Articles 45 – 48. 148
  VI. Article 45 - Delivery under an Ordinary Non-negotiable Transport Document or Record, or in the Absence of any Document or Record 149
  VII. Article 46 – Delivery When a Non-negotiable Transport Document That Requires Surrender Is Issued 152
  VIII. Essence of the Bill of Lading System Is the Legitimation 156
  IX. Article 47 – Delivery when a negotiable transport document or record is issued 157
  X. Article 48 - Goods Remaining Undelivered 161
  XI. Article 47(2) - An Alternative to Delivery Against a Letter of Indemnity 166
  XII. Some personal Conclusions and Recommendations 176

Part I, Chapter 4
Rotterdam Rules and Industries 181

  11 The Rotterdam Rules: The Carriers' Perspective 183
    I Introduction 183
    II General Remarks 183
    III. Concerns from the Carriers' Perspective and What Have To Be Done 184
    IV. Benefits from the Carriers' Perspective 189
  12 The Rotterdam Rules: The Cargo Interests' Perspective 190
    I. Introduction 190
    II. Cargo Claim 190
    III. Claims against a Carrier and a Ship Owner 193
    IV. Specific Issues 206
    V. Conclusion 209
  13 Rotterdam Rules: The Freight Forwarders' Perspective 211
    I. Preface 211
    II. Freight Forwarder as a Carrier 211
    III Freight Forwarder as a Shipper 215
    IV. Conclusion 218

14 The Rotterdam Rules: The Insures' Perspective ··· 219
  I. Introduction ··· 219
  II. Impact on Marine Insurance ··· 219
  III. Points in Favour of Cargo Interests ··· 220
  IV. Points in Favour of Ship Interests ··· 222
  V. General Average (Article 84) ··· 223
  VI. Salvage ··· 224
  VII. Uniformity ··· 225

Part I, Chapter 5
The Rotterdam Rules and Asia-Pacific States ··· 227

15 People's Republic of China ··· 229
16 The Rotterdam Rules in Japan ··· 231
17 Korea ··· 233
18 Singapore ··· 235
19 The United States ··· 237

Part II
Workshop on the Rotterdam Rules ··· 243

The Rotterdam Rules in the Asia-Pacific Region: Workshop ··· 245
  Q.1 Carrier's Obligation: Validity of Terms and Conditions in Standard Form Bill of Lading ··· 245
  Q.2 Period of Responsibility and Liabilities ··· 249
  Q.3 Carrier's Obligations and Liabilities and the FIO Clause ··· 253
  Q.4 Carrier's Liability (1): Basic Questions ··· 257
  Q.5 Carrier's Liability (2): Delay in Delivery, Loss of the Goods, and Non-performance ··· 260
  Q.6 Carrier's Liability (3): Various Liability in Connection with the Goods and the Convention ··· 265
  Q.7 Identity of the Carrier ··· 270
  Q.8 Parties Involved in a Contract of Carriage: Carrier, Performing Party, and Agent, etc. ··· 273
  Q.9 Liability of a Maritime Performing Party ··· 277
  Q.10 Multimodal Transport and Limited Network Principle ··· 282
  Q.11 Liability of the Shipper ··· 290
  Q.12 The Obligation to Accept Delivery ··· 293

Q.13 Delivery of the Goods ········· 298

Q.14 Volume Contracts ········· 302

Part III
The Text of United Nations Convention on Contracts for the International Carriage of Goods Wholly or Partly By Sea ········· 307

Corrections to the Original Text of the Rotterdam Rules ········· 309

United Nations Convention on Contracts for the International Carriage of Goods Wholly or Partly by Sea ········· 312

About authors

AMEMIYA, Masahiro

Attorney at Law, Partner of Yoshida & Partners, Visiting Professor of Law, Waseda University, Visiting Professor of Law, Dalian Maritime University. Mr. Amemiya was graduated LL.B (1986) and LL.M (1991) at Waseda University and worked at Nittsu Research Institute and Consulting, Inc. (1989-1992). After the legal training at the Legal Research and Training Institute (1999), he joined Yoshida & Partners.

Mr. Amemiya was seconded to maritime law firms in UK and China (2004-2005). He teaches maritime law at Waseda University as a lecturer (2011-present),

BEARE, Stuart

Mr. Stuart Beare practised as a solicitor with Richards Butler in the City of London specializing in shipping law for thirty years from 1966 to 1996, after which he remained associated with the firm for some years as a consultant. He is a Vice-President of the British Maritime Law Association and in 2008 was elected a Member *honoris causa* of the CMI.

Mr. Beare was the Chairman of the CMI International Sub-Committee on Issues of Transport Law which prepared the original CMI Draft Instrument. This Draft Instrument formed the basis of the discussions in UNCITRAL Working Group III – Transport Law. As a CMI Observer Mr. Beare attended all sessions of UNCITRAL Working Group III from 2002 to 2008 at which the Draft Convention (now known as the "Rotterdam Rules") was agreed; he was also a member of the Expert Group in UNCITRAL Secretariat. He then attended the 41st session of the UNCITRAL Commission in June 2008, when the Draft Convention was approved for submission to the UN General Assembly

CASTELLANI, Luca

After graduating in law (JD) in the University of Torino, Luca Castellani received a doctoral degree in comparative law (SJD) from the University of Trieste and a master in international law (LLM) from New York University. Admitted to the bar in Italy, he held lecturing positions in Italy and Eritrea. He joined the Office of Legal Affairs of the secretariat of the United Nations in New York in 2001, the UNCITRAL secretariat in Vienna, Austria, in 2004, and served as legal advisor to the United Nations Mission in Ethiopia and Eritrea (UNMEE) in Addis Ababa, Ethiopia, in 2008. He published in the fields of international trade law and comparative law.

Luca Castellani serves as a legal officer in the secretariat of the United Nations Commission on International Trade Law (UNCITRAL), where he has assisted in servicing Working Group III during the preparation of the Rotterdam Rules. From March 2012 to November 2013 he has been the Head of the UNCITRAL Regional Centre For Asia and Pacific. He is currently in charge of the secretary of UNCITRAL Working Group IV (Electronic Commerce), which is dealing with electronic transferable records, including dematerialized bills of lading.

FUJITA, Tomotaka

Professor of Law at Graduate Schools for Law and Politics, University of Tokyo. LLB, University of Tokyo (1988); Research Assistant at University of Tokyo (1988-1991); Lecturer and Associate Professor of Law at Seikei University (1991-1998); Associate Professor of Law at Graduate Schools for Law and Politics, University of Tokyo (1998-2004), Professor of Law at Graduate Schools for Law and Politics, University of Tokyo (2004-).

Professor Fujita was the Japanese Delegation to UNCITRAL Working Group III (Transport Law) (2002-2008). He attended the UNCITRAL 41st Session (2008) as a Vice Chairman of the Session and as the head of Japanese delegation when the Draft Convention was approved for submission to the UN General Assembly. He was also a member of the Expert Group in UNCITRAL Secretariat. Professor Fujita is a titularly Member of the Comite Maritime International (CMI) and the Chairman of CMI's International Working Group on Rotterdam Rules.

He is the author (with Michael Sturley and Gertjan van der Ziel) of THE ROTTERDAM RULES: THE UN CONVENTION ON CONTRACTS FOR THE INTERNATIONAL CARRIAGE OF GOODS WHOLLY OR PARTLY BY SEA.

GIRVIN, Stephen Darryl

Professor Stephen Girvin graduated at the University of Natal in South Africa (BA (1984), LLB (1986), LLM (1987)) and then took a PhD in Legal History (1991) at the University of Aberdeen. He is Professor of Law (2008-) and Vice Dean (Research) (2010-2014) at the National University of Singapore (NUS). He was previously an Associate Professor at NUS (2002-2005) and, before that, at the University of Natal (1986-88), at the University of Aberdeen (1989-1992), at the University of Nottingham (1992-2002), and at the University of Birmingham, where he was Professor of Maritime Law (2006-2008). He has been a Visiting

Lecturer and Visiting Professor at the University of Cape Town, a Parsons Fellow at the University of Sydney, MPA Visiting Professor of Maritime Law at NUS, Visiting Professor at the TC Beirne School of Law, University of and Queensland, and Visiting Professor at Direito Gv, Sao Päulo. He is the author of CARRIAGE OF GOODS BY SEA, 2ND ED (OXFORD UNIVERSITY PRESS, 2011), CHARLESWORTH'S COMPANY LAW 18TH ED (SWEET & MAXWELL, 2010), and is a contributor to D. RHIDIAN THOMAS (ED), A NEW CONVENTION FOR THE CARRIAGE OF GOODS BY SEA: THE ROTTERDAM RULES (LAWTEXT, 2009).

GOTO, Gen

Associate Professor of Law at Graduate Schools for Law and Politics, University of Tokyo; LLB, University of Tokyo (2003); Research Assistant at University of Tokyo (2003-2006); Lecturer of Law and Associate Professor of Law at Gakushuin University (2006-2010); Associate Professor of Law at Graduate Schools for Law and Politics, University of Tokyo (2010-present).

HAYASAKA, Tsuyoshi

Born in 1948, graduated the law faculty of Kyoto University and entered Kawasaki Kisen Kaisha Ltd. in 1975 and worked mainly for Liner Trade and Tramp Trade in the sphere of ship operation and chartering then in 1989 took a charge of legal affairs up to resignation in July, 2011. Arbitrator of the Japan Shipping exchange, Inc.

HIRATA, Ohki

Mr. Ohki Hirata practices law as a partner at SAH &Co. He graduated the law faculty of Nagoya University (L.L.B) (1981). After the legal training at the Institute of Legal Research and Practice (1983), he was admitted to the Bar (Tokyo Bar Association). He joined Yamamichi Uono & Nakada (1983), Tagawa Law Office (1990) and became a partner at Shimada Seno Amitani and Hirata (1993). The name of the firm was changed to SAH & Co. (1995). Mr. Hirata received Diploma in Shipping Law from London University (postgraduate course of University College of London) (1989). He teaches at Nanzan Law School as a lecturer since 2006.

HONKA, Hannu

Professor of International Commercial Law, Åbo Akademi University, Finland. Professor Honka is Member of the Board of the Scandinavian Institute of Maritime Law at the University of Oslo, Norway, and has previously chaired the Board; he has been visiting professor at Tulane Law School, New Orleans, USA, and full-time visiting professor at the Scandinavian Institute of Maritime Law. Professor Honka is Chairman of the Finnish Maritime Law Association; he is the Average Adjuster of Finland; he is invited Member of the Maritime Arbitration Commission at the Chamber of Commerce and Industry of the Russian Federation; he is also Member of the Council of Association Mondiale de Dispacheurs (AMD)

Professor Honka was the Representative and Delegate of Finland to UNCITRAL Working Group III (Transport Law) preparing a Convention that eventually came to the Rotterdam Rules. He also attended the 41st session of the UNCITRAL Commission in June 2008, when the Draft Convention was approved for submission to the UN General Assembly. He was also Member of the Expert Group in UNCITRAL Secretariat.

IKEYAMA, Akiyoshi

Attorney-at-law, Abe & Sakata, Tokyo; LLB (Tokyo) (1989); LLM with Merit (UCL) (1995); Nippon Yusen Kaisha, Tokyo (1989-1992); Legal Apprentice (1992-1994); Admitted to the Bar, Tokyo Bar Association (1994-present); Attorney-at-law, Abe, Mine & Sakata (1994); Attorney-at-law, Abe & Sakata (1994-present); Part-time Lecturer, Waseda Law School (2009-present).

ILLESCAS, Rafael

Professor of Comercial Law at Social Sciences and Law School and Director of the Master in Private Law, Carlos III University, Madrid (1990); LLB, Seville University, Spain (1966); PhD, Bologna University, Italy (1968); Associate Professor of Commercial Law, Seville University (1968-1979); Professor of Commercial Law, Universities of Saragossa (1980), Cadiz (1981-1985) and Seville (1986-1989).

Profesor Illescas was a member of the Spanish Delegation to UNCITRAL Working Group III (Transport Law) (2002-2008) and served as Chairman of the Working Group (2002-2008) and Chairman of the Commission (2008-2009) where the Draft Convention on Contracts for the International Carriage of Goods Wholly or Partly by Sea was negotiated and adopted.

ISHII, Masaru

After graduating from Hitotsubashi University he joined the Tokio Marine and Fire Insurance Co.,LTD. (now Tokio Marine and Nichido Fire Insurance Co.,LTD) in 1976.

He practiced in cargo claims settling and specialized in pursuing various kinds of cargo recovery cases (-2013).

He is a consultant at SAH&Co., a lecturer on Marine Insurance Law at Tokyo University of Marine Science and Technology and a member of The Maritime Law Association of Japan.

KIM, In Hyeon

Professor of Commercial Law at School of Law, Korea University; Bachelor of Engineering, Korea Maritime University (1982); LLM (1996), LLD (1999), and LLB (2007) College of Law, Korea University; LLM, University of Texas at Austin (2004); Navigational Officer and Master of Sanko Steamship Co. Ltd (1982-2002); Maritime Consultant, Kim & Chang, Law Firm in Korea (1996-1999); Associate and Assistant Professor, Mokpo National Maritime University (1999-2007); Associate Professor, College of Law Pusan National University (2007-2009); Full Professor, School of Law Korea University (2009-); A Vice President, Korea Maritime Law Association (2008-); A Korean Delegate to IOPC FUND and IMO Legal Committee.

Professor In Hyeon Kim was a Korean delegate to UNCITRAL Working Group III (Transport Law) (2002-2008) and attended the 41st session of the UNCITRAL Commission in June 2008, when the Draft Convention was approved for submission to the UN General Assembly. He is also a member of the Expert Group in UNCITRAL Secretariat.

SASAOKA, Manami

Lecturer of Law at Ryutsu Keizai University; LLB, Ritsumeikan University (2003); LLM, Keio University (2006); Withdrawal from the Doctoral Program with the completion of course requirements, Graduate School of Law, Keio University (2009).

SONG, Dihuang

Wang Jing & Co., Beijing, China. B.Sc. Dalian Maritime University (1983); LLM, University of Southampton (1995); Deputy Secretary General of China Maritime Law Association; Secretary General of Maritime Law Committee under All-China Lawyers' Association; Also Arbitrator of China Maritime Arbitration Commission and China International Economic and Trade Arbitration Commission; Supporting member of London Maritime Arbitrators' Association; Arbitrator of Chambre Arbitrale de Paris.

Mr. Song attended most sessions of CMI subcommittee on transport law issues (1999-2001), and was a member of Chinese Delegation to UNCITRAL Working Group III (Transport Law) where he attended all preparatory sessions of the Chinese Delegation, as well as some sessions of UNCITRAL Working Group III.

STURLEY, Michael.

Fannie Coplin Regents Chair in Law, University of Texas at Austin. BA (History), Yale University (1977), BA (Jurisprudence), Magdalen College, Oxford (1980), JD, Yale (1981); MA (Jurisprudence), Oxford (1984). Law Clerk, U.S. Court of Appeals, Second Circuit (1981-1982); Law Clerk, U.S. Supreme Court (1982-1983); Associate, Sullivan & Cromwell, New York (1983-1984); assistant professor, professor & chair-holder, University of Texas Law School (since 1984); visiting professor, University of London (1990).

Professor Sturley was the rapporteur for the CMI Working Group and the International Sub-Committee on Issues of Transport Law (which prepared the preliminary draft of what ultimately became the Rotterdam Rules) and was the senior advisor to the U.S. delegation to UNCITRAL Working Group III (which negotiated and drafted the Rotterdam Rules). He was also a member of the Expert Group in the UNCITRAL Secretariat. He also attended the 41st session of the UNCITRAL Commission in June 2008, when the Draft Convention was approved for submission to the UN General Assembly. He is the author (with Tomotaka Fujita and Gertjan van der Ziel) of THE ROTTERDAM RULES: THE UN CONVENTION ON CONTRACTS FOR THE INTERNATIONAL CARRIAGE OF GOODS WHOLLY OR PARTLY BY SEA.

TOZUKA Takehiko

Mr. Takehiko Tozuka practices law at Okabe & Yamaguchi law office. LLB, Kyoto University (1989). After the legal apprentices at the Legal Training and Research Institute, Mr. Tozuka admitted at Fukuokaken Bar Association (1991). Mr. Tozuka participated in Okabe & Yamaguchi law office in 1993 and has been its partner since 1998.

VAN DER ZIEL, Gertjan

Professor Van der Ziel worked for the Netherlands' Ministry of Transport, was for many years General Counsel of several transportation companies (a.o. Nedlloyd, European Rail

Shuttle) and lectured Transportation Law at the Erasmus University at Rotterdam.

He is Titulary Member of the Comite Maritime International, Maritime Arbitrator and former Chairman of the Netherlands' Association of Maritime and Transport Law.

He participated in the preparations of the Rotterdam Rules as the head of the Netherlands' delegation to UNCITRAL Working Group III. He also attended the 41st session of the UNCITRAL Commission in June 2008, when the Draft Convention was approved for submission to the UN General Assembly. He was also a member of the Expert Group in UNCITRAL Secretariat.

He is the author (with Michael Sturley and Tomotaka Fujita) of *The Rotterdam Rules: The UN Convention on Contracts for the International Carriage of Goods Wholly or Partly by Sea*.

YAMAGUCHI, Shuji

Attorney at Law, Partner of Okabe & Yamaguchi. After graduating the faculty of law at Kyoto University in 1980, Mr. Shuji Yamaguchi was admitted to the bar in 1982. He is a Member of The Maritime Law Association of Japan, The Air Law Institute of Japan, The International Bar Association, and The Inter-Pacific Bar Association. Mr. Yamaguchi was the Chair of Maritime Law Committee (2009-2011) of IPBA. He is also a Professional Partner of The International Union of Marine Insurance and the arbitrator of Tokyo Maritime Arbitration Commission of Japan Shipping Exchange and the arbitrator of Japan Commercial Arbitration Association.

Part I, Chapter 1

Introduction to the Rotterdam Rules

1

The Role of UNCITRAL and the Current Status of the Rotterdam Rules

Luca Castellani

The mandate of the United Nations Commission on International Trade Law (UNCITRAL, or the Commission) pertains to the promotion of the harmonization and modernization of international trade law.[1] Traditionally, UNCITRAL legislative activities have attracted significant attention: UNCITRAL is widely perceived as the global forum for the preparation of international legal standards, due to, inter alia, the fact that its universal composition ensures the broadest participation in the discussions and, consequently, legitimacy of the resulting texts.

However, drafting legislative texts is only one step in the international trade law harmonization process. Before that step, it is necessary to identify appropriate topics, and after it, it is necessary to effectively promote the use and the adoption of the uniform text. Finally, once the text enters into force, is widely enacted or otherwise commonly used, it is necessary to monitor its application. Such activity allows not only the promotion of uniform interpretation, but also the collection of important information for future revisions and preparation of complementary texts.

Although the importance of activities relating to the promotion of texts, and, more in general, technical assistance and cooperation was clear from the early days of UNCITRAL, a number of factors led to give priority to legislative work on the work agenda of UNCITRAL and its Secretariat. Those factors include the strict timing imposed by the periodical schedule of the meetings of the Commission and of its Working Groups, a certain attitude perceiving research and standard-making work as more appealing intellectual activities,

---

[1] United Nations General Assembly Resolution 2205 (XXI) of 17 December 1966, "Establishment of the United Nations Commission on International Trade Law"

and the fact that the resources in the Secretariat, including budget and staffing, remain largely designed around the necessity to service Commission and Working Group meetings. In this framework, non-legislative tasks had to be discharged more on an ad hoc basis.

In addition, work aimed at promoting UNCITRAL texts is hindered also by certain external constraints. International trade law reform is often not seen as a priority item both in the United Nations system, where it is perceived as rather peripheral to core activities despite its potential contribution to economic development and thus to the eradication of poverty, and in domestic contexts, where it is unlikely to attract significant political attention. International trade law reform is therefore not always featured prominently on the agenda of the executive and legislative powers. Legislative initiatives are therefore not always started in a timely manner and, when started, are sometimes left incomplete. In the latter case, work may be later duplicated or windows of opportunity may be lost.

Raising the profile of international trade law reform is a task of UNCITRAL and of its Secretariat. To achieve this goal, besides short visits to capitals, the UNCITRAL Secretariat makes use of two main communication channels: diplomats posted in Permanent Missions and delegates to meetings. Diplomats, however, are seldom trade law specialists and may be able to assist only to some extent given their many conflicting priorities. Delegates, on the other hand, are indeed experts in the field and are often familiar with the technicalities of the process of adoption of treaties and enactment of uniform model laws, but they do not set the agenda of their governments and therefore cannot necessarily influence the timing of law reform.

Moreover, the adoption of treaties poses an additional challenge beyond those associated with the enactment of model laws, as it requires coordination among a number of offices, i.e., at a minimum, the Ministry of Foreign Affairs and the substantive office(s). Such coordination requires additional time and resources that are scarce, especially in developing countries. Therefore, it is not unusual to see the substantive provisions of trade law treaties enacted domestically as if the source text were a model law.[2]

Aware of such challenges, the United Nations General Assembly decided a few years ago to allocate additional resources to the technical cooperation activities of the UNCITRAL Secretariat. Thus, a dedicated unit was established and best practices were compiled. This led to the definition of a strategic framework for technical cooperation activities,[3] identify-

---

[2] Thus, for instance, a number of provisions of the United Nations Convention on the Use of Electronic Communications in International Contracts, 2005, have been incorporated in national law, without formal adoption of that treaty in the concerned jurisdiction. *See*, for the list of those jurisdictions, http://www.uncitral.org/uncitral/en/uncitral_texts/electronic_commerce/1996Model_stat us.html (status of the UNCITRAL Model Law on Electronic Commerce, 1996), sub footnote (e).
[3] *See* UN Doc. A/CN.9/724, "Technical cooperation and assistance – Note by the Secretariat",

ing certain fundamental lines of action deemed particularly appropriate and effective: the promotion of those treaties already enjoying broad acceptance, namely, the Convention on the Recognition and Enforcement of Foreign Arbitral Awards, 1958 (the "New York Convention"),[4] and the United Nations Convention on Contracts for the International Sale of Goods, 1980 ("CISG");[5] the adoption of a regional approach in order to reach more stakeholders but also to ensure compatibility with similar initiatives promoted by regional economic integration organizations; and, finally, the dissemination of information on recently adopted texts with a view to facilitating their early entry into force and broad acceptance. This last category includes the promotional activities relating to the United Nations Convention on Contracts for the International Carriage of Goods Wholly or Partly by Sea, 2008 (the "Rotterdam Rules").[6]

In fact, experience shows that, unless they gather significant State participation in the years immediately after their adoption, treaties are unlikely to become widely adopted. Certain steps may be useful in drawing attention to recent texts.

Firstly, the organisation of a signature ceremony may provide an appropriate forum to show State support for a treaty. In fact, treaties are traditionally negotiated, or, at least, finalized at diplomatic conferences attended by delegates with full powers to sign them. That practice had to be discontinued at UNCITRAL for budgetary and other reasons. Currently, treaties drafted by UNCITRAL are, technically speaking, formally adopted by the United Nations General Assembly acting as a diplomatic conference. However, this approach does not allow for a dedicated signature ceremony. Since 2005, signature ceremonies were reintroduced in UNCITRAL practice and this approach led to a multiplication in the number of signatures to the concerned treaties.[7]

Secondly, effective communication on the treaty status during its first years is critical. This has taken place by introducing in the UNCITRAL secretariat the regular issuance of press releases, and with the compilation of dedicated webpages in the multilingual UNCITRAL website, providing a wealth of information ranging from status and purpose of the treaty to bibliographies.

Thirdly, efforts should be made to produce materials aimed at supporting countries wishing to consider the adoption of the treaty but facing limited capacity, so as to facilitate their research.

---

paras. 10-48, available at http://www.uncitral.org/uncitral/commission/sessions/44th.html.
[4] United Nations, Treaty Series, vol. 330, p. 38.
[5] United Nations, Treaty Series, vol. 1489, p. 3.
[6] UN Sales No. E.09.V.9 (treaty not yet in force).
[7] The website on the signature ceremony of the Rotterdam Rules is available at http://www.rotterdamrules2009.com/cms/index.php.

These measures have not yet, however, led to the desired results. Few of the treaties prepared by UNCITRAL – and of the international trade law treaties in general – enjoy broad participation. Some of those treaties that have entered into force remain marginal, and others have not yet done so despite having been concluded several years ago. Statistics for the most successful texts, the New York Convention and the CISG, show an adoption rate of about 2,7 accessions and ratifications per year. This is the best rate of international trade law treaty adoption that it is realistically possible to expect under current circumstances.

If this best adoption rate could apply to the Rotterdam Rules, they would enter into force in 2016. In reality, this cannot be the case because additional time is needed to prepare, discuss and approve an adequate legislative framework.[8] These timelines may not be easily shortened. This pushes the target date for entry into force even later in time.

Of course, additional measures to promote the early adoption of the Rotterdam Rules should be sought and implemented. However, in times of dwindling resources it is unlikely, though not in principle impossible, that the UNCITRAL Secretariat could devote extra staff to this task only. Moreover, the substantive expertise of the Secretariat is limited when compared to that of experts who have studied the matter for decades. At the same time, the Secretariat has an advantage in engaging governments to make suggestions for law reform and to advise at the policy level. In these areas the Secretariat may complement the work of other stakeholders interested in the promotion of the Rotterdam Rules in a particularly effective manner.

In fact, resources outside the Secretariat are actually plentiful. The UNCITRAL Secretariat needs therefore to focus on mobilizing those resources in order to benefit from them to the fullest. In particular, the Secretariat should ensure that those resources are made available to countries that do not independently have sufficient capacity to engage in maritime law reform.

Moreover, the UNCITRAL Secretariat is in constant communication with a variety of relevant public and private institutions, thus being in a position to monitor interest and possible opportunities for maritime law reform. Similarly, it is possible for the Secretariat to work with the organizers of general trade law meetings to schedule discussions of the Rotterdam Rules when appropriate, therefore seizing opportunities for promotion that would not arise otherwise. In this respect, the opening of the first UNCITRAL Regional Centre in Incheon, Republic of Korea, in charge of providing technical assistance to the Asia and Pacific region, offers an immediate opportunity to further increase support for the promotion

---

[8] In the same sense, *see*, e.g., D. Chard, *The Rotterdam Rules: two years on*, 106 BIMCO Bulletin 4 (2011), 38.

of the Rotterdam Rules in the region. As East Asia is seeking cross-border supply chain integration, including with respect to applicable legal provisions, the relevance of illustrating the potential central role of the Rotterdam Rules in the transport segment of that chain seems evident.

A number of practical steps may be envisaged to implement the above.

First, it seems of great importance to improve the level of communication on on-going adoption procedures. In fact, only some specialists seem aware of the steady progress towards accession and ratification of the Rotterdam Rules by certain countries. Broader dissemination of information on those processes, to the extent that this may be disclosed, would dispel the impression that the Rotterdam Rules are not being considered for adoption. This information would fill the hiatus between signature and ratification, attract further attention from the legal community and prevent criticisms and easy dismissals of the relevance of the treaty due to insufficient State support.

Secondly, it seems particularly important to collect the information relating to accession and ratification procedures. As already mentioned, a number of States, especially developing, face serious capacity deficits in the field of maritime law reform and would greatly benefit from advice in the consideration and possible adoption of the Rotterdam Rules. Existing comprehensive consultation papers may be used as a source of inspiration, especially when available from jurisdictions sharing the same legal principles with those seeking assistance. Such documents are not yet available for the Rotterdam Rules. While States in each region of the world embark in maritime law reform on a regular basis, in any given jurisdiction the occasion to pass new legislation in the field rarely presents itself. Hence, those States with limited capacity but nevertheless involved in maritime law reform are not in a position to examine the Rotterdam Rules alone, nor they can rely on existing consultation papers. Clearly, these States need support. Ideally, the compilation of information could lead to the preparation of an accession kit. Such a kit, in line with precedents, does not need necessarily to be prepared by UNCITRAL or its Secretariat. It should address practical issues as well, such as the arguments relating to lodging a declaration when becoming a party to the Rotterdam Rules. It could also go beyond a narrow discussion of the adoption of the Rotterdam Rules by illustrating related issues and providing guidance on complementary legislative choices drawing on examples provided by those countries already nearing accession or ratification. Ideally, it could reach as far as offering examples of practical implementation of the Rotterdam Rules, such as model clauses for bills of lading.

In fact, the effective implementation of the Rotterdam Rules requires interaction with national legislation. A number of questions may be pertinent in this respect, depending on the features, including at the constitutional level, of the concerned jurisdiction: to what extent may the Rotterdam Rules be considered self-executing? Which are the areas that are left outside the text but need to be coordinated with it? Which are the other treaties whose adoption could be considered in the framework of a comprehensive approach to maritime law reform? Those questions, too, could be addressed in an accession kit.

Last, but not least, is the issue of resources. Certain organisations are already cooperating with the Secretariat. Hopefully, they will be in a position to continue doing so. However, this may not be sufficient. It seems, therefore, particularly important to stress how the adoption of uniform trade law, including of the Rotterdam Rules, not only brings clear economic benefits, but also supports the rule of law and good governance. Such arguments are necessary to win the support of decision-makers outside the circle of maritime law specialists, to gather the attention of legislators, and to compete for a fraction of the many resources spent by the international community for international legal aid. Again, resources indeed exist: it is rather a matter of pleading effectively the case with potentially interested donors at the appropriate time by mainstreaming international trade law reform in the broader rule of law discourse. Given the importance of maritime transport for the global economy, this does not seem an impossible task.

2

The Need for Change and the Role of the CMI[*]

Stuart Beare

The United Nations Convention on Contracts for the International Carriage of Goods Wholly or Partly by Sea (the Rotterdam Rules) was adopted by Resolution 122 of the 63rd session of the United Nations General Assembly on 11th December 2008 and opened for signature in Rotterdam on 23rd September 2009. Twenty four states have so far signed the Convention and Spain has ratified it.

The preamble to the Resolution recites concerns that the current legal regime governing the international carriage of goods by sea lacks uniformity and fails adequately to take into account modern transport practices, including containerisation, door-to-door transport contracts and the use of electronic transport documents. The Resolution thus identifies three areas where there have been major changes in the industry that necessitate changes to the carriage of goods by sea regime.

At this point I shall not say very much about uniformity, but I shall refer to it again later in this paper. Much has been written about the present disharmony and the problems are well known[1]. These problems have long been the concern of the CMI, which has as its object contributing to the unification of maritime law in all its aspects. The most recent work began in 1988 when a sub-committee was set up under the chairmanship of Professor Francesco Berlingieri. A study of the then current problems, albeit based on the Hague-Visby Rules, was a major topic at the CMI's conference in Paris in 1990. Five years later a new sub-committee was formed, commonly known as the "Uniformity Sub-Committee", also under Professor Berlingieri's chairmanship. Professor Berlingieri's 1999 report[2] was the

---

[*] This is a revised and expanded version of a paper presented to the CMI Colloquium in Buenos Aires on 27 October 2010 and published in the 2010 CMI YEARBOOK 146)
[1] See, for example, Michael F Sturley, *The development of cargo liability regimes*, in HUGO TIBERG (ED) CARGO LIABILITY IN FUTURE MARITIME CARRIAGE (HASSELBY) 1997 10 at pp 60-64.
[2] Printed in 1999 CMI YEARBOOK 105.

starting point for work on the obligations and liabilities of the carrier to be included in the Draft Instrument which the CMI was then preparing for the UNCITRAL secretariat.

This Draft Instrument had its origins in the 29th session of the UNCITRAL Commission in 1996, when the Commission considered a proposal to include in its work programme a revision of current practices and laws in the area of carriage of goods by sea with a view to achieving greater uniformity of law. This proposal arose out of UNCITRAL's work on its Model Law on Electronic Commerce, which had exposed the fact that there were significant gaps regarding issues such as the functioning of bills of lading and sea waybills. The CMI took the lead in the preparatory stages of this project, which involved gathering information, ideas and opinions about the problems that arose in practice and possible solutions to them. Initially this work was primarily concerned with topics, such as electronic transport documents, that were not governed by existing conventions. However it became apparent that the work involved reviewing some provisions of the Hague-Visby and the Hamburg Rules, and this in turn led to a review of the obligations and liabilities of the carrier and the shipper, based on Professor Berlingieri's report.[3]

The CMI delivered a Draft Instrument to the UNCITRAL secretariat in December 2001.[4] The Preliminary Draft Instrument annexed to Working Paper 21 is substantially in the form of the CMI Draft and was the starting point for the subsequent inter-governmental negotiations in UNCITRAL Working Group III. During the six year period of these negotiations the Preliminary Draft Instrument was changed out of all recognition into the new Convention in terms of detailed drafting, but the basic structure of the Draft prepared by the CMI remains.

I shall now come back to modern transport practices. The Hague Rules were adopted in 1924 – almost ninety years ago. In 1924 the bulk of members of the United Kingdom P&I Club were operators of tramp steamers in the "6-10 Class". That is they steamed at 6-10 knots on 6-10 tons of coal a day and had a deadweight capacity of 6-10,000 DWT.[5] Twenty years later saw the construction of over two thousand Liberty ships which had a maximum speed of 11.5 knots and a deadweight capacity of 10,685 DWT. Many of these ships were still in commercial service in the early 1960s when I began to practise. Cargo was often handled by ship's gear. Winches were prone to breakdowns, giving rise to disputes over laytime and demurrage. Tally clerks checked the cargo as it was slung over the rail, noting bags that were torn, slack or stained, and the bills of lading were claused according to their re-

---

[3] For a full account of the development of the project between 1996 and 2001 see the Introduction to Working Group III Working Paper 21 (A/CN.9/WG.III/WP21).
[4] Printed in 2001 CMI YEARBOOK 532.
[5] SEE PETER YOUNG, MUTUALITY THE STORY OF THE UK P&I CLUB (GRANTA EDITIONS, 1995) 31

ceipts under article III rule 3 of the Hague Rules.

Fifty years later the *Emma Maersk* was launched. She has a speed in excess of 25.5 knots, a capacity of 157,000 DWT and she can carry 11,000 20ft containers.[6] Container transport was not dreamt of in 1924 and international container transport only began in the late 1960s[7]. New deep water ports were needed to accommodate the new container ships and terminal operators needed to make large investments in shore facilities. The days were gone when port authorities largely confined their operations to warehouses and stevedore companies simply employed dockworkers, often on a casual basis. When the *Emma Maersk* called at Felixstowe on her maiden voyage to Europe in November 2006, 300 dock workers unloaded 3,000 containers in 24 hours using six shore cranes.[8] The whole loading, unloading and stowage operation has been computerised and tally clerks have disappeared.

These changes in ship construction and operation demand changes to the carriage of goods regime. Let me give examples of how the necessary changes are reflected in the Rotterdam Rules. Article 25 develops the rather tentative changes to the deck cargo regime introduced by the Hamburg Rules. It brings the legal regime for deck cargo up to date to take account of cellular container ships, which are not built with the conventional decks of a Liberty ship. Article 40 re-writes article III rule 3 of the Hague Rules and introduces the concept of closed containers. Article 14(c) specifically extends article III rule 1(c) of the Hague Rules to containers supplied by the carrier.

These technical changes led to commercial change. Many of the containers discharged from the *Emma Maersk* in November 2006 would have been loaded onto trucks and taken direct to wholesalers' or major retailers' inland distribution depots pursuant to door-to-door transport contracts. Door-to-door transport, that is from the seller's factory to the buyer's warehouse, inevitably followed the container revolution. The CMI led the way in formulating a legal framework with the "Tokyo Rules", which were adopted in 1969[9]. These Rules formed the basis on which the container shipping industry developed its contracts for combined transport, that is sea carriage combined with inland carriage covered by a single contract.[10] These Rules provided for a network system which took account of the liability provisions in unimodal regimes for other modes of transport, in particular road and rail. These

---

[6] www.emma-maersk.com.
[7] The *Ideal-X* made the first containership voyage in April 1956 from Newark, New Jersey, to Houston, Texas. The first transatlantic container service was opened by Moore-McCormack Lines in March 1966. For an account of the "container revolution" see MARC LEVINSON, THE BOX HOW THE SHIPPING CONTAINER MADE THE WORLD SMALLER AND THE WORLD ECONOMY BIGGER (PRINCETON, 2006).
[8] *The Times* 6 November 2006.
[9] Printed in CMI REPORT OF THE TOKYO CONFERENCE, 1969.
[10] See, for example, the form of bill of lading code named "Combicon" issued by The Baltic and International Maritime Council (BIMCO).

concepts have been incorporated into the Rotterdam Rules in article 26, which provides for a limited network regime when loss or damage to the goods occurs during the carrier's period of responsibility, but before their loading onto the ship or after their discharge from the ship[11].

The Rotterdam Rules have thus expanded the scope of application of the carriage regime beyond tackle-to-tackle, as in the Hague and Hague-Visby Rules, and port-to-port, as in the Hamburg Rules, to door-to-door carriage. But it is important to stress that the application of the Rotterdam Rules is only so extended if the contract of carriage so provides. The contract may provide, for example, that the carrier receives the goods into his charge, and subsequently delivers them, when they pass the ship's manifold. Such a provision restricts the application of the Rules to tackle-to-tackle. However door-to-door carriage is today a major feature of container shipping and it needs to be accommodated in an up to date regime. I believe that this is one of the most important changes to the carriage regime that the Rotterdam Rules will bring about.

Maritime carriage of goods no longer simply involves the carrier and the shipper. The concept of the "actual carrier", as opposed to the contracting carrier, was introduced by the Hamburg Rules, but only in respect of performance of the carriage and only in the context of port-to-port transport. It was necessary to expand the concept in the Rotterdam Rules to take account of door-to-door transport contracts and the many parties involved in modern transport logistics, such as NVOCs, freight forwarders, terminal operators, stevedores and inland truckers and railroads. Hence the Rotterdam Rules refer to "performing parties", but the Rules draw a clear bright line in respect of liability between "maritime performing parties", who perform the carrier's obligations between the arrival of the goods at the port of loading of a ship and their departure from the port of discharge of a ship, and are covered by the Rules, and other, non-maritime, performing parties, such as inland truckers, that are not.

I believe that the Rotterdam Rules also clarify and codify an aspect of the law of the carriage of goods by sea that has given rise to some difficulty and lack of international uniformity. The unamended Hague Rules did not address the problem that was highlighted by the English case of *Adler v. Dickson – The Himalaya*[12]. This case involved the carriage of passengers, not the carriage of goods, but it was noted that there was a line of English case law that enabled the carrier's servants or agents to claim the benefit of the carrier's defences in carriage of goods cases. The decision in this case led to article IV bis being inserted into the

---

[11] For a general review, see Christopher Hancock QC, *Multimodal transport and the new UN Convention on the carriage of goods*, 14 JIML 484 (2008).
[12] Adler v Dickson, The Himalaya [1955] 1 QB 158.

Hague Rules in 1968 by the Visby Protocol, and the development of "Himalaya" clauses by carriers to give protection not only to their servants and agents, but also to their independent contractors.[13] The Rotterdam Rules reflect and codify industry practice. Article 18 specifically sets out the carrier's liability for other persons and article 4 applies the carrier's defences and limits of liability to the other persons so specified. Article 19 sets out the liability of maritime performing parties under the Rules. Other performing parties are not liable under the Rules; their liability is governed by applicable law.

The goods discharged from the *Emma Maersk* in November 2006 were mainly consumer goods which would not have been traded during the transit from China. Their carriage did not therefore need to be covered by negotiable transport documents. This development was noted in the Explanatory Note on the Hamburg Rules prepared by the UNCITRAL secretariat and the Hamburg Rules, in the context of port-to-port carriage, apply to all contracts of carriage by sea, as defined by article 1.6. At the 1990 Paris Conference the CMI adopted its "CMI Uniform Rules for Sea Waybills" for voluntary incorporation into contracts of carriage not covered by a bill of lading or other similar document of title.[14] These Rules apply to the contract of carriage any international convention, or national law, that would have been compulsorily applicable if a bill of lading or similar document of title had been issued. The Rules have been widely adopted by the industry[15] and, by applying the Hague, Hague-Visby or Hamburg Rules to such contracts, they have led to a degree of harmonisation between negotiable and non-negotiable documents. It was a natural development to extend the scope of application of the Rotterdam Rules to govern both negotiable and non-negotiable transport documents that evidence or contain a contract of carriage falling within the requirements of article 5.

Many of the consumer goods carried by the *Emma Maersk* to Felixstowe were destined for the Christmas market. She arrived in November after a voyage of about 22 days; arrival in January would have been too late. "Just in time" delivery of components is commonplace in construction projects. In 1924 it was unrealistic to expect a steamer making 6 – 10 knots to meet arrival deadlines. However the Explanatory Note on the Hamburg Rules says:

> However as a result of modern shipping technology, the proper charting of the oceans and sophisticated and efficient methods of navigation, voyages have become less subject to delays

---

[13] See clause 15 of the "Conlinebill 2000" issued by BIMCO.
[14] The Rules and the accompanying report of Lord Justice Lloyd are printed in CMI YEARBOOK 1990 PARIS II, 196-206.
[15] See the "Genwaybill" issued by BIMCO which is subject to the CMI Uniform Rules, although it contains a paramount clause applying the Hague Rules, or where necessary the Hague-Visby Rules.

and more predictable. Shippers have come to rely upon and expect compliance with undertakings by carriers to deliver the goods within a specified period of time.

What was said in 1978 can be said with even more force today.

The CMI Draft contained a provision imposing a liability on the carrier when the goods were not delivered within the time expressly agreed, but there was no consensus within the CMI regarding a further provision imposing liability when the goods were not delivered in a reasonable time. A provision to this effect was therefore included in square brackets in the CMI Draft for consideration by Working Group III. Initially the Working Group was in favour of both provisions and the square brackets were removed, but the issue was later reopened and almost reached an impasse. A compromise was finally agreed whereby the word "expressly" was deleted from the first provision, which is now article 21, and the second provision was deleted, as were all references to the shipper's liability for delay.

One commentator has observed that the Working Group has thus "agreed a form of words without reaching any agreement as to the effect those words were intended to produce."[16] It seems clear that the agreement referred to in article 21 need not be in writing or express; it may be implied, perhaps from pre-existing documents, such as a carrier's sailing schedule, or collateral undertakings. There is an issue as to whether such other documents and undertakings may be relied upon by the transferee of a negotiable transport document. There is also an issue as to whether damages can be claimed for breaches of articles 11, 13 and 14 for delay falling outside article 21. I believe that it is unfortunate that in this important area the Rotterdam Rules lack clarity, which will need to be given by the courts, and thus leave considerable scope for differences in application of the Rules in different jurisdictions.

I will end this brief review of the need for change on a more positive note. I have referred earlier to technical changes and I mentioned computerised loading and stowage. Nowadays the supply chain from the producer through the exporter, importer, wholesaler and retailer to the consumer is often totally computerised. The difficulties of accommodating a negotiable transport document into a paperless system are well known, but the Rotterdam Rules in chapter 3 provide for electronic communication in a way that is flexible and technologically neutral. The final text of the provisions in the Rotterdam Rules relating to electronic transport records was agreed following a joint meeting of experts from Working Group III

---

[16] Anthony Diamond QC, *The Rotterdam Rules*, [2009] LMCLQ 445 at p 479. See also Francesco Berlingieri, *Revisiting the Rotterdam Rules*, [2010] LMCLQ 583.

and Working Group IV (Electronic Commerce), which had prepared the Electronic Communications Convention.[17] The revisions recommended by these experts were largely adopted by Working Group III. I therefore believe that the Rotterdam Rules complement existing international instruments and consolidate international law in this complex and rapidly developing area in a flexible way that allows for future technical developments.[18]

In this short presentation I have outlined the most important changes that have taken place since 1924, mostly in the last 50 years, in ship construction and operation, and in technology. These changes have driven commercial changes, but the solutions developed by the industry have evolved piecemeal. In my submission the need for change in the international regime is unquestionable. The Rotterdam Rules attempt to bring the industry responses together into a single up-to-date and comprehensive code.

One final point. The changes that I have described have taken place worldwide. Due in large part to containerisation, the shipping industry is now truly global; much more so than in 1924. Regional attempts at solutions are not enough. I believe that only an international convention will provide a sound legal framework for the international maritime carriage of goods and meet the requirements of a fully globalized industry.

---

[17] United Nations Convention on the Use of Electronic Communications in International Contracts 2005.
[18] See Miriam Goldby, *Electronic alternatives to transport documents and the new Convention: a framework for future development?*, 14 JIML 586 (2008).

3

Basic elements and features of the Rotterdam Rules: Five Words on the Rules

Rafael Illescas

I. Introduction

It is an honor for me to have the opportunity to present you a general review of the basic elements and features of the Rotterdam Rules. I thank the organizers and sponsors of the conference for inviting me to Tokyo and participate in the event. A special mention goes out to Prof. Tomotaka Fujita who is not only the *deus ex* macchina of the conference but also a globally recognized drafter of the Rotterdam Rules, and one of its prominent commentators. The conference is the most relevant event since the rules organized in the Pacific Rim under uneasy national circumstances. To have so large and diversified audience makes my presentation particularly demanding, and I hope to be in accordance with the circumstances.

The basic elements and features of the Rotterdam Rules are multiple and operate in various fields mostly if we compare the Rotterdam Rules and their precedent rules, the 1924 Hague-Visby Rules, and the 1978 Hamburg Rules. This multiplicity of elements and features, however, can be reduced to five words that not only make the spirit of the rules apparent but also systematize the aims and the toolbox set up by the rules in order to formulate the best norms for the international carriage of goods wholly or partly by sea. The five words are the following: modernization, flexibility, freedom, comprehensivity and balance. Every one of these words has its precise meaning and content. We will check immediately.

II. Modernization

The UNCITRAL Convention opens the door to a new kind of thinking about global carriage regulation. From the tradition of the unimodal maritime and air conventions, formulated at the beginning of the past century, to the mirror of today's powerful and highly confident unimodal land instruments with a regional reach, there exists not one precedent to the approach that inspires the new text. Not even the failed 1980 UNCTAD Multimodal Convention [1] can be considered as a methodological precedent for the UNCITRAL Convention. At our convention, in fact, the starting point is not the parallel positioning of all the possible transport modes. The maritime mode is central to the UNCITRAL Convention, and it will not be applicable if a maritime leg is not found, whether it is isolated or embedded in door-to-door carriage contracts. This is a brand new approach to the legal regime of international transport without a proper precedent.

The Rotterdam Rules also explored a number of issues that had never been part of an international transport convention. As will be checked during the next minutes a number of features concerning the legal transport regime with regard to a uniform international instrument are first-time subjects of the rules. It is not necessary to insist, but only to mention, the electronification of documents of transport; the right of control and its circulation; the limited freedom contract; carrier's liability, or the obligations of shippers and carriers; among others, to reveal the high degree of innovative the rules enshrined by the new instrument.

As a powerful symbol of modernization, from the beginning of the negotiations, it has been necessary to resolve the issue of the electronic transport of documents. This attempt at modernization came about mostly after UNCITRAL's deployment of the authoritative instruments on electronic commerce in international trade – 1996 and 2000 Model Laws and the 2005 Convention (the latter is simultaneous with the debate on the Rotterdam Rules in Working Group (WG) III of the commission). However, the different stages of the technological development of maritime operators around the world quickly made it clear that the general rule on electronic contractual documentation –not previous parties consent for electronification- was not easily inserted into a convention whose aim was to harmonize world trade by sea. As a way out of the impasse, the WG started the formulation of the diverse provisions on electronic documentation with an unusual rule; Art. 8 (a) of Rotterdam Rules,

---

[1] United Nations Convention on International Multimodal Transport of Goods, Geneva, 24 May 1980.

which resolves the following:

> "Anything that is to be in or on a transport document under this convention may be recorded in an electronic transport record, provided the issue and subsequent use of an electronic transport record is agreed upon with the consent of the carrier and the shipper;"

The position adopted on the issue in Rotterdam Rules is based on the principle of a previously existing agreement among the parties to the contract of international carriage in order to use electronic contractual documentation. This is not consistent with the general UNCITRAL rules on e-commerce. According to those provisions, a previous agreement among the parties is not legally required in order to electronify the contract[2]. This approach proves the modernization of the rules; it is also proof of the delicate balance necessary to attribute the Rotterdam Rules as new and powerful content concerning the legal regime of sea carriage and the electronic formation, documentation, and partial performance of the contract.

As an additional expression of modernization and from a material point of view, the Rotterdam Rules also took into account the new realities of sea navigation and the carriage at large-. Among them, the massive irruption of containers in the industry, the constant progress in meteorology, the permanent control of vessels provided by GPS and similar, the proliferation of dangerous cargos, global monetary consolidation, and the digital tracking of the transported goods (tracking numbers and similar methods). All these new realities have a large impact on the navigation and, from a juridical point of view, facilitate the proof of claims and navigational incidents enormously. In parallel, the convention shows its ability to deduct consequences from the innovations and incorporate them to the sea carriage's legal regime[3].

---

[2] *Cfr.* Art. 11(1) in UNCITRAL Model Law on Electronic Commerce where the rule inserted is a rule of unnecessary previous agreement among the parties to an international contract in order to use electronic means to perform the different stages of the contract. The article states, "in the context of contract formation, unless otherwise agreed by the parties, an offer and the acceptance of an offer may be expressed by means of data messages. Where a data message is used in the formation of a contract, that contract shall not be denied validity or enforceability on the sole ground that a data message was used for that purpose." Almost the same terms are found in Article 8 of the 2005 United Nations Convention on the Use of Electronic Communications in International Contracts in force on 1 March 2013.

[3] The practical legal consequences of the proliferation of container use is found in the following Rules: Article 13(2) – "Specific obligations" of the carrier on charge and discharge and clause FIOS; Article 31(2) – "Information for compilation of contract particulars." Also, consequences are found in the rules governing the relevant aspects of door-to-door transport: Article 26 – "Carriage

III. Flexibility

The Rotterdam Rules have a much larger scope than merely solving the single and complex issue of the carrier's liability, as was the matter of the Hague-Visby Rules and, in a great deal, the Hamburg Rules. This wider scope of the instrument reflects the full diversity of the actual maritime carriage business to establish the full discipline of the contract providing for the international transport of goods wholly or partly by sea. That means that the scope at this stage is, at the very least, twofold, to establish norms with regard to the contract of carriage wholly by sea and norms with regard to the contract of carriage partly by sea. An addition to these two contracts is the well-known volume contract. Thus, it can be concluded that the Rotterdam Rules have the basic goal of regulating three different contracts of maritime carriage.

And all that is achieved without recourse to the multimodal formula. In fact, our convention creates a so-called "maritime plus" regime, not a multimodal regime. The provisions governing the "maritime plus" aspects of the Rotterdam Rules are included in Article 26 under the notation "Carriage preceding or subsequent to the sea carriage". Furthermore, Article 26 needs to be read in connection with Article 82, which includes the rules on the relationship between the Rotterdam Rules and other international conventions that govern the individual means of transport and contains some rules on multimodal aspects of the respective unimodal carriage of goods. Article 2 of the CMR Convention regulates the interference between road and maritime transports[4].

Both articles are not only the legal foundations of the above mentioned "maritime plus" nature of the Rotterdam Rules, they are also the core dispositions that allow a conclusion that the Rotterdam Rules establish a new regime not only for the international carriage contracts of goods by sea but also the regime of two other differentiated contracts: the interna-

---

preceding or subsequent to the sea carriage"; Article 40 – "Qualifying the information relating to the goods in the contract particulars"; and 48 –"Goods remaining undelivered"; among others. All these rules are the result of the new container carriage regulation under the Rotterdam Rules. Without containers, the mentioned norms are not easily conceivable.

[4] Convention on the Contract for the Carriage of Goods by Road, Geneva, 19 May 1956, amended by the 1978 and 2008 Protocols. CMR Article 2(1) is particularly interesting and states, "where the vehicle containing the goods is carried over part of the journey by sea, rail, inland waterways, or air, and except where the provisions of article 14 are applicable, the goods are not unloaded from the vehicle, this convention shall nevertheless apply to the whole of the carriage…" This is similar to the rule that while a more limited situation can be found in Article 38 of the Uniform Rules concerning the Contract for the International Carriage of Goods by Rail and the Appendix to the Convention concerning International Carriage by Rail, as amended by the 1999 Protocol (COTIF-CIM) "Liability in respect of rail-sea traffic."

tional carriage contract of goods partly by sea and the international contract of volume.

An additional foundation can be found in Article 19 on the liability of the maritime performing party. No mention of the non-maritime performing party is featured, and no liability of the non maritime performing party is established by the convention. The non- maritime performing party remains outside of the Rotterdam Rules.

In fact, we can conclude from both the articles mentioned that the Rotterdam Rules harmonizes not one but three contracts of international carriage and, especially for the "maritime plus" contract, determines the limits and connections between the Rotterdam Rules themselves and any other international, regional, or global instruments governing the non maritime, or door-to-door, dimensions of sea carriage.

Moreover, the rules allow the parties to a future contract to freely choose the most suitable contract for their needs among the three existing regimes. This implies the superior expression of the flexibility of the new convention.

IV. Freedom

Reference has been made to the volume contract and to the free choice of the parties among the three legal regimes included in the convention.

Precisely, the inclusion of volume contracts under the Rotterdam Rules responds to the legal engineering needed to incorporate the freedom of contract to international carriage law for goods by sea for the first time. It is true that the issue of freedom has been a very delicate one for many centuries, and its answer has been the same every time: the concerned convention should be mandatory, and the parties can only exercise their freedoms to augment, not to lower, the quantitative and monetary degree of liability of the carrier.

The Rotterdam Rules includes a couple of Articles (Arts.79 and 80) on the contentious matter of the freedom of contract in transport law and offers a positive and workable compromise for maritime transport. The parties will have the power to be exempt from many mandatory convention rules if the parties agree to enter into the so called "contract of volume" and if the entered contract observes all the conditions and requirements at this effect set up by the above mentioned articles of the treaty. They are the following:
  i. Inclusion in the volume contract of a prominent statement on derogation from the convention;
  ii. Individual negotiation of the contract or prominent specification the sections of the volume contract containing the derogations;
  iii. The shipper is given an opportunity to conclude a contract of carriage without deroga-

tions from the convention;
iv. The derogation cannot be incorporated by reference to the contract from another document; nor can it be included in a contract of adhesion that has not been subject to negotiation.[5]

From my point of view, the conventional requirements mean that a purely printed contractual formula does not comply with the mandate put forward by Article 80 of the rules.

V. Comprehensivity

Our convention includes a transport by sea convention, which is a comprehensive guide for the regime of the carriage contract. The new instrument offers an almost complete and regular set of features concerning the contract definition and discipline. It is not a question of merely solving the single and complex issues of the carrier's liability. Contrarily, the Rotterdam Rules have a much larger scope that reflects the full diversity of the actual maritime businesses legal necessities.

In so doing, the operated conventional approach is fully contractual, not partial or limited to some specific features of a contract that is subject to a larger extent to parochial legal systems. Definitions, the obligations of the parties, the liability of the parties, documentation, performance, electronic documents, and the related rights of the controlling party, time for suit, jurisdiction, and arbitration are the most relevant features encompassed in the convention. This complete, or almost complete, contractual regime is the core component of the comprehensive contractual approach to the discipline under the Rotterdam Rules.

These ideas have been developed before, and it is not necessary to repeat here.

VI. Balance

Some references to the balance between the interests of the carriers and the shippers have been already made. The utmost manifestation of the conventional balance and compromise is found, in my view, in the uniform rules of the carrier's liability.

---

[5] Art. 80(2) of Rotterdam Rules.

Article 17 of the Convention,[6] which changed numeration four times during negotiations, is the centerpiece of this balance; it was very controversial from the initial exchange of views inside the Working Group. In fact, the precedents were so divergent that the choice among them or the substitution with a new formula was a highly disputed decision from the beginning. The long list of The Hague and the elegant ellipsis from Hamburg offered everyone attractive reasons and enough sustained criticism to make difficult any decision on their respective substitution.

In this context, during the first three years of negotiations, the Working Group approached a complex and intermediate draft on the basis of carrier liability in which both historical elements (list and abstract rule) were kept, but its meaning was changed significantly. During this long process, new elements were added to the basic rules. The elements of the agreement as they appear in the final text of the Rotterdam Rules are as follows:

1. Seminal agreements were reached primarily on the determination of the liable persons, the dimension of the period of liability, and the causes and the legal nature of the liability. Liable persons are labeled the carrier (contractual carrier) and the maritime performing party[7]. No liability is attributed to the non maritime performing party. The period of the carrier's responsibility "begins when the carrier or a performing party receives the goods for carriage and ends when the goods are delivered"[8]. The carrier's liability is triggered by loss, damage to the goods, or delay in delivery of the goods[9].

The legal regime of the liability is contained in three relevant characters: (i) the liability is a liability by fault or negligence, not strict or so called objective liability; (ii) when two or more persons are liable, it is a joint and several liability[10]; and (iii) the liability is a presumed fault liability as the proof to be produced by the cargo interest only concerns, in principle, the occurrence of the damages during the period of the carrier's liability.

2. The carrier is liable for loss, damage, or delay in the delivery of the goods "if the claimant proves that the loss, damage, or delay, or the event or circumstance that caused or contributed to it took place during the period of the carrier's responsibility," as stated in Article 17(1) of Rotterdam Rules.

---

[6] From the beginning and during many sessions -- also during the session in which the final agreement was reached -- the article was Article 14. During the final meetings of the Working Group, some numeration changes occur, and at the end, the number was provided.
[7] Articles 14(1) and 19. The definition of carrier is found in Art. 1(5); for the definition of maritime performing party *cfr.* Art. 1(7).
[8] Article 12(1); for details, all of Chapter 4 must be read.
[9] Article 17(1).
[10] The conventional liability system and Art. 17 are based on the assumption that at any moment it can be proven by the defendant that there is a lack of fault or an exonerative event, and this proof will determine his exoneration. With regard to the joint and several liability, *see cfr.* Article 20.

This first element differs from the Rules of Hamburg only in the regime of the burden of the proof. In the Rotterdam Rules the proof should be borne by the cargo side. The proof should be extended to two main facts: (i) the fact of the actual occurrence of the loss, damage, or delay and (ii) the fact that it took place during the period of the carrier's responsibility. The possibility exists that the loss occurs after the end of this period, but the events or circumstances that caused or contributed to the loss took place during the period mentioned above. If this is the case, the proof should be extended to the connection between the subsequent loss and the adequate chronology of the causal or contributory event.

3. Against the proof produced by the cargo interests on the point mentioned above, the carrier can "counter-prove," as stated in Article 17(2). The carrier is relieved of its liability "if it proves that the cause or one of the causes of the loss, damage, or delay is not attributable to its fault or to the fault of any person referred to in article 18"[11]. This rule begins a sequential dance of proof and counter-proof that has to be alternatively produced by the carrier and the cargo interests. The dance constitutes the essence of Article 17 and its balance. In this situation, the proof is related to the non-attribution of the cause of the loss, damage, or delay to the carrier's fault.

4. The old Hague list of exonerating perils is now preserved in Article 17(3) of the Rotterdam Rules as an alternative means to counter-proof at the disposal of the carrier. The carrier can, in fact, choose among producing the counter-proof under Article 17(2) or proving that the loss, damage, or delay was the result of one of the items in the list.

The list is obviously adapted to the reality of our time, and it is very well known that the nautical fault disappears. Fire is restricted to fire on the ship. Also, other new circumstances, based on humanitarian and ecological grounds, have been added. However, the most relevant point to note is the evolution (and change) of the meaning and function of the events included in the current list under Art. 17(3). As it is emphasized under the Rotterdam Rules, the events are not a cause of the exoneration of liability for the carrier but a rebuttable presumption of innocence and due diligence in conducting his contractual duties, notwithstanding the occurred loss, damage, or delay with regard to the goods[12]. This is the conclusion to be obtained from Art. 17(4). The occurrence of any listed event has no effect

---

[11] The persons in Article 18 are the dependents of the carrier and any performing party. This article, as some others from the Rotterdam Rules, operates as a sort of legal Himalaya clause.

[12] *Cfr.* the oral presentations of Kofi Mbiah , The Rotterdam Rules: a new beginning? and F. Berlingieri, The carriers obligations and liability, "Congreso Internacional Las Reglas de Rotterdam, una nueva era en el Derecho uniforme del transporte," Universidad Carlos III de Madrid, Getafe, Madrid, Spain, 17-18 de Septiembre de 2009 –in the bilingual volume R. ILLESCAS ORTIZ, M. ALBA FERNANDEZ, LAS REGLAS DE ROTTERDAM: UNA NUEVA ERA EN EL DERECHO UNIFORME DEL TRANSPORTE. ACTAS DEL CONGRESO INTERNACIONAL,DYKINSON, MADRID, 2012, PP. 53 SS. AND 225 SS-. .

on the liability of the carrier if the claimant proves that the fault of the carrier caused or contributed to the event or circumstances the carrier relies on.[13]

5. Finally, without a direct relationship to the regime regulated under the four initial paragraphs of Art. 17 analyzed above, paragraph five of the same Article 17 includes other specific bases of liability for the carrier that are practically inexcusable. They are enumerated under Art. 17(5(a), which composes a second list of differentiated and much more powerful events than the events on the previous list under Article 17(3). I believe this list is much more powerful because the claimant proves and the carrier must produce a counter-proof for winning exoneration here. If the carrier fails in his task of producing the counter-proof, he will be liable for the loss, damage, or delay caused by any of the events on the list in Article 17(5)(a).

It is interesting to note that in Article 17 there are two lists, the long list and the shorter one. It is also interesting that the functioning of each list fulfilling its respective purpose is highly differentiated. In the case of the list under paragraph 3 of the article, the carrier alleges specific events, and the claimant has to prove that the alleged facts on which the allegation relies are wrong. In the give and take game of proof and counter-proof, with regard to the second list under paragraph 5 of Article 17, the proof of the event from the claimant operates as a rebuttable presumption of liability, but in the opposite way. Now, it is the carrier who becomes *prima facie* liable and, therefore, has to produce the counter-proof in order to avoid being declared liable.

The system of the basis of carrier liability encompassed in Article 17 is a balanced one. There are no exoneration causes in the convention, but only the rebuttable presumptions of the performance in due diligence even when they occur in a loss, damage, or delay.

As any balance at the beginning of the 21st Century, the design and operation of the reached *equilibrium* are not as simple or easy as they were at the beginning of the 20th Century. Law, economics, and commerce are much more complex today than 100 years ago. Thus, the search for simplicity in uniform law cannot be declared as an absolute priority. As usual, predictability, certainty, and fair treatment are much more important in uniform law and Maritime Law.

The carrier liability regime is not the only one of the conventional balances reached in 2008. Expressions of the balance featured by the convention can also be found in others

---

[13] Article 17(5)(a) provides "(i) unseaworthiness of the ship; (ii) the improper crewing, equipping, and supplying of the ship; and (iii) the fact that the holds or other parts of the ship in which the goods are carried, or any container supplied by the carrier in or upon which the goods are carried, were not fit and safe for reception, carriage, and preservation of the goods".

chapters of the Rotterdam Rules. The following rules are relevant: (i) the rules governing the electronification of the transport documents and (ii) the rules permitting the volume contract, and (iii) the rules on jurisdiction and arbitration. On these four innovative matters, the convention established specific safeguards that operate as a particular case permits, to preserve a satisfactory degree of equilibrium between the interest of the shipper and the carrier.

Turning to the electronification of the transport documents, balanced seminal norm is formulated by Article 8 (a) of the rules, to which reference was made at the beginning of this presentation[14]. I don't need to repeat the previous considerations, but it is interesting to annotate the fact that the required agreement between the parties in order to proceed to the electronification of the transport documents, and many other documents related to the performance of the carriage contract, is superior proof of the balance that the Convention reached: no one party to a contract of carriage can be obliged to substitute its paper documentation with electronic documentation. Previous consent is required from the text of the Rotterdam Rules, so every contract will adapt the documentation if the personal skills and equipment are available for both the parties to the contract. The bold advance into the modernization of contract documentation that the convention represents is, therefore, submitted to the abilities of shipper and carrier.

The volume contract and related partial reconnaissance of freedom of contract in the Rotterdam Rules, again, are found in the norm specific limits that make their way to an accurate balance between the parties and their opposed interests. Again, the rules that were previously referenced should be assessed because they have created the legal limit to the freedom of contract[15]. At this stage, only the result relevant to the moderation function that the legal limits of Article 80(2) to 80(4) of the rules provide concerning the use of contractual freedom and the free formation of the volume contract. In fact, the manifestation of balance is a requirement that before the formation of any volume contract, "the shipper is given an opportunity and notice of the opportunity to conclude a contract of carriage on terms and conditions that comply with this Convention without any derogation under this article"[16]. The obligation of the carrier to attribute to the shipper in the formation of a carriage contract the choice between a regular contract and a volume contract represents an additional illustration of the delicate balance that the rules contain. The weaker party, in

---

[14] Paragraph 1, Modernization.
[15] Paragraph 3, Freedom.
[16] Article 80(2).c of the rules. The reference made to "contracts that comply with terms and conditions of this convention" means that the carrier has to offer to the shipper a regular contract - a contract under Articles 17 and 59 - before offering him a second option, a derogating volume contract.

principle, has the right to choose the contract modality without any exception favorable to the carrier *a priori* the stronger party to the contract.

The final proof of the balance that the convention tried to reach, and reached effectively, can be found with regard to the innovative rules formulated on the jurisdiction and, consequently, on arbitration matters. As is already well-known, the rules in Chapter 14 on jurisdiction are not *prima facie* mandatory; "the provisions of this chapter shall bind only Contracting States that declare in accordance with article 91 that they will be bound by them,"[17] as stated in Article 74 of the Rules. The same situation is contemplated under Chapter 15 on arbitration, as a result of the rule formulated by Article 78[18]. The adopted formula was the way out of a complex negotiating situation characterized by the conflict between three different positions: (i) the European Union, whose member states' lack of treaty-making power with regard to commercial jurisdictions issues, was entitled to negotiate via the European Council and the European Commission on behalf of the Member States; however, not all of them were in agreement on the issue[19]; (ii) the position of the states that wanted to attribute the full validity to the jurisdiction's clauses in the liberal way permitted by the same silent, on the issue, Hague Rules, and (iii) the position of the negotiators favoring a high degree of legal restrictions on the choice of court agreements.

The results in Chapter 14 and 15 consist of an opt-in clause that allows all negotiators to keep their own interests alive with regard to jurisdiction and arbitration issues. Any contracting state interested in keeping the full validity of jurisdiction clauses or the choice of courts agreements celebrated by persons under its jurisdiction without the limitations specifically included in Article 66(a) of the Rotterdam Rules is allowed to not enter into the opt-in declaration. The opposite conduct is also permitted to any contracting state, making an opt-in declaration that the contracting state will be bound by the limits established in

---

[17] The mentioned Article 91 is a long and formalistic one related to the Law of Treaties and not to the Law of carriage. It is, however, interesting to check the applicable law and methods of the opting-in declarations of the states to be bound by both Chapter 14 and 15.

[18] "The provisions of this chapter shall bind only Contracting States that declare in accordance with article 91 that they will be bound by them"

[19] Explicit reference is made to the European Union Member States at the UNITED NATIONS, General Assembly, A/CN.9/572, 21 December 2004, Report of Working Group III (Transport Law) on the work of its fourteenth session (Viena, 29 November-10 December 2004), paragraph 112: "The Working Group heard that although the European Community had common rules in the area of jurisdiction as embodied in Brussels Regulation I (Council Regulation (EC) No 44/2001 od 22 December 2000 on jurisdiction and the recognition, and enforcement of judgments in civil and commercial matters), that would not prevent its members from negotiating rules in the draft instrument that derogated there from, if necessary." This final point, if necessary, "is a crucial one and the reason for the presence as negotiators, of the Commission and Council of the EU. The fact that Denmark is not bound by the mentioned EU Regulation Article 1(3) makes clear the statement above." To check the full text of the EU Regulation, visit *cfr.* OJEC, No. L 12/1, 16 January 2001.

Chapter 14. Turning to the European Union, not one of the member states can to produce any opt-in declarations in the absence of a common European position on the issue. This common position is nonexistent for the time being[20].

In view of these features, the balance of the adopted solution is quite clear. Even clearer is the comfort of the compromise reached on these points. The only difference among other balance expressions relies on the fact that, with specific regard to the jurisdiction and arbitration issues, the final decisions on the appropriate opt-in declaration is the choice of the states and not of the parties to the carriage contract. With the exception of the EU Member States, the competence is attributed to European governance institutions.

---

[20] This is the case of Spain, the only Contracting Party and EU Member Sate in the deposit of the Spanish Instrument of Ratification is not included in any opt-in declaration concerning Chapter 14 and 15 of the rules: Spain is waiting for the European common position.

Part I, Chapter 2

Coverage and the Parties Liabilities under the Rotterdam Rules

4

Scope of Application and Freedom of Contract

Michael F. Sturley[*]

Scope of application and freedom of contract are two sides of the same coin. The former defines the subjects that are covered by the Rotterdam Rules [1] while the latter defines the parties' ability to exclude subjects from the mandatory application of the Rules. It is therefore logical to consider the two issues together.

Scope of application was not controversial during the CMI and UNCITRAL negotiations. The principal discussion was about the best method to accomplish the agreed objective. Although the scope of the Rotterdam Rules is much broader than the scope of prior conventions, that expanded scope did not provoke any substantial disagreements.

Freedom of contract, on the other hand, was one of the most controversial issues during the negotiation of the Convention — even though an overwhelming majority in the Working Group ultimately supported the final compromise, which included freedom of contract. In my view, the freedom of contract provisions should not have been so controversial. The basic approach is substantially the same as the approach under the existing maritime conventions, i.e., the Hague,[2] Hague-Visby,[3] and Hamburg Rules.[4] Even the special rules for

---

[*] I write here solely in my academic capacity and the views I express are my own. They do not necessarily represent the views of, and they have not been endorsed or approved by, any of the groups or organizations (or any of the individual members) with which (and with whom) I have served.
[1] United Nations Convention on Contracts for the International Carriage of Goods Wholly or Partly by Sea, General Assembly Resolution 63/122, U.N. Doc. A/RES/63/122 (11 Dec. 2008).
[2] International Convention for the Unification of Certain Rules of Law Relating to Bills of Lading, Aug. 25, 1924, 120 L.N.T.S. 155 [hereinafter Hague Rules].
[3] The phrase "Hague-Visby Rules" describes the Hague Rules as amended by the Visby Amendments. *See* Protocol to Amend the International Convention for the Unification of Certain Rules of Law Relating to Bills of Lading, Feb. 23, 1968, 1412 U.N.T.S. 121, 128 (entered into force June 23, 1977). In many countries, the 1968 Hague-Visby Rules have been further amended by the 1979 Special Drawing Right (SDR) Protocol. *See* Protocol Amending the International Convention for the Unification of Certain Rules of Law Relating to Bills of Lading, Dec. 21, 1979, 1412 U.N.T.S. 121, 146 (entered into force Feb. 14, 1984).
[4] United Nations Convention on the Carriage of Goods by Sea, Mar. 31, 1978, 1695 U.N.T.S. 3

volume contracts are unlikely to result in any significant change in current practice.

I. Scope of Application[5]

One of the most fundamental issues for any legal instrument — whether it be a private contract, a domestic statute, or an international treaty — is defining when the instrument will apply. During the negotiations that produced the twentieth century's maritime conventions governing the carriage of goods by sea, defining the scope of application was often a controversial issue. In the 1920s, a principal dispute was whether the Hague Rules should regulate all forms of sea carriage, including carriage under charterparties, or whether the mandatory rules should be limited to liner shipments. Over forty years later, the single most contentious question in the negotiation of the Visby Protocol was whether the Hague-Visby Rules should govern inbound carriage *to* a contracting state (in addition to the traditional outbound carriage *from* a contracting state). And in the 1970s, the delegates negotiating the Hamburg Rules had to grapple with the extension of the regime to govern all contracts of carriage (except charterparties), without the traditional limitation to bills of lading.

The Rotterdam Rules' scope-of-application chapter was also extensively debated during the UNCITRAL negotiations, but not because of any serious disagreements over the substance of the chapter. On the contrary, a consensus quickly developed as to which transactions should be included and which should be excluded. The disagreement was instead over the best method to accomplish the agreed objective. Three different approaches were suggested and each one had its advocates. In the end, the scope-of-application chapter combined all three of the proposed approaches. That was not a compromise solution designed to satisfy the proponents of each approach. Rather, each approach had its advantages and disadvantages. By combining all three, the strengths of each one could offset the others' weaknesses. The combination thus enabled the final draft to define more clearly the transactions that are subject to the Convention.

[hereinafter Hamburg Rules].
[5] For a more detailed discussion of scope of application under the Rotterdam Rules, *see* Michael F. Sturley, Tomotaka Fujita & Gertjan van der Ziel, The Rotterdam Rules: The UN Convention on Contracts for the International Carriage of Goods Wholly or Partly by Sea ch. 2 (2010). The discussion here is largely drawn from that chapter. *See also, e.g.*, Michael F. Sturley, *Solving the Scope-of-Application Puzzle: Contracts, Trades, and Documents in the UNCITRAL Transport Law Project*, 11 J. Int'l Mar. L. 22 (2005).

1. The Documentary Approach in the Hague and Hague-Visby Rules

The Hague Rules were based on the idea that regulation was necessary for liner bills of lading but not for the charterparties used in the tramp trade. Thus the Hague Rules' coverage was defined in terms of the type of document issued in order to distinguish different types of trade.[6] The central phrase "contract of carriage" was limited to "contracts of carriage covered by a bill of lading or any similar document of title."[7] For charterparties, a compromise was agreed. To the extent that a charterparty governed the transaction (meaning, in effect, so long as the dispute remained between the original contracting parties under the charterparty), the Hague Rules would not apply. No need was seen to protect charterers automatically when the owners did not routinely have superior bargaining power. Sophisticated parties could protect themselves in the market. But when a bill of lading was issued under the charterparty and negotiated to a third-party holder, thus creating a new contract between the issuer and the third-party holder, then the Hague Rules would apply.[8] The rationale for excluding charterparties from the Hague Rules' scope of application did not apply to charterparty bills of lading. In that context, it was still appropriate to protect the holders that had played no role in the negotiation of the original charterparty.

The Hague-Visby Rules not only retained the documentary approach but also continued to govern only shipments from a contracting state.[9] The Visby Protocol did not change the charterparty exclusion or the treatment of charterparty bills of lading.

2. The Contractual Approach in the Hamburg Rules

The Hamburg Rules adopted a completely new scope-of-application approach. The Hamburg delegates decided that the documentary approach of the Hague and Hague-Visby Rules was too narrow, excluding too many transactions that were functionally equivalent to traditional liner bill of lading shipments. If the carrier issued a document that did not qualify as a "bill of lading or any similar document of title" under article 1(b) — which in some jurisdictions would include any non-negotiable document — or if the carrier issued no doc-

---

[6] In other words, the documentary approach became a surrogate for the trade approach. *Cf. infra* text at note 20.
[7] Hague Rules art. 1(b).
[8] Hague Rules arts. 1(b), 5.
[9] The Hague-Visby Rules have a slightly broader scope of application than the Hague Rules. Under article 10(c), the Hague-Visby Rules also apply to cases in which the clause paramount calls (directly or indirectly) for their application. *See infra* note 44 and accompanying text.

ument whatsoever, then the Hague and Hague-Visby Rules would not apply.

To address those concerns, the Hamburg Rules introduced in the maritime context what can be described as a "contractual approach."[10] The application of the convention depends on the parties' concluding a particular type of contract (without regard for the issuance of any particular document to evidence that contract). By its express terms, the provisions of the Hamburg Rules "are applicable to all contracts of carriage by sea" with a sufficient connection to a contracting state,[11] and a "contract of carriage by sea" is defined as "any contract whereby the carrier undertakes against payment of freight to carry goods by sea from one port to another."[12] Although the Hamburg Rules give the shipper the right to demand the issuance of a bill of lading[13] and recognize the possibility that a "bill of lading or other document [might] evidenc[e] the contract of carriage by sea,"[14] the issuance of a bill of lading is not a precondition to the application of the Rules. Indeed, the Hamburg Rules also recognized the possibility that no bill of lading would be issued.[15]

Despite the Hamburg Rules' reliance on a contractual approach, they do not entirely abandon the documentary approach. They retain the traditional charterparty exclusion[16] of the Hague and Hague-Visby Rules,[17] an exclusion that many would view as depending on the issuance of a particular type of document — a charterparty — to evidence a contract of carriage.[18] Moreover, they also retain the traditional treatment of charterparty bills of lading, which is generally recognized as a documentary approach. It provides that when "a bill of lading is issued pursuant to a charterparty, the provisions of the Convention apply to such a bill of lading if it governs the relation between the carrier and the holder of the bill of lading, not being the charterer."[19] In other words, the Hamburg Rules rely on a contractual approach to establish a broad general rule for the scope of application, but then follow a documentary approach perhaps for an exclusion from the broad general rule and at the very least for an exception to that exclusion.

---

[10] Transport law conventions governing other modes of carriage had previously adopted contractual approaches. *See, e.g.,* Convention on the Contract for the International Carriage of Goods By Road (CMR), art. 1(1), May 19, 1956, 399 U.N.T.S. 189.
[11] Hamburg Rules art. 2(1).
[12] Hamburg Rules art. 1(6).
[13] Hamburg Rules art. 14(1).
[14] Hamburg Rules art. 2(1)(d), (e).
[15] *See, e.g.,* Hamburg Rules art. 6(2)(a).
[16] Hamburg Rules art. 2(3).
[17] Hague Rules arts. 1(b), 5, Hague-Visby Rules arts. 1(b), 5.
[18] Others view a charterparty as a type of contract rather than a document evidencing a type of contract.
[19] Hamburg Rules art. 2(3).

3. The Introduction of a "Trade Approach"

During the negotiation of the Rotterdam Rules, a new proposal was made to adopt what can be described as a "trade approach," in which the application of the Convention would turn on the type of trade in which the carrier was engaged. Under that proposal, shipments in the liner trade would have been governed by the Convention on the theory that those transactions occur in a context that generally justifies the application of mandatory law. Contracts in the liner trade are less apt to be individually negotiated because form contracts (such as bills of lading and sea waybills) are the norm, and it has generally been assumed that an equality of bargaining power between the shipper and the carrier is less common in the liner trade. But the proposed trade approach would have excluded shipments in the tramp trade, a context in which individually negotiated charterparties and an equality of bargaining power are the norm.

Although the trade approach may appear novel, its theoretical justification goes back at least to the 1920s. The Hague Rules' distinction between bills of lading and charterparties was intended primarily to distinguish between liner and tramp shipments.[20] One goal of the trade approach was thus to accomplish directly what the Hague Rules' documentary approach was designed to achieve indirectly.

4. The Strengths and Weaknesses of the Documentary, Contractual, and Trade Approaches

The documentary, contractual, and trade approaches each have certain advantages and disadvantages in defining the scope of application for a maritime transport convention. Any one of them, standing alone, could have enabled the Convention to cover those transactions for which there was consensus support (albeit with some adjustments for special cases), at least to the extent that those transactions could be identified in advance. And each of the three would have been superior in some way to the other two. But by the same token, each of the three would have been inadequate in some way to accomplish all that needed to be done.

(1) The Documentary Approach

The documentary approach, having been in force for over eighty years, has the substantial

---

[20] See *supra* notes 6-7 and accompanying text.

benefit of being familiar to the industry. But the Hague and Hague-Visby version is too narrow for modern needs. Today's industry uses an array of documents in addition to the traditional bill of lading, many of which do not qualify as "similar documents of title" (at least in some legal systems). Furthermore, the Convention needs to facilitate the use of electronic commerce, which may operate without documents.

Perhaps both problems could have been solved with an updated list of covered documents (or their functional equivalents). Including explicit references to sea waybills, data interchange receipts, and electronic records would have been entirely straightforward. But that solution might quickly have become too narrow. The industry will undoubtedly develop new forms of documentation more quickly than the international legal community can develop a new convention (or even an amending protocol) to cover them. Perhaps the expanded list of covered documents could have ended with a general phrase, much as the Hague and Hague-Visby Rules cover not only bills of lading but also "similar" documents of title. The Convention might have covered "bills of lading, sea waybills, data interchange receipts, *and similar transport documents*" (along with their electronic equivalents). Although such a vague term might have permitted the courts to update the Convention to keep pace with a changing industry, it would have left the coverage at least somewhat ambiguous. Clarity would be obtained only through costly litigation that would be likely to produce different results in different jurisdictions.

On a more basic level, the documentary approach (no matter how broadly the covered documents are defined) is incapable of dealing with cases in which the parties do not intend that any document ever be issued for a specific shipment. To the extent that document-free transactions are increasingly common (in European short seas shipments, for example) and within the intended scope of the Convention, the documentary approach standing alone would inevitably have been inadequate to define the Convention's scope of application.

(2) The Contractual Approach

The contractual approach does not have the long history of the documentary approach, but it is still familiar to the industry. The Hamburg Rules have been in force in some countries since 1993, and there has been ample opportunity to study the approach and identify its weaknesses. Moreover, it solves the principal problem with the documentary approach. The serious gaps in coverage that have arisen under the Hague and Hague-Visby Rules would all be filled under a contractual approach. Even when no document is issued, the parties still have a contract of carriage.

The principal weakness with the contractual approach is its potential for being overly inclusive. It might accidentally cover transactions that are functionally equivalent to excluded transactions but that do not fall within the defined terms of the exclusion. For example, UNCITRAL readily agreed to exclude charterparties and considered a proposal to similarly exclude "contracts of affreightment, volume contracts, or similar agreements."[21] Heavy lift contracts were not specifically mentioned.[22] They are not charterparties, but would they have qualified as "similar agreements"? The argument for excluding them would have been indistinguishable from the argument for excluding charterparties, contracts of affreightment, and volume contracts. But a court might have decided to include heavy lift contracts (applying the broad contract of carriage definition) if they were not explicitly excluded. Although that immediate problem could have been solved by adding heavy lift contracts to the list of exclusions, there were serious concerns that the industry's next specialized, individually negotiated, non-liner contract — a new form of contract that UNCITRAL by definition could not have considered — might have been included within the scope of the Convention because a court did not believe that it was sufficiently "similar" to the listed agreements, or did not believe that it was "similar" in the proper way (particularly if it was impossible to define what sort of similarity would be relevant).[23]

(3) The Trade Approach

The trade approach has a strong logical appeal. The traditional distinction between bills of lading and charterparties was intended primarily to distinguish between liner shipments and tramp shipments.[24] The trade approach was thus designed to accomplish directly what the Hague Rules' documentary approach was intended to achieve indirectly. On a more practical level, the trade approach addresses the principal criticism of the contractual approach. It may be impossible to predict the industry's next specialized, individually negotiated contract comparable to a heavy lift contract.[25] But it can at least be recognized that those types of contracts, by their very nature, will not occur in the liner trade. Limiting the

---

[21] Transport Law: Draft instrument on the carriage of goods [wholly or partly] [by sea], art. 2(3), U.N. doc. no. A/CN.9/WG.III/WP.32 (4 September 2003); Transport Law: Preliminary draft instrument on the carriage of goods by sea, art. 3.3.1, U.N. doc. no. A/CN.9/WG.III/WP.21 (8 January 2002) [hereinafter Preliminary Draft Instrument WP.21].

[22] Heavy lift contracts were mentioned for the first time several years into the process. *See* Report of Working Group III (Transport Law) on the work of its fourteenth session ¶ 85 (Vienna, 29 November-10 December 2004), U.N. doc. no. A/CN.9/572 (2004). Not surprisingly, there was "broad agreement that . . . heavy lift contracts should be excluded from the application of the draft instrument." *Id.* ¶ 89. But of course heavy lift contracts are simply illustrations of the broader problem. Similar observations could be made with respect to other types of contracts that either were not explicitly discussed by UNCITRAL (such as supply contracts) or were not explicitly discussed until fairly late in the process (such as towage contracts).

[23] The Rotterdam Rules address the issue in article 6(2). *See infra* note 64 and accompanying text.

[24] *See supra* notes 6-7 and accompanying text.

[25] *See supra* notes 21-23 and accompanying text.

Convention's scope of application to the liner trade would avoid a major risk of inadvertent coverage.

The trade approach is nevertheless subject to several criticisms. First, it is a new approach, and thus does not have the long tradition of the documentary approach or even the more limited experience of the contractual approach. With no history, it is difficult to predict how courts will interpret it. Thus it might fail to bring the uniformity and predictability that the Convention strives to obtain. Distinguishing between liner shipments and tramp shipments, or between liner and non-liner shipments, might also be problematic. Although there should be little doubt in most cases in which category a transaction falls, the line can still be blurry at the margins.

In any event, the trade approach would be inadequate by itself to define the Convention's scope of application to give full effect to the substantive consensus about which transactions should be subject to the Convention. Most obviously, the industry has long accepted, at least since the adoption of the Hague Rules, that mandatory law should govern at least some transactions in the tramp trade, including cases in which a bill of lading issued under a charterparty has been negotiated to a third party.[26] Approaching the issue from the opposite perspective, there was a broad consensus that at least some transactions in the liner trade, such as slot charters and time charters, should not be covered.

Moreover, the liner and tramp trades do not constitute an exhaustive list. Some shipowners operate in a gap between the two trades essentially as liner carriers, but they do not fully satisfy the requirements of the liner trade.[27] For example, the liner trade is generally understood to require a regularly scheduled service, operating either on a timetable or at least on announced sailing dates.[28] But some carriers offer what would otherwise be recognized as liner services except that they operate on an "on demand" basis rather than as a regularly scheduled service. When shippers have a higher demand, they sail more frequently, and when shippers' demand is lower, they sail less frequently. But they issue traditional bills of lading (and thus are within the scope of the Hague or Hague-Visby Rules) and the policy justifications for applying a mandatory law to them apply just as strongly is in the strict liner context.[29]

---

[26] Hague Rules arts. 1(b), 5; Hague-Visby Rules arts. 1(b), 5; Hamburg Rules art. 2(3).
[27] The common-law distinction between "common carriage" and "private carriage" might better define the line that the trade approach seeks to draw, but those legal concepts would not be widely understood in all legal systems.
[28] *See infra* notes 71-72 and accompanying text (discussing the definitions of "liner" and "non-liner" trade).
[29] The Rotterdam Rules address the issue in article 6(2). *See infra* notes 65-67 and accompanying text.

5. The Rotterdam Rules' Combination of the Documentary, Contractual, and Trade Approaches

The three theoretical approaches to defining the scope of application for the Convention did not represent any disagreement among the UNCITRAL delegations on matters of substance. Each of the three was intended to include the same types of transactions within the scope of the Convention, and there was broad agreement on what those transactions should be. The issue was rather a practical one: which of the approaches would best accomplish the goal of clearly and predictably including the transactions that should be included and, just as important, excluding the transactions that should be excluded? Not only must the courts in a wide range of legal systems be able to recognize when the Convention applies, but commercial parties must be able to tell when they must conform their behavior to the mandatory rules (and know when they have the freedom to contract on terms of their own choosing).

Because each approach had advantages and disadvantages, it proved impossible to choose a single approach for the Convention. Any single choice would have been inadequate in some way. The Rotterdam Rules therefore combine all three approaches, taking advantage of each one's strengths to compensate for the others' weaknesses. Of course, combining different approaches to define the scope of application is not unprecedented. The Hamburg Rules already combined a contractual approach to establish a broad general rule with a documentary approach perhaps to create an exclusion from that general rule and at the very least to create an exception to the exclusion.[30]

The solution adopted was not by any means a political compromise. Indeed, the three alternatives did not represent competing values or substantive positions for which a compromise would have been appropriate. Rather, they each represented a somewhat different route to an agreed destination. The combination of the three approaches thus became an elegant solution to a perplexing puzzle. The hybrid solution deals with the contractual approach's overly broad coverage and inability to define which transactions should be excluded by using the documentary and trade approaches to define the exclusions. It deals with the documentary approach's inability to define all the transactions that should be included by relying on documents primarily to identify some, but not all, of the covered transactions. It deals with the problems of distinguishing trades at the margin by using the trade approach primarily to exclude transactions that do not fall at the margins, allowing the docu-

---

[30] See *supra* notes 16-19 and accompanying text.

mentary approach to do most of the work for close cases at the margins. And it deals with the conceptual problems of the documentary and trade approaches by using the contractual approach as the fundamental criterion for coverage under the Convention.

6. The General Scope-of-Application Rule: Broad Coverage Under the Contractual Approach

Article 5 establishes the general scope-of-application rule that initially defines transactions subject to the Convention. Article 5 is over-inclusive, however, identifying some transactions under its broad terms that should not be governed by the Convention. Articles 6 and 7 therefore fine-tune the general rule to exclude those transactions.[31] But before we can consider the details of the fine-tuning, we must first examine article 5's general rule.

(1) The Contractual Approach

The general scope-of-application rule in article 5 starts with the contractual approach: "this Convention applies to contracts of carriage."[32] "Contract of carriage," in turn, is defined in article 1(1) as "a contract in which a carrier, against the payment of freight, undertakes to carry goods from one place to another."[33] The definition continues with a clarifying sentence: "The contract shall provide for carriage by sea and may provide for carriage by other modes of transport in addition to the sea carriage."[34]

The "contract of carriage" definition includes several significant elements. Most fundamentally, the definition concerns the carrier's "undertak[ing] to carry goods," which refers to the promise to perform rather than the actual performance.[35] The contractual focus is also evident in article 1(5), which defines a "carrier" as the "person that enters into a contract of carriage with a shipper"[36] (i.e., the person that promises to carry the goods), not the person that in fact carries the goods, and in article 1(8), which defines a "shipper" as the "person that enters into a contract of carriage with a carrier"[37] (i.e., a person to whom a carrier's promise is owed), not the person that delivers the goods to a carrier for shipment.

---

[31] Article 5 thus opens with the recognition that it is "[s]ubject to article 6."
[32] Article 5(1). Even the formal title of the Convention – "Convention on Contracts for the International Carriage of Goods Wholly or Partly by Sea" – stresses the contractual approach.
[33] Article 1(1).
[34] Article 1(1).
[35] The contractual focus is important in the present context for establishing the Convention's scope of application, but the emphasis on the contract rather than its performance is important in many parts of the Convention.
[36] Article 1(5).
[37] Article 1(8).

The "contract of carriage" definition also introduces two substantive requirements that must be satisfied for the Convention to apply. The less significant is that the shipper must agree to pay for the carrier's service. If the carrier agrees to carry the goods other than "against the payment of freight," then the Convention does not apply. That is rarely an issue in practice, of course, because carriers almost inevitably insist on the payment of freight. But if a non-commercial, gratuitous transaction arises, it falls outside the scope of the Convention.

The more significant requirement in article 1(1) is the need for a maritime element to the transaction. To invoke the Convention, a contract must "provide for carriage by sea." But the contract need not be limited to sea carriage. It "may provide for carriage by other modes of transport in addition to the sea carriage." The permissive "may" establishes that additional modes are optional; a contract for sea carriage alone (i.e., a port-to-port contract) is undoubtedly covered. In the words of the Convention's official title, therefore, the Rotterdam Rules cover "contracts for the . . . carriage of goods *wholly or partly* by sea" (emphasis added). This is accordingly not a full multimodal convention (which would apply if two different modes of any kind were at issue), but rather a "maritime-plus" convention.

(2) The Internationality Requirements

Once a contract of carriage satisfies the article 1(1) definition, the three geographic requirements in article 5(1) must still be satisfied before the Convention will apply. The first two requirements ensure that the shipment is sufficiently international. As is true with all international transport conventions,[38] the Rotterdam Rules are not intended to govern purely domestic transactions.[39] It was understood from the beginning of the negotiations that an international shipment would be required in order to invoke the new regime. For purely unimodal regimes, this is an entirely straightforward requirement. Thus the Hamburg Rules, which govern only port-to-port ocean shipments, apply to "contracts of carriage by sea between two different States"[40] (if certain other requirements are also satisfied). The Rotterdam Rules, in contrast, may govern not only ocean shipments on a port-to-port basis but also multimodal shipments on a door-to-door, port-to-door, or door-to-port basis. The internationality requirement is accordingly more complex.

After extensive discussion, UNCITRAL decided that both the overall contractual ship-

---

[38] *See, e.g.,* Hague-Visby Rules art. 10; Hamburg Rules art. 2(1).
[39] A contracting state would, of course, be free to extend the Rotterdam Rules to govern purely domestic transactions as a matter of domestic law.
[40] Hamburg Rules art. 2(1). The Hague-Visby Rules similarly "apply to every bill of lading relating to the carriage of goods between ports in two different States" if certain other requirements are also satisfied. Hague-Visby Rules art. 10.

ment and its maritime component must be international.[41] Under the first internationality requirement, the Convention applies only if the contractual places of receipt and delivery are in different countries. In other words, the overall shipment must be international. This is consistent with prior transport conventions (which also look to the overall shipment, albeit within their unimodal scope) and with the Convention's emphasis on the contract (because the contract will inevitably specify the overall carriage).

Under the second internationality requirement, the Convention applies only if the contractual ports of loading and discharge are in different countries. In other words, the sea carriage must be international. This is consistent with prior transport conventions in a different sense because each of them focuses on the internationality of the mode of carriage that it governs. It is also consistent with the Convention's "maritime-plus" nature. The maritime leg is not simply one part of a door-to-door journey regulated by the Convention, it is the part of the shipment that triggers the Convention's application. Without the maritime leg, the Convention would not govern the other parts of the multimodal shipment.

(3) The Connection with a Contracting State

The third geographic requirement in article 5(1) ensures that a transaction has a sufficient connection with a contracting state before it is subject to the Rotterdam Rules. Over the years, different transport law conventions have demanded different levels of connection. The Warsaw Convention requires *both* the country of shipment *and* the country of destination to be contracting states.[42] No maritime convention has been so restrictive. The Hague Rules apply when the country of shipment is a party to the convention (without regard to the status of the country of destination).[43] In other words, the Hague Rules apply only to outbound shipments (shipments from a contracting state). The Hague-Visby Rules expanded the scope only slightly to include, in addition, cases in which the clause paramount calls (directly or indirectly) for their application.[44] The Hamburg Rules apply when *either* the

---

[41] There is no requirement or expectation that inland legs before or after sea carriage be international. Thus a shipment from Milan to Chicago via Genoa and New York would satisfy the internationality requirements. The overall shipment (from Milan to Chicago) is international and the sea carriage (from Genoa to New York) is international. Neither the domestic carriage from Milan to Genoa nor the domestic carriage from New York to Chicago is subject to an internationality requirement.
[42] Warsaw Convention art. 1(2).
[43] *See* Hague Rules art. 10. Strictly speaking, the Hague Rules "apply to all bills of lading issued in any of the contracting States." *Ibid.* As a practical matter, it was assumed that bills of lading would generally be issued in the country from which the goods were shipped.
[44] Hague-Visby Rules art. 10(c) (extending coverage to transactions in which the contract of carriage "provides that these Rules or legislation of any State giving effect to them are to govern the contract"). Article 10(c) filled the gap identified by the British Privy Council in *Vita Food Prod-*

country of shipment *or* the country of destination is a contracting state.[45] In other words, the Hamburg Rules apply to both inbound and outbound shipments (shipments to or from a contracting state).

The Rotterdam Rules continue the trend of expanding the scope of application by making the "connection requirement" easier to satisfy. Like the Hamburg Rules, they apply to both inbound and outbound shipments. For multimodal shipments, however, the scope of application may expand. The "country of shipment" could refer to either the place of receipt[46] (at the beginning of the initial inland leg before the sea carriage) or the port of loading[47] (where the sea carriage begins), and the "country of destination" could refer to either the place of delivery[48] (at the end of the final inland leg after the sea carriage) or the port of discharge[49] (where the sea carriage ends). The Rotterdam Rules apply if *any* of those four places is located in a contracting state.[50]

In two respects, the Rotterdam Rules' scope of application is narrower than that of prior maritime conventions because UNCITRAL rejected two connecting factors that had previously been accepted. The Hague-Visby[51] and Hamburg[52] Rules apply if the transport document is issued in a contracting state. But UNCITRAL recognized that the physical location in which documents are issued is largely irrelevant in the age of electronic commerce, and in any event does not have any necessary connection to the underlying transaction.

The Hague-Visby[53] and Hamburg[54] Rules also apply if the contract of carriage "provides that these Rules or legislation of any State giving effect to them are to govern the contract." That provision was originally introduced by the Visby Amendments to effectively overrule an unduly restrictive decision limiting the application of the Hague Rules[55] and then carried forward into the Hamburg Rules without extensive consideration. But UNCITRAL reject-

---

ucts, Inc. v. Unus Shipping Co., [1939] AC 277.
[45] Hamburg Rules art. 2(1). Some national enactments of the Hague and Hague-Visby Rules similarly apply to both inbound and outbound shipments. *See, e.g.,* U.S. Carriage of Goods by Sea Act § 13 ("This Act shall apply to all contracts for carriage of goods by sea *to or from* ports of the United States in foreign trade.") (emphasis added).
[46] Article 5(1)(a).
[47] Article 5(1)(b).
[48] Article 5(1)(c).
[49] Article 5(1)(d).
[50] For a port-to-port shipment, the place of receipt and the port of loading will be the same place. Similarly, the place of delivery and the port of discharge will be the same place. For port-to-port shipments, therefore, the geographic requirements would be the same for the Hamburg and Rotterdam Rules.
[51] Hague-Visby Rules arts. 10(a).
[52] Hamburg Rules art. 2(1)(d).
[53] Hague-Visby Rules arts. 10(c). *See also supra* note 44 and accompanying text.
[54] Hamburg Rules art. 2(1)(e).
[55] *See* Hague-Visby *Travaux Préparatoires* 714-741.

ed a draft provision[56] to incorporate substantially the same principle in the Rotterdam Rules. UNCITRAL concluded that it would be inappropriate to permit the parties to a transaction to agree by contract to the application of the Convention with the force of law, particularly when the Convention includes chapters on jurisdiction and arbitration. Such a result would be inconsistent with the choice-of-law rules in many jurisdictions and in any event could allow parties to override the procedural rules of a forum state.[57]

7. Using the Documentary and Trade Approaches to Limit the Scope of Application: Exclusions from the Broad General Rule and Exceptions to the Exclusions

Once article 5 and its contractual approach have broadly included every transaction that might plausibly be governed by the Convention, article 6 excludes transactions that should not be governed by the mandatory law. Article 6(2)(b) and article 7, however, recognize two exceptions to the article 6 exclusions, both of which are necessary to preserve the traditional coverage of the Hague, Hague-Visby, and Hamburg Rules.

Precisely and accurately defining the line between included and excluded transactions has long been a problem for the contractual approach,[58] particularly as modern industry recognizes more and varied types of contracts. Article 6 therefore combines the traditional documentary approach and the new trade approach to assist in making the necessary distinctions. As noted above, the Hague,[59] Hague-Visby,[60] and Hamburg[61] Rules all arguably use the documentary approach to exclude charterparty transactions from the general scope of application and in any event use the documentary approach to include charterparty bills of lading. Articles 6 and 7 build on that experience.

(1) The Charterparty Exclusion

When UNCITRAL began its negotiations, it was already well recognized that the traditional charterparty exclusion would continue; the industry is strongly in favor of retaining it, and no one expressed a compelling reason to change it. Implementing that consensus was nevertheless more complicated than it had been in the 1920s. The key term "charter-

---

[56] *See, e.g.,* Transport Law: Draft convention on the carriage of goods [wholly or partly] [by sea], art. 8(1)(c), U.N. doc. no. A/CN.9/WG.III/WP.56 (8 September 2005).
[57] *See* Proposal by Japan on scope of application, U.N. doc. no. A/CN.9/WG.III/WP.65 (27 January 2006) (explaining the difficulties).
[58] *See supra* notes 21-23 and accompanying text.
[59] Hague Rules arts. 1(b), 5.
[60] Hague-Visby Rules arts. 1(b), 5.
[61] Hamburg Rules art. 2(3).

party" was never satisfactorily defined (despite efforts to achieve a definition), even in the 1920s (when commercial practices were less complicated). With the growth of new commercial practices, carriers and cargo owners now enter into a broad range of contracts that bear a closer resemblance to traditional charterparties than to bills of lading, but that do not really fit into either category. To the extent that the parties to the "new" contracts are sophisticated commercial actors with comparable bargaining power, it makes sense to treat them in the same way that the law treats those who conclude charterparties.[62] But it is not always easy to define which of the new contracts are sufficiently like charterparties and which are not, particularly in the absence of any agreement on the relevant criteria. The discussion of heavy lift contracts[63] illustrates how difficult it is to anticipate every possibility.

To avoid the weaknesses associated with any individual approach, UNCITRAL ultimately decided to implement the charterparty exclusion with a combination of the trade and (arguably) documentary approaches. Transactions in liner trades that otherwise qualify are generally within the Rotterdam Rules' scope of application, but UNCITRAL recognized that charterparties and charterparty equivalents are sometimes used in liner trades. Thus article 6(1)(a) excludes from coverage all "charterparties" in liner trades and article 6(1)(b) excludes other contracts in liner trades "for the use of a ship or any space thereon" (such as slot charters or space charters).

As a practical matter, "charterparties" covered by article 6(1)(a) will also be excluded by the broader definition in article 6(1)(b), thus making article 6(1)(a) superfluous in most cases. The charterparty exclusion is so well-established (and strongly supported), however, that it was thought wiser to risk the inclusion of a superfluous sub-paragraph than to draft an exclusion that might not cover all charterparties. Similarly, any document satisfying article 6(1)(b)'s definition would probably be considered a "charterparty" under article 6(1)(a) in any event, thus making article 6(1)(b) redundant in most cases. Once again, the desire to exclude transactions under slot charters or space charters, even if they might not literally qualify as "charterparties" in some legal systems, was so strong that it was preferable to include a possibly redundant sub-paragraph to ensure the desired result.

Article 6(1) does not address non-liner transactions, the trade in which most charterparties have traditionally been used. Article 6(2) thus excludes all non-liner transactions as a general rule, but relies on the documentary approach to create a limited exception (because a blanket exclusion would have been too broad). By excluding most non-liner transactions,

---

[62] The treatment of "volume contracts" created an entirely different set of problems, which will be discussed in part II of this paper. See *infra* notes 112-166.
[63] See *supra* notes 21-22 and accompanying text.

the trade approach straight-forwardly resolves most of the cases covered by the traditional charterparty exclusion. In addition, it resolves otherwise difficult cases involving contracts that are sufficiently like charterparties that they should be similarly excluded from the scope of application.[64] Heavy lift contracts, for example, are used only in the non-liner trade. Article 6(2) thus excludes them without needing to resolve potentially complicated questions about other ways in which they might be similar to charterparties.

In one regard, the total exclusion of all non-liner cases would be too broad. Although UNCITRAL agreed that all tramp shipping should be excluded, "tramp" shipping is somewhat narrower than "non-liner" services. For example, "on demand" carriers operate essentially as liner companies in the sense that they offer their services to the public generally and issue bills of lading, but they do not operate on a regular schedule.[65] Because they issue bills of lading rather than concluding charterparties, their shipments have typically been within the scope of the Hague, Hague-Visby, and Hamburg Rules. In order to ensure their continued coverage, the general exclusion of non-liner transactions in article 6(2) is qualified by an exception that preserves the Convention for cases in which no charterparty or similar document is used[66] but instead a bill of lading or its modern equivalent is issued.[67]

To summarize, then, the Rotterdam Rules extend the traditional charterparty exclusion so that it now excludes from the Rotterdam Rules three types of transactions that are functionally similar to traditional charterparties: (1) transactions under a charterparty (in liner or non-liner transportation),[68] (2) transactions under contracts "for the use of a ship or of any space thereon" (in liner or non-liner transportation),[69] and (3) other transactions in non-liner transportation in which no "transport document or . . . electronic transport record is issued."[70]

(2) Defining Liner and Non-Liner Trade

For the trade approach to work, it must be reasonably clear what is meant by "liner" and "non-liner" trade. Article 1(3) defines "liner transportation" as

---

[64] *See supra* notes 21-23 and accompanying text.
[65] *See supra* text at notes 27-29.
[66] Article 6(2)(a).
[67] Article 6(2)(b).
[68] Article 6(1)(a) (excluding charterparties in liner transportation), 6(2)(a) (excluding charterparties in non-liner transportation). This category simply represents the continuation of the charterparty exclusion of the Hague, Hague-Visby, and Hamburg Rules.
[69] Article 6(1)(b) (liner transportation), 6(2)(a) (non-liner transportation).
[70] Article 6(2)(b). When a "transport document or an electronic transport record is issued," article 6(2)(b) preserves the traditional coverage of the Hague, Hague-Visby, and Hamburg Rules.

a transportation service that is offered to the public through publication or similar means and includes transportation by ships operating on a regular schedule between specified ports in accordance with publicly available timetables of sailing dates.[71]

"Non-liner transportation" is not independently defined, but is simply "any transportation that is not liner transportation." [72]

To qualify as "liner transportation," a transportation service must satisfy two requirements (each of which is phrased in general terms to preserve enough flexibility to accommodate future commercial and regulatory developments). First, the service must be offered to the public through publication or similar means. In some jurisdictions, legislation specifies how liner services are offered (for example, by filing a tariff). In any event, the customary method of offering a liner service is generally well-known in most jurisdictions. Second, the service must include transportation by regularly scheduled ships following published timetables. The definition requires only that the transportation service "include" this element because a liner service may also offer additional services, such as warehousing.

8. The Treatment of Third Parties in Excluded Transactions

As noted above,[73] the traditional charterparty exclusion affects only the original contracting parties. If the carrier issues a bill of lading that passes to a third party (a person other than the original charterer), then the Hague, Hague-Visby, and Hamburg Rules would all govern the relationship between the carrier and that third party (in an otherwise appropriate case).[74] In a second exception to article 6's charterparty exclusion, article 7 preserves the traditional treatment of charterparty bills of lading. But the Convention's expanded scope requires a broader approach (which is not limited to charterparties or bills of lading).

The article 7 exception is not limited to the charterparty context because article 6's exclusion is not so limited. Just as article 6 excludes arrangements comparable to (but arguably distinct from) charterparties, so article 7 applies the Convention as between the carrier and a third party that is entitled to assert the shipper's rights under *any* of the excluded arrangements.

Similarly, just as the Convention as a whole is not limited to bills of lading, so the article

---

[71] Article 1(3).
[72] Article 1(4).
[73] See *supra* notes 8 & 19 and accompanying text.
[74] See Hague Rules art. 1(b); Hague-Visby Rules art. 1(b); Hamburg Rules art. 2(3).

7 exception does not depend on the issuance or transfer of a bill of lading.[75] Indeed, article 7 does not even depend on transport documents or electronic transport records (as many other provisions in the Convention do). Article 7 instead lists the parties that could acquire the relevant status under any of the excluded arrangements — consignees, controlling parties, and holders. Together, those are the parties that can by virtue of their status assert the original shipper's rights,[76] and are thus the parties that functionally correspond to the holder of a charterparty bill of lading under the narrower traditional analysis. Because the Rotterdam Rules permit a shipper to be a consignee, controlling party, or holder, however, article 7 concludes with the clarification that its special treatment does not apply as between the original contracting parties.

9. Nationality of the Parties or the Ship

Fifty years ago, during the preparation of what ultimately became the Hague-Visby Rules, a question arose whether an international convention could properly apply in an action between two nationals of the same state. To avoid any possible ambiguity, a clause was added at the end of the scope-of-application article to clarify that "the nationality of the ship, the carrier, the shipper, the consignee, or any other interested person" was irrelevant.[77] Substantially the same language was carried forward to the Hamburg Rules[78] and somewhat broader language (to recognize the broader scope of the Convention) has now been repeated in article 5(2). Although the provision is probably unnecessary today, UNCITRAL feared that if the language were deleted it could be seen as a signal that the nationality of the vessel or the parties might indeed be relevant to the Convention's scope of application.[79]

---

[75] Cf. Hague Rules art. 1(b); Hague-Visby Rules art. 1(b); Hamburg Rules art. 2(3).
[76] The consignee, for example, is simply the person entitled to delivery of the goods. *See* article 1(11). A "controlling party" is defined in article 1(13), which further refers to article 51. A "holder" is defined in article 1(10).
[77] *See* Hague-Visby Rules art. 10.
[78] *See* Hamburg Rules art. 2(2).
[79] Article 5(2) is one of several provisions that are retained in the Rotterdam Rules primarily to avoid any implication that their omission — after consistently appearing in prior maritime conventions — might be significant. *See also*, e.g., Article 79(1)(c) (preserving the ban on benefit-of-insurance clauses previously included in article 3(8) of the Hague and Hague-Visby Rules and article 23(1) of the Hamburg Rules); *infra* note 139 (discussing article 79(1)(c) and benefit-of-insurance clauses).

II. Freedom of Contract[80]

"Freedom of contract" has long been the general caption for the debate over the extent to which the rules of an international convention will be mandatory — *i.e.*, the extent to which the parties to a transaction within the convention's scope of application will be required to follow the convention's rules and will be prohibited from varying those rules by contract. Nothing about a "convention" inevitably requires that all its rules must be mandatory. The parties to an international sales transaction, for example, can entirely avoid the application of the Vienna Sales Convention if their contract so provides.[81] But the tradition established by the twentieth century's carriage conventions was, to a considerable extent, for mandatory rules. The Rotterdam Rules, however, reexamined and refined that tradition.

1. The Mandatory Character of the Existing Maritime Conventions

Understanding freedom of contract under the Rotterdam Rules requires a review of some history. In the early nineteenth century, carriers were subject to what has often been described (somewhat inaccurately) as "insurer" liability. A carrier was liable for all cargo damage unless it could prove one of a small list of exceptions.[82] Starting in the middle of the nineteenth century, carriers reacted to that responsibility by drafting their bills of lading to include broad exculpatory clauses that were designed to excuse them from liability for most cargo damage.[83] The nineteenth century British courts, in deference to "freedom of contract," would enforce those broad exculpatory clauses, even to the point of excusing carriers from liability for their own negligence.[84] European and Commonwealth countries

---

[80] For a more detailed discussion of freedom of contract under the Rotterdam Rules, see STURLEY, FUJITA & VAN DER ZIEL, *supra* note 5, ch. 13; Michael F. Sturley, *The Mandatory Character of the Convention and Its Exceptions: Volume Contracts*, in LAS REGLAS DE ROTTERDAM: UNA NUEVA ERA EN EL DERECHO UNIFORME DEL TRANSPORTE: ACTAS DEL CONGRESO INTERNACIONAL [THE ROTTERDAM RULES: A NEW ERA IN UNIFORM TRANSPORT LAW: PROCEEDINGS OF THE INTERNATIONAL CONGRESS] 271 (Rafael Illescas Ortiz & Manuel Alba Fernández eds. 2011). The discussion here is largely drawn from those sources.

[81] *See* United Nations Convention on Contracts for the International Sale of Goods, art. 6, 1489 U.N.T.S. 3, 11 April 1980 ("The parties may exclude the application of this Convention or, subject to article 12, derogate from or vary the effect of any of its provisions.").

[82] *See generally, e.g.*, Jan Ramberg, *Freedom of Contract in Maritime Law*, 1993 LLOYD'S MAR. & COM. L.Q. 178, 178 (1993); Michael F. Sturley, *The History of COGSA and the Hague Rules*, 22 J. MAR. L. & COM. 1, 4-5 (1991) [hereinafter *History*].

[83] *See generally, e.g.*, Ramberg, *supra* note 82, at 179.

[84] *See* Sturley, *History, supra* note 82, at 5 & n.23.

generally followed the British example.[85] In the United States and some other countries, however, freedom of contract was limited: Carriers could not escape liability for the consequences of their own negligence or for their failure to furnish a seaworthy vessel.[86] Against that background, the U.S. Congress enacted the Harter Act[87] in 1893, adopting the famous compromise[88] that ultimately became the basis for the Hague Rules.[89] Several other countries followed the U.S. example during the next two decades and adopted Harter-style legislation.[90]

During the negotiation of the Hague Rules in the early 1920s, freedom of contract was the primary focus of the discussion. The single biggest question at that time was whether the new regime should be mandatory and, if so, to what extent. The principal debate was between those representing cargo interests, who sought mandatory rules that would impose minimum obligations on carriers for cargo loss or damage, and those representing carrier interests, who argued for unrestricted freedom of contract.[91] That debate was ultimately resolved with a commercial compromise whereby some transactions (generally[92] those evidenced by bills of lading) were subject to mandatory rules while other transactions (primarily those between a vessel owner and a charterer) enjoyed substantial freedom of contract.

In subsequent decades, the liner trade showed less concern with freedom of contract. When the Visby Amendments were negotiated in the late 1950s and the 1960s, two dozen different proposals to change the Hague Rules were considered,[93] but there was no serious

---

[85] See id. at 5 & nn.24-25.
[86] See id. at 5-6.
[87] The Harter Act is now codified at 46 U.S.C. §§ 30701-07.
[88] Under the Harter compromise, the carrier is responsible for negligence in the care and custody of the cargo but so long as it uses due diligence to furnish a seaworthy vessel it is not liable for the crew's navigational faults. See generally, e.g., Sturley, History, supra note 82, at 12-14.
[89] See generally, e.g., Ramberg, supra note 82, at 179; Sturley, History, supra note 82, at 18-21.
[90] See Sturley, History, supra note 82, at 15-18 (discussing legislation in New Zealand, Australia, Canada, and Morocco).
[91] At the first committee meeting to address the proposed new regime, for example, members began by considering four questions to establish the project's broad parameters. The first of those was "[w]hether the freedom of contract on the part of the shipowner with regard to carriage of goods by sea should be absolute or should be limited by legislation?" 2 International Law Association, Report of the 30th Conference, at xxxix (Hague Conference 1921) [hereinafter Hague Conference Report], reprinted in 1 THE LEGISLATIVE HISTORY OF THE CARRIAGE OF GOODS BY SEA ACT AND THE TRAVAUX PRÉPARATOIRES OF THE HAGUE RULES 94 (Michael F. Sturley ed. 1990) [hereinafter HAGUE RULES TRAVAUX PRÉPARATOIRES].
[92] Some exceptional transactions evidenced by bills of lading, such as the carriage of live animals and most deck cargo, were also excluded from the mandatory application of the Hague Rules. See Hague Rules art. 1(c).
[93] See COMITÉ MARITIME INTERNATIONAL, REPORT OF THE 26TH CONFERENCE 74-102 (Stockholm Conference, 1963) (discussing 24 proposals made prior to the Stockholm Conference).

effort to increase the freedom-of-contract possibilities. If anything, the Visby Amendments decreased the theoretical possibilities by tightening the scope-of-application procedures.

The Hamburg Rules further restrict freedom of contract (when compared to the Hague and Hague-Visby Rules) because they expand the mandatory application of the regime. Most significantly, the Hamburg Rules apply to all contracts of carriage by sea (subject to the traditional charterparty exclusion[94]), not just contracts evidenced by a bill of lading or similar document of title.[95] But the focus of the Hamburg debates was on the substantive changes to the liability regime, not the tangential impact on freedom of contract.

2. Commercial Practice Under the Existing Maritime Conventions

Despite the freedom that carriers retain under the Hague and Hague-Visby Rules, they have generally made little effort to escape the constraints that those regimes impose upon them. On the contrary, the norm has been to extend the Hague or Hague-Visby Rules by contract to transactions (or portions of transactions) in which the mandatory rules would not otherwise apply.[96] For example, charterparty forms routinely incorporate the Hague or Hague-Visby Rules notwithstanding the well-established charterparty exclusion.[97] When possible,[98] multimodal bills of lading often extend the maritime regime[99] to the inland portions of shipments notwithstanding the freedom that exists under article 7 to adopt some other liability regime. And sea waybills — which in some jurisdictions do not qualify as bills of lading or similar documents of title under article 1(b),[100] and thus are not mandatorily subject to the Hague or Hague-Visby Rules in those jurisdictions — routinely incorporate the Hague or Hague-Visby Rules as a matter of contract.[101]

---

[94] *See* Hamburg Rules art. 2(3).
[95] *See id.* arts. 2(1), 1(6).
[96] *See generally* Michael F. Sturley, *The Application of COGSA as a Matter of Contract*, 2A BENEDICT ON ADMIRALTY § 43 (7th rev. ed. 2013).
[97] *See, e.g.*, The New York Produce Exchange Time Charter 1993 (NYPE 93), clause 31(a); BIMCO Standard Grain Voyage Charter Party (GRAINCON), clause 34 (2003) (incorporating BIMCO's Standard General Clause Paramount (1997).
[98] In many countries, mandatory law applicable to road and rail transport makes it impossible to extend the maritime regime to inland carriage. In Europe, for example, regional treaties known as CMR (*see supra* note 10) and CIM-COTIF govern road and rail transport.
[99] To be sure, the inland extension of the maritime regime is not always on precisely the same terms as the international convention. In the United States, for example, it is not unusual for the inland extension of the one-year time-for-suit provision to include an additional service-of-process requirement that is not included in article 3(6) of the Hague and Hague-Visby Rules. *See generally* Michael F. Sturley, *Time-for-Suit Provisions*, 2A BENEDICT ON ADMIRALTY § 163, at 16-14 to 16-15 & nn.29-30 (7th rev. ed. 2013).
[100] *See, e.g.*, Ramberg, *supra* note 82, at 187.
[101] *See, e.g.*, Combined Transport Bill of Lading 1995 (COMBICONWAYBILL), clause 11(2).

It is possible to imagine many different explanations for the carriers' failure to take greater advantage of the freedom-of-contract opportunities that are available to them (and different explanations may well apply in different contexts and for different carriers). One possible explanation is simple marketing.[102] As a legal matter, a carrier might avoid the application of the Hague and Hague-Visby Rules by issuing only a sea waybill, data freight receipt, or other document that does not qualify under article 1(b).[103] But if customers object to that treatment and take their business elsewhere, it would be a hollow victory. Lawyers who handle cargo recovery actions seem to discount the possibility that carriers would ever do anything for the benefit of cargo owners, presumably because their views of carriers' motives have been colored by the negotiating positions that carriers have taken in the sometimes combative world of litigation. As a general rule, however, most businesses treat their customers and prospective customers more generously than they treat those who have sued them when things have gone wrong. The distinction becomes even more compelling when one remembers that, in many cases, litigation no longer involves either the carrier or the original customer (because insurers are conducting the litigation on both sides).

The well-known benefits of uniformity[104] suggest another possible explanation for the carriers' failure to take greater advantage of the opportunities to be free of mandatory rules. It is easier for a carrier to conduct its business on the assumption that every container on the ship is pretty much the same,[105] and therefore can be handled in pretty much the same way. Carriers effectively discourage shippers from declaring higher values (by charging high ad valorem rates), even though they miss an opportunity for higher profits in the process. For much the same reason, they may have little interest in having some of their cargo subject to lower liability limits (or at least have little interest in making any other concessions to obtain lower liability limits). The benefits that carriers might receive in a few[106] cases from the potential lessening of liability could be more than offset by the spe-

---

[102] Carriers have undoubtedly relied on liability terms as part of their marketing efforts. When Sealand was still an independent company, it offered its customers higher package limits than the governing liability regime required. *See, e.g., Sea-Land Hikes Its Liability For Damaged, Lost Cargoes*, Journal of Commerce, July 18, 1991, at 8B (announcing the plan to accept higher liability limits). The company concluded that the benefit of the increased business attracted by the promise of higher package limits more than offset the cost of the greater liability that it assumed.
[103] Even more strikingly, the carrier could adopt a paperless approach and decline to issue any document whatsoever.
[104] *See generally*, e.g., Michael F. Sturley, *Uniformity in the Law Governing the Carriage of Goods by Sea*, 26 J. Mar. L. & Com. 553, 556-559 (1995) (noting that the benefits of uniformity in the rules governing the carriage of goods by sea have been widely recognized and documented).
[105] Of course some containers will need to be treated differently as a practical matter. Dangerous goods, for example, may be subject to special stowage requirements.
[106] Anyone reading only the reported decisions could be left with the impression that little if any cargo ever arrives safely at its intended destination. In practice, of course, lost or damaged cargo

cial treatment that would be required in every case.[107] Thus non-uniform lower limits may be a pleasant windfall in a particular case but not a potential source of any systemic benefit.

Whatever the explanation for the carriers' actions over the years, it is significant to note that carriers have had opportunities for decades to avoid the "mandatory" restrictions of the Hague and Hague-Visby Rules but they have not made any real effort to take advantage of the opportunities. Even if we are unsure of the explanation, we at least have some evidence of how carriers have reacted in the past when faced with the opportunity to avoid the mandatory rules of an international convention.

3. Freedom of Contract in the Rotterdam Rules

During the negotiation of the Rotterdam Rules, freedom of contract returned to center stage. Although article 79 substantially continues the traditional "one way"[108] mandatory nature of the Hague,[109] Hague-Visby,[110] and Hamburg Rules,[111] at least for carrier liability, article 80 introduces a new commercial compromise to define when the parties to a contract of carriage will enjoy broader freedom of contract.

(1) The CMI Negotiations

The freedom-of-contract issue arose in conjunction with the Rotterdam Rules' need to update and modernize the existing liability regimes. Current law permits freedom of contract under a charterparty but not in a bill of lading transaction.[112] That simple dichotomy worked well enough when most commercial transactions fell neatly into one category or the other. During the preparatory work for the new Convention, however, the CMI recognized that today many transactions do not fit very comfortably into either category. It therefore considered how volume contracts, contracts of affreightment, service contracts, towage

---

represents the exceptional case.

[107] Carriers that have publicly announced their support for the Rotterdam Rules have stressed the benefits of uniformity and predictability. *See, e.g.*, Knud Pontoppidan, *Shipowners' View on the UNCITRAL Convention on Contracts for the International Carriage of Goods Wholly or Partly by Sea*, 2009 CMI YEARBOOK 282.

[108] Prior maritime regimes have been considered "one way" mandatory because they limited the parties' freedom to contractually *reduce* the carrier's liability but permitted contractual *increases* to the carrier's liability. That risk allocation was based on the premise that carriers in liner trade almost inevitably had superior bargaining power in negotiations with individual shippers.

[109] Hague Rules art. 3(8).

[110] Because the Visby Amendments did not amend the Hague Rules in this regard, article 3(8) of the Hague-Visby Rules is identical to article 3(8) of the Hague Rules.

[111] Hamburg Rules art. 23.

[112] *Cf. supra* note 92 and accompanying text.

contracts, and non-traditional "charterparties" (such as slot charters and space charters) should be treated.[113] Only some of those ambiguous arrangements could plausibly be called charterparties,[114] but all of them resemble charterparties in some respects. In particular, the transactions at issue tend to involve sophisticated parties with substantial bargaining power, thus suggesting that they do not require the protection of mandatory law.[115] During most of the preparatory work in the CMI and during the early negotiations at UNCITRAL, the relevant issue was whether the ambiguous arrangements should therefore be analogized to charterparties and similarly excluded from the coverage of the new regime.[116]

In November 2001, at the final meeting of the CMI's International Sub-Committee on Issues of Transport Law,[117] shortly before the CMI submitted its draft to UNCITRAL,[118] the debate began to change. The National Industrial Transportation League (NITL) and the World Shipping Council (WSC) — the principal industry organizations representing shipper and carrier interests in the United States[119] — made an entirely new proposal that addressed the modern contracting forms and reintroduced the freedom-of-contract debate.[120]

---

[113] See, e.g., Report of the Fourth Meeting of the International Sub-Committee on Issues of Transport Law (London, 12-13 Oct. 2000), 2000 CMI YEARBOOK 263, 267; CMI Draft Instrument on Transport Law, 2001 CMI YEARBOOK 532, 544-545. Cf. supra notes 21-23 and accompanying text.

[114] Part of the problem, of course, is the lack of an accepted definition of a charterparty. During the negotiations leading to the Rotterdam Rules, some argued for including a definition of "charterparty" in article 1. The Working Group ultimately rejected the suggestion. It did not appear that the Working Group could formulate an effective and beneficial definition when industry practice itself was so unclear.

[115] See, e.g., Ramberg, supra note 82, at 180 (noting that for contracts of affreightment and volume contracts "the need to provide protection by mandatory rules is even less than in many charterparty situations").

[116] Thus article 3.3.1 of Preliminary Draft Instrument WP.21, supra note 21, like the CMI Draft Instrument on Transport Law, 2001 CMI YEARBOOK 532, 544, on which UNCITRAL's Preliminary Draft Instrument was based, repeats the traditional charterparty exclusion and also lists "contracts of affreightment, volume contracts, or similar agreements" in square brackets (to indicate the need for further discussion). The commentary explains the issue in more detail. See Preliminary Draft Instrument WP.21, supra note 21, ¶¶ 37-43; see also 2001 CMI YEARBOOK at 544-545.

[117] See Report of the Sixth Meeting of the International Sub-Committee on Issues of Transport Law (Madrid, 12-13 Nov. 2001), 2001 CMI YEARBOOK 305 [hereinafter Report of the Sixth Meeting of the International Sub-Committee].

[118] See CMI Draft Instrument on Transport Law, 2001 CMI YEARBOOK 532.

[119] The National Industrial Transportation League (NITL) is the principal industry organization representing U.S. shippers. It was already well-established in the 1920s when it served as the principal voice for shippers in the U.S. debates over the ratification of the Hague Rules. See, e.g., Sturley, History, supra note 82, at 41 n.320 (noting NITL's early role in the U.S. ratification debates in the 1920s and 1930s). The World Shipping Council (WSC), a much newer organization, represents the principal liner carriers serving the United States.

[120] In September 2001, NITL and WSC had agreed on a Joint Statement of Common Objectives on the Development of a New International Cargo Liability Instrument (available at http://www.worldshipping.org/jointstatement.pdf). The freedom-of-contract proposal is contained in paragraph B(11) of the Joint Statement. Five years earlier, the Maritime Law Association of the United

Under the NITL-WSC proposal, the new regime would govern "service contracts"[121] on a default basis, but the parties to a service contract would have the freedom to contract out of coverage if they wished.[122] Mandatory law would still protect the rights of third parties (much as it does today in the context of charterparty bills of lading[123]), but the immediate parties to the agreement could define the terms on which they would work with each other.

(2) The UNCITRAL Negotiations

Although the CMI's International Sub-Committee rejected the NITL-WSC proposal,[124] the U.S. delegation to UNCITRAL's Working Group III made a very similar proposal early in the UNCITRAL negotiations.[125] In substance, that freedom-of-contract proposal should not have been considered particularly radical. The Working Group had already expressed support for extending the charterparty exclusion[126] so that it would also exclude analogous arrangements (such as volume contracts) from the scope of the new Convention.[127] If that

---

States (USMLA) had proposed a number of amendments to the U.S. Carriage of Goods by Sea Act (COGSA), including an amendment that would have provided similar treatment for service contracts. *See generally, e.g.,* Michael F. Sturley, *Proposed Amendments to the Carriage of Goods by Sea Act,* 18 HOUSTON J. INT'L L. 609, 655-656 (1996) (discussing USMLA proposal's treatment of service contracts).

[121] The "service contract" is a defined term in the federal statutes that regulate U.S. shipping. Under the current codification, which is derived from section 3(21) of the Shipping Act of 1984, the term means

   a written contract, other than a bill of lading or receipt, between one or more shippers, on the one hand, and an individual ocean common carrier or an agreement between or among ocean common carriers, on the other, in which —
   (A) the shipper or shippers commit to providing a certain volume or portion of cargo over a fixed time period; and
   (B) the ocean common carrier or the agreement commits to a certain rate or rate schedule and a defined service level, such as assured space, transit time, port rotation, or similar service features.

46 U.S.C. § 40102(20). A slightly different "service contract" definition applied when NITL and WSC initially made their proposal. *See* 46 U.S.C. app. § 1702(21) (2000) (codifying section 3(21) of the Shipping Act of 1984). Considerable work in the UNCITRAL negotiations involved the need to move the U.S.-centered definition to one that would be suitable for an international convention. *Cf. infra* note 137.

[122] *See Report of the Sixth Meeting of the International Sub-Committee, supra* note 117, 2001 CMI YEARBOOK at 315-317, 343-347.

[123] Articles 1(b) and 5 of the Hague and Hague-Visby Rules and article 2(3) of the Hamburg Rules protect the third-party holders of charterparty bills of lading. *See also supra* notes 8, 19, 26 & 73-74 and accompanying text.

[124] *See Report of the Sixth Meeting of the International Sub-Committee, supra* note 117, 2001 CMI YEARBOOK at 347.

[125] *See* Proposal by the United States of America, ¶¶ 18-29, U.N. doc. no. A/CN.9/WG.III/WP.34 (7 Aug. 2003).

[126] *See supra* notes 113-116 and accompanying text.

[127] *See, e.g.,* Report of the Working Group on Transport Law on the work of its ninth session ¶ 62 (New York, 15-26 April 2002), U.N. doc. no. A/CN.9/510 (2002) [hereinafter Ninth Session Re-

traditional exclusionary approach had been adopted, the contracting parties would still have been able to extend the Convention to cover those excluded transactions (as is commonly done in charterparties today[128]). The practical effect of the freedom-of-contract proposal was thus to shift the default rule that applies in the absence of any contrary action by the parties. Parties that chose to address the issue explicitly could reach their preferred result, whatever it might be (potential liability defined either by the Convention's terms or by individually negotiated terms), equally well under either the freedom-of-contract approach or the exclusionary approach. They need simply specify the liability rules that they wish to have govern their transaction. The significant distinction between the two approaches is that the freedom-of-contract proposal would broaden the reach of the new Convention by applying it when the parties did not explicitly address the issue.[129] Broadening the application of the new Convention should not have been controversial.

Whatever the practical realities may have been, a number of delegations reacted negatively to the suggestion that the parties should be permitted any freedom of contract with respect to transactions that would otherwise by subject to the new Convention.[130] Indeed, the freedom-of-contract proposal became one of the most controversial issues of the entire negotiation. Some of the opposition was essentially visceral, with delegates complaining that it would be too "revolutionary" to permit freedom of contract in the context of an international convention on the maritime carriage of goods.[131] Other opposition went primarily to the details of creating a system that could work fairly in different legal systems.[132] The most compelling opposition focused on the difficulty of defining the class of transactions in

---

port]; *see also* Preliminary Draft Instrument WP.21, *supra* note 21, ¶ 37.
[128] *See supra* notes 96-97 and accompanying text.
[129] See generally Michael F. Sturley, The United Nations Commission on International Trade Law's Transport Law Project: An Interim View of a Work in Progress, 39 TEXAS INTERNATIONAL LAW JOURNAL 65, 90-92 (2003) (discussing the details of the proposal).
[130] *See, e.g.*, Ninth Session Report, *supra* note 127, ¶ 69; Report of Working Group III (Transport Law) on the Work of its Eleventh Session (New York, 24 Mar. to 4 Apr. 2003), ¶¶ 208-211, U.N. doc. no. A/CN.9/526 (9 May 2003) [hereinafter Eleventh Session Report].
[131] *See, e.g.*, Eleventh Session Report, *supra* note 130, ¶¶ 209, 211. It was never explained why it would be too "revolutionary" to permit freedom of contract in certain defined transactions when it would not be too revolutionary to entirely exclude those same transactions from the scope of the mandatory regime. *Cf. supra* notes 113-116 and accompanying text.
[132] *See, e.g.*, Eleventh Session Report, *supra* note 130, ¶ 210. FIATA's principal concern was to ensure that freight forwarders and non-vessel operating carriers (NVOCs) would have the same right as vessel operating carriers (VOCs) to enter into transactions in which freedom of contract would be permitted. Otherwise, VOCs might receive a competitive advantage over freight forwarders and NVOCs. That was not an objection to freedom of contract as such but a definitional concern. If UNCITRAL had instead extended the charterparty exclusion to cover modern equivalents, *see supra* notes 113-116 and accompanying text, the same concern would have arisen in the same way when the Working Group decided how to define the transactions that were sufficiently similar to charterparties to justify exclusion from the scope of the mandatory regime.

which broader freedom of contract would be permitted,[133] but the same definitional difficulties would also have arisen under the traditional exclusionary approach when it came time to draw the line between those transactions subject to mandatory coverage and those that would be excluded.[134]

In the end, a version of the U.S. freedom-of-contract proposal was accepted with almost no dissent — but only after provoking some of the most heated criticism[135] and extensive discussion[136] of the negotiation, going through dozens of revisions to ensure that it applied only when true freedom to contract was possible,[137] and being included in the final compromise package at the end of the Working Group's final session.[138]

(3) The Convention's Treatment of Freedom of Contract

The Rotterdam Rules' final resolution of the freedom-of-contract debate is found in articles 79 and 80 of the Convention. Under article 79(1), the general rule for carrier liability is the familiar "one-way mandatory" approach of the Hague, Hague-Visby, and Hamburg Rules.[139] The parties may agree to increase the carrier's liability but may not directly or indirectly reduce it. The Working Group discussed the possibility of adopting a "two-way mandatory" approach, as exists in the CMR (the regional convention governing road car-

---

[133] See, e.g., Eleventh Session Report, *supra* note 130, ¶ 208.

[134] *Cf. supra* notes 131 & 132. Perhaps the exclusionary approach would also have become controversial if the Working Group had pursued that option to the point of resolving the details of its application.

[135] See, e.g., Joint Proposal by Australia and France on Freedom of Contract under Volume Contracts, U.N. doc. no. A/CN.9/612 (22 May 2006).

[136] For a summary of the principal deliberations on the freedom-of-contract proposal, *see, e.g.*, Report of Working Group III (Transport Law) on the Work of its Nineteenth Session (New York, 16-27 Apr. 2007), ¶¶ 164-170, U.N. doc. no. A/CN.9/621 (2007) [hereinafter Nineteenth Session Report]; Report of Working Group III (Transport Law) on the Work of its Twenty-First Session (Vienna, 14-25 Jan. 2008), ¶¶ 235-242, U.N. doc. no. A/CN.9/645 (30 Jan. 2008) [hereinafter Twenty-First Session Report].

[137] Even the terminology used to describe the covered transactions went through a number of iterations. The original NITL-WSC focus had been on "service contracts," *see* 2001 CMI YEARBOOK at 315, but the terminology quickly shifted to "ocean transportation contracts," *id.* at 343. In the U.S. Proposal, *see supra* note 125, the term was "ocean liner service agreements." In the end, the Rotterdam Rules use the term "volume contracts" to describe the arrangements in which freedom of contract is permitted. *See* art. 80.

[138] *See* Twenty-First Session Report, *supra* note 136, ¶ 197.

[139] *See* Hague Rules art. 3(8); Hague-Visby Rules art. 3(8); Hamburg Rules art. 23(1). Indeed, article 79(1) so closely follows the substance of the earlier conventions that it even includes a provision prohibiting benefit-of-insurance clauses. *See* article 79(1)(c). That provision represents a solution to a problem that has not existed in practice for over ninety years. *See* Michael F. Sturley, *Benefit of Insurance Clauses*, 2A BENEDICT ON ADMIRALTY § 165, at 16-28 & n.2 (7th rev. ed. 2013). But UNCITRAL did not wish to risk resurrecting the problem by repealing the well-established prohibition.

riage in and near Europe),[140] under which the carrier's liability but may be neither increased nor reduced.[141] After discussion, however, the Working Group concluded that there was no general need to protect carriers from the superior bargaining power of large shippers.[142] There has been no evidence of abuse under the current maritime regimes, all of which permit voluntary increases in the carrier's liability.

Article 79(2) declares the general rule that the shipper's obligations may not be increased or decreased, thus adopting a "two-way mandatory" approach.[143] The more obvious half of the general rule — providing that the shipper's obligations may not be increased — follows both well-established tradition and the underlying principle of article 79(1) to protect shippers in cases of unequal bargaining power.[144] An increase in the shipper's obligations would generally mean a decrease in the carrier's obligations, which article 79(1) expressly prohibits. The Working Group concluded that it was also appropriate in this context to protect carriers from the superior bargaining power of large shippers,[145] primarily to ensure that all shippers met their obligations with respect to dangerous goods[146] but also to ensure that shippers delivered cargo to the carrier in appropriate condition[147] and furnished the information necessary for carriage.[148] Thus the parties may not contractually decrease the shipper's obligations.

Article 80 then sets out the "[s]pecial rules for volume contracts." Although volume contracts are subject to the Convention as a default rule,[149] the parties have the freedom to alter that risk allocation (as between themselves[150]) by contract.[151] A short list of "super-manda-

---

[140] *See* CMR, *supra* note 10, art. 41(1).
[141] *See, e.g.*, Report of Working Group III (Transport Law) on the Work of its Fifteenth Session (New York, 18-28 Apr. 2005), ¶¶ 45-48, U.N. doc. no. A/CN.9/576 (13 May 2005) [hereinafter Fifteenth Session Report].
[142] *See, e.g.*, Fifteenth Session Report, *supra* note 141, ¶ 49.
[143] *Cf. supra* note 140 and accompanying text.
[144] *See, e.g.*, Eleventh Session Report, *supra* note 130, ¶ 205; Fifteenth Session Report, *supra* note 141, ¶ 79; Report of Working Group III (Transport Law) on the Work of its Seventeenth Session (New York, 3-13 Apr. 2006), ¶ 151, U.N. doc. no. A/CN.9/594 (2006) [hereinafter Seventeenth Session Report]; Nineteenth Session Report, *supra* note 136, ¶ 159.
[145] *See, e.g.*, Nineteenth Session Report, *supra* note 136, ¶ 160.
[146] *See* Rotterdam Rules art. 32. The Working Group felt so strongly about that obligation of the shipper that it designated it as one of the "super mandatory" provisions for which derogation is impermissible even in transactions governed by volume contracts. *See id.* art. 80(4); *see also infra* note 152 and accompanying text.
[147] *See* Rotterdam Rules art. 27.
[148] *See id.* arts. 28-29, 31.
[149] *See id.* art. 79.
[150] Third parties are bound by derogations only if they consent to them. *See id.* art. 80(5). *See generally, e.g.*, Fifteenth Session Report, *supra* note 141, ¶¶ 24-28, 101-103; Seventeenth Session Report, *supra* note 144, ¶¶ 163-168.
[151] *See* Rotterdam Rules art. 80(1).

tory" provisions are not subject to derogation,[152] but otherwise a volume contract may provide for greater or lesser rights if certain requirements (designed to protect the small or unsuspecting shipper) are satisfied.[153] Most obviously, there must be a "volume contract,"[154] which guarantees that the contracting parties will at least be repeat players (and thus more likely to be sophisticated).[155] In addition, procedural safeguards ensure that the shipper does not agree to a derogation inadvertently,[156] that the shipper has the choice of shipping on the Convention's terms (without derogation),[157] and that the agreed derogation is not part of a contract of adhesion.[158] The Working Group also attempted to define a minimum quantity of cargo that would need to be shipped to qualify for "volume contract" status,[159] but it proved impossible to identify a single quantity that would serve the intended purpose across all trades.

Article 81 completes the chapter with two special rules that apply in two exceptional situations. Article 81(a) gives the parties the ability to exclude or limit the carrier's obligations or liability for the carriage of live animals, even outside the volume contract context,[160] but the exclusion or limitation may be broken in the same circumstances as the carrier may lose the benefit of unit limitation.[161] Although article 81(a) departs from the approach taken under either the Hague and Hague-Visby Rules[162] or the Hamburg Rules,[163] it was not controversial.[164] Article 81(b) simply continues the rarely used option, first created in article 6 of the Hague Rules,[165] to avoid the application of the mandatory rules for non-

---

[152] *See id.* art. 80(4). For example, the carrier's obligation under article 14(a)-(b) to exercise due diligence to furnish a seaworthy vessel may not be reduced by agreement. *See generally, e.g.,* Fifteenth Session Report, *supra* note 141, ¶¶ 20-23; Seventeenth Session Report, *supra* note 144, ¶¶ 158-162.
[153] *See id.* art. 80(2)-(3).
[154] *See id.* art. 80(1).
[155] *See id.* art. 1(2) (defining "volume contract" to require "a series of shipments").
[156] *See* id. art. 80(2)(a)-(b).
[157] *See* id. art. 80(2)(c).
[158] *See* id. art. 80(2)(d)-(3).
[159] *See* Twenty-First Session Report, *supra* note 136, ¶ 246.
[160] If live animals are carried under a volume contract, then the rules in article 80 still apply. Article 81 applies "without prejudice to article 80."
[161] The carrier may lose the benefit of unit limitation for deliberate or reckless misconduct. *See* Rotterdam Rules art. 61.
[162] The Hague and Hague-Visby Rules exclude coverage entirely for the carriage of live animals. *See* Hague Rules art. 1(c); Hague-Visby Rules art. 1(c).
[163] The Hamburg Rules cover the carriage of live animals, see Hamburg Rules arts. 1(5), but excuse the carrier from all liability for losses "resulting from any special risk inherent in that kind of carriage," *id.* art. 5(5).
[164] *See, e.g.,* Eleventh Session Report, supra note 130, ¶¶ 216-217; Fifteenth Session Report, *supra* note 141, ¶¶ 105-109; Seventeenth Session Report, *supra* note 144, ¶¶ 171-172; Nineteenth Session Report, *supra* note 136, ¶¶ 173-174; Twenty-First Session Report, *supra* note 136, ¶¶ 254-255.
[165] *See* Hague Rules art. 6; Hague-Visby Rules art. 6.

commercial shipments. Although the Hamburg Rules contain no corresponding provision, article 81(b) was also not controversial.[166]

4. The Likely Impact of the Rotterdam Rules' Freedom of Contract

With the Rotterdam Rules still some time away from entering into force,[167] any discussion of the likely impact of the new freedom-of-contract provisions is necessarily speculative. During the debates, opponents predicted that article 80 would effectively immunize carriers from virtually all liability for cargo damage because they would force most shippers to agree to volume contracts in which the limitation amounts were reduced to zero.[168] Supporters, on the other hand, suggested that article 80 would rarely be used. The provision was important only because it could play a valuable role in those exceptional cases in which it would be appropriate.[169] It is possible to imagine scenarios under which either of those predictions could turn out to be true. The best evidence that we have, however, suggests that the opponents' predictions of doom are unlikely to be accurate.

Even under current law, a carrier could already price its services so that every shipper was effectively required to enter into a slot or space charter for the portion of the ship necessary to carry the cargo in question. With a high enough tariff rate, even the consumer shipper of a single container of household goods would rationally prefer a charterparty for a single container slot on a single voyage over the more expensive bill of lading. And once that shipment is carried under a charterparty,[170] none of the current conventions would apply,[171] thus leaving the carrier (assuming it had superior bargaining power) free in most countries to insist on terms exonerating it from all liability for cargo loss or damage. Alternatively, a carrier could operate a service in which no documents were issued that could possibly qualify as bills of lading under article 1(b) of the Hague and Hague-Visby Rules.[172]

---

[166] *See, e.g.*, Eleventh Session Report, *supra* note 130, ¶ 218; Fifteenth Session Report, *supra* note 141, ¶ 109; Seventeenth Session Report, *supra* note 144, ¶ 172; Nineteenth Session Report, *supra* note 136, ¶¶ 175-176; Twenty-First Session Report, *supra* note 136, ¶ 255.
[167] The Convention enters into force approximately one year after twenty countries have become parties to it. *See* Rotterdam Rules art. 94(1).
[168] *See, e.g.*, Eleventh Session Report, *supra* note 130, ¶ 209.
[169] The new freedom of contract could also be valuable in dealing with unanticipated problems that the Rotterdam Rules might otherwise be poorly equipped to resolve.
[170] Although slot and space charters may not be traditional charterparties, it seems likely that most courts would still recognize them as charterparties. (Whatever hesitation the Working Group might have had in treating volume contracts or towage contracts as charterparty equivalents, everyone seemed to accept that slot and space charters were already charterparties.) Indeed, the law has long recognized the possibility of chartering less than an entire ship.
[171] *See* Hague Rules art. 5; Hague-Visby Rules art. 5; Hamburg Rules art. 2(3).
[172] Although article 3(3) of the Hague and Hague-Visby Rules requires the carrier to issue a bill of

Once again, the most popular of the current conventions would not apply, leaving a carrier that has sufficient bargaining power free to insist on its exoneration clauses.

In practice, of course, neither of those attempts to evade the otherwise mandatory terms of the existing regimes is known to have occurred. Many explanations are possible, and many of those would be plausible.[173] But I have trouble imagining any plausible explanation for why carriers that make no effort to avoid the mandatory rules under current law — and even incorporate those rules contractually to govern situations in which the rules are not mandatory[174] — would suddenly force unwilling customers to accept volume contracts in an unprecedented effort to avoid otherwise mandatory rules. My own speculation, therefore, is that the freedom of contract permitted under article 80 will be used to derogate from the carrier's obligations only in exceptional cases.

5. Observations on Mandatory Rules in a Half-Regulated Market

Even if my speculation is wrong, article 80 would not undermine the fundamental principles on which the international regulation of cargo liability regimes has been based for over eighty years. The occasional[175] loss or damage of cargo is a commercially inevitable cost of transporting goods.[176] The legal system can play some role in controlling those costs, but its primary function in this particular context is simply to allocate costs among the participants in a transaction. (Indeed, it is by allocating costs — and thus creating the incentive to

---

lading on the shipper's demand, that provision would not apply unless either the Hague or Hague-Visby Rules applied. If the carrier operates a service in which no "bill of lading or any similar document of title" (art. 1(b)) is ever issued, neither the Hague nor Hague-Visby Rules would apply.
[173] *See supra* notes 102-107 and accompanying text.
[174] *See supra* notes 96-101 and accompanying text.
[175] *Cf. supra* note 106.
[176] It is possible to envision extreme precautions that would significantly reduce the risk of any cargo being lost or damaged. For example, a carrier could pad each item with cotton wool and paper, secure it in a sturdy packing case, slide that first case into a second case, and then slide everything into a waterproof, dustproof van designed to float (in case anything should happen to the vessel on the voyage). Three experts in international transportation (all with extensive experience in that type of work) could design a procedure for loading and unloading the cargo to ensure that it was not dropped, or even jarred. And armed guards could protect the cargo from thieves during the entire operation. Under those circumstances, the cargo would be very likely to arrive safely. But even if the precautions would be 100% effective, most goods carried by sea are worth significantly less than a carrier would have to spend to provide that level of protection. Thus as a commercial matter only the most exceptional cargo would justify such an extraordinary level of care. In fact, the procedures described are exactly what the Italian Line did when it carried Michelangelo's incomparable Pietà — perhaps the most exceptional cargo ever carried on a trans-Atlantic ocean liner — from the Vatican to New York for the 1964 World's Fair. *See Pieta to Get Massive Protection*, New York Times, Jan. 16, 1964, at L33, col. 4. For most cargo carried by sea, some loss or damage is commercially inevitable.

avoid those costs — that the legal system plays a role in controlling costs.) Many different risk allocations can be imagined, from a simple one in which either shippers or carriers assume the entire cost of any loss or damage to the more complex risk allocations that the law has long adopted whereby shippers and carriers divide the risk, and thus the costs, depending on the cause of the loss or damage.

The desire to ensure that carriers assume some minimum level of liability on a mandatory basis in order to protect small shippers may be understandable, but that is not the goal of any of the current conventions. Indeed, the Hague, Hague-Visby, and Hamburg Rules do little if anything to ensure that small shippers are actually treated "fairly."[177] Starting with the Hague Rules and continuing though the Hague-Visby and Hamburg Rules, the idea has long been to require carriers to offer at least a certain minimum level of protection when dealing with cargo loss or damage. But no international regime even attempts to comprehensively regulate the relationship between shippers and carriers. In particular, none of the regimes regulates freight rates (which is a far more important topic for most carriers and shippers).[178]

If governments were truly serious about protecting small shippers, or truly believed that the free market did not work because there was a gross inequality in bargaining power between shippers and carriers, they would not stop with imposing minimum liability terms on carriers. They would regulate the entire industry, much as governments have done with other monopolies and oligopolies (such as public utilities). The governments not only would define the level of service that must be offered (as the current international regimes do) but also would determine the price that carriers would be allowed to charge for that ser-

---

[177] It is in any event open to debate whether a concept such as "fairness" plays any meaningful role in the context of liability rules for cargo loss or damage. This is not a field in which widows and orphans are subject to frequent abuse. (Maritime conventions involving passengers, for example, would raise entirely different concerns. *See, e.g.*, Ramberg, *supra* note 82, at 183, 184-185.) Only international shipments are governed by any of the existing conventions, and that limitation still applies under the Rotterdam Rules. Thus by definition the players on both sides will at least be sophisticated enough to participate in international trade. A high proportion of the litigation is in any event between two insurance companies, meaning that the entire dispute is over which insurance company should be responsible for a loss. Of course insurance companies have rights, too. Most would agree that it would be "unfair" to change the rules in the middle of the game, for example, thus requiring an insurance company to bear a loss that it had never agreed to assume. But it is often difficult to see why an insurance company — or any other commercial actor — has any fairness-based right to more than the law provides or than it negotiated to receive.

[178] The later CMI and earlier UNCITRAL drafts included a chapter on freight. *See, e.g.*, Preliminary Draft Instrument WP.21, *supra* note 21, ch. 9. The UNCITRAL Working Group decided to omit the chapter from the instrument on the theory that it was too ambitious. *See* Report of Working Group III (Transport Law) on the Work of its Thirteenth Session (New York, 3-14 May 2004), ¶¶ 162-164, U.N. doc. no. A/CN.9/552 (24 May 2004). But even that early (and ambitious) attempt to address the subject did not attempt to regulate freight rates.

vice.

The Hague, Hague-Visby, and Hamburg Rules instead create a half-regulated system. Carriers are told that they must provide a certain level of service — a service that satisfies the minimum obligations imposed by the relevant mandatory regime — but they are then free to charge whatever price the market will bear for that service. A shipper who wishes to purchase a lower level of service[179] does not have that choice. It must either pay the unregulated price established by the carrier or forego the service entirely. In other words, the current system "bundles" a defined service level with the basic transportation and forces a shipper to buy both even if it wants only the basic transportation. It then forces the shipper to pay the price set by the carrier (and the market) with no regulatory protection. Whatever the purpose behind such a system, it is unlikely to be the protection of small shippers.

The true goal of the Hague, Hague-Visby, and Hamburg Rules was never to protect small shippers from carriers but rather to facilitate commercial transactions.[180] The commercial party that is protected is the third-party purchaser who succeeds to a shipper's interest (but did not have the shipper's opportunity to contract with the carrier).[181] By ensuring that carriers must satisfy defined minimum obligations in every bill of lading transaction, the Hague, Hague-Visby, and Hamburg Rules enable third parties to rely on the bill of lading. They know that they can purchase the bill of lading (or lend money in reliance on the bill of lading), confident in the minimum level of protection that they will receive, without the need to examine each bill of lading in detail. That protection, in turn, facilitates commercial transactions,[182] which are able to occur in a free (and more efficient) market.[183]

The Rotterdam Rules may seem inconsistent with the principles discussed here to the extent that article 80 permits any derogation from the carrier's obligations. But safeguards

---

[179] For example, a shipper may wish to purchase a service with a lower package limitation amount because it prefers to buy cargo insurance from an underwriter who offers a better price with no concern for its potential subrogation rights.
[180] *See, e.g., Hague Conference Report, supra* note 91, at 45 (statement of Sir Norman Hill), *reprinted in* 1 HAGUE RULES TRAVAUX PRÉPARATOIRES, *supra* note 91, at 151.
[181] *See, e.g.,* 2 International Law Association, *Report of the 31st Conference* 3 (Buenos Aires Conference 1922) (report of the Maritime Law Committee) (noting the interests of bankers and underwriters), *reprinted in* 2 HAGUE RULES TRAVAUX PRÉPARATOIRES, *supra* note 91, at 243; *Hague Conference Report, supra* note 91, at 92-93 (statement of Sir James Hope Simpson) (discussing bankers' interests), *reprinted in* 1 HAGUE RULES TRAVAUX PRÉPARATOIRES, *supra* note 91, at 198-199.
[182] To the extent that any of the international regimes represents an acceptable risk allocation between carrier and cargo interests, the existence of the regime facilitates commercial transactions by saving the carrier and shipper the trouble and expense of negotiating their own risk allocation.
[183] In some ways, the idea here is similar to the *numerus clausus* principle, which limits the types of interests that may be created in property. By standardizing, to some extent, the liability terms in bills of lading, the Hague, Hague-Visby, and Hamburg Rules facilitate the market in bills of lading.

in article 80 prevent that result. First, and most importantly, no derogation will affect a third party (unless the third party consents to the derogation).[184] Thus the parties that the Hague, Hague-Visby, and Hamburg Rules actually protect will continue to be protected. Second, no derogation can be forced on an unwilling or uninformed shipper.[185] Thus the market will continue to function efficiently. Indeed, in those exceptional cases in which the benefits of a special transaction are worth the costs of negotiating that special transaction, the market will function more efficiently than it does today.

III. Conclusion

The Rotterdam Rules' changes to existing law are not (and were not intended to be) earth-shaking. The Convention is deliberately evolutionary, not revolutionary. The focus is on updating and modernizing the existing legal regimes that govern the carriage of goods, filling in some of the gaps that have been identified in practice over the years, and harmonizing the governing law when possible. And like the Convention as a whole, the provisions addressing the scope of application and freedom of contract are also evolutionary, not revolutionary.

Although scope of application was a controversial issue in the negotiation of the Hague Rules, in the negotiation of the Rotterdam Rules it was primarily a technical issue. The principal goal was to update and modernize the law to reflect current commercial practices, now that the traditional dichotomy between bills of lading and charterparties is no longer adequate. UNCITRAL easily agreed which transactions should generally be included and which should be excluded, so the challenge was to draft provisions that would accomplish that goal as we move into the twenty-first century.

During the negotiation of the Rotterdam Rules, freedom of contract also became an issue as the result of the need to update and modernize the law to reflect current commercial practices. Although it became a controversial issue during the negotiations, the Convention's provisions for greater freedom of contract are ultimately unlikely to make a significant difference in practice. Existing conventions already permit an under-recognized degree of contractual freedom. Not only have carriers failed to take advantage of that freedom to reduce their liability, they have instead extended the mandatory regimes when they were under no compulsion to do so. It seems safe to predict that article 80 will be

---

[184] *See* Rotterdam Rules art. 80(5). *See supra* note 150 and accompanying text.
[185] *See* Rotterdam Rules art. 80(2)-(3). *See supra* notes 153-158 and accompanying text.

used, as it was intended, to address only exceptional cases.

5

Period of Responsibility and Multimodal Aspects

Tomotaka Fujita

I. Introduction

"Door-to-door" is a phrase often used to describe the basic character of the Rotterdam Rules. During his speech this morning, Professor Illescas rightly pointed out that "door-to-door" is the important feature of the Rotterdam Rules. Mr. Beare explained why the liability regime that covers "door-to-door" is desired. I do not wish to repeat these points in my short speech. Instead, I will address the following three topics related to "door-to-door" coverage under the Rotterdam Rules[1].

First, I will explain the technical aspect of the Rules that is related to "door-to-door" coverage of the carrier's period of responsibility. Second, I will refer to the "multimodal" aspect that necessarily follows from the "door-to-door" coverage. Finally, I will mention the persons other than the carrier who are covered by the Rotterdam Rules. The last topic is not exactly a part of the issue of "door-to-door," but it is closely related to it, and if I do not mention it, no other speaker will cover the topic.

---

[1] For the detail discussion on the issues referred to in this paper, see, Tomotaka Fujita, *The Comprehensive Coverage of the New Convention: Performing Parties and the Multimodal Implications*, Texas International Law Journal, vol. 44, p.349 (2009) and MICHAEL F. STURLEY, TOMOTAKA FUJITA AND G.J. VAN DER ZIEL, ROTTERDAM RULES: THE UN CONVENTION ON CONTRACTS FOR THE INTERNATIONAL CARRIAGE OF GOODS WHOLLY OR PARTLY BY SEA, SWEET & MAXWELL, 2010, ¶¶4.001-4.044, 5.139-5.195.

II. The Carrier's Period of Responsibility: "Door-to-door" Application of the Convention

1. The Period of Responsibility under Article 12

Let us confirm how the text of the Rotterdam Rules extends its period of responsibility to "door-to-door." Article 12(1) provides that *"the period of responsibility of the carrier for the goods under this Convention **begins when the carrier or a performing party receives the goods for carriage** and **ends when the goods are delivered.**"*(emphasis added) There is no restriction to the place of receipt or place of delivery. Therefore, if the carrier receives goods at the inland depot according to the contract terms, the period of responsibility begins there even if the depot is outside the port area. The period ends when the carrier delivers the goods at the consignee's factory according to the contract terms, the period of responsibility ends there even if the factory is outside the port area.

2. The Convention Does Not Force a Multi-modal Contract

Please note that the fact that the Rules adopt a "door-to-door" period of responsibility *does not* mean that the parties are prohibited from entering into a traditional "tackle-to-tackle" or "port-to-port" contract of carriage. The parties may agree on the time and location of the receipt and delivery of the goods as they wish. Article 12(3) clarifies that point. The only restriction is the proviso in Article 12(3), which says that the time of receipt of the goods cannot be after the beginning of their initial loading, and the time of delivery of the goods cannot be before the completion of their final unloading. Therefore, it is perfectly possible for the parties to enter into a traditional "port-to-port" contract of carriage in which the shipper delivers the goods to the container yard of the port of loading, and the carrier unloads them at the container yard of the port of discharge. In this example, the receipt of the goods at the container yard occurs before the "initial loading" of the goods and delivery takes place after the "final unloading" of the goods, under the contract of carriage. Therefore, these contract terms are valid and the carrier is only responsible for the carriage between the two container yards.

More difficult question arises in the following situation. Let us assume that the carrier received the goods for carriage at the inland depot and carried them to the port by the truck. The goods were loaded onto the ship at the port. The contract of carriage provided that the goods were received alongside of the ship when they were loaded onto the ship. When does the carrier's period of responsibility begin? There are two questions: (i) the relationship between Article 12(1) and (3), and (ii) the interpretation of "initial loading" in Article 12(3)(a).

Let us examine the first question. One might argue that, despite the agreement in contract of carriage, the period of responsibility begins at the inland depot because the carrier, in fact, received the goods there. On the other hand, one could also argue that according to Article 12(3), the receipt under Article 12(1) occurs only when the goods were received at the time and location agreed in the contract of carriage. Under the latter view, the carrier's period of responsibility begins when the goods are loaded onto the ship. The issue was vigorously debated at the 41st Session of UNCITRAL at which the Draft Convention was finalized but the delegates could not reach the consensus and the text was left open to the interpretation[2]. The former view sees that the carrier's period of responsibility continues the whole period where the goods are under the custody of the carrier. However, the carrier's period of responsibility ends when the goods are not delivered at the time and location agreed in the contract even if the carrier's custody under the Rotterdam Rules (Although the carrier is not totally exonerated from the liability with respect to the goods under Article 48(5), it is the liability as a bailee etc., rather than the carrier). The latter view under which the carrier's period of responsibility is decided, subject to the proviso of Article 12(3), according to the contract of carriage irrespective of the physical possession of the goods seems more consistent with the structure of the Rotterdam Rules.

The second question relates to the meaning of "initial loading" under Article 12(3)(a). Can the party agree that the carrier's period of responsibility begins when the goods are loaded onto the ship despite the fact that the goods are already loaded onto the truck? The answer is yes. Article 12(3)(a) provides that "the time of receipt of the goods is subsequent to the beginning of their initial loading *under the contract of carriage*" (emphasis added). If the contract of carriage in question is the carriage of goods by sea beginning from the loading onto and ending at the discharge from the ship, then the initial loading is the loading onto the ship, not the loading onto the truck[3]. Therefore, nothing in the above agreement contradicts with Article 12(3)(a).

---

[2] Report of the United Nations Commission on International Trade Law on its forty-first session (New York, 16 June-3 July 2008), A/63/17 and Corr.1 (UNCITRAL YEARBOOK Volume XXXIX (2008), pp.12-13), paras.39-43.
[3] Sturley, Fujita and Van der Ziel, *supra* note 1, ¶¶ 4.008.

3. The Treatment of "FIO"

In practice, the carrier and shipper sometimes agree that the shipper will load and unload the goods onto or from the ship. Such an arrangement is called "free in/free out" (FIO). The validity of an FIO clause has been discussed under the Hague-Visby Rules. In some jurisdictions, an FIO clause is understood as determining the scope of the contract of carriage. As such, the mandatory regulation does not apply to activities under a FIO clause because they are outside the scope of the contract of carriage[4].

However, under the Rotterdam Rules this justification is no longer valid. Article 12(3) clearly states that the parties cannot agree on a time and location of the receipt of the goods beginning after the commencement of the initial loading, or a time and location of the delivery of the goods ending before the completion of the final unloading. This is why Article 13(2) specifically provides that the carrier and the shipper may agree that the loading, handling, stowing, or unloading of the goods may be performed by the shipper, the documentary shipper or the consignee. Article 13(2) explicitly authorizes the validity of FIO clauses and Article 17(3)(i) provides an explicit exoneration for the carrier from liability as a result of such activities.

Although one might simply see the Convention's approach as an alternative way of authorizing FIO clauses, it might be more than that. If one justifies FIO clauses, like English courts, as determining the scope of the contract of carriage, it becomes unclear how far such freedom of contract goes. Is there any geographic restriction for the parties to decide the period of the contract of carriage (e.g., can the party agree on the period of responsibility being only a part of ocean voyage)? Can the parties agree any activity performed by persons employed by the carrier as being outside the scope of the contract of carriage? The Convention's approach to FIO clauses is restrictive in that it allows only the activities listed in Article 14(2) ("the loading, handling, stowing or unloading of the goods") to be performed by the shipper or the consignee, and also provides limits to the freedom of contract to shorten the period of responsibility (Article 12(3)). Moreover, the carrier is liable for the activities under FIO clause if they are performed by the carrier or anyone employed by him/her (Article 17(2)(i)). Therefore, it is fair to say that the Convention not only confirms the validity of FIO clauses but also specifically regulates the extent to which freedom of con-

---

[4] For instance, English case law has adopted this approach (*Pyrene v. Scindia Navigation* [1954] 2 QB 402; *Jindal Iron and Steel Co,Ltd,and Others v. Islamic Solidarity Shipping Company* (The JORDAN II"), [2005] 1 Lloyd's Rep 57). Although there is no case explicitly refers to the point, this is also the majority view in Japan.

tract applies to such arrangements.

III. Multimodal Aspects

1. Possible Conflicts between Conventions

The extended period of responsibility inevitably introduces a multimodal aspect and possibly might create conflicts with other liability regimes. For example, let us assume that a contract of carriage in question includes a road carriage and the Convention on International Road Carriage (called "CMR") applies to that part of the carriage. The Rotterdam Rules provides for a time-bar of two years (Article 62(1)) while CMR provides for a one year time-bar (Article 32(1)). Therefore, when an action is brought before a court in a contracting state to both conventions with respect to the goods lost or damaged during the road leg 15 months after the delivery of the goods, and the both conventions apply at the same time, the court will violate either of the conventions whether or not it applies the time-bar. This is a typical situation referred to as a "conflict of conventions."

It is difficult to say whether the concern over the conflict of conventions is real or a purely theoretical possibility because the answer depends on the interpretation of each convention. For example, it is uncertain as to whether CMR applies to an international road carriage that constitutes part of a multimodal transport. If it does not, no conflict of convention exists in the example I have just mentioned. In fact, this is the interpretation in several European countries[5]. However, delegations to the UNCITRAL Working Group thought it was necessary to avoid possible conflicts, even if those conflicts are only theoretical, and the Rotterdam Rules include two provisions that serve that purpose: Article 26 and Article 82.

2. Article 26 and the "Limited Network" Principle

Article 26 provides, "When loss of or damage to goods etc. occurs ... before their loading onto the ship or after their discharge from the ship, then provisions of this Convention

---

[5] For example, the German Supreme Court recently held that CMR, according to its own scope rules, does not apply to the international road haulage portion of a multimodal transport contract. See BGH July 17, 2008, Transport Recht 2008, S.365; see also, e.g., The Hague Court of Appeal, June 22, 2010, S&S 2010, 104. In contrast, an English court has held that CMR, according to its own scope rules, applies to the international road haulage portion of a multimodal transport contract. See Quantum Corp, Inc v. Plane Trucking Ltd., [2001] 2 Lloyd's Rep. 25 (Eng. C.A.).

do not prevail over those provisions of other international instruments." This is a formula for a "network" principle. However, it should be noted that Article 26 introduces the network principle in as limited a way as possible. Three conditions are enumerated in subparagraphs (a)-(c). Since the structure of Article 26 is fairly complicated, it might be helpful to use several examples to show how the article operates in practice.

Case #1   **Assume a contract from New York to Berlin with a sea carriage from New York to Rotterdam and a road carriage from Rotterdam to Berlin. The goods were damaged during the road carriage.**

Since the damage occurred after the goods were discharged from the ship, the requirement in the chapeau of Article 26 is met. The conditions set forth in paragraphs (b) and (c) are satisfied because CMR provides specific provisions on the carrier's liability, limitation of liability, and time for suit, and these provisions are mandatory rules. Finally, the requirement under paragraph (a) is also fulfilled because if the parties enter into "a separate and direct contract" for the carriage by road from Rotterdam to Berlin, this contract for international road carriage would be subject to CMR. Therefore, the provisions of this Convention do not supersede the provisions of CMR. The court can safely apply the provisions of CMR instead of the Rotterdam Rules.

Let us take a slightly different example.

Case #2   **Assume a contract of carriage from New York to Berlin via Rotterdam. The goods were damaged somewhere during the transport but the exact location is unknown.**

In this case, the carrier's liability for the damage of the goods is governed by the Rotterdam Rules and the provisions of CMR do not apply. For Article 26 to be applied, the loss of or damage to the goods must occur before the goods are loaded onto the ship or after their discharge from the ship. In other words, Article 26 does not apply when the location where the damage occurred is not specified[6].

---

[6] Please note that the loss of, damage to the goods rather than the event or circumstance that caused or contributed to the loss or damage should occur before the goods are loaded onto the ship or after their discharge from the ship. Compare the wordings in Article 26 with those in Article 17(1). Please also note that the loss or damage should occur "solely" during the period in question. Therefore, Article 26 does not apply to the case where the damage occurs progressively during the sea leg and land leg.

3. The Provisions in the Rotterdam Rules "do not prevail over" the provisions in Another International Instrument

It should be noted that Article 26 provides that "provisions in this convention *do not prevail over* those provisions of another international instrument"(emphasis added) when conditions under Article 26 are met. Some view that, despite this wording, courts *should* apply "the provisions of another international instrument" (in Case #1, CMR) if the conditions under Article 26 are satisfied[7]. They understand that Article 26 provides a substantive incorporation of the provisions of another international instrument and such provisions are applied by the force of the Rotterdam Rules[8]. Others interpret Article 26 more literally. They argue that since Article 26 clearly states that provisions of the Rotterdam Rules "do not prevail", if the court see that the provisions of another international instrument do not apply to the contract of carriage in question, it can safely apply the provisions of the Rotterdam Rules. The question whether the court should apply the provisions of another international instrument is decided in accordance with the rules on conflict of laws. They argue that although the court may apply provisions of CMR if conditions under Article 26, there is no reason to prohibit the court to apply the Rotterdam Rules when it does not have to apply CMR[9].

These views could lead to different solutions when the court is located in a state which is not a contracting state of "another international instrument"[10]. For example, if the claimant sues the NVOC as a contracting carrier in New York in Case #1. Courts in the United States are not bound by CMR. Under the former view, the court should always apply the provisions of CMR. Under the latter view, the court applies CMR if and only if the U.S. conflict of laws rule requires it to do so. The author believes that it is too demanding that a court of a contracting state of Rotterdam Rules is always required to apply CMR (or any other international instrument) to which the state is not a contracting state. Drafting history also seems to support the conclusion. In the 41st Session of UNCITRAL (18 June 2008) where the text of the Rotterdam Rules was finalized, it was proposed to change the word "prevail"

---

[7] Gertjan Van der Ziel, *Multimodal aspects of the Rotterdam Rules*, CMI Yearbook 2009, pp.306-307.
[8] Van der Ziel, *supra* note 7, pp.306-307.
[9] Fujita, *supra* note 1, pp.360-361.
[10] Please note that a similar problem could happen even if a court located in a contracting state of CMR. As is already mentioned, views are divided whether CMR applies to sea leg under multimodal transportation that includes international road leg. *See*, III.1 above. If a court in a contracting state of CMR interpret that CMR does not apply, it would face the same question as a court in a non-contracting state of CMR.

in Article 26 to "apply"[11]. If the Article 26 is designed to work as a substantive incorporation of the provisions in another international instrument, the word "apply" is much more suitable. The fact that the proposal was explicitly declined at the final stage suggests that Article 26 is not intended to introduce a substantive incorporation and that a court does not obliged to apply provisions of another instrument if it is not required to do so according to the force of such instrument or the conflict of laws rule of the court.

4. Article 82

Although the limited network system largely eliminates the concern over any potential conflict of conventions, nevertheless, Article 26 alone leaves open the possibility that in some specific situations a contracting state could face incompatible obligations under the Rotterdam Rules and other conventions. This is why Article 82 provides a further safeguard for the contracting states to avoid any possible conflicting obligation. The following example will illustrate why this provision is necessary.

Case #3   The parties contract for carriage from Nairobi to Tokyo via Singapore. **The goods are carried by air from Nairobi to Singapore and by ship from Singapore to Tokyo. The goods are actually damaged during the sea carriage by a cause that occurred during the air carriage. The consignee sues the carrier in Singapore (a contracting state of the Montreal Convention which regulates carriage by air).**

The Rotterdam Rules apply because the damage occurred during the sea carriage. The Montreal Convention also applies because the cause of the damage occurred during the air carriage. Article 18(1) of the Montreal Convention provides "the event *which caused the damage* ...... took place during the carriage by air." Therefore, the Singapore court faces an

---

[11] Summary record of the 870th meeting, held at Headquarters, New York, on Wednesday, 18 June 2008, at 3 p.m., A/CN.9/SR.870 and Corr.1, paras. 10 (UNCITRAL YEARBOOK Volume XXXIX (2008), pp.958) . The delegation from Germany proposed to change the word "prevail" to "apply". The reason for the change, the delegation explained "was to make it clear that draft article 27 [article 26 in the final text] was not a conflict of conventions provision. Provided it was known where the damage had occurred and provided it had occurred where another international instrument applied, the provisions of the latter instrument would apply." (*ibid.*, para.22) Although it was supported by one delegation (Switzerland) (*ibid.*, para.18), many delegations disagreed. Norway, the Netherlands, Belarus, and Japan expressly preferred the word "prevail". Others (the U.K. France, Spain, Greece, Chile) approved the text without specific mention to the choice between "prevail" and "apply" (*ibid.*, paras. 15-21). Some delegations (Belarus and Japan) explicitly supported the word "prevail" because the court should be allowed to apply the Rotterdam Rules if there is no conflict of convention and the court sees it should apply then (*ibid.*, paras. 20-21)

incompatible obligation to apply both conventions. Article 82(a) allows the court to apply the provisions of the Montreal Convention. Articles 82(b)-(d) address similar problems with the carriage by road, rail, and inland water.

IV. The Regulation of "Performing Parties"

Let us turn to the final topic: the persons other than the carrier who are covered by the Rules. Three sub-questions should be considered with respect to those persons: *(1) Who, other than the carrier, is liable under the Rotterdam Rules?; (2) Whose acts or omissions are attributable to the carrier?; and (3) Who is entitled to a defense and limitation of liability under the Rotterdam Rules?*

1. Who is Liable under the Rotterdam Rules?

The Hague and the Hague-Visby Rules regulate only the liability of the carrier. The Hamburg Rules extended their scope to the "actual carrier" who undertakes the sub-carriage. The Rotterdam Rules move even further by introducing a new concept of "performing party."

Article 1(6) defines the term "performing party" as "a person who performs or undertakes to perform any of the carrier's responsibilities under a contract of carriage and who acts, either directly or indirectly, at the carrier's request or under the carrier's supervision or control." This notion is broader than "actual carrier" used in the Hamburg Rules in the sense that it includes not only the sub-carrier who performs the actual carriage, but also other persons—such as stevedores or terminal operators—involved in the performance of the carriage.

However, please note that the Rotterdam Rules do not impose liability on all performing parties. Rather, they provide for liability only for those referred to as a "maritime performing party." (See, Article 19) Article 1(7) defines "maritime performing party" as "a performing party to the extent that it performs or undertakes to perform any of the carrier's obligations during the period between the arrival of the goods at the port of loading of a ship and their departure from the port of discharge of a ship. An inland carrier is a maritime performing party only if it performs or undertakes to perform its services exclusively within a port area." Although the definition is lengthy, roughly speaking, it is a performing party that offers services related to sea carriage[12].

Why should the Rotterdam Rules restrict their liability regime to the "maritime performing party"? Because delegations to the UNCITRAL Working Group thought it was too far-reaching if the Rotterdam Rules covered purely domestic land transportation. If the Rules cover the liability of all performing parties, they could apply to a truck driver who carries the goods to a neighboring town. Such a result is beyond the ordinary expectations of a small carrier who engages exclusively in domestic land transport. Moreover, each state has its own domestic policy for regulating such a transport, and it was thought unwise for the Rotterdam Rules to intervene.

Let me show how the Rotterdam Rules apply to performing parties using the following example.

Case #4 **The shipper entered into a contract of carriage from Berlin to Chicago with NVOC. The goods were carried by road from Berlin to Antwerp, by ship from Antwerp to New York, and by rail from New York to Chicago. The United States is a contracting state to the Convention while Germany and Belgium are not. When the goods were damaged, who can the consignee sue, and on what basis?**

Because the contract of carriage satisfies the conditions in Article 4, the NVOC is liable as the "carrier".

The ocean carrier that carried the goods from Antwerp to New York is liable as a maritime performing party, if the goods were damaged during the sea carriage (Article 19(1)).

Stevedores who worked at the port of New York are liable under the Rotterdam Rules, while stevedores in the port of Antwerp are not. Maritime performing parties who provide services in a port of a non-contracting state are not liable under Article 19(1) of the Rotterdam Rules.

If the goods were damaged between Berlin and Antwerp, the trucker would not be liable under the Convention. A trucker is a performing party but is not a maritime performing party. CMR applies to the road carriage between Berlin and Antwerp, but CMR does not provide for a direct cause of action for a person with no contractual relationship. The consignee can sue the trucker only in torts.

---

[12] Article 19(4) provide that nothing in the Rotterdam Rules imposes liability on the master or crew of the ship or on an employee of the carrier or of a maritime performing party. The persons listed in Article 19(4) may, if not always, fall under the definition of maritime performing party in Article 1(7). The UNCITAL Working Group was reluctant to provide for a direct cause of action against the individual employee under the Rotterdam Rules and introduced an explicit provisions for the purpose. For the details of the problem, see, Fujita, *supra* note 1, pp.369-371.

If the goods were damaged between New York and Chicago, the liability of the railroad would be governed by law of the United States and not by the Rotterdam Rules. If the Carmack Amendment (U.S. domestic law)[13] does not offer a direct cause of action against the sub-carrier for the benefit of the consignee, the consignee can sue the railroad only in torts.

2. Whose Acts or Omissions are Attributable to the Carrier?

The second sub-question is *whose acts or omissions are attributable to the carrier?* Article 18 provides that a carrier is liable for the breach of its obligation under the Convention caused by the acts or omissions of not only any performing party, but also other persons that perform or undertake to perform any of the carrier's obligations under the contract of carriage. If the concept of "performing party" alone can completely define the scope of the persons whose acts or omissions are attributable the carrier, it would be most elegant. Unfortunately, because there may be "residual" people who cannot be completely covered by the term "performing party," a fine-tuning was necessary to make sure no one would be missing from the list[14].

3. Who is Entitled to a Defense and Limitation ("Himalaya Protection")?

Finally, *who, other than the carrier, is entitled to the defense or limitation of liability that the carrier enjoys?* Such protections for a person other than the carrier are known as a "Himalaya protection[15]." Article 4 provides a list of persons who are entitled to a defense and limitation of liability under the Rotterdam Rules[16].

---

[13] 49 U.S.C. § 14706

[14] For example, a master or the crew of a ship under time charter may not be an employee of the carrier (time charterer) and they may not be a performing party. Therefore, it was thought necessary for Article 18 to explicitly refer to such persons to make sure their acts or omissions are attributable to the carrier. The treatment of individual employees (natural persons) of the carrier or a performing party was discussed and the UNCITRAL Working Group decided to make an explicit reference in each provision. *See, supra* note 12. One cannot interpret Article 18(b) and (c) as meaning that employee is not performing party.

[15] The name "Himalaya" came from a famous English case *Adler v Dickson (The Himalaya)*, [1954] 2 Lloyd's Rep 267, [1955] 1 QB 158 [1]. The case involved in a passenger claim rather than cargo claim. A passenger injured during the embarking sued the master and the boatswain. The defendant argued that the exoneration clause agreed between the carrier and the passenger effectively protected them. Although the House of Lords dismissed the claim by the master and the boatswain, it acknowledged that if the contract of carriage contained an agreement that gave exemption for the benefit the carrier's employees, it was effective to protect the employees.

[16] Article 4(1) provides that "any provisions of this Convention that may provide a defence for, or limit the liability of, the carrier" applies to the persons listed in subparagraph (a) – (c). If a carrier agreed a higher or lower (in case of volume contract) limitation than the amount in article 59(1), the

When you look at the persons other than the carrier that are mentioned in Article 4, you can see that they are divided into two categories. First, the maritime performing party is entitled to a defense and limit of liability under the Convention. This is because maritime performing parties are liable under the Rotterdam Rules and it is simply logical that they also enjoy the benefits under the Rules. Strictly speaking, this is not a "Himalaya protection". The second category is employees of the carrier or maritime performing party (Article 4(1)(c)), as well as masters, crew, or other persons offering services on board the ship (Article 4(1)(b)). These people need a different justification for protection because the Rotterdam Rules do not impose any liability on them. The reason they receive this protection is that the employees are economically dependent on their employers. In this context, their disadvantages are ultimately borne by the employer. Due to their economic dependency, if we denied the defense and limit of liability for the employees, it would, in fact, result in depriving the carrier or maritime performing party of the defense and limit of liability.

If economic dependency is the reason, we cannot automatically extend Himalaya protection to all performing parties. An inland carrier, such as a railroad, is not economically dependent on the carrier, at least not to the same degree as the carrier's employees. This is why the list in Article 4 does not refer to "performing parties" itself but only to a portion of them. Of course, this does not mean that the Rotterdam Rules prohibit the parties from agreeing on a Himalaya clause in their contract. However, save for specific contract provisions, persons not listed in Article 4 cannot automatically enjoy the benefit of a defense and limitation of liability.

---

persons listed in Article 4(1)(a)-(c) can invoke such higher or lower limitation agreed by the carrier. The Himalaya protection gives an agent or an employee (except for a maritime performing party) the same protection as the carrier enjoys. "Any provisions of this Convention that may provide a defence for, or limit the liability of, the carrier" should be read as a defence or a limitation which is available for the carrier under the Rotterdam Rules in a particular case. If there is any valid limitation agreed under the Rotterdam Rules, it is the limit available under Article 4.

However, a maritime performing party is not bound by the higher limitation agreed by the carrier and can assert the limitation amount provided under Article 59 (1) unless it expressly agrees to accept such limitation (Article 19(2)). A maritime performing party can limit its liability because it is liable under the Convention. Therefore, a maritime performing party's right to limit its liability is not exactly a Himalaya protection. The employee of the maritime performing party, just like maritime performing party, can also enjoy the limitation amount of the Convention rather than the higher limitation agreed by the carrier under Article 4(1) unless the maritime performing expressly agrees to accept such limitation. Otherwise, the employees of the maritime performing party owes higher limitation than the maritime performing party.

V. Conclusions

In this short speech, I have addressed three aspects with respect to the coverage of the liability regime under the Rotterdam Rules. The Rules expand the coverage of liability regime to "door-to-door transport" in response to modern containerized transportation and provide the solution to possible problem of "conflict of conventions" that necessarily results from such expansion. The Rules include a more comprehensive reference to the persons involved in the performance of carriage during the carrier's extended period of responsibility. In summary, my short presentation deals with the extended coverage of the liability regime under the Rotterdam Rules. However, I did not talk about the substance of the liability regime. The next speaker will explore this important subject.

6
The Obligations and Liability Of The Carrier

Hannu Honka

I. Background

The Rotterdam Rules deal with a number of issues on obligations and liabilities which concern the carrier, the shipper and certain third parties.

As far as the carrier is concerned, the obligations and liabilities can be divided into different categories. The main ones are those relating to cargo and those relating to documents, including electronic transport records. My task is to concentrate on cargo issues connected with the carrier's obligations and liability. As has been explained earlier, these issues are largely, but not completely, covered by one-way mandatory provisions in the Rotterdam Rules.

All international liability regimes concerning carriage of goods are results of difficult and delicate negotiations ending in compromise solutions. In a certain way it might be an optimal choice to place the whole risk of loss of or damage to the goods on either the carrier or the cargo interests. One insurance would suffice, i.e. two separate ones would not be needed.

Such solutions in either extreme nevertheless have substantial problems. They would go against general principles of a fair risk division in a legal perspective, but, foremost of all, from the market evaluation point of view they would be and are unrealistic.

To divide the risk between the parties is an understandable and defendable option. The difficulty is where to draw the line between the carrier's risk and the cargo's risk. This, of course, is a classic point of debate, also typical in negotiating the Rotterdam Rules.

There has been a lot of support and a lot of criticism of these Rules. But, particularly in view of the critics who maintain that other solutions on this and that should have been reached, it should be remembered that whatever an *individual* concept of a proper risk division is, it is the *collectively* reached understanding of a proper risk division that is decisive. This is exactly what has happened in creating the Rotterdam Rules.

In the following, I shall on a general level deal with the carrier's obligations concerning the carriage of goods and the carrier's liability due to loss of or damage to the goods. At the end of my presentation the carrier's delay liability will be touched upon. There is no possibility to go into details, and I shall leave many provisions outside my presentation. Some important aspects of the liability provisions are dealt with by others.

II. The carrier's obligations concerning carriage of goods

The Rotterdam Rules specify the carrier's many obligations. Chapter 4 deals with them in six articles. These provisions are, however, not complete in the sense that they relate to the movement of the goods, but they do not relate to documentary and corresponding electronic issues, found elsewhere in the Rotterdam Rules. Out of the obligations found in Chapter 4, familiar concepts can be found.

The obligation of the carrier to provide a seaworthy ship is age-old. We know this requirement from common law as being an implied term of the contract and its importance in relation particularly to general exception-from-liability clauses in the contract. The overriding breach doctrine would exclude the exception clause. The Hague and the Hague-Visby regimes give independent importance to unseaworthiness of the ship before and at the beginning of the voyage as a cause of loss or damage. The Hamburg regime is different. But, once the Hague/Hague-Visby *ex lege* independent exception of nautical fault (error in navigation) has been omitted from the Rotterdam Rules and the exception of fire been adjusted as compared with the Hague/Hague-Visby regimes, the matter of the unseaworthiness of the ship before and at the beginning of the voyage would have either become moot, as in the Hamburg Rules, or would have to be adjusted to maintain some kind of independent importance. The latter option was chosen in the Rotterdam Rules. One part of this option is that the Rotterdam Rules require the carrier not only to make the ship seaworthy before and at the beginning of the voyage, but also to maintain the seaworthiness during the voyage by exercising due diligence, article14 of the Rotterdam Rules.

The other observation concerning the carrier's obligations is that the period of responsibility is extensive with a door-to-door rule applied, Article 12 of the Rotterdam Rules. This gives rise to the question to what extent clauses placing loading and/or stowing and/or discharging functions and risk on the cargo interests are possibly affected. In previous regimes these clauses have been accepted, be it with some modifications. In spite of the period of responsibility mentioned, these clauses, known as FIO clauses or variations, still have relevance, Article 13(2) of the Rotterdam Rules. Again, this is better seen under the liability provisions, where an exception from the carrier's liability covers the FIO issue as further specified in the respective provision.

III. The carrier's liability for loss of or damage to the goods

This is the major aspect of the liability system.

1. Who is the carrier?

There is not much use in applying the Rotterdam Rules liability provisions, if it is not known who the carrier is. This might in a complicated chain of operators become a difficult issue. In the liability regimes preceding the Rotterdam Rules, the carrier has been defined, but nevertheless certain legal problems have arisen, not least within a time charter concept, where the bill of lading has been signed on the basis of "for the Master". Is it the time charterer or the owner proper/or somebody comparable with the owner proper who is the carrier?

Article 1(5) of the Rotterdam Rules defines the carrier as a person that enters into the contract of carriage with a shipper. The person who has given the respective promise to carry has to be found. It was realized that a transport document or an electronic transport record should not be without relevance in this respect. It is required in the Rotterdam Rules that the transport document or the electronic transport record include the name and address of the carrier, Article 36(2)(b) of the Rotterdam Rules. The importance of such information is emphasized by the fact that any identity-of-carrier clause pointing to another person as carrier is irrelevant, Article 37(1) of the Rotterdam Rules. There is an emergency exit rule should there be a failure to identify the carrier. In the end, under specified preconditions, it is the registered owner of the ship named in the transport document or the electronic transport record that is presumed to be the carrier, Article 37(2) of the Rotterdam Rules. Notwithstanding such provisions, the cargo interests may prove that another person is the carrier, Article 37(3) of the Rotterdam Rules.

The Rotterdam Rules have seriously tried to create a system that aims to facilitate proper identification.

Cargo interests might wish to direct the claim against another person than the carrier as understood above. Within the sea carriage, this possibility might arise, as indicated above, in time chartered situations where the time charterer has contracted for carriage, but where performance is fulfilled by another, i.e. the owner. Another possibility is that the carrier only part-performs and the rest of the carriage is performed by another operator, such as in feeder traffic. Both of these situations contain another performer than the carrier. Again, details have to be omitted, but in a pure sea carriage context the Rotterdam Rules have recognized this other performer under the term "maritime performing party", the Rotterdam Rules article 1(7), cf. article 1.6. This is the person who performs or undertakes to perform any of the carrier's obligations. Interestingly, the definition covers also port operators/stevedores even if they do not perform the voyage itself.

As the maritime performing party has a special legal role to play, it is naturally necessary for the Rotterdam Rules to include provisions under what conditions that party's liability arises Article 19 of the Rotterdam Rules. This is not only related to substantive provisions on liability, but also to scope of application and jurisdictional matters, Article 19(1) (a) and 68 of the Rotterdam Rules respectively.

2. The basis of the carrier's liability

Chapter 5 of the Rotterdam Rules deals with the carrier's liability concerning cargo claims.

It is generally known that the previous liability regimes have adopted the principle of presumed fault as the basis of the carrier's liability, be it that the Hamburg Rules have clarified the application of the principle only through an expression of "common understanding". It was more or less clear from the start that the Rotterdam Rules would continue this tradition. The Hague and Hague-Visby q) - clause on presumed fault in the catalogue is an independent provision in the the Rotterdam Rules, Article 17(2). (*See* also, Article 17(1)).

In cargo liability cases, once cargo interests have proved that goods have been lost or damaged during the carrier's period of responsibility, by, for example, reference to a "clean" transport document, the carrier is relieved from its liability totally or in part to the extent the carrier proves that the loss or damage is not attributable to the carrier's fault.

3. Exceptions

So far tradition prevails. When it comes to *ex lege* exceptions from liability, it is true that a Hague type of catalogue is included in the Rotterdam Rules, but with certain modifications, the Rotterdam Rules Article 17(3). By far the most important modification of the catalogue is that the Hague and Hague-Visby exception of nautical fault or more precisely the exception of "Act, neglect, or default of the master, mariner, pilot, or the servants of the carrier in the navigation or in the management of the ship" is not included in the Rotterdam Rules. The Hamburg Rules do not include this exception either. The rest of the catalogue in the Rotterdam Rules has many similarities with the Hague and Hague-Visby system. Omitting the nautical fault exception from the Rotterdam Rules is in many jurisdictions a true change, but in some others perhaps not completely so. The conclusion depends on how the concept of seaworthiness-unseaworthiness before and at the beginning of the voyage is understood. The larger that concept is, the less importance the nautical fault exception has had.

The fire exception has undergone an adjustment in the Rotterdam Rules, Article 17(3) (f). Fire on the ship - without further specification is an excepted peril, but cargo interests may rebut the exception by proving fault with the carrier. The burden of proof thus lies with the cargo interests. This legislative approach is not far from the solution accepted in the Hamburg Rules.

The above-mentioned FIO acceptance under the Rotterdam Rules is combined with one of the exceptions in the Rotterdam Rules catalogue that specifies the exception as loading, handling, stowing, or unloading of the goods performed pursuant to an agreement in accordance with article 13(2) of the Rotterdam Rules, unless the carrier or a performing party performs such activity on behalf of the shipper, the documentary shipper or the consignee, Article 17(3)(i) of the Rotterdam Rules. There are several terms under this exception that cannot be further explained in this context, but a general reference can be made to article 1 of the Rotterdam Rules where the terms are defined.

New exceptions in the Rotterdam Rules catalogue include, for example, loss or damage due to reasonable measures to avoid or attempt to avoid damage to the environment, Article 17(3) (n) of the Rotterdam Rules.

In addition to the catalogue, it was necessary to clarify the Rotterdam Rules on how the liability provisions stand in view of proof, rebuttal and counter-proof. The role of the catalogue in the Hague and Hague-Visby systems has, as it seems, been somewhat unclear in certain jurisdictions, but in the Rotterdam Rules the carrier's proof of no-fault or the carrier's proof of a cause included in the catalogue of exceptions can be overturned by the cargo interests, Article 17(4) of the Rotterdam Rules.

As said, unseaworthiness as a cause of loss of or damage to the goods does not play the same role in the Rotterdam Rules as in the Hague and Hague-Visby regimes. According to the Rotterdam Rules, the cargo interests may prevail by proving that the loss of or damage to the goods was *probably* caused by the unseaworthiness of the ship as this concept is understood in Article 17(5) of the Rotterdam Rules. The level of proof required by the cargo interests is lower than in "normal" situations. Even in case of such unseaworthiness the carrier has a possibility to prove either lack of causation or lack of fault by proving that due diligence has been exercised. The unseaworthiness rule is relevant whether unseaworthiness existed before or at the beginning of the voyage or arose during the voyage.

Finally, the Rotterdam Rules take into consideration the fact that more than one cause gave rise to loss or damage, Article 17(6) of the Rotterdam Rules. In such a case the carrier is liable only to the extent that the cause that the carrier is liable for attributed to the loss or damage.

The main provisions in the Rotterdam Rules concerning the basis of the carrier's cargo liability represent a fairly complicated setting. There were doubts during the preparatory stages that this "liability package" was over-detailed and that a more streamlined version would have been preferable. But, the view emphasizing the need to have a kind of an all-coverage regulation prevailed. Some of the provisions of course leave and have to leave room for discretion.

4. Particular situations

The Rotterdam Rules take certain specific situations into consideration, i.e. deviation, deck cargo, multimodal carriage, live animals, special carriage in need of a special agreement and general average.

Most of them are familiar from the older liability regimes, but in substance there are certain differences, not possible to go into now.

I would just like to comment first on the deviation provision in Article 24 of the Rotterdam Rules. As you know there are or might be national differences concerning the concept of deviation and also differences concerning the consequences of breach of contract by deviation. The Rotterdam Rules aim to prohibit the use of nationally based rules and principles, by requiring the Rotterdam Rules to be applied in all cases where the goods have been lost or damaged. This means that efforts by the cargo interests to give priority to national deviation rules are not possible under the Rotterdam Rules. It is another matter that a deviation might affect the discretion when applying the Rotterdam Rules.

My second note is on general average. According to Article 84 of the Rotterdam Rules, general average is not affected. But, this might not quite be the case in reality. General average (GA) is adjusted by objective factors. This is particularly emphasized in Rule D of the York-Antwerp Rules 2004 and previous versions. General average is relevant at least where the Hague and Hague-Visby regime are applicable and where the cause of loss of or damage to the goods is nautical fault, this being an *ex lege* exception. As the nautical fault exception is not included in the Rotterdam Rules, it is not impossible that this will affect the GA system. There is no point in declaring general average if the result is that no contribution will be received or that paid contribution is reclaimed. Furthermore, the Rotterdam Rules are silent on the question of the status of cargo interests in view of contribution in general average. This seems to remain a national issue. The Hamburg Rules are clear on the point: According to Article 24(2), the provisions of the Hamburg Rules relating to the liability of the carrier for loss of or damage to the goods also determine whether the consignee may refuse contribution in general average and the liability of the carrier to indemnify the consignee in respect of any such contribution made or any salvage paid. This provision in the Hamburg Rules clarifies the issue on contribution by cargo interests. It is to be hoped that such an interpretation would be accepted on a national basis.

5. The amount of compensation

The amount of compensation in cases of loss of or damage to the goods does not follow the line of general contract law, whereby a contracting party may claim costs arisen and profit lost due to the breach of contract by the other contracting party. Instead, a value based compensation system prevails. This has been explicitly so since the Hague-Visby Rules.

The Rotterdam Rules follow the pattern, but the value is decided according to the place and time of delivery as specified, Article 22(1) of the Rotterdam Rules. The value is alternatively the commodity exchange price, market price or the normal value of the goods of the same kind and quality at the place of delivery, Article 22(2) of the Rotterdam Rules.

There has been some doubt in some jurisdictions whether or not loss of profit can be claimed under general rules (certain profit might, nevertheless, be included in the value assessment). The Rotterdam Rules disallow such a possibility, unless otherwise agreed by the parties within the limits of the mandatory provisions, Article 22(3) of the Rotterdam Rules.

Limitation of liability has existed internationally in sea carriage since the Hague Rules. The permanent debate seems to be on what level to place the limitation level. This is of course both difficult and not only legal by nature. It is at least partly a question of politics, remembering that the limitation question is a certain kind of a shop window to any liability regime.

Since the Visby protocol, which adjusts the Hague Rules, there has been a dual limitation system based on the shipping unit and the weight of the goods, where the higher limitation is applied. The unit limitation has been specified for consolidated goods, such as in containers. The specification in the transport document has been decisive in this respect. This pattern is also accepted in the Rotterdam Rules, but the limits are higher than under the Hague-Visby system, where they are 666,67 SDR per unit or 2 SDR per kilo. Now, under the Rotterdam Rules the limits are 875 SDR per unit and 3 SDR per kilo respectively Article 59(1) the Rotterdam Rules. See Article 59(2) of the Rotterdam Rules on unit limitation.

Often the weight limitation is referred to and it has been said that it is very low in comparison with other modes of transport. The CMR (Convention relative au contrat de transport international de marchandises par route = CMR; Convention on the Contract for the International Carriage of Goods by Road), for example, has 8,33 SDR per kilo for road carriage. That criticism has the flaw that it does not consider the unit limitation in sea carriage. The fact is that, as long as the goods are specified properly in the transport document or the electronic transport record, the unit limitation not rarely ends in a higher limitation than when applying the kilo limitation. Each unit would have to weigh 292 kg or more before the kilo limitation would be applied. If, for example, manufactured goods, such as mobile phones or TV sets in packages, have been damaged it would probably be the unit limitation that would apply. It is quite another matter to what extent as such limitation levels relating to any mode of transport de facto have followed inflationary development.

There is one further important aspect with limitation of liability: Under the Hague and Hague-Visby regimes limitation is referred to when loss of or damage to the goods has taken place, but also when there has been loss "in connection with the goods". The meaning of these last words has at least in some jurisdictions been unclear, or they have been ignored. And, it often seems to be a general understanding that limitation refers only to the loss of or damage to the goods (delay is a different matter). This dilemma was solved in a more clarified way in the Rotterdam Rules than before. Now the limitation provisions are included in an independent Chapter 12 in order to show their all-coverage nature in the Rotterdam Rules regime. The reference is to "the carrier's liability for breaches of its obligations under this Convention", Article 59(1) of the Rotterdam Rules.

IV. The carrier's liability for delay in the delivery of the goods and certain other matters

One of the big problems in preparing the Rotterdam Rules was the question of the carrier's and the shipper's liability for delay. Concerning the carrier, there was strong opposition to include a general definition of delay. This means delay in the delivery of the goods. The result is that delay under the Rotterdam Rules results only when the goods are not delivered at the place of destination provided for in the contract of carriage within the time agreed, Article 21 of the Rotterdam Rules. What is the time agreed? It could be explicit, but the contract may also be interpreted as including such a timely delivery obligation. An implied term of this kind might be clarified in national law.

Once delay as described occurs, the carrier's liability follows what has been said above about loss of or damage to the goods. Calculation of compensation is not specified in the Rotterdam Rules and it is thus possible to apply general principles including foreseeability aspects, with the restriction that the carrier's liability is limited to an amount equivalent to 2.5 times the freight payable on the goods delayed, but there being a total amount corresponding to what has been said about limitation due to loss or damage, Article 60 of the Rotterdam Rules.

There is no conversion provision in the Rotterdam Rules. It might be possible to add nationally a rule, whereby the goods after a certain time are considered to be lost, if not delivered at all.

There are provisions on notification in case of loss, damage or delay and specific time-bar provisions not possible to deal with now.

V. Conclusions

Concerning the carrier's cargo liability, the Rotterdam Rules include both traditional solutions, adjusted traditional solutions and novelties. By thoroughly going through the liability issues and debating them at the preparatory stages of the Rotterdam Rules, it was thought that the Rotterdam Rules approach would satisfy the market.

In general, the Rotterdam Rules are a product of years of work and it is unlikely that any renewed effort of creating a modern liability regime would be initiated on a global level. The choice now lies between previous liability regimes and the Rotterdam Rules. The Rotterdam Rules aim for global solutions. This is extremely important. It would be an unhappy choice if legal fundamental issues concerning carriage of goods wholly or partly by sea would be regulated by regional or national solutions.

7

Shipper's Obligation

In Hyeon Kim

I. Introduction

The two parties in a contract for the carriage of goods by sea are the carrier and the shipper. The carrier promises the shipper that it will transport the goods from the loading port to discharging port. In return, the shipper promises to pay the freight charges to the carrier. While discharging its duty under the contract, the carrier may inflict damages on the cargo interests. The carrier then may be held liable for the cargo damages. It is a general rule among countries, such as Japan, Korean and China, that the carrier's liability is based on the presumed fault liability, which means that the carrier is liable unless it can be proved that the damages were not caused by its negligence.

The various kinds of cargo transported by the carrier include both bulk cargo and boxed cargo. However, with regard to containerized cargo, the carrier may not have a chance to check the condition of the cargo inside the container received by the carrier. Without information about the cargo, the carrier cannot care for the cargo properly. When a cargo accident occurs, and the cargo suffers damages, the carrier may not escape liability. The carrier's fault is presumed under national law, such as the Japanese COGSA, the Maritime Law Section in the Korean Commercial Code (hereinafter KCC), the Chinese Maritime Code, or the Hague-Visby Rules, even though the cargo damages may have been caused by the shipper. These legal regimes have only two or three provisions, such as for dangerous cargo and the accuracy of information furnished by the shipper. In this context, there is call for regulating the shipper's obligation and liability in a clearer manner than the current national laws and international conventions currently articulate.

During the 2000s, the legal regime of the shipper's obligation and liability was challenged by the drafters of the Rotterdam Rules. Consequently, under the Rotterdam Rules, the existing rules on the shipper's obligation and liability are articulated in a more precise manner. Furthermore, several new rules imposing heavier obligation and liability upon the shipper than in other conventions were adopted. The present author would like to introduce the new legal regime of the shipper's obligation and liability under the Rotterdam Rules.

II. Various Cargo Interests

1. Shipper and documentary shipper

Under the Rotterdam Rules, the shipper is a person that enters into a contract of carriage with a carrier (Art. 1(8)). Therefore, it is one party in the contract for the carriage of goods by sea.

Under the KCC, the shipper is also a party in the contract for the carriage of goods by sea (Art. 791). The carrier and the shipper are the two parties in the contract for the carriage of goods (Art. 827). However, in a voyage charter party, the ship owner and the charterer are the two parties. In other words, the carrier in a common carriage is the equivalent to the ship owner in a voyage charter party, and the shipper in a common carriage is the equivalent to the charterer in a voyage charter party.

The term, "the consignor," is no longer used in the Rotterdam Rules although it is widely used in Korean practice. The term "consignor" has long been used as equivalent to the term, the shipper. However, depending on the situation, the term means the person who sends the goods to the consignee. Under the CIF terms, the consignor as the exporter is obliged to enter into the contract for the carriage. Thus, the consignor becomes the shipper by entering into the contract. On the other hand, the consignee becomes the shipper under the FOB terms.

In a Korean Supreme Court case *2000.8.18. Docket No. 99da48474*, the consignor was sued by the carrier for unpaid freight. The Court decided that the consignor, under FOB terms, acted as the agent of the consignee, and thus the parties under the contract were the carrier and the consignee. As a result, the consignor was not responsible for the unpaid freight (because it was not the shipper who is responsible for the freight) The Court rejected the carrier's claim.

Under the Rotterdam Rules, the documentary shipper means a person, other than the shipper, that accepts being named the shipper in the transport document or electronic transport record (Art. 1.9). In the above Korean Supreme Court case, the FOB seller becomes a documentary shipper, only if it accepted to be named as the shipper in the bill of lading (B/L). Under the Rotterdam Rules, the documentary shipper is subject to the obligations and liabilities imposed upon the shipper if the several requirements are fulfilled.[1]

2. Consignee

Under the Rotterdam Rules, the consignee is the person who is entitled to delivery of the cargo (Art. 1(11)). When the negotiable B/L is issued, the holder of the B/L is the person who is entitled to claim the cargo. The carrier has obligation to deliver the cargo to the consignee with exchange of the B/L and thus when the negotiable B/L is issued, the carrier should deliver the cargo to the holder of the B/L with the exchange of the B/L.

Under the FOB terms, the consignee as an importer is the person who should make the contract for the carriage of goods. Therefore, the consignee becomes the shipper in the contract for the carriage. Under Korean law, the consignee is not different from that under the Rotterdam Rules.

3. Holder of the Bill of Lading

When the B/L is issued, the holder of the B/L becomes the consignee, who then is the person eligible to claim the cargo from the carrier.

III. Shipper's Obligation Subject to Fault Liability

1. General

When we address the shipper's obligation and liability, we should focus on two special circumstances involved in the transportation of the cargo.

First, the shipper is the person who requests the carrier to transport the cargo to the des-

---

[1] Art. 33 Assumption of shipper's rights and obligations by the documentary shipper
    (1) A documentary shipper is subject to the obligations and liabilities imposed on the shipper pursuant to this chapter and pursuant to article 55, and is entitled to the shipper's rights and defences provided by this chapter and by chapter 13.
    (2) Paragraph 1 of this article does not affect the obligations, liabilities, rights or defences of the shipper.

tination. This person knows the quantity, weight and nature of the cargo to be transported. Relying on the information furnished by the shipper, the carrier issues the B/L with statements on the description of the cargo. Without the information from the shipper, the carrier may not know the nature of the cargo within the container box that was handed over by the shipper in a sealed condition. We can say safely that the shipper rather than the carrier is in an easy position to provide information on the condition of the cargo to be transported.

Second, from the perspective of protecting the parties involved in the contract, since the Harter Act in 1893, the carrier has been regarded as having bargaining power over the shipper. Hence, the Hague-Visby Rules have only the provision that prohibits the carrier from derogating its obligation and liability stipulated in the Rules, but it allows the carrier to increase its obligation or liability (Art. 3(8)).

Under previous conventions, such as the Hague-Visby Rules, there are only a few provisions on the obligation and liability of the shipper. Only three provisions are relevant. First, the shipper guarantees the accuracy of the information on the weight, quantity, and nature of the cargo furnished by it (Art. 3(5)). Second, the shipper has the obligation to notify the carrier of the nature of the dangerous cargo (Art. 4(6)). Third, the shipper is liable for loss or damage sustained by the carrier as a result of any fault of neglect by the shipper or his agent or servants (Art. 4(3)). It is interpreted that the shipper is strictly liable for the damages caused by the inaccuracy of the information of the cargo and failure of such notification in case of dangerous cargo.[2]

As the successor of the Hague-Visby Rules, the Hamburg Rules maintained the position of the Hague-Visby Rules with respect to the shipper's obligation and liability. The Hamburg Rules re-stated in detail two provisions (Art. 13 Dangerous Good and Art. 17 Guarantees by the Shipper) on the shipper's obligation and liability in the Hague-Visby Rules. It maintained a general rule on the shipper's liability (Art. 12) that originated from Art. 4(3) of the Hague-Visby Rules. Even though containerization began in the early 1970s, the Hamburg Rules did not reflect the circumstances in the new method of transport.

During the 1980s, 1990s and 2000s, containerized cargo became widely used in transportation. In common carriage, almost all cargo is currently transported packed in a container box. Carriers unfortunately have experienced several fire and explosion cases in con-

---

[2] Article 3(5)
The shipper shall be deemed to have guaranteed to the carrier the accuracy at the time of shipment of the marks, number, quantity and weight, as furnished by him, and the shipper shall indemnify the carrier against all loss, damages and expenses arising or resulting from inaccuracies in such particulars. The right of the carrier to such indemnity shall in no way limit his responsibility and liability under the contract of carriage to any person other than the shipper.

tainer vessels due to the dangerous nature of the goods in the container box.[3] As a result, it is inevitable that a new regime will be required to be spelled out in the R/R.

Shipper's liability can be divided by the fault based liability and the strict liability.

2. Delivery ready for carriage under Article 27(1) and (3)

Article 27(1)

Unless otherwise agreed in the contract of carriage, the shipper shall deliver the goods ready for carriage. In any event, the shipper shall deliver the goods in such condition that they will withstand the intended carriage, including their loading, handling, stowing, lashing and securing, and unloading, and that they will not cause harm to persons or property.

Article 27(3)

When a container is packed or a vehicle is loaded by the shipper, the shipper shall properly and carefully stow, lash and secure the contents in or on the container or vehicle, and in such a way that they will not cause harm to persons or property.

Under Article 27(1) and Article 27(3), these obligations are very similar to the carrier's duty to provide a seaworthy vessel for the carriage. If the cargo is not capable of withstanding the intended voyage, the carrier cannot complete its duty under the contract. The obligations imposed under Article 27(1) and (3) of the Rotterdam Rules upon the shipper seem natural and reasonable. Even though these provisions are newly inserted in the Rotterdam Rules, the obligations under Article 27(1) and (3) are not regarded as newly invented.[4] It is

---

[3] Under Korean jurisdiction, the Hyundai Fortune explosion case on March 21, 2006 is very famous. According to Wikipedia, the explosion might have been caused by dangerous cargo: "Theories concerning the cause of the explosion vary. The pool chemical calcium hypochlorite reacts violently when exposed to moisture or heat, and has been involved or suspected in other explosions aboard container ships in recent years. Notable examples include *Sea Elegance*, M/V *Hanjin Pennsylvania*, *CMA Djakarta*, *Aconcagua*, *Sea Land Mariner* and M/V DG *Harmony*. Investigators also considered the possibility that volatile cargo (specifically, the 7 containers of fireworks) may have detonated due to heat, triggering the larger explosion that crippled the ship. According to a statement to the Homeland Security Appropriations Subcommittee, Committee on Appropriations, United States House of Representatives, "The cause of the fire is believed to have been a container loaded with petroleum-based cleaning fluids stowed near the engine room. The shipper failed to indicate the hazardous nature of this shipment to *Hyundai Fortune*, undoubtedly to avoid the special handling fees associated with transporting hazardous materials"(http://en.wikipedia.org/wiki/MV_Hyundai_Fortune).

[4] MICHAEL STURLEY, TOMOTAKA FUJITA AND GERTJAN VAN DER ZIEL, THE ROTTERDAM RULES (SWEET & MAXWELL, 2010), p. 181. The authors say that the ROTTERDAM RULES simply codifies and harmonizes the existing practice rather than creating novel obligations.

understood that the same obligation can be found in accordance with the general obligation of the shipper under the contract.

The obligation under Article 27(1) is not subject to the mandatory application of Article 79(2) because it starts with the wording, "unless otherwise agreed in the contract of carriage." The obligation under Article 27(3) focuses on containerized cargo, which reminds the shipper of the importance of stowing and securing the goods in the container to withstand the voyage.[5]

Pursuant to Article 30(1), the shipper's liability for the breach of obligation under Article 27(1) and (3) is fault-based. In the case that a shipper did not pack a box containing liquids securely, and the liquid leaked into the cargo hold, with the result that (i) hold cleaning expenses were incurred to the carrier, or (ii) the neighboring cargo was damaged. The shipper then is liable for the damages that the carrier paid if the carrier proves that the damage was caused by the breach of the shipper's obligation under Article 27(1).

Even under the current Korean law, the shipper is interpreted to have a general obligation to provide cargo strong enough to withstand an intended voyage. Under the Korean law, the shipper may exclude these obligations by agreement. However, under the Rotterdam Rules Article 27(3), the shipper is not allowed to exclude these obligations by agreement in the case of containerized cargo because the agreement is against the compulsory provision of Article 79(2), which differs from the Hague-Visby Rules.

3. FIO under Article 27(2)

Article 27(2)

The shipper shall properly and carefully perform any obligation assumed under an agreement made pursuant to article 13, paragraph 2.

This obligation is not found in the Hague-Visby Rules. Under the Rotterdam Rules, the carrier is legally allowed to shift its obligation of loading, stowing and discharging to the shipper (Art. 13(2)).[6] In the situation of FIO agreements,[7] the shipper should discharge its

---

[5] UNCITRAL Working Group III 16th Session Report (A/CN. 9/591, 28 Nov.- 9 Dec., 2005, Vienna), par. 111-112.
[6] Article 13(2)
Notwithstanding par. 1 of this article, and without prejudice to the other provisions in chapter 4 and to chapters 5 to 7, the carrier and the shipper may agree that the loading, handling, stowing or unloading of the goods is to be performed by the shipper, the documentary shipper or the consignee. Such an agreement shall be referred to in the contract particulars.
[7] In a voyage charter party, the shipowner and the charterer make an agreement to the effect that the cargo shall be brought into the holds, loaded, stowed and/or trimmed, tallied, lashed and/or se-

obligation in accordance with Article 27(2). [8]

The shipper's liability is regulated by Article 30. It is based on the fault-based liability. If the carrier sustained damages due to a negligent act of the shipper, the shipper is liable for the carrier's damages if the carrier proves that the damages were caused by the breach of the shipper' obligation.

Article 27(2) is applicable to only the relation between the shipper and the carrier. If the unloading of goods was carried out by the consignee in a non-negotiable transport document situation, the carrier is not allowed to make claims against the consignee under Article 27(2).[9] The carrier may have a cause of action in the applicable governing law. However, in case that the consignee became the holder of the B/L, Article 27(2) is applied in conjunction with Article 58(2), and thus the consignee is liable in accordance with Article 27(2) and Article 30(1).

4. To provide information, instruction and documents under Article 29

> Article 29 Shipper's obligation to provide information, instruction and documents
>
> 1. The shipper shall provide to the carrier in a timely manner such information, instruction and documents relating to the goods that are not otherwise reasonably available to the carrier, and that are reasonably necessary:
>
> (a) For the proper handling and carriage of the goods, including precautions to be taken by the carrier or a performing party; and
>
> (b) For the carrier to comply with law, regulations or other requirements of public authori-

---

cured, and taken from the holds and discharged by the charterer, free of any risk, liability and expense whatsoever to the owners. Gencon 1994 Art. 5(a). This clause is called the FIO (Free In and Out) clause. Under the voyage charter party, when the shipowner issues the B/L, then the relation between the shipowner as the carrier and the holder of the B/L falls within the scope of the application of the Rotterdam Rules (Art. 7).

[8] Several court cases show the tendency in Korean practices that the carrier and the shipper insert the simple wording of FIO on the front of the B/L without any full paragraph on the back of the B/L. In the Korean Supreme Court case 2010.4.15. *Docket No. 2007da50649*, the Court held to the effect that, in the case that only the wording of FIO existed, the Korean custom and practice was for the charterer to pay the expense of loading and discharging, in addition to arranging with stevedores for loading and discharging, and on some occasions, giving instructions to the stevedores for cargo works and supervising their works. Therefore, the FIO BASIS in the B/L should be interpreted such that the charterer had made an agreement that it assumes the expenses and liability as well. Please refer to In Hyeon Kim, *Korean Maritime Law Update: 2010, Journal of Maritime Law and Commerce*, Vol. 42. No. 3(July 2011), pp. 423-425. For the general situation in Korea on the FIO clause, please refer to IN HYEON KIM, TRANSPORT LAW IN SOUTH KOREA (WOLTER KLUWER, 2011), pp. 81-82 (Kim, Transport Law).

[9] Sturley, Fujita and Van der Ziel, *supra* note 4, p. 181.

ties in connection with the intended carriage, provided that the carrier notifies the shipper in a timely manner of the information, instructions and documents it requires.

2. Nothing in this article affects any specific obligation to provide certain information, instructions and documents related to the goods pursuant to law, regulations or other requirements of public authorities in connection with the intended carriage.

This article imposes the obligation of providing information, instruction and documents upon the shipper. Under current liner shipping business, especially in FCL cargo, the cargo within the container is delivered in a sealed condition by the shipper. Therefore, the carrier does not have a chance to look at the content within the container. The carrier should passively rely on the information provided by the shipper. Without such information, the carrier cannot carry out the promised contract for the carriage. In addition, without instruction from the shipper on the care of the cargo during the carrier's custody, the carrier is not able to transport the goods as expected or promised. Document on the goods should be provided for the carrier's formality. However, in the case that the information, instruction and documents are reasonably available to the carrier without the shipper's help, Article 29 is not applicable.

The first draft of the Convention imposed strict liability upon the shipper for a breach of the shipper's obligation to furnish information.[10] However, it was finally decided that these obligations under Article 29 should be subject to the fault liability rule (Art. 30). The shipper is liable if the carrier proves that the breach of the shipper under Article 29 caused the loss or damage that the carrier sustained, unless the shipper can prove it was (not caused by) its fault. For example, if the shipper did not give the carrier information about how to care for a special cargo, and the carrier stowed it on the top of a hot bunker tank, which caused an explosion, the shipper will be liable for the carrier's damages unless it can prove that such damages were not caused by its fault.

5. Shipper's basic liability under Article 30

Article 30 Basis of shipper's liability to the carrier

1. The shipper is liable for loss or damage sustained by the carrier if the carrier proves that such loss or damage was caused by a breach of the shipper's obligation under this Convention.

---

[10] Please refer to A/CN.9/WG III/WP 21(Preliminary draft instrument on the carriage of goods by sea). Art. 7.5 and para. 115.

2. Except in respect of loss or damage caused by a breach by the shipper of its obligation pursuant to articles 31, paragraph 2, and 32, the shipper is relieved of all or part of its liability if the cause or one of the causes of the loss or damage is not attributable to its fault or to the fault of any person referred to in article 34.

3. When the shipper is relieved of part of its liability pursuant to this article, the shipper is liable only for that part of the loss or damage that is attributable to its fault or to the fault of any person referred to in article 34.

Article 30(1) addresses the shipper's liability. The liability under this Article is fault-based as opposed to strict liability under Article 31(2) and Article 32. If we make a rule corresponding to the carrier's obligation and liability in accordance with Article 17, the shipper's liability should be presumed fault liability,[11] which means that the shipper is liable for the damage to the carrier unless it proves that the damage was not caused by its breach of the duty. During the UNCITRAL working group meeting, this rule was heavily discussed. [12] It was finally decided that the carrier must first establish a breach of the shipper's obligations under the Convention and that the breach caused the loss or damage.[13]

Article 30(2) covers how the shipper is relieved of the liability if it proves that its negligence did not contribute to the loss or damage of the carrier. A breach of the shipper's obligations does not necessarily mean the presence of the shipper's fault. Under Article 30(2) the shipper's fault rather than the breach of the shipper's obligation is the subject to be proved. Under Article 30, the shipper's liability is treated differently from that in the carrier's liability under Article 17 in that the shipper' breach of the obligation is separated from the fault of the shipper[14]. The burden of proof of the existence of the fault is not explicitly

---

[11] During the negotiations, it was alleged by some delegations that the liabilty of the shipper should mirror the liability of the carrier. Please refer to Johan Schelin, Obligations of the Shipper to the Carrier, in ALEXANDER VON ZIEGLER, STEFANO ZUNARELLI AND JOHAN SCHELIN (EDS.), THE ROTTERDAM RULES 2008 (WOLTER KLUWER, 2010), p. 156.

[12] Please refer to the 16th session report (A/CN. 9/591, 28 Nov.-9 Dec. 2005, Vienna), para. 136-153; 17th session report (A/CN. 9/594, 3-13 April 2006, New York, para. 199-207; 18th session report (A/CN.9/616, 6-17 Nov. 2006, Vienna), para. 83-113; 19th session report (A/CN. 9/621, 16-27 April, 2007, New York), para. 220-243; 21st session report (A/CN. 9/645, 14-25, Jan. 2008, Vienna), para. 220-243.

[13] Sturley, Fujita and Van der Ziel, *supra* note 4, p. 183.

[14] Art. 17(2) The carrier is relieved of all or part of its liability pursuant to paragraph 1 of this article if it proves that the cause or one of the causes of the loss, damage, or delay is not attributable to its fault or to the fault of any person referred to in article 18.

It seems to the author that, in this paragraph, the breach of the obligation of the carrier is contained in the fault of the carrier referred to in the same paragraph.

stated in Article 30(2).[15,16]

The cargo damage caused by the shipper's negligence cannot be compensated by the carrier. If claims are raised against the carrier, the carrier may be exempted from liability in accordance with Article 17(3)(h)(i)(k). The scope of the application of Article 30 is limited to the liability of the shipper against the carrier. It will include the direct loss or damage of the carrier and indirect loss or damage of the carrier. The direct damage to the vessel itself due to the explosion of the goods is a good example of the former. A good example of the latter is the carrier's loss or damages by paying cargo damages for the third party cargo owner due to the shipper's negligence. In this case, the carrier may have a recourse claim against the shipper.

Article 30(2) also makes it clear that the shipper is strictly liable for the damages against the carrier in the cases of Article 31 (2) and Article 32.

Article 30(3) provides for the shipper's partial exemption from liability when loss or damage was incurred due to concurring causes of both the carrier and the shipper. The shipper is responsible only to the extent of its own fault.

Loss or damage caused by delay is not included in Article 30 as opposed to Article 17(1). It is the result of deliberate omission the language. The UNCITRAL Working Group decided that the shipper's liability against the carrier in connection with the loss or damage caused by delay should not be included in the Rotterdam Rules but left to the national law.[17]

IV. Shipper's Obligation Subject to Strict Liability

1. General

Under the Hague-Visby Rules and Hamburg Rules, two obligations on the accuracy of the information furnished by the shipper and dangerous goods were based on strict liability.

---

[15] According to Professors Sturley, Fujita and Van der Ziel, who should bear the burden of the proof on the presence of the fault was the result of a compromise during the negotiation. It was deliberately left to the national courts (Sturley, Fujita and Van der Ziel, *supra* note 4, p. 188).
[16] However, Prof. Girvin explained that the burden of the proof under Art. 30(2) is imposed upon the shipper. He says that the shipper would have to prove the fault of the other person in such circumstances (STEPHEN GIRVIN, CARRIAGE OF GOODS BY SEA, THE 2ND EDITION (OXFORD, 2011), P. 377). Jose Vincente Guzman also supports imposing the burden of the proof upon the shipper (Vincente Guzman, *Rotterdam Rules Shipper's Obligations and Liability*, CMI Yearbook 2000, p. 160).
[17] Sturley, Fujita and Van der Ziel, *supra* note 4, p. 186.

Like its predecessors, the Rotterdam Rules maintains the above two obligations and imposes strict liability upon the shipper in a more precise manner.

2. Accuracy on the information shipper provided

> Article 31. Information for compilation of contract particulars
>
> 1. The shipper shall provide to the carrier, in a timely manner, accurate information required for the compilation of the contract particulars and the issuance of the transport documents or electronic transport records, including the particulars referred to in Art. 36(1); the name of the party to be identified as the shipper in the contract particulars; the name of the consignee, if any; and the name of the person to whose order the transport document or electronic transport record is to be issued, if any.
>
> 2. The shipper is deemed to have guaranteed the accuracy at the time of receipt by the carrier of the information that is provided according to par. 1 of this article. The shipper shall indemnify the carrier against loss or damage resulting from the inaccuracy of such information

Article 31(1) imposes the obligation of providing the information for the compilation of contract particulars, such as leading marks, numbers of packages, quantity of goods or the weights of goods under Article 36(1) in addition to the name of the consignee upon the shipper. These lists in Article 36(1) are not exhaustive.[18] If incorrect weight, quantity or name of shipper caused damages to the carrier, the shipper is liable for the damages if the carrier proves that the breach of duty under Article 31(1) caused loss or damage to the carrier.

Article 31(2) is a very famous and traditional provision that imposes strict liability upon the shipper for the accuracy of the information that the shipper provides to the carrier.[19] Article 31(2) is essentially the same as Article 3(5) of the Hague-Visby Rules and Article 17(1) of the Hamburg Rules. The liability of the shipper is triggered only when the shipper provided one of the listed information to the carrier items but it was (i) either inaccurate or (ii) accurate but it was provided in an untimely manner. Because of the wording of "deemed to have guaranteed the accuracy" in Article 31(2), the shipper is strictly liable for loss or damage against the carrier.[20] Even though the shipper mistakenly misunderstood the number or weight, the shipper will be strictly liable for the loss or damages that the carrier sustains.

The KCC has the same provision in Article 853(3), and the Japanese COGSA also has the

---

[18] Sturley, Fujita and Van der Ziel, *supra* note 4, p. 189.
[19] Schelin, *supra* note 11, p.157.
[20] Sturley, Fujita and Van der Ziel, *supra* note 4, p. 190.

same provision in Article 8(3).

3. Dangerous goods

> Article 32 Special rules on dangerous goods
> When goods by their nature or character are, or reasonably appear likely to become, a danger to persons, property or the environment:
> (a) The shipper shall inform the carrier of the dangerous nature or character of the goods in a timely manner before they are delivered to the carrier or a performing party. If the shipper fails to do so and the carrier or performing party does not otherwise have knowledge of their dangerous nature or character, the shipper is liable to the carrier for loss or damage resulting from such failure to inform; and
> (b) The shipper shall mark or label dangerous goods in accordance with any law, regulations or other requirements of public authorities that apply during any stage of the intended carriage of the goods. If the shipper fails to do so, it is liable to the carrier for loss or damage resulting from such failure.

The Rotterdam Rules followed the tradition of the Hague-Visby Rules[21] and the Hamburg Rules.[22] It imposed the obligation to inform the carrier of the dangerous nature of the goods and to mark or label dangerous goods. In comparison with that in the Hague-Visby Rules, the obligation of labeling dangerous goods is added in the Rotterdam Rules. While the Hamburg Rules require the shipper to inform the carrier "if necessary, of the precaution to be taken," the Rotterdam Rules do not require it. As a result, it can be interpreted that al-

---

[21] The Hague-Visby Rules Article 4(6)
Goods of an inflammable, explosive or nature dangerous to the shipment whereof the carrier, Master or agent of the carrier has not consented with knowledge of their nature and character, may at any time before discharge be landed at any place, or destroyed or rendered innocuous by the carier without compensation, and the shipper of such goods shall be liable for all damage and expenses directly or indirectly arising out of or resulting from such shipment. If any such goods shipped with such knowledge and consent shall become a danger to the ship or cargo, they may in like manner be landed at any place or destroyed or rendered innocuous by the carrier without liability on the part of the carrier except to general average, if any.

[22] The Hamburg Rules Article 13
(1) The shipper must mark or label in a suitable manner dangerous goods as dangerous.
(2) Where the shipper hands over dangerous goods to the carrier or an actual carrier, as the case may be, the shipper must inform him of the dangerous character of the goods and, if necessary, of the precautions to be taken. If the shipper fails to do so and such carrier or actual carrier does not otherwise have knowledge of their dangerous character, (a) the shipper is liable to the carrier and any actual carrier for the loss resulting from the shipment of such goods, and (b) the goods may at any time be unloaded, destroyed or rendered innocuous, as the circumstances may require, without payment of compensation.

though the shipper may be required to inform the carrier of the necessary precautions under Article 29, the liability of the shipper is based on not strict but on fault liability.[23]

The Rotterdam Rules states that (i) the shipper is liable to the carrier for loss or damages resulting from failure to inform the carrier of the dangerous nature or character of the goods; and (ii) the shipper is also liable to the carrier for loss or damages resulting from the failure to mark or label dangerous goods without mentioning about the fault or negligence.[24] Accordingly, it can be said that the shipper's liability under Article 32 is based on strict liability.[25,26]

The term, dangerous goods, is not fully defined in the Rotterdam Rules. However, for the goods to fall within the scope of the application of Article 32, they must be "by nature or character" dangerous. The International Maritime Dangerous Goods (IMDG) Code can be of guidance in determining whether certain goods are considered dangerous. In addition, the shipper should be careful about the wording in Article 32 "or reasonably appear to likely become" a danger. If goods are loaded together with certain types of cargo such that the goods become dangerous, the shipper should inform the carrier of this characteristic of the goods.[27]

In the following scenario, the shipper purchased certain goods (cargo A) without knowing their dangerous nature. The carrier then received a container in which they were stowed with other cargo (B) on board the vessel for the carriage. During the voyage, cargo A exploded, causing heavy damage to cargo B inside the container, and the ship itself was also damaged. Under the Rotterdam Rules, the shipper, as the owner of cargo A, is not allowed to make claims against the carrier if the damages were caused by the dangerous nature of cargo A itself pursuant to Article 17(3)(h). In accordance with Article 17(1), the carrier may be liable for the cargo damages that the owner of cargo B suffered unless it proves that the cause of the loss is not attributable to the carrier. Subsequently, the carrier may have a re-

---

[23] Sturley, Fujita and Van der Ziel, *supra* note 4, p. 196; Girvin, *supra* note 16, p. 379; Guzman, *supra* note 16., 161.
[24] Furthermore, Art. 30(2) starts with qualification that except in respect of loss or damage caused by a breach by the shipper or its obligations pursuant to article 31, paragraph 2, and 32, the shipper is relieved of all or part of its liability if the cause or one of the causes of the loss or damage is not attributable to its fault.
[25] Sturley, Fujita and Van der Ziel, *supra* note 4, p. 193.
[26] In Compania Sud Americana De Vapores Sa v Sinochem Tianjin Import and Export Corp (The "Aconcagua"), the dangerous cargo's IMDG number was correctly informed to the carrier. However, due to the mistake of the manufacturer, the shipper handed over cargo to the carrier that was more sensitive than informed. The UK Court of Appeal (December 9, 2010) decided that the shipper was still liable for the carrier's damages caused by the cargo's explosion. Compania Sud Americana De Vapores (CSDV) was a time charterer and the carrier. CSDV as the plaintiff sought for indemnification from the shipper after it paid the damages to the owner caused by the explosion.
[27] Schelin, *supra* note 11, p. 158.

course claim against the shipper. The shipper is strictly liable for the compensation that the carrier paid to the owner of cargo B pursuant to Article 31(a).[28,29] The repair cost of the ship itself is one example of damage to be compensated under the term of "loss or damage resulting from such failure to inform" under Article 31.

V. Freedom of Contract and its Limitation

1. General

Under the Hague-Visby Rules Article 3(8), the agreement in which the carrier tries to derogate from its obligation and liability stipulated in the Hague-Visby Rules is null and void. The agreement in which the carrier assumes much more obligation or liability than that stipulated in the Hague-Visby Rules is valid because it does not put the shipper in an unfavorable position but it instead benefits the shipper.

In the modern liner service, the shipper with volume cargoes who has bargaining power over the carrier appeared. The old idea that the carrier prevails over the shipper in bargaining power became no longer sustainable.[30] Reflecting this practice, the Rotterdam Rules adopted a so-called two-way compulsory provision. Neither the carrier nor the shipper are allowed to be derogated from their obligation and liability stipulated under Article 79 in the Rotterdam Rules. While Article 79(1) is related to the carrier's obligation and liability, which is borrowed from Article 3(8) in the Hague-Visby Rules, Article 79(2) is a newly invented provision in relation to the shipper's obligation and liability.

---

[28] Even though Korea incorporated most of the provisions in the Hague-Visby Rules, it did not adopt the liability provision. Therefore, there is no statutory provision regarding whether the shipper is strictly liable for the cargo damages caused by the dangerous cargo. Art. 801 deals only with the permission of the carrier's discharging of the dangerous cargo. The latter part of Art. 4(6) under the Hague-Visby Rules is missing in the KCC Art. 801. In this regard, split views exist in Korea. The prevailing view is that the shipper may hold liability when it acts negligently because Korean law is based on the fault liability principle, and there is no express provision that imposes strict liability upon the shipper. For details, please refer to Kim, *supra* note 8, Transport Law, p. 101.
[29] The Japanese COGSA has one provision on dangerous goods. Art. 11 (2) says that the preceding paragraph shall not bar the carrier's claim against the shipper for damages.
[30] Please refer to a more detailed explanation in Sturley, Fujita and Van der Ziel, *supra* note 4, pp. 366-367.

2. Compulsory Provision

> Article 79(2)
> Unless otherwise provided in this Convention, any term in a contract of carriage is void to the extent that it:
> (a) Directly or indirectly excludes, limits or increases the obligations under this Convention of the shipper, consignee, controlling party, holder or documentary shipper; or
> (b) Directly or indirectly excludes, limits or increases the liability of the shipper, consignee, controlling party, holder or documentary shipper for breach of any of its obligations under this Convention.

Article 79(2) is assessed as one of the Rotterdam Rules's innovations.[31] It extends the mandatory regime to cargo interests. For example, if the shipper enters into an agreement with the carrier, saying that it will not hold any obligation or liability on the dangerous goods stipulated in Article 32, this agreement will be null and void because it directly or indirectly excludes the shipper's obligation and liability under this Convention in accordance with Article 79(2).

Article 79(2) does not simply mirror Article 79(1) because the wording "increase" is retained in the provision.[32] After a lengthy debate, the UNCITRAL working group III decided that there was still a need to protect the shipper in the new Rotterdam Rules regime.[33] As a result, an agreement between the carrier and the shipper to increase the shipper's obligation and liability is null and void. For example, if the carrier successfully makes an agreement that the shipper is held strictly liable in the case of a breach of the obligation under Article 27(1), which is subject to fault-based liability in accordance with Article 30, it is null and void because the agreement tried to increase the shipper's liability, which is against Article 79(2).

Taking into consideration that the agreement to increase the carrier's liability is valid because it is not against Article 79(1), we can safely say that Article 79(2) is a kind of protective measure for the shipper as opposed to the carrier.[34]

---

[31] Sturley, Fujita and Van der Ziel, *supra* note 4, p. 370.
[32] ibid.
[33] 19th Session Report para. 159.
[34] Japanese COGSA 15 and KCC Art. 799 address only the carrier's derogation of the obligation and liability.

VI. Shipper's Vicarious Liability

1. General

Under the contract law principle, the agent or subcontractor's negligence is regarded as the principal's negligence (Korean Civil Code Art. 391), and thus the carrier is liable for the cargo damages if the cargo's damage was caused by the negligence of its crew during the discharging of carrier's obligation instead of the carrier (KCC Art. 135 & 795) (Japanese COGSA Art. 3(1)).[35]

Under the Hague-Visby Rules, the shipper's liability was not dealt in depth. However, now that the Rotterdam Rules addresses the shipper's obligation and liability in a detail, the shipper's vicarious liability should be dealt in response to the carrier's vicarious liability.

2. Vicarious Liability of the Shipper

> Article 34. Liability of the shipper for other persons
> The shipper is liable for the breach of its obligation under this Convention caused by the acts or omissions of any person, including employees, agents and subcontractors, to which it has entrusted the performance of any of its obligations, but the shipper is not liable for acts or omissions of the carrier or a performing party acting on behalf of the carrier, to which the shipper has entrusted the performance of its obligations.

Just as Article 18 stipulates that the carrier is liable for the acts or omissions of certain other persons, so Article 34 stipulates that the shipper is liable for the acts or omission of the persons to which it entrusts the performance of its obligation.[36]

When the shipper's agents or subcontractors act negligently against the obligation stipulated in Article 27, 29, 31 and 32, the shipper is liable for the damage that the carrier suffers. However, if the agents or subcontractors acted outside the scope of entrusted obligation of the shipper, the shipper is not liable for the damages.

For example, when the shipper's agent gives the carrier wrong information on the goods, and the carrier thus suffers damages, the shipper will be liable for the damages pursuant to

---

[35] Under tort law theory, the carrier may be vicariously liable for the cargo damage caused by its servant, such as crew, when the cause of action is based on tort.

[36] Sturley, Fujita and Van der Ziel, *supra* note 4, p. 183.

Article 34.

VII. Other Issues

1. Limitation of Liability

The shipper does not have a right to limit its liability under the Rotterdam Rules. Taking into consideration that the carrier is allowed to invoke the package limitation or kg limitation) under Article 59, it seems to the author that the absence of a limitation system for the benefit of the shipper is a disadvantage to the shipper as opposed to the carrier.[37]

During the negotiations for the draft of the Rotterdam Rules, there was serious discussion on whether the shipper should be allowed to limit its liability and how the shipper calculates the limitation amount in relation to damage resulting from delay. Whether the shipper should be liable for loss or damage caused by delay was debated in depth at the fall 2005 meeting (16th) of the UNCITRAL Working Group.[38] This topic was discussed continuously at the next two meeting, along with the carrier's liability for delay.[39] Many delegations were nervous about the scenario of the shipper's being held liable for the loss caused by delay. Accordingly, the UNCITRAL Working Group seriously attempted to set a sensible limitation on the shipper's liability for delay.[40] When those attempts were not successful, the Working Group decided that all reference to delay was deleted as part of a compromise package.[41]

2. Time Bar

Article 62 is applicable to the carrier's claim against the shipper. Article 62 (1) says that no judicial or arbitral proceedings with respect to claims or disputes arising from a breach of an obligation under this Convention may be instituted after the expiration of a period of two

---

[37] At the 41st Commission session (A/63/17, 16 June to 3 July, 2008, New York), the German delegation reiterated the importance of the adoption of a limitation regime for the shipper in connection with Art. 79. The argument was not accepted. Refer to para. 103, para. 236-241. There was discussion to delete the wording of "limit" in Art. 79(2).
[38] Refer to 16th Session Report para. 143-146.
[39] Refer to 17th Session Report para. 199-207; 18th Session Report para. 83-113; 19th Session Report para. 233-243.
[40] Refer to 18th Session Report para. 105-106.
[41] Sturley, Fujita and Van der Ziel, *supra* note 4, p. 187.

years. Article 62 does not have any limitation on the person subject to it, which means that it is applicable in the case of the shipper's claim against the carrier as well as that of the carrier's claim against the shipper. Accordingly, if the carrier does not bring about a law suit against the shipper within two years after the day on which the carrier delivered the goods or the last day on which the goods should have been delivered, the carrier no longer institutes the claims against the shipper for the loss or damages arising from the breach of an obligation under the Rotterdam Rules.

VIII. Conclusion

The shipper's general obligation is subject to the fault liability under Article 27, 29 and 31(1), and the shipper's two obligations regarding the accuracy of information and dangerous goods are subject to strict liability under Article 31(1) and 32, which are similar to those in the Hague-Visby Rules and the Hamburg Rules. However, these obligations and liabilities should be interpreted in conjunction with the newly invented mandatory provision of Article 79(2). The shipper is not allowed to make any arrangement to derogate from its obligation and liability. Accordingly, it can be said that the shipper's obligation and liability are heavier than those under the Hague-Visby Rules and the Hamburg Rules.[42]

Two major obstacles for shipowners or carriers in East-Asian countries with regard to ratifying the Rotterdam Rules may be the deletion of error in navigation and the imposition of a continuous duty of seaworthiness upon the carrier. However, when we take into consideration the newly imposed heavy burden upon the shipper, the Rotterdam Rules can be evaluated as being well balanced convention between the carrier and the shipper's interest.

---

[42] Refer to the different opinions of the author; (i) Sturley, Fujita and Van der Ziel, *supra* note 4, p. 201. They say that by taking all of these elements into account, it is implausible to suggest that the shipper's obligations and liabilities are substantially increased under the Rotterdam Rules compared with prior conventions; (ii) Guzman, *supra* note 16, p. 162. He says that shipper's obligation and liability do not worsen the shipper's contractual position under the existing regime but give more certainty to the regulation, for the benefit of the market and the parties involved.

Part I, Chapter 3

Aspects of Transport Regulated by the Rotterdam Rules

8

Transport Documents and Electronic Transport Records

Stephen Girvin

I. Introduction

International maritime law conventions concerned with cargo liabilities, in their drive towards harmonisation and unification of law, have sought to achieve solutions which will be acceptable to a wide range of states, thereby promoting uniform interpretation in all the countries in which the relevant international instruments are in force. In the case of the new Rotterdam Rules[1], there has been a unique collaboration between the CMI[2] and UNCITRAL in the most far-reaching cargo convention of them all[3]. One of the features of the new Rules are a number of innovative provisions concerning transport documents and the extension of the Rules to cover the use of electronic transport records. These aspects of the Rules form the focus of this paper and I shall start by considering the usage of electronic transport records.

---

[1] The United Nations General Assembly on 11 December 2008 passed Resolution 63/122 adopting the "United Nations Convention on Contracts for the International Carriage of Goods Wholly or Partly by Sea".
[2] The CMI connection goes back many years, starting arguably in 1995, when it set up an International Sub-committee (ISC) on Uniformity of the Law of Carriage of Goods by Sea under Professor Francesco Berlingieri, the CMI's President *ad honorem*. *See* Stephen Girvin, *The 37th Comité Maritime International Conference: a report.* [2001] *Lloyd's Maritime & Commercial LQ* 406, 409.
[3] *See*, generally, STEPHEN GIRVIN, CARRIAGE OF GOODS BY SEA 2ND ED (2011), PARA 17.10.

II. Electronic Transport Records

Electronic data interchange (EDI), the computer-to-computer transmission of standard business documents now covers the whole gamut of dealings between businessmen in their commercial relationships with each other.[4] While used very successfully in a number of financial contexts, including banking,[5] the move to electronic documentation and transfer in the carriage of goods by sea context has been remarkably slow, despite the relative success stories of the well-known system, Bolero, ESS-Databridge™, and others.[6] This is now one of the most important features of the new Rotterdam Rules[7] and was clearly identified at an early stage in the CMI's work project. Thus, in 2000 it was noted that "the growing use of electronic means of communication in the carriage of goods further aggravated the consequences of those fragmentary and disparate laws and also created the need for uniform provisions addressing the issues particular to the use of new technologies".[8] A particular concern was to therefore to ensure consistency with the text of the UNCITRAL Model Law on Electronic Commerce, with respect to both substance and terminology.[9]

That electronic communications is a central feature of the Rotterdam Rules[10] is highlighted by the definitions of 'electronic communication',[11] 'electronic transport record',[12] 'negotiable electronic transport record', and 'non-negotiable electronic transport record'.[13]

---

[4] These are tellingly set out in Nicholas Gaskell, *Bills of lading in an electronic age*, [2010] Lloyd's Maritime & Commercial LQ 233.
[5] i.e. SWIFT, or The Society for Worldwide Inter-Bank Financial Telecommunications was established in 1972 to "facilitate the transmission of bank-to-bank financial transaction messages".
[6] For a brief introduction to Bolero, *see* Mariika Virrankoski, *Bolero.net – A solution for electronic trade documentation*, CMI Newsletter No 1/2000, 12. See also Girvin, *supra* note 3, para 13.24; Malcolm Clarke, *Transport documents: their transferability as documents of title; electronic documents*, [2002] Lloyd's Maritime & Commercial LQ 356.
[7] *See* too Girvin, *supra* note 3, para 13.28; RICHARD AIKENS, RICHARD LORD & MICHAEL BOOLS, BILLS OF LADING (2006), PARA 2.117. For more detailed consideration, *see* Miriam Goldby, *Electronic alternatives to transport documents and the new Convention: a framework for future development?*, 14 JIML 586 (2008); Manuel Alba, *Electronic Commerce Provisions in the UNCITRAL Convention on Contracts for the International Carriage of Goods Wholly or Partly by Sea*, 44 Texas International LJ 287 (2008-2009). *See* also Gaskell, *supra* note 4, 269.
[8] *See* "Transport Law: Possible future work", United Nations Commission on International Trade Law, thirty-third session, 12 June-7 July 2000, A/CN.9/476, para 2.
[9] *See* Report of the Working Group on Transport Law on the work of its ninth session (New York, 15-26 April 2002) A/CN.9/510, para 35.
[10] For detailed analysis, *see* now MICHAEL F STURLEY, TOMOTAKA FUJITA, AND GERTJAN VAN DER ZIEL, THE ROTTERDAM RULES: THE UN CONVENTION ON CONTRACTS FOR THE INTERNATIONAL CARRIAGE OF GOODS WHOLLY OR PARTLY BY SEA (2010), CH 3.
[11] Article 1(17).
[12] Article 1(18).
[13] Article 1(20).

Although the main provision dealing with electronic communications is to be found in Chapter 3 of the Rules, other provisions are to be found scattered throughout the Rules, including the provisions on deck cargo,[14] compilation of the contract particulars,[15] transport records,[16] delivery,[17] the rights of the controlling party,[18] and the transfer of rights.[19] So the electronic provisions are not a mere bolt-on to the Rules, but are woven into the very fabric of the Rules. Indeed, not to have done so, would have undermined this feature of the Rules.

In essence, the Rules rely on the so-called "functional equivalence approach".[20] Article 8(a) of the Rules provides that:[21]

> (a) Anything that is to be in or on a transport document under this Convention may be recorded in an electronic transport record, provided the issuance and subsequent use of an electronic transport record is with the consent of the carrier and the shipper.

Such issuance, exclusive control or transfer of an electronic transport record is stated to have the same effect as the issuance, possession, or transfer of a transport document.[22] The importance of these provisions are that they confirm that anything in the Rules which can be done with a traditional paper transport document may be recorded in an electronic transport record provided that this is with the consent of the carrier and shipper and so long as the issuance, exclusive control, or transfer of such a record has the same effect as with a paper document.

Article 9 of the Rules lay down a number of specific procedures which must be followed in relation to negotiable electronic transport documents. Thus, under this provision of the Rules, the relevant procedures must provide for the issuance and transfer of the electronic record to an intended holder; an assurance that the negotiable electronic transport record retains its integrity; the manner in which the holder is able to demonstrate that it is the holder; the manner of providing confirmation that delivery has been effected or the electronic transport record has ceased to have any effect or validity. Moreover these procedures must be referred to in the contract particulars and be readily ascertainable. There is no

---

[14] *See* Article 25(4).
[15] *See* Article 31(1).
[16] *See* Chapter 8 of the Rules.
[17] Article 45.
[18] Article 51(4).
[19] Article 57.
[20] *See* the UNCITRAL Model Law and the "Guide to Enactment" of that Model Law.
[21] *See* too BENJAMIN'S SALE OF GOODS 8TH ED (2010), PARA 18-249.
[22] *See* Article 8(b).

equivalent provision concerning non-negotiable transport records.

Article 10 of the Rules allows for the replacement of a negotiable transport document by an electronic transport record and vice versa. The substitution of a non-negotiable record is not possible. Article 10(1) deals with the former case and lays down various safeguards. Thus, the holder must surrender the negotiable transport document – all of them if there is more than one original – to the carrier. The carrier is obliged to issue an electronic record which includes a statement that it replaces the negotiable transport document. Once issued the paper original ceases to have any effect or validity. Article 10(2) deals with the latter case and, where this occurs, the carrier must issue to the holder a negotiable transport document which includes a statement that it replaces the negotiable electronic transport record. The electronic transport record no longer has any effect or validity.

Now, it will be obvious that these provisions are drafted at the level of some generality and I would submit that this is correct. The Rules do not require the use of electronic transport records; they provide a mechanism for enabling their coverage if they are issued.

III. Transport Documents

The Hague and Hague-Visby Rules[23] apply to "contracts of carriage covered by a bill of lading or any similar document of title in so far as such document relates to the carriage of goods by sea".[24] This definition, enshrined in an international convention drafted not too many years following the end of the First World War, could never have envisaged the momentous changes which would occurred in the transportation of cargoes immediately following World War Two.[25] In due course, it became necessary for courts in many jurisdictions, including those in the common law world, to consider the definition of "contract of carriage" in this new context. Thus, reported cases in England[26] and Australia[27] confirmed that straight bills of lading and consignment notes were included in this definition.[28]

---

[23] The original Hague Rules and the Hague-Visby Rules are substantially similar, save for amendments effected in relation to limitation of limitation of liability (*see* Article IV, r 5), limitation of time (Article III, r 6), and the legal effect of the Rules (*see* Article X).
[24] Article I(b). *See*, generally, Girvin, *supra* note 3, para 19.16; Aikens et.al., *supra* note 7, para 2.36.
[25] *See* Girvin, supra note 3, para 1.15.
[26] *See J I MacWilliam Co Inc v Mediterranean Shipping Co SA* (The Rafaela S) [2005] UKHL 11; [2005] 2 AC 423, at [57] (Lord Rodger).
[27] *See Comalco Aluminium Ltd v Mogal Freight Services Ltd* (1993) 113 ALR 677, 700 (Sheppard J). *See* Article 1(1)(g) of the Carriage of Goods by Sea Act 1991 (Cth).
[28] I have suggested elsewhere that liner booking notes, tally clerk's receipts, mate's receipts, and ship's delivery orders are excluded: *see* Girvin, *supra* note 3, para 19.20.

The Rotterdam Rules takes a broader, more modern, approach, as befits an international convention enacted in the first decade of the twenty-first century.[29] The test for determining whether a document is a "transport document" is whether such is issued under a contract of carriage[30] and "evidences the carrier's or performing party's receipt of goods under a contract of carriage and evidences or contains a contract of carriage".[31] Accordingly, the two principal requirements are, first, evidence of receipt and, second, evidence of a contract of carriage. These requirements broaden the scope of the Rotterdam Rules beyond the limitations of the Hague and Hague-Visby Rules. The fundamental definition of "transport document" is, moreover, buttressed by definitions of "negotiable transport document"[32] and "non-negotiable transport document".[33] The latter is exclusionary, referring to any document which is not a negotiable[34] document. Negotiability, on the other hand, requires the wording "to order" or "negotiable" or "other appropriate wording"[35] and also an indication as to whether the goods are consigned to the order of the shipper, to the order of the consignee, or to bearer.[36] Note, in particular, the emphasis on transport documents which perform certain functions – thus we are no longer limited to bills of lading. Moreover, problems associated with determining whether a document is a "bill of lading or similar document of title" will be avoided and a much wider range of documents will be covered.

IV. Excluded Documents

The Rotterdam Rules, like the Hague and Hague-Visby Rules[37] and the Hamburg Rules,[38] do not apply to charterparties but will be applicable to bills of lading issued under charter-

---

[29] For detailed analysis, see now Sturley et. al., *supra* note 10, ch 7.
[30] See Article 1(1).
[31] Article 1(14). The reference to "evidences or contains ..." was deliberate, to accommodate different techniques in various countries. See, e.g., Report of the Working Group on Transport Law on the work of its ninth session (New York, 15-26 April 2002), A/CN.9/510, para 110.
[32] Article 1(15).
[33] Article 1(16).
[34] This has a limited meaning in English law, namely the fact of the transferability of the bills of lading: *Kum v Wah Tat Bank* [1971] 1 Lloyd's Rep 439 (PC), 446 (Lord Devlin).
[35] Bills of lading in these various forms operate as a symbol of the goods and give constructive possession of the goods: see, e.g., *Sanders Bros v Maclean* (1883) 11 QBD 327, 341 (Bowen LJ); *The Prinz Adalbert* [1917] AC 586 (PC), 589 (Lord Sumner).
[36] These specifics have an impact on how the bills of lading are transferred to others. See Girvin, *supra* note 3, para 5.11.
[37] See Article I(b) and Article V (second sentence). See Girvin, *supra* note 3, para 19.23.
[38] Article 2(3).

parties.[39] The reason for this has always been that charterparties, especially those involving the bulk trades, are contracts where freedom of contract should prevail because charterers and owners negotiate such contracts individually.[40] There is no need to protect a weaker party from another who is in a stronger bargaining position. Charterparties are not defined in the Rotterdam Rules[41] but it is also made clear that "other contracts for the use of a ship or of any space thereon" are not covered by the Rules.[42] This would accordingly exclude slot charterparties[43] and conforms with the general approach of the Rules, which is to regulate liner transportation.[44] However, the Rotterdam Rules also go further by providing that in the case of non-liner transportation, the Rules will apply where there is no charterparty (or other contract) between the parties and where a transport document or an electronic transport record is issued.[45] In so far as transport documents are issued pursuant to charterparties, the Rules provide that the Rules will apply as between the carrier and the consignee, controlling party or holder who is not an original party to the charterparty.[46]

V. Issuing Transport Documents

Under the Hague and Hague-Visby Rules,[47] a carrier is only obliged to release a bill of lading with the relevant information specified in Article III, r 3 where there is a "demand" from the shipper to this effect.[48] As was pointed out by the ISC,[49] it is not clear which of the

---

[39] Article 6(1)(a).
[40] Typically through their brokers. For a detailed study, see EDWIN ANDERSON III, SHIPBROKERS AS INTERMEDIARIES, AGENTS AND THIRD PARTIES (2006).
[41] But clearly should include the main types and their variants, viz. time charterparties and trip charterparties, voyage charterparties and consecutive voyage charterparties, and demise (bareboat) charterparties. See, as to these, Girvin, supra note 3, para 1.45.
[42] Article 6(1)(b).
[43] See Metvale Ltd v Monsanto International SARL (The MSC Napoli) [2008] EWHC 3002 (Admlty); [2009] 1 Lloyd's Rep 246, at [11] (Teare J).
[44] See Article 1(3).
[45] See Article 6(2).
[46] See Article 7.
[47] For the Hamburg Rules, see Article 14(1). See generally Girvin, supra note 3, para 27.04; Aikens et.al., supra note 7, para 5.5.
[48] See Vita Food Products Inc v Unus Shipping Co Ltd [1939] AC 277 (PC), 288 (Lord Wright); Noble Resources Ltd v Cavalier Shipping Corporation (The Atlas) [1996] 1 Lloyd's Rep 642, 646 (Longmore J); Agrosin Pte Ltd v Highway Shipping Co Ltd (The Mata K) [1998] 2 Lloyd's Rep 614, 618 (Clarke J).
[49] i.e. the International Subcommittee of the CMI, which was set up by its Executive Council on 12 November 1999 with the brief to "consider in what areas of transport law, not at present governed by international liability regimes, greater international uniformity may be achieved; to prepare the outline of an instrument designed to bring about uniformity of transport law; and thereafter to

parties that might be described as "shipper" is entitled to make this demand, viz. the contracting shipper, the consignor, or some other party.[50] The solution adopted in the Rotterdam Rules is found in Article 35. This specifies that the shipper or, at this consent, the documentary shipper is entitled to "obtain" from the carrier (a) a non-negotiable transport document (or its electronic version) or (b) an appropriate negotiable transport document (or its electronic version), unless the carrier and the shipper have agreed not to use a transport document or it is the custom, usage or practice of the trade not to use one. This is important because it prioritises the agreement between the original parties to the contract and allows custom, usage or practice, to determine the issue. This seems to me to accord well with commercial practice; under some types of sale contract, particularly c.i.f. contracts,[51] the seller has the responsibility for arranging shipment, while in others, such as f.o.b. contracts,[52] he merely has to bring alongside a designated vessel the cargo for shipment, with the buyer having the responsibility of ensuring that an effective vessel is nominated to which the seller can deliver the goods.[53]

VI. Information Contained in the Transport Document

The Hague and Hague-Visby Rules requires the carrier to include quite limited information in a bill of lading, of course only following on from a demand by a shipper.[54] This includes "the leading marks necessary for identification of the goods as the same are furnished in writing by the shipper before the loading of such goods",[55] either the "number of packages or pieces, or the quantity, or weight, as the case may be ...",[56] and "the apparent order and condition of the goods".[57] The Hamburg Rules, by contrast, requires much more detailed information.[58] The Rotterdam Rules has followed the model of the Hamburg Rules, al-

---

draft provisions to be incorporated in the proposed instrument including those relating to liability": *see* CMI Newsletter No 1/2000, 3.
[50] *See* "Possible future work on transport law", United Nations Commission on International Trade Law, thirty-fourth session, 25 June-13 July 2001, A/CN.9/497, para 35.
[51] *See*, e.g. INCOTERMS A3(A); MICHAEL BRIDGE, THE INTERNATIONAL SALE OF GOODS: LAW AND PRACTICE 3RD ED (2013), PARA 4.07.
[52] *See*, e.g. INCOTERMS A4; Bridge (2013), para 3.02.
[53] Bridge (2013), para 3.11.
[54] Article III, r 3. *See* Girvin, *supra* note 3, para 27.05; Aikens et.al., *supra* note 7, para 4.6.
[55] Article III, r 3(a).
[56] Article III, r 3(b). The choice of what is shown lies with the carrier.
[57] Article III, r 3(c).
[58] Article 15(1) specifies fifteen pieces of information. This was criticized as imposing on the parties "a rigid set of obligations which may well be commercially unrealistic and unwanted, and may produce undesirable and even dangerous consequences": C W H Goldie, "Documentation – The

though with modifications, taking into account the more ambitious, maritime-plus, extent of the Rules. During the deliberations within the ISC it was noted that while existing international conventions required certain core information to be included, many important aspects, such as the date and the significance of an ambiguous date were omitted.[59] Nevertheless, during the deliberations of the Working Group there was a view that the list of mandatory requirements should be limited as much as possible to strictly necessary items because parties were free to agree on further requirements in the contract particulars should their commercial needs require them.[60] The final list of requirements for the contract particulars, whether in a transport document or electronic transport document, is as follows:

a. A Description of the Goods as Appropriate for the Transport

This provision reproduces a similar provision from the Hamburg Rules[61] although the information required would invariably be provided by the shipper and accepted by the carrier in standardized transport documents. One issue which the Working Group had to address was how to achieve a balance between the increasing tendency of shippers to provide lengthy and detailed technical descriptions of goods and how to impose a limit on the amount of information which a shipper might include.[62] The final wording, "as appropriate",[63] was selected so as to cover situations such as where import restrictions applied in respect of certain goods and to provide sufficient information, particularly in relation to dangerous goods[64] but may not fully address concerns raised by some that there should be a more overt limit to the description required.[65]

---

writing on the bill" in SAMIR MANKABADY (ED), THE HAMBURG RULES ON THE CARRIAGE OF GOODS BY SEA (1987), 209.
[59] See "Transport Law: Possible future work", United Nations Commission on International Trade Law, thirty-third session, 12 June-7 July 2000, A/CN.9/476, para 24; "Possible future work on transport law", United Nations Commission on International Trade Law, thirty-fourth session, 25 June-13 July 2001, A/CN.9/497, para 34.
[60] Report of Working Group III (Transport Law) on the work of its seventeenth session (New York, 3-13 April 2006), A/CN.9/594, para 227.
[61] Cf. Article 15(1)(a) of the Hamburg Rules which specifies that there must be a statement as to the "general nature of the goods".
[62] See Report of Working Group III (Transport Law) on the work of its nineteenth session (New York, 16-27 April 2007), A/CN.9/621, para 271.
[63] Originally it was suggested that the words "as furnished by the shipper" should be added: see Report of Working Group III (Transport Law) on the work of its seventeenth session (New York, 3-13 April 2006), A/CN.9/594, para 228.
[64] At para 272.
[65] See, e.g., Comments of the International Chamber of Shipping (ICS), BIMCO and the International Group of P&I Clubs on the draft convention, A/CN.9/WG.III/WP.87, 4. See too the proposal of Denmark, Norway, and Finland that the words should be qualified with the words "in general

b. The Leading Marks Necessary for the Identification of the Goods

The requirement to state the leading (or loading) marks for carriage[66] will be familiar territory as this is information also required by the Hague and Hague-Visby Rules[67] and under the Hamburg Rules.[68]

c. The Number of Package or Pieces, or the Quantity of Goods

This information is also required under the Hague and Hague-Visby Rules[69] and under the Hamburg Rules.[70]

d. The Weight of the Goods, if Furnished by the Shipper

This information may be provided under the Hague and Hague-Visby Rules[71] in the sense that the carrier need only supply this as an alternative to "the number of packages or pieces, or the quantity"[72] but the information as to weight is mandatory under the Hamburg Rules.[73] This is important in the case of bulk goods and containerized goods and hardly a matter of surprise that this information should be required also under the Rotterdam Rules.

e. A Statement of the Apparent Order and Condition of the Goods at the Time the Carrier or a Performing Party Receives Them for Carriage

Information as to the condition of the goods is required information under both the Hague and Hague-Visby Rules[74] and under the Hamburg Rules.[75] This has been understood in many jurisdictions as referring to the external and apparent condition of the goods,[76] re-

---

terms": *see* Proposal of the delegations of Denmark, Norway and Finland on draft article 37 (1)(a) regarding contract particulars, A/CN.9/WG.III/WP.86, 2.

[66] i.e. the marks which identify the shipment rather than any marks of identity of the commercial character of the goods or, as described by AL Smith MR, "identify to the holder of the bill of lading ... the goods which that holder is entitled to demand": *see Parsons v New Zealand Shipping Co* [1901] 1 KB 548, 557. See also Collins LJ at 564-565.

[67] *See* Article III, r 3(a).
[68] Article 15(1)(a).
[69] Article III, r 3(b).
[70] Article 15(1)(a).
[71] i.e. as an alternative to the "... number of packages or pieces, or the quantity ...": *see* Article III, r 3.
[72] As the requirement is that the carrier need only attest to one of the items, a reservation can validly be inserted in respect of the others: *see*, e.g., *Pendle & Rivet Ltd v Ellerman Lines Ltd* (1927) 29 Ll L Rep 133, 136 (Mackinnon J). *See* also Girvin, *supra* note 3, para 27.07.
[73] Article 15(1)(a). This was criticized as being "mistaken policy": *see* Goldie, *supra* note 58, p. 211.
[74] Article III, r 3(c). *See* Girvin, *supra* note 3, para 27.08.
[75] Article 15(1)(b).
[76] *Compania Naviera Vascongada v Churchill & Sim* [1906] 1 KB 237, 245; *The Peter der Grosse* (1875) 1 PD 414, 420.

quiring an accurate statement of fact. It has been described as an absolute contractual undertaking and not merely a duty to take reasonable care, except that, where the making of the statement requires some skill, then the duty is cast as one to take reasonable care.[77] Article 36(4)(a) of the Rotterdam Rules requires a "reasonable external inspection of the goods as packaged at the time that the shipper delivers them to the carrier or a performing party". However the Rules provide, at Article 36(4)(b), that this also means "any additional inspection that the carrier of a performing party performs before issuing the transport document or electronic transport record". This is intended to reflect the position that if the carrier undertakes more inspection than is required, such as inspecting the contents of packages or opening a closed container, then he should be responsible for whatever such an inspection should have revealed.[78]

f. The Name and Address of the Carrier

This information is not required by the Hague and Hague-Visby Rules, but is required under the Hamburg Rules[79] and is industry practice in most standard form bills of lading.[80] The Working Group took the view that this information should be required so as to conform with the requirements of the UCP 600.[81]

g. The Date on Which the Carrier or a Performing Party Received the Goods, or on Which the Goods Were Loaded on Board the Ship, or on Which the Transport Document or Electronic Transport Document Was Issued

This is a new requirement which was not part of the Hague and Hague-Visby Rules or the Hamburg Rules but in practice is very important because the value of the cargo or the price to be paid or the underlying sales transaction is governed by the date of issue of the bill of

---

[77] See *Oceanfocus Shipping Ltd v Hyundai Merchant Marine Co Ltd (The Hawk)* [1999] 1 Lloyd's Rep 176, 185 (Judge Diamond QC); *Trade Star Line Corp v Mitsui & Co Ltd* [1996] 2 Lloyd's Rep 449 (CA), 458 (Evans LJ).
[78] See Report of Working Group III (Transport Law) on the work of its eleventh session (New York, 24 March to 4 April 2003), A/CN.9/526, para 30.
[79] Article 15(1)(c). The name of the carrier is required in China, Germany, Italy, Japan, Lebanon, Norway, Poland, Spain and Turkey while his address is also required in China, Germany, Lebanon and Norway: *see* "Transport Law: Possible future work", United Nations Commission on International Trade Law, thirty-third session, 12 June-7 July 2000, A/CN.9/476, para 30.
[80] e.g. in Argentina, Australia, Canada, Hungary, Indonesia, the Netherlands, New Zealand, the United Kingdom and the United States: *see* "Transport Law: Possible future work", United Nations Commission on International Trade Law, thirty-third session, 12 June-7 July 2000, A/CN.9/476, para 30.
[81] Although under the UCP 600 only the carrier's name is required, not his address: *see* Article 20(a)(i). *See*, e.g., Report of Working Group III (Transport Law) on the work of its eighteenth session (Vienna, 6-17 November 2006), A/CN.9/616, para 18.

lading.[82] This was considered on a number of occasions by the Working Group and its predecessors. Thus, the ISC initially felt that this should not be considered an essential element of the bill of lading and an undated bill of lading should be considered valid[83] but there was a view that there should be a harmonized provision seemingly because in some countries a dated bill of lading was a mandatory requirement[84] while in others this was merely common practice.[85] In settling on a mandatory date requirement, Article 39(2) states that if date is specified but the significance is not indicated then the date is deemed to be the date on which all of the goods indicated in the transport document or electronic transport record were loaded on board the ship (if the contract indicates that the goods have been loaded on the ship) or the date on which the carrier or a performing party received the goods if the contract particulars do not indicate that the goods have been loaded on board the ship. This wording conforms more or less to similar wording in the UCP 600.[86]

h. If the Transport Document Is Negotiable, the Number of Originals of the Negotiable Transport Document, When More than One Original Is Issued

Though much criticized in the past,[87] it has been standard commercial practice for centuries[88] for bills of lading to be issued in sets,[89] usually of three originals.[90] So as to avoid the potential for fraud[91] the standard wording in bills of lading is that "one ... being accomplished,[92] the others stand void". Many bills of lading also require the number of bills

---

[82] *See*, e.g., *Novorossisk Shipping Co v Neopetro Co Ltd (The Ulyanovsk)* [1990] 1 Lloyd's Rep 425 where a difference of a few days in the bill of lading date involved an enormous fluctuation in the commodity price and saw the shipowners liable for contractual damages of US$865,591.42 for disobeying the charterer's voyage instructions.
[83] *See* "Transport Law: Possible future work", United Nations Commission on International Trade Law, thirty-third session, 12 June-7 July 2000, A/CN.9/476, para 27.
[84] e.g., Argentina, China, the Democratic People's Republic of Korea, Germany, Indonesia, Lebanon, Netherlands, Norway, Poland, Spain and Turkey: at para 25.
[85] e.g., Australia, Canada, New Zealand, the United Kingdom and the United States: at para 25.
[86] *See* Article 20(a)(ii).
[87] *See Glyn, Mills & Co v East & West India Dock Co* (1882) 7 App Cas 591, 605 (Lord Blackburn).
[88] *See*, e.g., GERARD MAYLNES, CONSUETUDO VEL LEX MERCATORIA (1686), 97.
[89] *In Sanders v Maclean* (1883) 11 QBD 327, 342, Bowen LJ suggested that "if [the practice] survives it is probably that the commercial world still finds it more convenient or less troublesome to preserve it than to change it".
[90] The UCP 600 requires that, for the purpose of a credit, a full set, as indicated in the bill of lading, must be provided: Article 20(iv).
[91] Reported instances of fraud are very rarely heard of, save for the above case of *Sanders v Maclean* (1883) 11 QBD 327.
[92] i.e. delivery of the cargo as against one of the set. It has been said that by "accomplishing" is meant completing performance of the contract of carriage by delivery against surrender of one original bill of lading: *see*, e.g., *Carewins Development (China) Ltd v Bright Fortune Shipping Ltd* [2009] 3 HKLRD 409, at [33] (Ribeiro PJ); *Glyn, Mills & Co v East & West India Dock Co* (1882) 7 App Cas 591, 599 (Lord Cairns).

of lading to be stated on their face.[93] The Hamburg Rules requires this information[94] and the decision was made in the Working Group to require that the number of originals should be inserted because it was thought that this would protect third party holders of the negotiable transport document by indicating how many originals were in circulation.[95] This problem may be more imagined than real, particularly as it is often practice for all three originals to be kept together and dealt with together.

i. The Name and Address of the Consignee, if Named by the Shipper

This provision is in similar terms to the Hamburg Rules[96] and was highlighted for possible inclusion both in 2006[97] and in 2007.[98]

j. The Name of a Ship, if Specified in the Contract of Carriage

This requirement is new and is not found in the Hague and Hague-Visby Rules or the Hamburg Rules. It conforms with the UCP 600 which requires that a bill of lading indicates that the goods have been shipped on board "a named vessel"[99] although there were concerns that while such a requirement was possible in a port-to-port context, but almost impossible in the door-to-door context when a carrier was often not the ship owner but instead a non-vessel operating carrier (NVOC).[100]

k. The Place of Receipt and, if Known to the Carrier, the Place of Delivery

This information is not required under the Hague or Hague-Visby Rules and is a multimodal variant of the provisions in the Hamburg Rules which requires that the port of loading and discharge are named.[101] This information was suggested for inclusion in the Rules because this is relevant for determining the scope of application of the Rules[102] as well as for the purpose of the applicability of the provisions on jurisdiction and arbitration.[103]

---

[93] See, e.g., Conlinebill 2000; Congenbill 2007.
[94] See Article 15(1)(h).
[95] See Report of Working Group III (Transport Law) on the work of its seventeenth session (New York, 3-13 April 2006), A/CN.9/594, para 230.
[96] See Article 15(1)(e). Note, however, that this provision does not require the consignee's address.
[97] See, e.g., Report of Working Group III (Transport Law) on the work of its seventeenth session (New York, 3-13 April 2006), A/CN.9/594, para 227.
[98] See Report of Working Group III (Transport Law) on the work of its nineteenth session (New York, 16-27 April 2007), A/CN.9/621, para 274.
[99] Article 20(a)(ii).
[100] Report of Working Group III (Transport Law) on the work of its nineteenth session (New York, 16-27 April 2007), A/CN.9/621, para 274.
[101] i.e. Article 15(1)(f)(g).
[102] See Article 5(1).
[103] See e.g. Article 66(a); Article 75(2). See, Report of Working Group III (Transport Law) on the

I. The Port of Loading and the Port of Discharge, if Specified in the Contract of Goods

As was noted in relation to place of receipt, this provision combines the two separate requirements of the Hamburg Rules.[104]

VII. Requirement for a Signature

In many jurisdictions, it is a requirement of domestic law that bills of lading must be signed.[105] In other jurisdictions it is merely the practice to do so.[106] That there should be a prvision was accepted quite early in the Working Group's deliberations.[107] Article 38(1) therefore makes it mandatory for a transport document to be signed by the carrier "or a person acting on his behalf". This is clearly included because it is standard practice for bills of lading to be presented to the master for signature or to his agent or the charterer's agent in the case where the vessel is under charterparty.[108] In the case of an electronic document, an electronic signature must be provided which indicates the carrier's authorization of the electronic transport record. This wording was adopted partly to reflect the similar wording in the UCP 600[109] although it was pointed out that this had a different purpose to the Rules because the former was concerned with facilitating the system of documentary credits, while the latter set out legal rules with legal consequences.[110]

---

work of its seventeenth session (New York, 3-13 April 2006), A/CN.9/594, para 231.

[104] *See* Article 15(1)(f)(g).

[105] Argentina, China, the Democratic People's Republic of Korea, Hungary, Italy, Japan, Lebanon, Netherlands, Norway, Poland, Spain and Turkey: *see* "Transport Law: Possible future work", United Nations Commission on International Trade Law, thirty-third session, 12 June-7 July 2000, A/CN.9/476, para 28.

[106] e.g. Australia, Canada, New Zealand, the United Kingdom and the United States: "Transport Law: Possible future work", United Nations Commission on International Trade Law, thirty-third session, 12 June-7 July 2000, A/CN.9/476, para 28. Generally as to signature and the insertion of qualifying words, *see The David Agmashenebeli* [2002] EWHC 104; [2003] 1 Lloyd's Rep 92.

[107] Although a suggestion that there should be a definition of signature was rejected because the view was taken that this could be determined by commercial needs: *see* Report of Working Group III (Transport Law) on the work of its eighteenth session (Vienna, 6-17 November 2006), A/CN.9/616, para 11.

[108] *See Girvin, supra* note 3, para 12.08 and *see* particularly SIR GUENTER TREITEL & FMB REYNOLDS, CARVER ON BILLS OF LADING 3ʳᴅ ED (2011), PARA 4-036.

[109] A bill of lading under the UCP is required to be signed "by the carrier or a named agent for or on behalf of the carrier or the master or a named agent for or on behalf of the master" (Article 20(a)(i).

[110] Report of Working Group III (Transport Law) on the work of its nineteenth session (New York, 16-27 April 2007), A/CN.9/621, para 291.

VIII. Qualifications of the Information Provided

Art III, r 3 of the Hague and Hague-Visby Rules,[111] which requires the carrier to issue, on demand, a bill of lading with certain information, also contains an important proviso, that "no carrier, master or agent of the carrier shall be bound to state or show in the bill of lading any marks, number, quantity, or weight which he has reasonable ground for suspecting not accurately to represent the goods actually received or which he has had no reasonable means of checking." The effect of qualifying statements or qualifying endorsements on the face or margins of bills of lading can cause real potential for dispute and controversy.[112] Indeed, in practice, this has been one of the most troublesome issues in transport documents[113] though it may be noted that the effect of such negative statements is generally thought not to infringe the Hague and Hague-Visby provision which declares void clauses or covenants that relieve the carrier or ship from liability.[114]

This is now dealt with in the Rotterdam Rules in Article 40. It will be mandatory[115] for a carrier to qualify the information to be inserted in a transport document if he has "actual knowledge that any material statement in the transport document or electronic transport document is false or misleading" or he has "reasonable grounds to believe that a material statement ... is false or misleading" (Article 40(1)).[116] The carrier may qualify the information so as to indicate that he does not assume responsibility for the accuracy of the information provided by the shipper (Article 40(2)).[117] What is not clear from these provisions is what form such a "qualification" should take. Moreover this would appear not to deal with the standard types of exemptions (some of them printed) which carriers include in their bills of lading, e.g. "particulars declared by the shipper but not acknowledged by the carrier",[118]

---

[111] For the Hamburg Rules, *see* Article 16(3).
[112] For a US perspective, *see* THOMAS J SCHOENBAUM, ADMIRALTY AND MARITIME LAW 5ᵀᴴ ED (2011), §10-12.
[113] *See* "Possible future work on transport law", United Nations Commission on International Trade Law, thirty-fourth session, 25 June-13 July 2001, A/CN.9/497, para 37.
[114] i.e. in Article III, r 8. *See Agrosin Pte Ltd v Highway Shipping Co Ltd (The Mata K)* [1998] 2 Lloyd's Rep 614, 617 (Clarke J).
[115] viz. "the carrier shall qualify ..."
[116] This provision was originally included in a separate article: *see* Report of Working Group III (Transport Law) on the work of its eighteenth session (Vienna, 6-17 November 2006), A/CN.9/616, para 44.
[117] A suggestion that the carrier should give reasons for the qualification was, fortunately, rejected, as was any requirement of good faith: *see* Report of Working Group III (Transport Law) on the work of its eighteenth session (Vienna, 6-17 November 2006), A/CN.9/616, paras 34-37.
[118] Conlinebill 2000.

"weight, contents and value when shipped unknown",[119] or "said to contain".[120] One eminent commentator[121] has suggested that these statements do not amount to qualifications, unlike statements such as those which were the subject of litigation in an English case called *The David Agmashenebeli*,[122] where the master insisted on certain wording being used[123] and the case turned upon whether the master's clausing of the bills of lading amounted to a breach by the shipowners of the contract of carriage.[124]

Remaining with this point, the Rules also make a fundamental distinction between containerized and non-containerized goods, notwithstanding some doubts as to the efficacy of such a distinction.[125] If the goods are *not containerised* or where there is an actual inspection of the goods, the carrier may qualify the information if he had no physically practicable or commercially reasonable means of checking the information furnished by the shipper or if he has reasonable grounds for believing that the information provided is inaccurate (Article 40(3)). But if the goods are *containerized* in a closed container, the carrier may qualify the information specified in Article 36(1)(a)-(c)[126] if the goods have not actually been inspected and neither he nor a performing party has actual knowledge of its contents before issuing the transport document (Article 40(4)(a)).[127] He may qualify the information in Ar-

---

[119] *Attorney-General of Ceylon v Scindia Steam Navigation Co Ltd* [1962] AC 60 (PC); [1961] 3 WLR 936.
[120] *See*, eg, *El Greco (Australia) Pty Ltd v Mediterranean Shipping Co SA* [2004] FCAFC 202; [2004] 2 Lloyd's Rep 537; *The River Gurara* [1998] 1 Lloyd's Rep 225; *Marbig Rexel Pty Ltd v ABC Container Line NV (The TNT Express)* [1992] 2 Lloyd's Rep 636; *Ace Imports Pty Ltd v Companhia De Navegacao Lloyd Brasileiro (1987)* 10 NSWLR 32; *Rosenfeld Hillas & Co Pty Ltd v The Ship Fort Laramie* (1923) 32 CLR 25, 38. Although nothing turned on it in the case, in *Compania Sud Americana de Vapores SA v Sinochem Tianjin Import & Export Corp (The Aconcagua)* [2009] EWHC 1880 (Comm); [2010] 1 Lloyd's Rep 1 the bill of lading acknowledged the shipment of one container said to contain "Calcium Hypochlorite 65 per cent".
[121] Anthony Diamond QC, *The Rotterdam Rules*, [2010] Lloyd's Maritime & Commercial LQ 445, 506.
[122] [2002] EWHC 104; [2003] 1 Lloyd's Rep 92.
[123] "Cargo discoloured also foreign materials e.g. plastic, rust, rubber, stone, black particles found in cargo".
[124] The court held that though a small proportion of the cargo was discoloured, the master was not entitled to use words which conveyed the meaning that the whole or a substantial part of the cargo was thus affected; nor was he entitled to clause the mate's receipts or bills of lading to suggest that the presence of a miniscule quantity of contaminants rendered the cargo otherwise than in good order and condition: [2002] EWHC 104; [2003] 1 Lloyd's Rep 92, 114.
[125] *See* Report of Working Group III (Transport Law) on the work of its eighteenth session (Vienna, 6-17 November 2006), A/CN.9/616, para 32.
[126] i.e. in relation to the description of the goods, the leading marks, and the number of packages or pieces, or the quantity of goods.
[127] This was discussed at some length at a late stage in the deliberations of the Working Group: *see* Report of Working Group III (Transport Law) on the work of its twenty-first session (Vienna, 14-25 January 2008), A/CN.9/645, paras 135-137.

ticle 36(1)(d)[128] if neither he nor a performing party weighed the container or vehicle and there was no agreement prior to shipment that the container or vehicle would be weighed and the weight included in the contract particulars or there was no physically practicable or commercially reasonable means of checking the weight of the container or vehicle (Article 40(4)(b)).

IX. Effect of Deficiencies

Article 39(1) provides that the absence or inaccuracy of the information specified in Article 36(1)-(3) does not "of itself affect the legal character or validity" of the transport document. But there are certain specific provisions. If the date is provided, but there is no indication of its significance, the date is deemed to be the *date of loading on board*, if the contract particulars state that the goods have been loaded on board (Article 39(2)(a)) OR the date on which the goods *were received* if the contract particulars do no indicate the goods have been loaded on board (Article 39(2)(b)). Furthermore, if there is no statement in the contract particulars at the time of receipt of the condition of the goods, the contract particulars are deemed to have stated that the goods were in apparent good order and condition at the time of receipt (Article 39(3)).

X. Evidentiary Effect

The Hague and Hague-Visby Rules regards a bill of lading which states the information required in Art III, r 3 as being prima facie evidence of receipt by the carrier (Art III, r 4).[129] The same provision in the Hague-Visby Rules (though not the Hague Rules),[130] goes on to say that contrary evidence cannot be admitted in the case where the bill of lading has been transferred to a third party in good faith.[131] It is recognized that the carrier is only so bound in relation to those items enumerated in Art III, r 3, but where the description of the goods is the shipper's then he is not so bound.[132] Nor would the carrier be so bound where the bill

---

[128] i.e. in relation to the weight of the goods.
[129] *See* too Article 16(3)(a) of the Hamburg Rules.
[130] This, then, is a further difference between the Hague and Hague-Visby Rules.
[131] Also Article 16(3)(b) of the Hamburg Rules.
[132] *See Ace Imports Pty Ltd v Companhia de Navegacao Lloyd Brasileiro (The Esmeralda 1)* [1988] 1 Lloyd's Rep 206 (NSW), 210-211 (Yeldham J).

of lading is appropriately claused.[133]

One of the issues highlighted at an early stage of the deliberations on the Rotterdam Rules was whether the evidentiary rule should be limited to negotiable transport documents transferred to a third party acting in good faith or whether it should be extended to any third party acting in good faith who had paid value or otherwise altered its position in reliance on the description of the goods in the transport document.[134] This debate continued at various stages during the work of the Working Group.[135]

The final version Article 41 provides that a transport document[136] (or its electronic equivalent) is prima facie evidence of the carrier's receipt of the goods as stated in the contract particulars (Article 41(a)). Although in many respects resembling the previous Hague and Hague-Visby regime, there are some important points to note. The first of these is the obvious one that a wider group of transport documents is covered under the new Rules than under the Hague and Hague-Visby Rules.[137] The second point is, as we have seen, that there is a much more extensive list of particulars mandated under the Rules.

In relation to third parties, the Rules provide that contrary proof is not admissible where the contract particulars are included in a negotiable transport document[138] which is transferred[139] to a third party acting in good faith.[140] For non negotiable documents, contrary proof is not admissible where the document requires surrender in order to obtain delivery and is transferred to the consignee acting in good faith (Article 41(b)). Proof to the contrary is also not admissible against a consignee in good faith acting in reliance on the contract particulars included in a non-negotiable transport document as follows: (i) those specified in Article 36(1), when these particulars are furnished by the carrier; (ii) in relation to the number, type, identifying numbers of the containers, but not the identifying numbers of the container seals; (iii) in relation to the contract particulars specified in Article 36(2)(Article

---

[133] *See*, e.g., *Sea Success Maritime Inc v African Maritime Carriers Ltd* [2005] EWHC 1542 (Comm); [2005] 2 Lloyd's Rep 692, 699 (Aikens J).

[134] *See* "Possible future work on transport law", United Nations Commission on International Trade Law, thirty-fourth session, 25 June-13 July 2001, A/CN.9/497, para 36.

[135] *See*, e.g., Report of Working Group III (Transport Law) on the work of its eighteenth session (Vienna, 6-17 November 2006), A/CN.9/616, para 49.

[136] i.e. as defined in Article 1(14).

[137] Under the Hague-Visby Rules the House of Lords has confirmed that coverage includes straight bills of lading: see *J I MacWilliam Co Inc v Mediterranean Shipping Co SA (The Rafaela S)* [2005] UKHL 11; [2005] 2 AC 423. See, generally, Stephen Girvin, *Straight bills of lading in international trade: principles and practice*, [2006] Journal of Business Law 86.

[138] *See* the definition in Article 1(15).

[139] On the transfer of rights in a negotiable document (or negotiable electronic transport record), *see* Article 57.

[140] i.e. this provision is the "conclusive evidence" of the equivalent Hague-Visby provision (in Article III, r 4).

41(c)).

XI. Other Matters: Who Is the Carrier?

A final important issue dealt with in the Rotterdam Rules is a provision (Article 37) which seeks to deal with the important issue of identifying the carrier in a transport document.[141] A shipper or consignee must not only identify the carrier against whom the cargo claim can be pursued, but must establish the precise terms of the contract of carriage.[142] Surprising, the first of these requirements has often been a major difficulty for many claimants because bills of lading may be issued in the name of the shipowner, the charterer, a sub-charterer or the agent of any one of them. An additional complication is that the bill will often be signed by or on behalf of the ship's master as agent of the shipowner. It is particularly important for the shipper to make the correct choice of person to sue as many common law jurisdictions specify that only one party may be liable as carrier under any individual contract of carriage. Of further significance, if the contract is governed by the Hague-Visby Rules, by Art III, r 6 any cargo claim[143] is time-barred unless it is brought within the prescribed 12-month period.[144] There have been many cases in the past on which the wording on the reverse combined with statements on the face of the bills of lading have led to fine distinctions been made by the courts, sometimes leading to somewhat incongruous results.[145] Nevertheless, so far as English law is concerned, the matter has been authoritatively settled in *Homburg Houtimport BV v Agrosin Private Ltd (The Starsin)*.[146] In that case Lord Bingham restated the importance of construing legal documents commercially and of reading documents in a "business sense"[147] so as not to frustrate the reasonable expectations of businessmen.[148] Thus the House of Lords confirmed that one should look for the identity of the

---

[141] For detailed analysis, *see* now Sturley et. al., *supra* note 10, para 7.044.
[142] *See* Girvin, *supra* note 3, para 12.08.
[143] This means that both the remedy and the right to claim are extinguished: *see Aries Tanker Corporation v Total Transport (The Aries)* [1977] 1 WLR 185, 188 (Lord Wilberforce).
[144] In the case of the Hamburg Rules the time bar is two years (Article 20(1), as it now is also for the Rotterdam Rules (Article 62(1)).
[145] *See* e.g. *See The Berkshire [1974]* 1 Lloyd's Rep 185; *The Venezuela* [1980] 1 Lloyd's Rep 393; *The Rewia* [1991] 2 Lloyd's Rep 325; *MB Pyramid Sound NV v Briese Schiffahrts GmbH & Co KG MS Sina (The Ines) (No 2)* [1995] 2 Lloyd's Rep 144; *Sunrise Maritime Inc v Uvisco Ltd (The Hector)* [1998] 2 Lloyd's Rep 287; *Fetim BV v Oceanspeed Shipping Ltd (The Flecha)* [1999] 1 Lloyd's Rep 612.
[146] [2003] UKHL 12; [2004] 1 AC 715. *See* Edwin Peel, *Actual carriers and the Hague Rules*, 120 LQR 11 (2004).
[147] At [10]. *See* also Lord Millett at [188].
[148] At [12].

carrier on the face of the bill rather than the clauses on the reverse,[149] such as demise clauses.[150]

A provision on the identity of the carrier was closely considered by the Working Group at several points and three points were identified: (i) problems when the face of the transport document or electronic transport record was unclear and contained only the trade names of the carrier or his booking agents; (ii) problems with the small print on the reverse of the bills of lading; (iii) problems caused by the transport document being signed by or on behalf of the master, without stating the basis of the master's authority.[151]

Article 37(1) of the Rotterdam Rules accordingly provides that where the carrier is identified by name in the contract particulars, any other information in the transport document, or electronic transport document to the extent that it is inconsistent "shall have no effect". Where, however, no person is identified but the contract particulars indicate that the goods have been put on board a named ship, there is a presumption[152] that the registered owner is the carrier.[153] The onus will be on the registered owner to prove that the ship was under bareboat charter or to otherwise rebut the presumption of being the carrier by identifying the carrier and indicating his address (Article 37(2)). A claimant may also prove that any other person is the carrier (Article 37(3)).

XII. Conclusion

The provisions of the Rotterdam Rules which relate to transport documents and their electronic equivalents are an important element in the innovative and important changes contained in the Rules. The overall scheme of the Rules contains much which may, at first sight, appear to be new to shipping lawyers. Closer scrutiny of the provisions of the Rules reveals, however, that although this is indeed the case, many of the changes introduced conform with established commercial practice. It is to be hoped that the provisions on transport

---

[149] At [126]. *See* Lord Bingham at [16]; Lord Steyn at [47]; Lord Hoffmann at [77]-[80]; Lord Millett at [188].
[150] On the history of such clauses, *see* Lord Roskill, *The Demise Clause*, 106 LQR 403 (1990).
[151] Report of Working Group III (Transport Law) on the work of its eighteenth session (Vienna, 6-17 November 2006), A/CN.9/616, para 119.
[152] There were strong objections to such a presumption, inter alia, by the ICS, BIMCO, and the International Group of P & I Clubs: *see* Comments of the International Chamber of Shipping (ICS), BIMCO and the International Group of P&I Clubs on the draft convention, A/CN.9/WG.III/WP.87, 4.
[153] For discussion of these points, *see* particularly the Report of Working Group III (Transport Law) on the work of its nineteenth session (New York, 16-27 April 2007), A/CN.9/621, paras 278-288.

documents and electronic transport documents will assist in harmonising these areas of shipping practice and, together with the Rules as a whole, will be readily accepted by signatory states in the years to come.

9

Right of Control and Transfer of Rights

Dihuang Song

I. Introduction

At the 67th Plenary Meeting of the UN General Assembly on 11 December 2008, it was discussed and finally decided that the United Nations Convention on contracts for the International carriage of Goods Wholly or Partly by Sea be adopted, known as "Rotterdam Rules". This convention was opened for signature at a ceremony in Rotterdam on 23 September 2009.

Up to the time of writing this paper, there are 24 signatures and two ratification[1] of Rotterdam Rules. It is the first time ever in the history that a maritime convention attempts to include provisions on right of control and transfer of right though many conventions on other modes of transportation have done so already. However, in order to avoid any misunderstanding, it should be noted that CMI has already made various attempts to include such important issue, for example, in CMI Rules for Electronic Bill of Lading and CMI Uniforms Rules for Sea Waybill.

---

[1] See http://treaties.un.org/Pages/ViewDetails.aspx?src=TREATY&mtdsg_no=XI-D-8&chapter=11&lang=en

II. Why Right of Control is Necessary under Rotterdam Rules

1. The Concept of Right of Control

First of all, it is to be noted that the use of wording "Right of Control" is interchangeable with "Right of Controlling Party" in this paper. The draft chapter preceding March 2007 by UNCITRAL was titled "right of control", and during the elaboration, it was thought that the right of control was not limited to those that can be exercised unilaterally, and it could include the right to re-negotiate with the carrier on the contract of carriage. Thereafter, the chapter was changed as "Right of Controlling Party".

This concept is slightly different from right of disposal in other conventions, as well as the provisions in CMI Rules for Electronic Bill of Lading and/or CMI Uniform Rules for Seaway Bills.

In the CMI Rules for Electronic Bill of Lading, it is provided that:

> "7. Right of Control and Transfer
> a) The Holder is the only party who may, as against the carrier:
> (1) claim delivery of the goods;
> (2) nominate the consignee or substitute a nominated consignee for any other party, including itself;
> (3) transfer the Right of Control and Transfer to another party;
> (4) instruct the carrier on any other subject concerning the goods, in accordance with the terms and conditions of the Contract of Carriage, as if he were the holder of a paper bill of lading.

In the CMI Uniforms Rules for Sea Waybills, "Right of Control shall mean the rights and obligations referred to in rule 6, and it is provided that:

> "6. Right of Control
> (i) Unless the shipper has exercised his option under subrule (ii) below, he shall be the only party entitled to give the carrier instructions in relation to the contract of carriage. Unless prohibited by the applicable law, he shall be entitled to change the name of the consignee at any time up to the consignee claiming delivery of the goods after their arrival at destination, provided he gives

the carrier reasonable notice in writing, or by some other means acceptable to the carrier, thereby undertaking to indemnify the carrier against any additional expense caused thereby."

In the CMR, the right of control is called "right of disposal" and Article 12 provides that:

"1. The sender[2] has the right to dispose of the goods, in particular by asking the carrier to stop the goods in transit, to change the place at which delivery is to take place to deliver the goods to a consignee other than the consigned indicated in the consignment note."
2. This right shall cease to exist when the second copy of consignment note is handed to the consignee or when consignee exercises his right under article 13 paragraph 1; from that time onward, the carrier shall obey the orders of the consignee;…"

In COTIF-CIM 1999, Article 18 on Right to Dispose of the Goods provides that:

"1. The consignor shall be entitled to dispose of goods and to modify the contract of carriage by giving subsequent orders. He may in particular ask the carrier
a) to discontinue the carriage of the goods;
b) to delay the delivery of the goods;
c) to deliver the goods to a consignee different from the one entered on the consignment note;
2. the consignor's right to modify the contract of carriage shall, notwithstanding that he is in possession of the duplicate of the consignment note, be extinguished in cases where the consignee
a) has taken possession of the consignment note;
b) has accepted the goods;
c) has asserted his rights in accordance with article 17 section 3;
d) is entitled, in accordance with section 3, to give orders from that time onwards, the carrier shall comply with the orders and instructions of consignee.
…"

In CMNI, Article 14 on Holder of the right of disposal provides that:

"1. The shipper shall be authorized to dispose of the goods; in particular, he may require the carrier to discontinue the carriage of the goods, to change the place of delivery or to deliver the

---

[2] Different conventions adopt different terminology of "shipper" or "consignor" or "sender".

goods to a consignee other than the consignee indicated in the transport document.

2. The shipper's right of disposal shall cease to exist once the consignee, following the arrival of the goods at the scheduled place of delivery, has requested delivery of the goods and...."

In Warsaw Convention, Article 12 provides that

"1. Subject to his liability to carry out all his obligations under the contract of carriage, the consignor has the right to dispose of the cargo by withdrawing it at the airport of departure or destination, or by stopping it in the course of the journey on any landing, or by call for it to be delivered at the place of destination or in the course of the journey to a person other than the consignee originally designated, or by requiring it to be returned to the airport of departure. He must not exercise this right of disposition in such a way as to prejudice the carrier or other consignors and he must repay any expenses occasioned by the exercise of this right..."

2. Commercial Need from the Industry

The lack of laws of right of control in the current international maritime conventions was partly due to the fact that goods carried by sea were usually consigned to order (or to order of a named person) and consequently, there was no urgent need, as compared with other modes of transportation, for a unified rule on right of control. However, there have been some rules of practice that prevail and are recognized in the shipping industry. For example, where the shipper/seller wish to have the cargo telex release to the consignee/buyer, they must surrender full set of original bill of lading[3]; where there is any need to switch for a different bill of lading (which might be required under chains of sales) for cargo in transit, full set of original bill of lading must be collected before such new set of bill of lading can be issued.

Such practice is not problem-free. Indeed, under some circumstances, the right to demand delivery (under contract of carriage) by the lawful holder of the bill may conflict with, say, the right of stoppage in transit which is vested in the unpaid seller (under sales contract), and in fact, it was one of the issues that CMI had taken into consideration from the outset on whether and how we can reconcile the right of seller under sales contract with the right of control under contract of carriage by sea.

In fact, during the past decades, there are constant market demands for unification of

---

[3] This is so in China even if the bill of lading is not yet issued, and in such circumstances, bill of lading must be issued first, and then surrendered for exercising the right to give such instruction to the carrier.

laws on right of control in sea transportation, particularly because of great changes that have taken place since Hague Rules, in both the trade patterns and the customs of shipping.

Obviously, from the perspective of a cargo side, the right of control (over the cargo) originated from its right under sales contract, are not the same as those from the contract of carriage. Existing convention concerning other modes of transportation have been drafted to cater for this commercial need. When the cargo is in the custody of a carrier, the parties interested in the cargo may wish to give instructions to the cargo for the performance of the contract of carriage (so as to complete the sales transaction or otherwise to take necessary protective measures when transaction is or will be frustrated). Needless to say, the e-commerce calls for speedy and convenient rule in right of control so as to facilitate the modern trade.

Similarly, ocean carrier on the other hand may also wish that the right of control (by controlling party against him) be clarified/unified so that it does not have to face with uncertainties of different national laws in different jurisdictions. Further, it may, in certain circumstances, need to make sure who is entitled to re-negotiate the contract (e.g. change of destination, return of cargo back to loading port etc), or in other cases, need to obtain further information/instructions with respect to the cargo from the controlling party (e.g. action is required in order to avoid potential damage to other cargo, and/or to take care of the cargo).

A financing institution may also wish to see clear and unified rules on right of control, and in particular, its right and obligation vis-à-vis a carrier when the bill of lading is, e.g. pledged for the transaction.

Thus, as mentioned above, CMI has in the past decades made some attempts to unify practice of right of control, notably in the CMI Rules for Electronic Bill of Lading and Uniforms Rules for Sea Waybills.

During the preparation and drafting of these Rotterdam Rules, it was agreed that it is now both commercially and legally necessary and feasible to include a provision on right of control, though at some stage, concerns were expressed as to whether we should maintain the unilateral nature of the instruction given to the carrier by the controlling party, as opposed to any modification of the contract which would require mutual agreement of the parties[4].

Thus, in the Preliminary Draft Instrument on Carriage of Goods by Sea - Note by Secretariat (A/CN.9/WG.III/WP.21) on 8 January 2002, it was noted that "Unlike under other

---

[4] *See* Transport Law: Draft instrument on the carriage of goods [wholly or partly] [by sea], U.N. doc. no. A/CN.9/WG.III/WP.32

transport conventions, the subject of right of control is not dealt with in maritime conventions. Practices that have developed under the bill of lading system may have been the reason that in the past no urgent need was felt. Today, the situation in maritime transport is different. In many trades the use of negotiable transport documents is rapidly decreased or has entirely disappears. Furthermore, a well defined and transferable right of control may play a useful role in the development of e-commerce systems, where no electronic record as defined in this draft instrument is used."[5] In the Report of the Secretary General of UNCITRAL dated 31 March 2000, it was decided that the scope of work for Working Group III on transport law issue may include the rights of disposal and right to give instruction to the carrier[6]. Unlike other conventions concerning other modes of transportation on the right to modify/renegotiate new terms with the carrier, it is observed that the ocean carrier should be free to reject or accept such changes in the contract, but the existing conventions provide at least a basis for possible further unification in carriage by sea[7].

III. Who is Controlling Party

Article 1(13) of Rotterdam Rules defines a controlling party as "the person that pursuant to article 51 is entitled to exercise the right of control".

Article 51 of the Rotterdam Rules provides that following persons may become the controlling party:

(1) Shipper;

(2) Other person designated by shipper when the contract of carriage was concluded, such as documentary shipper, or consignee or other person;

(3) Holder of the negotiable transport document or electronic transport record;

It is utmost important to ascertain who and under which circumstances are the controlling party. The Rotterdam Rules have considered the issue under three different scenarios:

(1) Where negotiable transport document or negotiable electronic record is issued;

(2) Where non-negotiable transport document is issued, and it will be surrendered in order to take delivery of the cargo;

---

[5] *See* Transport Law: Preliminary draft instrument on the carriage of goods by sea, U.N. doc. no. A/CN.9/WG.III/WP.21, para.185.
[6] *See* Transport Law: possible future work: Report of the Secretary-General, U.N. doc. no. A/CN.476, para.51-52..
[7] *See supra* note 5, at paragraph 51.

(3) In any other cases (including where no transport document is required to take delivery of cargo or even no transport document is issued at all).

Apparently, great efforts have been made to harmonize the practice of Rotterdam Rules with other conventions concerning other modes of transportation[8] though difference between Rotterdam Rules and other conventions are apparent and even different terminology were used. However, unique feature of maritime transport is properly preserved where negotiable transport document or electronic record is issued. As a consequence, due consideration of a bank or other person who merely holds the bill of lading, but does not wish to exercise the right of control would have to be made. This will be briefly discussed below, but, suffices it that there was no intention to interfere with the important function of a negotiable transport document and/or the banking practice when this was drafted.

IV. Exercise and execution of right of control

The Rotterdam Rules provide that the right of control may only be exercised by the controlling party and is limited to:

(a) The right to give or modify instructions in respect of the goods that do not constitute a variation of the contract of carriage;

(b) The right to obtain delivery of the goods at a scheduled port of all or in respect of inland carriage, any place en route; and

(c) The right to replace the consignee by any other person including the controlling party.[9]

However, the rights as list above in the Rotterdam Rules do not relate to any modification or variation of a contract. Where there is any need to modify or verify the contract of carriage, it is only the controlling party (and not anyone else) that may agree with carrier. This is important, particularly when buyer and seller have disputes as to the ownership of a cargo (and hence dispute over the right of disposal under sales contract), and obviously, carrier is not interested to get involved in the trade dispute. However, doubts and concerns are also

---

[8] See Comparative Tables by UNCITRAL, A/CN.9/WG.III/WP.27 dated 30 December 2002.

[9] Article 50(1) of Rotterdam Rules. However, according to Article 56, the right of control in Article 50(1)(b) and (c) above is not mandatory and can be modified by the parties. Thus, concerns are expressed in China that this would undermine the efforts of UNCITRAL to unify the law/practice, since it is suspected that a carrier may insert whatever they wish into printed clauses of a bill of lading.

expressed that this may conflict with general principle of property laws in civil law countries, and more importantly, may facilitate a fraud which would otherwise be impossible.

Article 52 of the Rotterdam Rules imposes an obligation on part of the carrier to execute the instructions from the controlling party if the instructions can be reasonably executed according to their terms when it is received by the carrier, provided that the instructions will not interfere with the normal operation of the carrier, including its delivery practice.

This does not mean that a carrier will execute the instruction at a loss of his interest or cost. Thus, Article 52(2) provides that the controlling party will in any event reimburse the carrier for any reasonable additional expenses and will indemnify the carriage against any loss/damage as a result of diligently executing any instructions. Further, under Article 52(3), the carrier is also entitled to obtain a security from the controlling party for any additional expense or loss or damages that may be reasonably expected, failing which the carrier may refuse to carry out the instruction.

Finally, the right of control only exists during time when cargo is in the custody of the carrier, and shall cease when that period expires[10].

V. Transfer of right under Rotterdam Rules

Transfer of right under Rotterdam Rules is actually dealt with in both Chapter 10 and 11. However, Chapter 11 which is more specifically titled as "transfer of right", deals only with the transfer of right where a negotiable transport document or negotiable transport record is issued. Transfer of right under other scenarios are of no material difference with other conventions which only deal with the transfer of right of disposal where non-negotiable transport document is issued.

Obviously, a bank may hold a negotiable transport document as security for the financing of the sales transaction, but it has no interest in getting involved in the contract of carriage (nor in the sales contract). There appears to have few arguments as to whether an innocent bank should be protected in order to maintain current long-established practice. The mere fact that a bank holds the bill of lading (or the buyer pledges the bill of lading to the bank) does not necessarily mean that it exercises any rights under it.

During the discussion and elaboration, it was also discussed on the difference between "transfer" and "assignment". In other words, whilst in many jurisdiction including China,

---

[10] Article 50(2) of Rotterdam Rules. Again this is not mandatory and can be varied by the parties. *See* Article 56. Again concerns are expressed that this may jeopardize the effort for uniformity, since different carrier may insert different provisions to reflect different period of control.

any assignment of a contractual right by a creditor can be exercised unilaterally by giving the debtor a proper notice, whereas assignment of obligation by a debtor needs prior approval of the creditor[11]. Obviously, a negotiable transport documents may goes with it both right (document of title) and obligation (such as unpaid freight, demurrrtage, liability for the improper packing of cargo etc). Thus, it is important to make clear whether a bank or other person has indeed exercised its right by replacing the negotiable transport document with an electronic record (or vice versa), or by transferring the right under it to the buyer (or other person).

VI. Impact on Laws in Peoples Republic of China (PRC)

1. The Legal Regime of PRC laws on Contract of Carriage by Sea

As it is known, China did not ratify, nor accede to any of the existing maritime conventions. Instead, in its coded maritime law 1992, China based its law on Hague Visby Rules, and in the meantime, absorbs some provisions from Hamburg Rules. Notably it includes the adoption of "contractual shipper" which refers to the person who contracts with carrier[12] and "actual shipper" who actually deliver the cargo to carrier for shipment[13]. As a comparison, Hamburg Rules provides that a shipper "means any person by whom or in whose name or on whose behalf a contract of carriage of goods by sea has been concluded with a carrier, **or** any person by whom or in whose name or on whose behalf the goods are actually delivered to the carrier in relation to the contract of carriage by sea" (emphasis added).

Likewise, we also have "contractual carrier"[14] and "actual carrier" as their respective counterparts[15].

Similarly, there is no "right of control" and/or "transfer of right" in the Maritime Code of China. However, Article 308 and 309 of Contract Law of China provides that:

"**Article 308**: Before the carrier delivers the goods to the consignee, the consignor may request

---

[11] E.g. Articles 79-80, and Articles 84-85 of the Contract Law of China.
[12] See Article 42(3)(a) of Maritime Code of PRC.
[13] See Article 42(3)(b) of Maritime Code of PRC.
[14] See Article 42(1) of Maritime Code of PRC.
[15] See Article 42(2) of Maritime Code of PRC.

the carrier to suspend carriage, return the goods, change the place of destination or deliver the goods to another consignee, but he shall compensate the carrier for the loss suffered as a result thereof.

Article 309: When the goods carried have arrived at the place of destination, the carrier shall notify the consignee (if known to him) in a timely manner, and the consignee shall take delivery in a timely manner. If the consignee fails to take delivery within the time limit therefor, he shall pay the carrier custody fees etc."

The aforesaid shipper under PRC laws have for years created some problems. For example, a shipper is entitled to demand a bill lading from the carrier. However, when both contractual shipper and actual shipper so demands, the carrier will be in a dilemma as to whom the bill should be issued? Further, whether the right of demanding a bill of lading only applies to carrier or to both carrier and actual carrier who has no contract with the shipper?

This issue was discussed as early as in CMI when it starts drafting the instrument on transport law. There was no much dispute that the new instrument should have only "one shipper" who contracts with the carrier[16]. There was no much dispute either that a FOB seller should be considered, and the term "documentary shipper" was used in the Rotterdam Rules[17]. However, doubts and concerns are expressed in China as to how this innovative "documentary shipper" can in practice protect the interest of a FOB seller.

2. Judicial Practice in China

There are limited reported cases concerning right of control in China. This is partly due to the lack of express provision under Maritime Code of China. Further, it is to be noted that China is not a case-law country, and the discussion below does not represent the case-law of China.

In (2004) Hu Hai Fa Shang Chu Zi No. 567 before Shanghai Maritime Court, one of the issue before the court was that whether Article 308 of the Contract Law could be applied where Maritime Code is silent on the right of control. The answer was in the affirmative. However, in hearing the argument on whether the unpaid seller was entitled as a legal right to demand the return of the cargo from the carrier. It was quite an interesting interpretation of the Contract Law by the court, and the court held that the shipper was only able to make a "request", and since it was a variation of the contract, carrier was free to accept or to re-

---

[16] *See* Article 1(8) of the Rotterdam Rules.
[17] *See* Article 1(9) of the Rotterdam Rules.

fuse such a "request". In other words, the Shanghai Maritime Court has in this particular case decided that there was no such statutory obligation of "returning the goods" by a carrier upon request by the shipper.

In another case – (2003)Hu Gao Min Si Hai Zhong Zi No. 71 before Shanghai High People's Court, it was again decided that the shipper's request to return the goods after the goods have arrived in its destination was a variation of the contract, and this cannot be unilaterally made by the shipper.

An interesting case rests with (2002) Yue Gao Fa Min Si Zhong Zi No. 75, where it was heard and held that Article 308 only applies to the straight bill of lading where consignee can be identified before delivery. For an "to order" bill of lading, shipper cannot exercise its right of stoppage in transit, unless it surrender full set of the bill of lading for cancellation.

In a more recent case – (2009) Hu Gao Min Si Hai Zhong Zi No. 131, a logistics company A was a NVOCC for a shipment of cargo by the shipper B who sold its cargo on FOB terms (payment term T/T) to the buyer C. It was said that a booking note was once sent to A, requesting that B was named as shipper. Apparently, C as FOB buyer had the obligation of making a contract of carriage by sea, and it contracted with D who in turn also entrusted A for the shipment. At the request of D, the bill of lading indicating C as shipper was issued, but it was held until D paid the ocean freight before it was released to D. During the interval, B requested from time to time that A release the bill of lading to him, but A refused to follow the order, and insisting that it was entrusted by D and had to follow D's order. The court found that A deprived B of its right of control over the cargo when it issued the bill of lading indicating C as the shipper and released the bill to D. This typically shows the difference that can be achieved in finding of the role of a FOB seller vis-à-vis the buyer in the contract of carriage.

3. Comments and Attitude towards the Rotterdam Rules

Given the controversies in preparation of and after adoption of the Rotterdam Rules, it is not surprising that the comments and attitude from China are also diversified.

Therefore, Chinese government has so far not yet signed the Rotterdam Rules, nor ratified it. However, Ministry of Commerce and Ministry of Department had entrusted universities/institutes to carry out an independent research on the Rotterdam Rules and how the rules may affect the current laws and industries.

In 2010, a research study[18] by China University of Politic Science and Law indicated that

---

[18] See "Research report about the influence of the Rotterdam Rules on China's import and export"

while there were some doubts and suspicions among Chinese cargo interests on the Rotterdam Rules, positive attitude towards the Chapter on Right of Controlling Party was taken by majority of those interviewed.

Similar researches were conducted by Peking University and Dalian Maritime University respectively. While the result of their researches are yet to be publicized, it appears that general view of the public is that Chinese government should take a cautious approach towards the Rotterdam Rules.

---

by Prof. Zhang Liying, Annual of China Maritime Law, vol 21, December 2010.

10

DELIVERY OF THE GOODS

Gertjan Van der Ziel

I. Preliminary Remarks[1]

1. New Subject

Delivery is a new subject that is not addressed in earlier conventions.[2] The Hague and Hague-Visby Rules pay little attention to the delivery of the goods. The notice-of-claim period and the time-for-suit period begin running on delivery,[3] but that is the only context in which the issue is addressed. As a result, both leave open the question whether delivery of the goods is an obligation of the carrier under the Convention. As a consequence of that omission, it is questionable whether the provisions on limitation of liability,[4] for example, apply in case of misdelivery. Thus no uniformity exists on the issue. In view of the provision allowing the carrier to exclude its liability after discharge,[5] it is even arguable that those Conventions permit a carrier to exclude its liability for misdelivery. The legal uncer-

---

[1] The discussion in this paper is to a large extent drawn from Ch. VIII of MICHAEL F. STURLEY, TOMOTAKA FUJITA AND GERTJAN VAN DER ZIEL, THE ROTTERDAM RULES, THE UN CONVENTION ON CONTRACTS FOR THE INTERNATIONAL CARRIAGE OF GOODS WHOLLY OR PARTLY BY SEA, SWEET & MAXWELL, 2010. See also ALEXANDER VON ZIEGLER ET AL. (EDS), THE ROTTERDAM RULES 2008, KLUWER LAW INTERNATIONAL, 2010, CH.9.
[2] To my knowledge, there is not much literature on the subject of 'delivery' generally. Most of the writings are restricted to partial subjects, see note 148. One of the few exceptions is the PhD thesis of YINGYING ZOU, DELIVERY OF GOODS BY THE CARRIER UNDER THE CONTRACT OF CARRIAGE BY SEA, A FOCUS ON CHINA, ERASMUS LAW SCHOOL PUBLICATIONS, 2005.
[3] *See* Hague-Visby Rules Article 3(6).
[4] *See* Hague-Visby Rules Article 4(5).
[5] *See* Hague-Visby Rules Article 7.

tainties have given rise to substantial litigation.

2. Applicability to Charterparties

The subject of delivery is normally part of the relationship between the carrier and the consignee, controlling party or holder of a negotiable transport document. Article 7 explicitly declares the Rotterdam Rules applicable to this relationship also in respect of contracts of carriage which are otherwise excluded from the application of the Convention, such as charterparties.[6] Therefore, the Rotterdam Rules provisions on delivery will often be relevant even for contracts of carriage excluded from the application of the Convention, such as charterparties.

3. Statutory Obligation

Delivery has now under the Rotterdam Rules become a statutory obligation of the carrier, because they explicitly provide that the carrier's basic obligations under the contract of carriage are not only to carry the goods to the place of destination but also to deliver them to the consignee.[7] As a consequence, if the carrier delivers the goods to a person that is not entitled to them, it breaches one of its obligations under the Convention. In the event of misdelivery, the goods are not "lost" in the physical sense, and it is unclear whether misdelivery constitutes "loss of the goods" under Article 17. One might argue that the basis of the carrier's liability for misdelivery must be found in otherwise applicable law.[8] Once liability for misdelivery has been established, however, it is a breach of obligation under the Convention and the carrier's liability is subject to limitation,[9] time bar,[10] and mandatory regulation[11] under the Rotterdam Rules.

4. Mandatory Law

The obligation of the carrier to deliver the goods to the consignee at their destination is mandatory law. Article 79 provides that any term in a contract of carriage is void to the ex-

---

[6] Except when the consignee is an original party to the charterparty or other contract of carriage excluded from the Convention's application, *see* Article 7.
[7] *See* Article 11.
[8] *See* 17th Session Report paras 118-120.
[9] *See* Article 59(1).
[10] *See* Article 62(1).
[11] *See* Article 79(1).

tent that it directly or indirectly excludes or limits the obligations of the carrier under the Convention. In practice, contracts of carriage often contain a clause that permits the carrier to discharge the goods at a different place than the original destination under exceptional situations in which it becomes physically impossible or economical impractical for the carrier to complete the carriage.[12] The question arises whether such clauses are valid under the Rotterdam Rules. It may be argued that the obligation of the carrier to deliver at destination is qualified by the phrase "in accordance with the contract of carriage" (in Article 11) and that the exception "unless otherwise provided in this Convention" (in Article 79) may apply.

Answering the above question it is submitted that the starting point is that a carrier must deliver the goods at the place as originally agreed. However, the exceptional situation that has been arisen during the carriage may be of such a nature that a carrier may reasonably invoke the contingency clause. When the goods are destined for Sendai and this port is closed due to an earthquake, it is reasonable that a carrier discharges the goods in an alternative nearby port and that the consignees accepts delivery of the goods in such alternative port. However, when, for example, during a voyage from Tokyo to Rotterdam the vessel incurs a fire in the engine room and has to be towed to Singapore as a port of refuge, it may be held unreasonable if a carrier discharges the goods there and regards the carriage as completed. If the ship would not be able to continue the voyage within a reasonable time, a carrier should, as a matter of principle, take care of an alternative carriage of the goods to Rotterdam.

Having regard to the above, it must be noted that the Rotterdam Rules do not deal with freight and charges. A contractual clause that would permit a carrier to charge additional freight or costs in case of a contingency might be held valid under the law that is otherwise applicable to the contract of carriage.

II. What is Delivery?

1. No Definition of "Delivery"

The Rotterdam Rules do not define "delivery." Both from a practical perspective and as a matter of legal doctrine, properly defining delivery is notoriously difficult. The Convention

---

[12] Such a clause is often referred to as 'Caspania Clause'. For an example, see Question 1 in "Rotterdam Rules in the Asia-Pacific Region: Workshop" contained in this book at pp. 245.

circumvents the potential problem in two ways.

First, Article 12 defines the end of the carrier's period of responsibility for the goods, which is normally the agreed time of delivery.[13] For example, when a charterparty relating to the carriage of liquid cargo includes the clause that "the cargo shall be delivered when it passes the ships manifolds" this cargo is delivered by the carrier when it is pumped out the vessel and it passes the ships manifolds. As from that moment the responsibility for the cargo is for account of the consignee. Another example is a charterparty containing the clause "delivery shall take place alongside the vessel as fast as she can deliver." When the cargo is bundles of timber, the time and place of delivery of any bundle of timber is when it is placed on the quay alongside the vessel. As from that moment the responsibility for this bundle of timber is for the consignee. It is important to note that upon the agreed end of the period of the carrier's responsibility for the goods, the contract of carriage has come to an end. Consequently, the carrier has as from that moment no contractual responsibility for the goods anymore. This applies irrespective of the type of transport document used.

Second, Article 48 (addressing "goods remaining undelivered") regulates the situation in which the goods are still under the carrier's supervision after its period of contractual responsibility has ended and no delivery took place.[14]

For all practical purposes, these provisions combine to make a definition of delivery less important.

2. Transfer of Responsibility

It may be concluded that, either under the Articles 45 – 47[15] or under Article 48[16] of the Convention, delivery of the goods is essentially equivalent to the transfer of the responsibility for the goods from the carrier to a person entitled to them.

There may be a physical element to the delivery of the goods, but not necessarily. Sometimes the consignee collects the goods at the agreed time and location of delivery. Then the transfer of responsibility and the transfer of physical custody coincide. But often the goods are in the hands of an agent and remain so even after the transfer of the responsibility. In that case, the agent acts on the carrier's behalf before delivery and on the consignee's behalf after delivery. Or upon delivery the goods may physically remain with the carrier (or its subcontractor), with the result that after delivery the carrier acts as the consignee's agent.

---

[13] *See* Article 12(2)(b) and (3).
[14] *See* below X.
[15] These articles address the delivery under the contract of carriage, *see* below VI, VII, IX and XI.
[16] *See* below X.

Also in respect of a delivery under Article 48 the physical element of delivery may be absent. It should be noted that, in the event that the carrier after delivery still has custody over the goods, this period of continued custody is outside the Rotterdam Rules.

III. The nature of the contract of carriage

For a proper understanding of the substantive provisions relating to delivery[17] it might be useful to remind some of the fundamental features of a contract of carriage generally as follow hereunder:

(a) A contract of carriage is a contract by which the carrier undertakes to carry goods from one place to another[18].

(b) It is a two parties contract: the shipper[19] and the carrier[20] make the agreement, but:

(c) there is always a third party involved: the consignee,[21] and

(d) the shipper determines who that person is. This person may already be known at the time of conclusion of the contract (and accordingly named in the transport document) or, when this person at that time unknown yet, it must eventually be known upon arrival of the goods at destination.[22]

(e) The consignee is defined as a person entitled to the goods, which implies that

(f) there is no obligation of the consignee to accept delivery of the goods.

From the nature of the contract of carriage as outlined above it may be concluded that:

(i) delivery of the goods is the responsibility of the carrier;

(ii) deliverability of the goods, i.e. bringing the carrier in a position to perform its obligation to deliver, is the responsibility of the cargo side, and

(iii) when after arrival of the goods at destination there is no consignee or the consignee does not take delivery of the goods, the carrier has no option but to address itself to the shipper, being its contractual party.

It must be noted that the above nature of the contract of carriage as well as the conclu-

---

[17] *See* Articles 43-47.
[18] *See* definition Article 1(1).
[19] *See* definition Article 1(8).
[20] *See* definition Article 1(5).
[21] *See* definition Article 1(11).
[22] For the traditional method to make the identity of the consignee known to the carrier, *see* below VIII.

sions resulting thereof relating to delivery, apply generally. They are irrespective of whether, and if so, which type of transport document is used for the carriage.

IV. Article 43 – Whether, When and Where the Consignee Must Accept Delivery

1. Discussion in UNCITRAL

It is easy to understand that the potentially conflicting matter that the carrier is obliged to deliver, while the consignee has no absolute obligation to accept delivery, raised extensive discussions within UNCITRAL. Article 43 was the result of that discussion.[23]

UNCITRAL firmly rejected a proposal to impose an unqualified obligation on the consignee.[24] Recognising that also the opposite extreme – no obligation for the consignee at all – is unworkable, it was felt that the consignee should be obliged to accept delivery when it had some degree of involvement with the carriage of the goods. The discussion then focused on the degree of the consignee's involvement that should trigger its obligation to accept delivery.[25] Many delegates favoured the view that "the exercise of (any) rights under the contract of carriage by the consignee" should trigger the obligation. For example, if a consignee requested a sample of the goods in order to decide whether to reject them under the sales contract, it should be obliged to accept delivery under the contract of carriage. Even if the consignee rejected the goods under the sales contract, those delegates argued, it should nevertheless accept delivery on the seller's behalf.[26] In the end, however, UNCITRAL decided that only a "demand for delivery" would trigger the obligation to accept delivery.[27] It means that in case a buyer/consignee on the basis of the result of the sampling rejects the goods under the contract of sale, it is entitled not to demand delivery and thereby

---

[23] UNCITRAL's discussion of Article 43 is reported in 11th Session Report paras 65-72; 16th Session Report paras 209-219; 20th Session Report paras 15-23; 21st Session Report paras 145-151; 2008 Commission Report paras 139-141.
[24] *See* 16th Session Report paras 211-212; 20th Session Report para. 19. An unqualified obligation to accept delivery might have enabled the absurd result that a person could dispose of garbage simply by shipping it to somebody else.
[25] *See* 20th Session Report, paras 20-23; 2008 Commission Report paras 139-140.
[26] The delegates advocating a broad rule argued that it was in line with the United Nations Convention on Contracts for the International Sale of Goods, 1980 (CISG). *See* CISG Article 86(2) (first sentence).
[27] *See* 2008 Commission Report para. 142.

leaving the goods with the carrier.[28]

In the context of the consignee's obligation to accept delivery, UNCITRAL also discussed whether the carrier should be obliged to send a "notice of arrival"[29] to the consignee. UNCITRAL concluded that the introduction of that new obligation was unnecessary because sending a notice of arrival is already standard practice in the industry for the benefit of both carriers and consignees and it does not raise any legal problems.[30]

2. The Consignee's Obligation

If the consignee demands delivery, it is obliged to accept delivery "at the time or within the time period and at the location agreed in the contract of carriage." This phrase is substantially the same as the language used in Article 12(3) — "the parties may agree on the time and location of . . . delivery of the goods" — to determine the end of the carrier's period of responsibility.[31] The principal difference is Article 43's addition of the phrase "or within the time period," which recognize that the contract of carriage sometimes permits the consignee to have the goods stored in the port of discharge for a specified period before their delivery. If the contract of carriage omits the time or location of delivery, the consignee must take delivery "at the time and location at which" the "delivery could reasonably be expected." Reasonable expectations should be informed by (i) "the terms of the contract," (ii) "the customs, usages or practices of the trade," and (iii) "the circumstances of the carriage."

If a consignee declines to properly accept a delivery that it previously demanded, Article 48 (which addresses goods that remain undelivered) determines the consequences.[32] Because the Convention addresses the consignee's legal position under the contract of carriage only in specific cases and does not include a general provision on the consignee's liability towards the carrier,[33] the consignee's liability for a breach of its obligation under Article 43 must be based on otherwise applicable law.[34]

---

[28] For the consequences thereof, *see* Article 45(c) below VI.3 and 4, Article 46(b) below VII.2, and 47(2)(a) below XI.4, respectively.
[29] A "notice of arrival" is a message providing details about the arrival of the goods at their destination. The carrier sends a notice of arrival in advance of the arrival to the consignee and to any other person designated in the document. A person designated as a party to which this message should be sent is a "notify party."
[30] *See* 16th Session Report para. 214.
[31] *See* above note 13 and accompanying text.
[32] *See* Article 48(1)(a); below notes 116-118 and accompanying text.
[33] Unlike Article 30 that regulates the liability of the shipper towards the carrier.
[34] The otherwise applicable law may, for some cases, extend the application of Article 30 to the liability of the consignee.

3. Practical Value

Because the consignee is implicitly entitled not to demand delivery of the goods, the practical value of Article 43 seems rather limited. For example, if on the basis of the result of the sampling the buyer/consignee would decide to reject the goods under the contract of sale, it may not demand delivery of the goods under the contract of carriage and Article 48 determines the consequences.[35] Nevertheless, Article 43 may be useful because it can avoid or reduce delays in the collection of goods from ports of discharge, which is sometimes a cause of port congestion.

For sake of clarity, it is observed that Article 43 applies irrespective of whether, and if so, what type of transport document is used for the carriage.

V. To Whom the Goods Must Be Delivered – The Structure of the Articles 45 – 48.

The matter to whom the goods must be delivered by the carrier is addressed in the Articles 45-47. These rules differ depending on the type of transport document used. Article 45 is the main provision and applies when the transport is performed (i) under an ordinary non-negotiable transport document or electronic record or (ii) without the use of any transport document or electronic transport record.[36] The Articles 46 and 47 are the exceptions to Article 45. They apply when the transport is performed under a non-negotiable transport document "that requires surrender"[37] (Article 46[38]) or under any negotiable transport document or electronic transport record (Article 47). Accordingly, when the Articles 46 and 47 are not applicable, Article 45 applies as the default rule.

Article 48 applies when under the Articles 45–47 the carrier is entitled or required to refuse delivery of the goods to the consignee.

Furthermore, the application of Article 48 is, at the option of the carrier, the alternative

---

[35] *See* above note 32.
[36] Situations in which no documents are issued may include e-commerce business models in which the electronic cargo data record does not qualify as an "electronic transport record" under Article 1(18).
[37] As opposed to an "ordinary" non-negotiable transport document to which Article 45 applies.
[38] Although Article 45's chapeau does not expressly exclude cases governed by Article 46, the structure of the chapter accomplishes the same result. The provisions of Article 45 either are inapplicable in the context of an Article 46 document or are pre-empted by the more specific provisions of Article 46.

for the application of the provisions of Article 45(c), (d), Article 46(b), (c) and 47(2). In the case of Article 47(2) the negotiable transport document or electronic record must, in addition, be qualified by the condition included in the heading of this section of Article 47. But Article 48 applies again when these alternatives do not lead to proper delivery.

VI. Article 45 - Delivery under an Ordinary Non-negotiable Transport Document or Record, or in the Absence of any Document or Record

1. The Carrier's Obligation to Deliver

Article 45[39] follows fully the principles according to the nature of the contract of carriage.[40] The first sentence of Article 45(a) repeats the carrier's general obligation to deliver the goods to the consignee[41] and specifies that it must do so "at the time and location referred to in Article 43."[42]

Under a non negotiable transport document, the consignee claiming delivery does not necessarily possess the right of control.[43] If a party other than the consignee has control of the goods, that right of control will not cease when the consignee demands delivery but at the (often later) delivery to the consignee that marks the end of the carrier's period of responsibility.[44]

Misdelivery is a carrier's risk. To prevent misdelivery to the extent possible, the second sentence of Article 45(a) gives the carrier the right to request the consignee to identify itself.[45] If the consignee does not properly identify itself, the carrier is entitled to refuse delivery.

---

[39] UNCITRAL's discussion of Article 45 is reported in 11th Session Report paras 74-77; 16th Session Report paras 223-230; 20th Session Report paras 25-28; 21st Session Report para. 153; 2008 Commission Report paras 143-144, 166, 168.
[40] *See* above III.
[41] *See* Article 11.
[42] *See* above note 31 and accompanying text.
[43] This follows from Article 51(1)(a)-(b).
[44] *See* Article 50(2).
[45] Because, in practice, identification of the consignee is not always needed, the request of the carrier for identification by the consignee was drafted as a carrier's right and not as its obligation. *See* 16th Session Report para. 226. When the carrier does not request for identification, however, it does so at its own peril.

2. The Duty to Advise the Carrier of the Name and address of the Consignee

Normally, when a carrier issues a non-negotiable transport document, the shipper has advised the carrier of the consignee's name and address, which will accordingly be stated in the document. When this is not the case,[46] Article 45(b) states, as a matter of principle,[47] that the controlling party has a duty to advise the carrier of the consignee's name and address. The controlling party may be the shipper, but because the right of control is transferable it may be any person (provided that the carrier has been notified).[48]

Obviously, the controlling party must *timely* advise the carrier of the consignee's particulars. The wording of Article 45(b), which simply specifies that the information must be given "prior to or upon the arrival of the goods at the place of destination," leaves room for otherwise applicable law to further specify the timing that is required.[49]

3. Procedures When the Goods Are Not Deliverable

Because the carrier has a duty to deliver, an active role may be expected from the carrier when the goods are not deliverable. Article 45(c) addresses three different situations in which the goods are undeliverable. In case (i), the consignee does not claim delivery in conformity with Article 43[50] after the carrier sends a notice of arrival.[51] In case (ii), the carrier refuses delivery because the consignee does not properly identify itself. And in case (iii), which is new, "the carrier is, after reasonable effort, unable to locate the consignee in order to request delivery instructions." This third case presupposes that the carrier does some active research to find the consignee and that the consignee is generally able (when found) to provide the required clarity as to what the carrier must do with the goods.

The requirement that the carrier must seek delivery instructions follows the industry practice. Normally, the carrier is represented at the place of destination by an agent that is part of the local business community. The agent, or the carrier itself, generally knows the

---

[46] Note that Article 45 also applies in situations in which no document at all is used.
[47] *See* 11th Session Report para. 75.
[48] *See* Article 51(1)(a)-(b).
[49] *See* 16th Session Report para. 225. Local authorities may for customs or safety purposes wish to avail of the data relating to the consignee and may require the carrier to submit these data to them at a specified time before arrival of the goods.
[50] *See* above IV.
[51] *See* above note 29.

trade patterns of its customers and, with some effort, is able to locate the (probable) consignee. Communication between those two persons may be of great assistance in finding a practical and legally sound solution.

If despite the carrier's efforts it turns out that a serious impediment to delivery remains, the carrier must request instructions from the controlling party. The logic behind this is that the controlling party is the person interested in the goods[52] and is known to the carrier.[53] If the controlling party does not provide instructions — which may well happen if the controlling party is not in a position to give meaningful instructions[54] — or the controlling party cannot be located, then the carrier must request instructions from the shipper.[55]

Although Article 45(c) is an extensive provision, it does not enumerate all possible cases in which the goods might be undeliverable. For instance, case (iii) refers only to the inability to locate the controlling party and does not explicitly cover the situation in which the controlling party can be located but is unwilling or not reasonably able to provide adequate delivery instructions. The intention of the subsection is to provide a certain order of persons whom the carrier must contact for a practical solution when difficulties arise. If the approach to one person does not produce a satisfactory result, the carrier must contact the next person in line. In view of this intention, the three cases should not be regarded as an exhaustive list. The procedural rules of Article 45(c) should be applied in all cases in which the goods are undeliverable under Article 45.

Although the procedural rules look very practical, they cannot guarantee success. The persons mentioned may be untraceable and a carrier is not required to make in-depth investigations. A "reasonable" effort, which is a relative duty, is sufficient.[56] It may be that nobody wants any involvement with the goods, as may be the case if they have a negative value.[57] In that context, a carrier has no option but to dispose of the goods as best it can.[58]

Article 45(c) begins with the phrase "without prejudice to Article 48."[59] The phrase appears only in the first sentence, but — as Article 45(c) establishes a cumulative series of options — the qualification applies to the entire paragraph. The intent is to ensure that when

---

[52] *See* Articles 50(1) and 54(1).
[53] *See* Article 51.
[54] For example, when the controlling party is a holder of security rights in the goods, such as a bank. If the bank knows the identity of the consignee, however, it may have an interest to assist the carrier in locating that person.
[55] Further down the line, the carrier may apply to the documentary shipper, if any.
[56] *Cf.* below XI.6.
[57] This may be the case either from the outset, for example when the goods are destined for recycling, or as a result of an event occurring during the carriage, for example when the goods are contaminated or damaged otherwise.
[58] *See* Article 48(2)-(4); below X.2.
[59] *See* above notes 56-58 and accompanying text.

the goods are undeliverable, the carrier has the option either (i) immediately to invoke Article 48 or (ii) first to apply the provisions of Article 45(c) and, if still necessary, thereafter to invoke Article 48. Sometimes, it will be clear from the outset that it would be pointless for the carrier to seek instructions from any of the persons mentioned in Article 45(c).[60] Or the carrier may have other reasons not to follow the procedure of Article 45(c) and instead prefers to apply Article 48.[61]

4. The Carrier's Discharge

A carrier that follows Article 45's procedures and delivers the goods on instruction of the controlling party, shipper, or documentary shipper is thereby discharged from its obligation to deliver the goods. The opportunity to be discharged may create an additional[62] incentive for the carrier to be active and do some reasonable research in order to overcome what may be mere carelessness on the cargo side. Article 45 should also induce the consignee not to be completely inattentive to its goods because it may run the risk that another person, such as the shipper, will instruct the carrier to deliver the goods to another person.[63] In this connection, it may be reiterated that delivery of the goods is the carrier's obligation, but the carrier's contractual counterpart is responsible for ensuring that they are deliverable.[64]

VII. Article 46 – Delivery When a Non-negotiable Transport Document That Requires Surrender Is Issued

Article 46 applies when the carrier issues a non-negotiable transport document[65] that indi-

---

[60] For example when the goods are seized upon their arrival by the customs authorities because they must be regarded as illegal.
[61] Under Article 48 (*see* above notes 56-58 and accompanying text), the carrier does not have complete flexibility. The carrier must advise the "notify party" (*see* above note 29) and the consignee, the controlling party, or the shipper (if known) of any intended action with regard to undeliverable goods.
[62] The obligation to deliver the cargo already creates an incentive for the carrier to be diligent.
[63] Any instruction given by the shipper to the carrier may have an impact on the relation between the shipper/seller and consignee/buyer under the contract of sale. Whether an instruction to the carrier in respect of delivery would constitute a breach under the contract of sale depends on the terms of the latter contract.
[64] *See* above III(ii) and VI.2.
[65] Unlike most other provisions in the Convention, Article 46 does not deal with electronic equivalents. Draft Convention WP.81 included a provision relating to "delivery of the goods when a non-negotiable electronic transport record that requires surrender has been issued." Draft Convention WP.81 Article 48. But that article was subsequently deleted because no existing practice uses that

cates that it must be surrendered to obtain delivery of the goods.[66]

1. The Evolution of Article 46

To understand Article 46, it is first necessary to understand the specific characteristics of the type of document that is governed by Article 46 — "a non-negotiable transport document... that indicates that it shall be surrendered in order to obtain delivery of the goods." The Convention's early drafts did not address such a document.[67] Most delegates had felt that it would be adequate to establish rules for negotiable and non-negotiable transport documents and electronic transport records.[68] In some legal systems, however, a third type of transport document is used that falls somewhere between the negotiable and non-negotiable transport documents.[69] Thus UNCITRAL was forced to recognize the existing practice and finally addressed those documents, which were commonly called "recta bills of lading."

A formal proposal to address the hybrid documents was submitted at the 2006 spring meeting of the UNCITRAL Working Group.[70] One of the first problems to overcome was terminology. The term "recta bill of lading" is unknown in many parts of the world.[71] Terms that are sometimes used as synonyms have very different meanings in different legal systems. While in Scandinavia a "straight bill of lading" might be equivalent to a "recta bill of lading," in the United States a "straight bill of lading" is something entirely different (and much closer to what would be described as a "sea waybill" in Scandinavia). Other suggestions — "bill of lading consigned to a named person," "nominative bill of lading" — had similar problems. In addition, UNCITRAL had already concluded that the term "bill of lading" had become too ambiguous to be suitable for use in the Convention. In the end, therefore, UNCITRAL decided to create a completely new term that describes what is in-

---

sort of electronic record. *See* 20th Session Report paras 36-38; 21st Session Report para. 157; *cf.* below notes 72-73 and accompanying text.

[66] UNCITRAL's discussion of Article 46 is reported in 11th Session Report para. 73; 17th Session Report paras 208-215; 20th Session Report paras 29-35; 21st Session Report paras 154-156; 2008 Commission Report paras 145,166,168.

[67] *See* Draft Instrument WP.21; Draft Instrument WP.32; Draft Instrument WP.56.

[68] Because the Rotterdam Rules reinforce the use of non-negotiable documents with an explicitly defined right of control with enhanced transferability, there might be no real need for other forms, such as the non-negotiable transport document requiring surrender.

[69] *See* WP.68, para. 2.

[70] *See* WP.68.

[71] Efforts to define "recta" bills of lading also revealed ambiguities in the usage. The term "recta" itself simply indicates that the document is non-negotiable, but the distinguishing feature of "recta" bills of lading in the present context is that they (unlike other non-negotiable transport documents) must be surrendered in order to obtain delivery of the goods.

tended. A 19-word phrase may not be elegant, but at least it defines the relevant characteristics.

Once the terminology was established, UNCITRAL agreed to cover the document solely because it exists and is used in practice.[72] A principal goal of the Rotterdam Rules is to provide legal certainty while meeting the needs of commerce. If recta bills of lading and other hybrid documents are used in practice, the Convention should provide the legal framework to enable that commercial practice to work more efficiently.[73]

A principal problem with many of the documents that fall into the gray area between negotiable and non-negotiable transport documents is whether they must be surrendered in order to obtain delivery of the goods. No uniformity exists.[74] In some jurisdictions, surrender is required while in others there is no such obligation. And often there is legal uncertainty within a single jurisdiction whether surrender is required.[75] Because of the uncertainty and lack of uniformity, some carriers are deliberately vague in their standard transport documents about the requirement of presentation.[76] To solve those problems, the Convention is fairly precise on the matter: presentation of a non-negotiable transport document is not required to obtain delivery *unless the document itself indicates that it must be surrendered*. Documents that include that requirement are then governed by Article 46.

UNCITRAL discussed whether a document sufficiently "indicates" that it must be surrendered if it merely bears the heading "bill of lading" — a term used in some (but not all) legal systems for a document that must be presented and surrendered — with no further indication of the requirement of presentation and surrender.[77] One conclusion of the discussion was to defer to the courts to decide whether the word "indicates" is sufficiently flexible for that interpretation. If courts follow such a wide interpretation of the word "indicates," however, the Convention will not achieve the intended uniformity. Article 46 cannot achieve its goal unless the courts require a document to include a more specific indication

---

[72] A provision addressing the issue was first included in Draft Convention WP.81, art. 47.
[73] *See* 17th Session Report paras 208-211.
[74] For a general overview *see* Pejovic, cited below at note 148, p. 456-459.
[75] For circumstances under which in Hongkong no surrender is required, *see* the recent judgement of the Court of Appeal in *Forsa Multimedia Ltd. vs. C&C Logistics (HK) Ltd* , HCMP 683/2011
[76] For example, two of the three main Japanese container carriers include in their standard bill of lading the phrase: "*If required by the carrier*, this bill of lading duly endorsed must be surrendered in exchange for the goods or delivery order." The bill of lading of the third carrier states: "one of the original bills of lading must be surrendered duly endorsed in exchange for the goods or delivery order *unless otherwise provided herein*," and in an indirect way this bill of lading so provides. Clearly, all three carriers contractually reserve the right to deliver the goods, under circumstances, without surrender of the bill of lading. *See* also below XII.5(b).
[77] *See* 17th Session Report paras 212-214; 20th Session Report paras 31-33; 21st Session Report paras 154-156.

that surrender is required before applying Article 46. If a document is simply headed "bill of lading" and made out to a named person (while being vague about the requirement of presentation and surrender), then Article 46 does not apply.[78]

The Rotterdam Rules are silent on one of the main controversies relating to an Article 46 document, which is whether it incorporates rights and thus whether a transfer of the document between the shipper and the consignee includes the transfer of those incorporated rights.[79] The Convention provides only that a transfer of an Article 46 document between the shipper and consignee transfers the right of control, which includes the right to obtain delivery of the goods.[80]

2. The Substantive Rules of Article 46

It follows from the hybrid character of the "non-negotiable transport document that must be surrendered to obtain delivery" that Article 46 must contain aspects of Article 45[81] and aspects of Article 47[82] to the extent that those provisions are appropriate. In addition, Article 46 incorporates some other parts of those articles with minor adjustments as necessary for the nature of the Article 46 document. Thus Article 46(b) is very similar to Article 45(c), while Article 46(a) is similar to Article 47(1)(a), with appropriate adjustments for the non-negotiable nature of the Article 46 document.

In contrast, Article 46(b) does not incorporate the caveat in the chapeau of Article 47(2) that delivery without surrender of the transport document is allowed only if the document itself includes a statement to that effect.[83] A statement designed to warn a third-party holder would be pointless in the context of an Article 46 document, which can involve no parties on the cargo side other than the shipper and the consignee.

---

[78] Carriers and shippers themselves are generally in a position to ease the problem by paying due attention to the question of surrender requirements when they issue or accept transport documents. *See* also below XII.5(b).

[79] For negotiable transport documents, the chapeau of Article 57(1) explicitly provides for the transfer of incorporated rights. Because of the hybrid character of the Article 46 document and the doctrinal aspects of the issue, UNCITRAL made no serious attempt to reach a consensus on the question.

[80] *See* Article 51(2). Article 41(b)(ii) deals with the evidentiary value of the non-negotiable transport document that must be surrendered to obtain delivery. In Article 1(10), however, the use of the notion "holder" is not extended to the Article 46 document.

[81] *See* above VI.

[82] *See* below IX, XI.

[83] *See* below notes 161-163 and accompanying text.

VIII. Essence of the Bill of Lading System Is the Legitimation

Before turning to the provisions of Article 47 it may be useful to remind the fundamental function of the bill of lading[84] as a contract of carriage. The essence of the bill of lading is its legitimation function, meaning that the document itself identifies the person that is entitled to the rights incorporated in the document, such as delivery of the goods at destination.[85] This person is not identified by name, but by holding the document.[86]

According to the definition of holder[87] this person, who is in physical possession of the document, can only be (i) the person named in the document as shipper or as consignee, (ii) the final endorsee, when there is an uninterrupted list of endorsements on the back of the document, or (iii) anyone, when the document is a bearer document[88] or it is endorsed in blank.[89]

This legitimation function creates certainty for both sides:

(a) The consignee, in possession of the document, can learn from the document that it is a person entitled to the rights incorporated in it. It must be one of the persons listed in the previous paragraph. If that is the case, he may exercise the rights. If not, even if it is in possession of the document, it is not entitled to exercise any rights under the document.[90]

(b) The carrier knows that, when it delivers to goods to the holder – either a bearer or a person named in the document – it is discharged of his delivery obligation under the contract of carriage.

This legitimation function dates back from ancient times.[91] Because this function put the

---

[84] Note that the Convention uses the term "negotiable transport document." Because in practice, however, this type of document traditionally is referred to as a 'bill of lading,' this word or the word "document" is used in this Chapter VIII.
[85] The legitimation by the negotiable document gives the relevant person only a formal entitlement. Whether a holder is ultimately entitled to exercise the rights is a subsequent question that is left to the law otherwise applicable to the document. For this reason a proposal to add the word "lawful" before "possession" was rejected. *See* 9th Session Report para. 91.
[86] When the holder is a person named in the document – *see* below at para. X.2(4). – such person may have to identify itself as well.
[87] *See* Article 1(10).
[88] Bearer transport documents are exceedingly rare in practice.
[89] On endorsements, *see* Article 57.
[90] For example, a forwarder to whom a carrier has issued the document and who is not stated as shipper therein. As long as the document has not been endorsed by the shipper as named in the document (or by the consignee if the document is made out to the order of the consignee) to the forwarder (or is endorsed in blank), it cannot exercise any right under the document against the carrier.
[91] Already the old Roman literature refers to the following custom in the grain trade between Alexandria, Egypt, to Rome, Italy, some two millennia ago. When the ship was loaded in Alexandria,

holder - in the context of the contract of carriage - in such a strong position towards the goods, over times the transport document could develop into 'the key to the warehouse', or, more generally, into its title function – in the context of a contract of sale or trade financing contract – providing to the holder symbolic possession of the goods.[92]

Obviously, a transport document can only exercise its legitimation function if it is timely available, namely when the goods have arrived at destination and are ready for delivery, and is surrendered to the carrier. Otherwise, a carrier cannot know to whom to deliver the goods.

This does not mean that a holder always has to present a bill of lading when the goods arrive at destination. It was already set out in IV.1 that a consignee has no legal duty to take delivery and, therefore, is allowed not to present the bill of lading. However, in my view, the holder has a <u>systematical</u> duty – based on the essential legitimation function of the document that goes to the roots of the system – to make itself known to the carrier (by producing the bill of lading) when the goods have arrived at destination and to instruct the carrier on delivery in such a way that the carrier may become discharged from his delivery obligation under the contract of carriage.[93]

IX. Article 47 – Delivery when a negotiable transport document or record is issued

When the carrier issues a negotiable transport document[94] or electronic transport record,[95] Article 47 establishes the delivery rules.[96]

---

the captain issued a receipt to the Egyptian grain exporter, stating that it, the named captain, had received on board a specified quantity of grain for carriage to Rome. Then, this receipt was torn in two pieces. One piece was retained on board and carried with the ship to the port of destination. The other piece was sent through the Roman mail system, mainly overland, to the port of destination of the grain. When finally the ship had arrived, the merchant that could present to the captain the piece of the receipt that fitted to the piece carried on board of the ship, was the person entitled to receive the cargo. Such receipt torn in two pieces was named in Latin: 'charta partita'. The word 'charterparty' stems from this old Latin expression.

[92] When the owner or the pledgee of goods in transit wishes to exercise its right in the goods towards the carrier, it needs under the Rotterdam Rules to be in possession of the right of control; see Articles 50-54.

[93] *See* also III(ii). In most cases this may result in a surrender of the bill of lading to the carrier, but not necessarily so. For example, the holder may instruct the carrier to return the goods to the shipper, while returning the bill of lading to the shipper accordingly.

[94] Article 1(15) defines the 'negotiable transport document.'

[95] Article 1(19) defines the 'negotiable electronic transport record.'

[96] UNCITRAL's discussion of Article 47 is reported in 11th Session Report paras 78-90; 16th Session Report paras 231-239; 17th Session Report paras 80-89; 20th Session Report paras 42-67; 21st

1. Rule of Application of Article 47

The first section of the Article follows the classic bill of lading system. Its general rules apply to all negotiable transport documents or electronic transport records. As soon as the transport document qualifies as a negotiable one in conformity with its definition in Article 1(15) the first section applies, irrespective of the name that a carrier may have given to the document in its heading or whether it includes a contractual obligation of surrender to obtain delivery.

In addition, the specific provisions of the second section apply when the negotiable document or record "expressly states that the goods may be delivered without the surrender of the transport document or the electronic transport record." Because the chapeau of Article 47(2) requires a negotiable transport document or electronic transport record, the general rule of application stated in Article 47(1) for negotiable transport documents or electronic transport records necessarily applies to Article 47(2). The second section applies to negotiable transport documents that are undeliverable under the first section[97] and, as an additional condition for its applicability, include an express statement to the effect that the goods may be delivered without surrender of the transport document or electronic record. [98]

2. The Heart of the Classic Bill of Lading System

In conjunction with the definition of holder,[99] Article 47(1)(a) lays down the heart of the classic bill of lading system. Together, those two provisions contain the "legitimation"[100] function of the document and provide that the person legitimated by the negotiable transport document or electronic transport record has the right to claim delivery of the goods from the carrier. Similarly, the carrier has a duty to deliver the goods to that person when it claims delivery.

It may be noted that the holder of the negotiable transport document may – under another contract than the contract of carriage - have become owner or pledgee of the goods, but not necessarily so. In any event, under the Convention possession of such proprietary rights in the goods is no (additional) condition for a person to become entitled to claim delivery of

---

Session Report paras 158-161; 2008 Commission Report paras 146-165.
[97] *See* Article 47(2)(a).
[98] *See* below notes 161-163 and accompanying text.
[99] *See* above notes 87-89 and accompanying text.
[100] *See* above VIII.

the goods from the carrier. These rights are separate from the rights that a person may have under a contract of carriage. Under the latter contract holdership of the document alone is sufficient for being entitled to delivery of the goods, represented by this document, from the carrier.

The description of the system in Article 47(1)(a) and (b) is rather straight-forward. Nevertheless a few phrases deserve some further attention:

(1) "is entitled to"[101]

This wording follows the same principle expressed in Article 43. Generally, a consignee is not obliged to accept delivery, but once it has claimed delivery, it is obliged to accept delivery at the time and location referred to in Article 43.[102]

(2) "*after* they have arrived at the place of destination"[103]

The word "after" is not meant to mean "at any time after." Because the holder must claim delivery before the carrier can deliver, and Article 47(1)(a) requires the carrier to deliver "at the time . . . referred to in Article 43," the word "after" necessarily refers to the time between the goods' arrival at the place of destination and the agreed time of delivery. Thus "after" in Article 47(1)(a) has the same effect as "when" in Article 43. Unless the parties explicitly agree otherwise,[104] the negotiable transport document or electronic transport record should perform its legitimation function when the goods arrive at their destination and the carrier is ready to deliver them at the time and location referred to in Article 43.

(3) "surrender of the . . . document"[105]

This obligation applies regardless of the wording of the transport document.[106] When a document is negotiable, as determined under the Convention's definition of "negotiable transport document,"[107] it must be presented and surrendered to the carrier, even if the document does not explicitly state that obligation or includes the caveat referred to in the chapeau of Article 47(2).[108]

---

[101] Article 47(1)(a).
[102] *See* above IV.
[103] Article 47(1)(a) (emphasis added).
[104] For example, when the carrier has agreed to temporary storage of the goods prior to delivery.
[105] Article 47(1)(a)(i).
[106] For a negotiable electronic transport record, the procedures required by Article 9 will provide an electronic counterpart to "surrender." *See* Articles 9(1)(d), 47(1)(c) (second sentence).
[107] *See* Article 1(15).
[108] *See* below notes 161-163 and accompanying text.

(4) "the holder properly identifying itself"[109]

Unless the transport document is endorsed in blank or is a bearer document,[110] the person presenting it must be named in the document and, on the carrier's request, must properly identify itself. Although the wording on identification here is not the same as in Articles 45(a) and 46(a), the intention is the same — to avoid misdelivery to the extent possible.[111] Therefore, the carrier has a right (and not a duty) to request identification, in which case the consignee has a duty to properly identify itself.

When the holder does not surrender the transport document or does not properly identify itself on the carrier's request, the carrier has a duty to refuse delivery of the goods. In view of the certainty that the system aims to provide, Article 47(1)(b) intentionally uses the word "shall," while in Article 45(a) the word "may" suffices. For the carrier, however, the risk is the same under the two provisions: if it does not request identification and, as a result, the goods are misdelivered, it may be held liable.

3. More than One Original Having Been Issued

Despite numerous recommendations by industry organizations and others not to use multiple originals, the widespread practice still exists that transport documents are issued in a set of three (or more) originals. The Rotterdam Rules follow the current practice that the consignee's surrender of one original of a set is sufficient to obtain delivery of the goods.[112] Thus the carrier (which usually delivers on "first come, first served" basis) is discharged of its obligation to deliver the goods when one original has been surrendered and the other originals in the set of documents then cease to have any effect or validity.

The severity of the rule voiding subsequent originals is mitigated by the requirement that the number of originals must be stated in the document. This requirement follows from the carrier's obligation to state the number of originals on the transport document when it issues more than one original.[113] When no number is stated, the holder may assume that only one original has been issued.[114] But when a larger number is stated, each holder will be on notice of the risk that it takes if it fails to acquire the full set of originals.

---

[109] Article 47(1)(a)(i).
[110] *See* above notes 87-89 and accompanying text.
[111] *See* above note 45 and accompanying text.
[112] *See* Article 47(1)(c).
[113] *See* Article 36(2)(d).
[114] The subsection is not explicit about the consequences of the case that no number is stated and a second presenter of an original would show up. Presumably, a carrier may be liable towards the second presenter under otherwise applicable law for breach of its obligation to state the number of originals.

X. Article 48 - Goods Remaining Undelivered

In Chapters IV, VI, VII and IX above we discuss cases in which the goods remain undelivered in a factual sense (even if the carrier has technically satisfied its "delivery" obligation). In that context, the question arises what the carrier may or must do with those goods if it still has possession of them after its period of responsibility has ended and no delivery took place. Article 48 deals with the issue, providing a general regulation of undelivered goods.[115] We address that general regulation here. For situations in which Article 48 does not offer a practical solution, however, Article 47(2) may offer an alternative avenue to deal with the problem. We discuss that alternative in Chapter XI below.

1. Scope of application

Article 48 starts with the phrase "for the purposes of this article" and then lists five cases for which the fiction is introduced that "goods shall be deemed to have remained undelivered." The opening phrase and the fiction of undeliverability illustrate that Article 48 addresses the specific situation in which the contractual period of responsibility has come to an end, while the goods, in one form or another, remain in the carrier's custody under the Rules.[116] In the normal course of events, delivery marks the end of the performance of the contract of carriage. The Convention refrains from putting a doctrinal label on the carrier's legal status during the potential subsequent period when it, beyond the contract of carriage, still has custody of the goods. Article 48 instead provides only practical legal rules.

The first three enumerated cases to which Article 48 applies are cases of non-delivery that are addressed in the Convention. The first case[117] occurs when the consignee is in default by failing to accept delivery as required by the Convention.[118] In the second case,[119] the goods are undeliverable and the carrier cannot find the controlling party, the holder, the shipper, or the documentary shipper, or else those persons would not give the carrier ade-

---

[115] UNCITRAL's discussion of Article 48 is reported in 11th Session Report paras 91-99; 17th Session Report paras 90-113; 20th Session Report paras 68-83; 21st Session Report paras 162-165; 2008 Commission Report paras 167-172.
[116] *See* above note 14 and accompanying text and V.
[117] *See* Article 48(1)(a).
[118] *See* Article 43; *see* also above IV.
[119] *See* Article 48(1)(b).

quate instructions.[120] The third case[121] arises when the carrier is entitled or required to refuse delivery pursuant to Articles 44, 45, 46, or 47.[122]

The last two enumerated cases are more open-ended. The fourth case,[123] arising outside the scope of the Convention, occurs when the carrier is not allowed to deliver the goods to the consignee pursuant to the law or regulations where delivery is requested. Finally, the fifth case is a catch-all provision covering any situation in which "[t]he goods are otherwise undeliverable by the carrier."[124]

According to the chapeau of Article 48, its substantive rules apply only to the five listed cases. The word "only" suggests that the list is intended to be exhaustive. The inclusion of a final catch-all provision, however, effectively makes the list open-ended.

2. Carrier's rights related to undelivered goods

When the goods are undeliverable, the carrier has become involuntarily responsible for them for an undefined period. Article 48 thus grants the carrier a very wide discretion.

It may "take such action in respect of the goods as circumstances may reasonably require."[125] Although circumstances vary widely, the Convention gives three examples. The carrier may (a) "store the goods at any suitable place,"[126] (b) "unpack the goods if they are packed in containers or vehicles," or "act otherwise in respect of the goods, including by moving them,"[127] and (c) "cause the goods to be sold or destroyed."[128]

The listed examples are derived from traditional bill of lading clauses and pre-existing national law, so commercial practice is already consistent with the Convention's approach. But the listed cases are merely examples. The key provision is that the carrier's actions must be "reasonably require[d]" under the circumstances. The discretion given to the carrier is wide enough to include delivering the goods against a letter of indemnity.[129] In practice, there may be many instances in which delivery against a letter of indemnity is reason-

---

[120] See Articles 45, 46 and 47; above notes 50-58, 79-80 and accompanying texts; below notes 165-167 and accompanying text; XI.6.
[121] See Article 48(1)(c).
[122] See above notes 45, 81-83 and 111-112 and accompanying texts.
[123] See Article 48(1)(d).
[124] Article 48(1)(e).
[125] Article 48(2).
[126] Article 48(2)(a).
[127] Article 48(2)(b). Under well-established principles of interpretation, the phrase "act otherwise" authorizes actions comparable to unpacking the goods or moving them. It would not authorize more extreme acts, such as selling or destroying the goods, which are covered by Article 48(2)(c).
[128] Article 48(2)(c).
[129] See below notes 150-151 and accompanying text.

ably required.[130]

The carrier may take its authorized actions "[w]ithout prejudice to any other rights that the carrier may have against the shipper, controlling party or consignee,"[131] thus emphasizing that the carrier's Article 48 rights are not the exclusive remedies. If the goods are undeliverable because a listed person is in default under the contract of carriage, for example, the carrier may have a claim for damages against that person. Other contractual arrangements may also exist. If, for example, circumstances reasonably require to postpone delivery for a short period, a carrier may have a claim for demurrage.

As a general principle of contract law in many jurisdictions, the risk shifts to a creditor that wrongfully refuses to accept a debtor's performance of its obligation. When goods are undeliverable, it is generally[132] due to some fault on the cargo side. The risks and expenses of the carrier's actions under Article 48 are accordingly for the account of "the person entitled to the goods."[133]

The phrase "the person entitled to the goods" is also part of the definition of "consignee."[134] A consignee is a party entitled to the goods *under* a contract of carriage, however, while Article 48 deals with the period *after* the contract of carriage has been completed. Within the scope of Article 48, the person entitled to the goods may be the consignee, but not necessarily so. It may be a different person, such as an owner of the goods or the holder of a security interest.

3. Conditions and Procedures for the Carrier When Acting under Article 48

When the carrier exercises its rights under Article 48, it must satisfy the conditions and follow the procedures provided in Article 48.

(1) Reasonable Notice

Before exercising any rights, the carrier must give reasonable notice of the intended action (i) to the notify party,[135] if any, and (ii) to the consignee, or the controlling party, or the

---

[130] For typical examples, *see* Sturley *et al*, cited note 1, Illustrations 8-20, 8-21, p.264-265.
[131] Article 48(2).
[132] The fault for undeliverable goods is not always on the cargo side. For instance, if the goods suffer damage during the carriage due to the carrier's fault and have a negative value as a result, the cargo side is not at fault when it refuses delivery. In that situation, any claim for reimbursement of costs by the carrier might (under otherwise applicable law) be set off against the claim for cargo damages.
[133] Article 48(2).
[134] *See* Article 1(11) and III(b)-(f) above.
[135] *See* above note 29. The notice under Article 48 must be clearly distinguished from the ordinary

shipper (in the order indicated), if known to the carrier.[136] The notice is intended to ensure, to the extent possible, that the "person entitled to the goods" will not be prejudiced by irreparable actions by the carrier.

The notice must be "reasonable." What is reasonable in a given case will depend on the circumstances. In view of the intention of the notice, a reasonable notice will generally specify the intended action and, if possible, give the party being notified a reasonable time to arrange an alternative if it wishes to prevent the carrier's proposed action.

(2) Local Law and Regulation

If the goods are sold or destroyed, the carrier must act "in accordance with the practices or pursuant to the law and regulations of the place where the goods are located at the time."[137] Some form of court supervision is often required in those cases.

(3) Proceeds of Sale

If the goods are sold, the carrier must hold the proceeds of sale for the benefit of the person entitled to the goods.[138] The article allows a deduction of any costs incurred by the carrier and any other amounts that are due to the carrier in connection with the carriage, but only insofar as the deductions are related to the goods sold. Whether other costs or amounts due to the carrier may be deducted from the proceeds of sale, for instance through set-off, is left to otherwise applicable law.

4. Carrier's Liability

Because the carrier's custody of the undeliverable goods generally results from a fault on the cargo side,[139] the general rule is that "the carrier shall not be liable for loss of or damage to goods that occurs during the time they remain undelivered pursuant to this article."[140] Because the words "remain undelivered" are the same as used in the chapeau of Article 48(1) and the words "pursuant to this article" refer to the cases listed in Article 48(1)(a)-(e), the period of exclusion of liability starts with the occurrence of any of those cases.[141]

---

notice of arrival sent to the notify party. The Article 48 notice must refer to the intended action upon non-delivery and therefore, by necessity, is a later and separate notice.
[136] *See* Article 48(3).
[137] Article 48(2)(c).
[138] *See* Article 48(4).
[139] *See* above note 132.
[140] Article 48(5).
[141] *See* above notes 117-124 and accompanying text.

The exclusion of the carrier's liability does not apply when the claimant proves that the carrier failed to take reasonable steps for the preservation of the goods while "the carrier knew or ought to have known that the loss or damage to the goods would result from its failure to take such steps."[142, 143]

The formula in Article 48(5) establishing the exception to the exclusion of liability differs from the wording in Article 61 relating to the loss of the benefit of limitation of liability.[144] The effect of the one formula is nevertheless to a large extent similar to that of the other, because in both cases the carrier must know or have constructive knowledge that the loss or damage (probably) would result from its act or failure to act. That element of consciousness carries with it that in both cases the act or failure to act is made intentionally or recklessly.

Because the carrier's obligations under the contract of carriage have been completed when the Article 48 period begins, the joint and several liability of the carrier and the maritime performing party[145] does not apply under Article 48. The performing party is defined as "a person ... that performs ... any of the carrier's obligations under a contract of carriage with respect to receipt, loading, handling, stowage, carriage, care, unloading or delivery of the goods ... ,"[146] That definition restricts the activities of a performing party within the period of the contract of carriage.

Also, for a similar reason, the carrier's general vicarious liability applies only to acts or failures to act by the master and crew of the ship and by the carrier's employees.[147] And if a claim is instituted directly against one of the persons entitled to automatic Himalaya protection under Article 4(1), it includes the carrier's exclusion of liability under Article 48.

---

[142] Article 48(5).
[143] If the goods are rapidly deteriorating perishables, such as bananas, the carrier knows or ought to know that it may have to take immediate steps to preserve the goods or such steps as otherwise reasonable in the circumstances. Those steps may include, for example, delivery of the bananas to the fruit importer while accepting a letter of indemnity (preferably to be co-signed by a first class bank) in lieu of the surrender of the transport document or a prompt sale of the bananas to the highest bidder and holding the proceeds of sale for the party entitled to the bananas.
[144] Article 61 refers to "a personal act or omission of the person claiming a right to limit done with the intent to cause such loss or recklessly and with the knowledge that such loss would probably result."
[145] *See* Article 20.
[146] Article 1(6).
[147] *See* Article 18.

XI. Article 47(2) - An Alternative to Delivery Against a Letter of Indemnity

The matter of delivery without production of a the negotiable document, including the widespread practice of the letter of indemnity (LoI) system, was intensively discussed within UNCITRAL for the purpose of whether making specific provision on it in the Convention. [148] Article 47(2) is the result of this discussion.

1. The Problem

One of the most frequent reasons for non-delivery is that the holder of a negotiable transport document (i) does not demand delivery after the arrival of the goods at the destination or, more often, (ii) demands delivery at that time but does not present (and surrender) the transport document. The frequency of those cases should not be underestimated. In the carriage of commodity goods, the transport document is unavailable when required about half of the time. In oil and related trades, the transport document is absent close to 100 percent of the time.

The cause of the transport document's absence may be inadvertent, such as delays in the mail or in the document processing in the banking system. In many cases, however, the cause is related to contingencies in the underlying sales or trade-financing contract, such as the buyer/consignee may wish to reject the goods, or has not taken up the documents from the bank, for instance, because an envisaged resale has not yet taken place. Even more seriously, the cause of the unavailability of the transport document may be structural and inherent to the particular trade. For example, (standard) credit terms under the sale contract may last longer than the voyage of the goods. Or it may be usual in a particular trade that long chains of buyers and sellers prevent the timely availability of the transport docu-

---

[148] For a general overview of the different problems in the Asia-Pacific region connected with this subject, see Caslav Pejovic, *Delivery of goods without a bill of lading: revival of an old problem in the Far East*, 9 JIML 448-460 (2003). In Japan, Takashi Hiraizumi made various publications on the subject. *See* Takashi Hiraizumi, *The ocean carrier's liability for delivery to a person not entitled to the goods without production of bills of lading in Japanese law*, Kyorin University Journal of Social Sciences Vol.14, No.1 (1998); *Ocean carrier's limitation of liability for delivery to a person not entitled to the goods without production of B/L (Revised)*, The Chuo Law Review Vol.108, No.9-10 (2002; *Delivery without production of the original bill of lading and the exclusion clauses in the UK*, The Chuo Law Review Vol.111 No.5-6 (2005). For China, *see* Zou, cited above note 2, p. 144-243.

For conferences on the subject *see* CMI Colloquium on Bills of Lading, Venice, May/June, 1983; Annual Conference of Japanese Maritime Law Association, Tokyo, October 2002.

ment.[149]

When the cause is trade-related, Article 48 is often not the proper solution for the parties. This is particularly true for commodity goods, which usually are carried in large quantities per vessel. In those cases, carriers have traditionally delivered the goods against a letter of indemnity issued by either the shipper or the person to whom the goods are delivered.[150] In the letter of indemnity, the issuer/indemnifier promises the carrier to present the transport document in due course and to hold the carrier harmless for any damages that it may incur due to the delivery of the goods without the presentation and surrender of the transport document.[151]

2. Discussions in UNCITRAL

UNCITRAL extensively discussed whether the Rotterdam Rules should address the practice of delivering the goods without surrender of the negotiable transport document.[152] Indeed, the Final Draft Convention approved by the UNCITRAL Working Group and submitted to the Commission in 2008 for final approval included provisions that would — in limited circumstances — have permitted delivery without surrender of the negotiable transport document.[153] Throughout the process, views were sharply divided.

Those who opposed the treatment of the subject in the Final Draft Convention argued that "legalising" delivery without presentation and surrender of the transport document would undermine the key function of the traditional bill of lading system that has been a long-standing business practice in international trade. It would weaken the entire system, reduce the value of the transport document, and institutionalise an undesirable practice of delivery. Those adverse consequences would also significantly impact banking practices. Article 48, which deals generally with undeliverable goods, is sufficiently flexible to cover whatever solution the parties might adopt for handling cases in which no transport document is available at destination. Furthermore, giving the shipper the authority to instruct the carrier to deliver the goods when a negotiable transport document had been issued would introduce a risk that the shipper might collude with the carrier to deliver the goods to

---

[149] These chains can also include pre-shipment sales and may even include future (i.e., pre-production) sales. It may take weeks and sometimes months or even years before the final buyer receives the transport document.
[150] *See* note 130.
[151] These terms are often already included in charterparties as a standard clause. Transport documents issued under a charterparty usually incorporate the terms of the charterparty by reference.
[152] *See* discussion cited above note 96.
[153] *See* Final Draft Convention art. 49(d)-(h). These provisions formed the basis for Article 47(2) in the final text of the Convention.

a person not entitled to them. The better long-term solution for the problems, it was argued, would ultimately be the wide-spread use of electronic transport records.

Proponents of the treatment in the Final Draft Convention agreed that the delivery practices without presentation and surrender of the transport document are undesirable. In their view, however, those practices had already undermined the traditional system because they were widespread and had created many legal uncertainties for both carrier and cargo interests, including banks. Indeed, for cargo interests the legal uncertainties extended beyond the contract of carriage *per se*. To save the costs involved with these practices, therefore, the better option should be to include a solution in the Convention that would, as much as possible, restore legal certainty for all parties concerned. The fact that those parties, including banks, may have to change some existing practices under the new system should be seen as an advantage precisely because the current practices are so undesirable. Consultations with those parties, it was said, had confirmed that view. The flexibility of Article 48 was not seen as a solution, because many national laws already include rules for undeliverable goods that are comparable to Article 48, but those existing rules are inadequate to remedy the problems. A solution through the Convention would admittedly be subject to fraud, but so is the traditional system. Under the letter of indemnity system many specific types of fraud are possible, and the Convention could prevent some of them. Electronic transport records must also be produced at delivery, one way or another, and are therefore not the solution to the problem when the absence of the transport document is part of the structure of the trade in question.

During the very final stage of the negotiations in June 2008, the Commission agreed on a compromise solution. It retained the controversial provisions, which were reorganized to become Article 47(2),[154] with some essential practical corrections to the text.[155] Under the reorganization, Article 47(2) included all the provisions addressing the situation when the holder of a transport document does not claim delivery of the goods or does not identify itself as the holder.[156] But to satisfy the opponents' concerns, the chapeau of Article 47(2) conditioned its application on the parties' inclusion of an express statement in the transport document or electronic transport record to permit delivery without surrender.[157]

---

[154] *Cf.* above notes 152-153 and accompanying text. The noncontroversial provisions of Final Draft Convention art. 49 — paragraphs (a) to (c) — became Article 47(1). *See* above IX.1 and 2.
[155] *See* 2008 Commission Report paras 153-154.
[156] *See* below XI.4-5.
[157] *See* below XI.3.

3. The Chapeau of Article 47(2)

Like Article 45(c)[158] and 46(b),[159] the chapeau of Article 47(2) starts with the phrase "without prejudice to Article 48."[160] The phrase ensures that if the goods are undeliverable under Article 47(1)(a), the carrier has the option either (i) immediately to invoke Article 48 or (ii) first to apply the provisions of Article 47(2) and, if still needed, thereafter to invoke Article 48.

For Article 47(2) to apply, the transport document or electronic transport record must expressly state that the goods may be delivered without the surrender of the document or record.[161] Looking merely at the wording of the condition, it seems to conflict with the principles laid down in Article 47(1). As discussed above,[162] presentation and surrender of the document to obtain delivery are essential elements of the "legitimation" function, which in itself is the basis of the title function of the document. The purpose of the condition, therefore, cannot be the creation of a type of transport document without a legitimation function. That would undermine the entire purpose of Article 47.

In the context of Article 47, the chapeau's condition operates as a warning. Article 47(2) is intended to provide a solution for the problems that arise if a transport document is unavailable when it should perform its legitimation function. In other words, Article 47(2) is a safety valve that operates only when Article 47(1) is unworkable.

Following the application of Article 47(2), a transport document may remain in circulation after a delivery of the goods without the surrender of a transport document. The cesser provision of Article 47(1)(c) does not apply but the holder is nevertheless no longer entitled to delivery of the goods. To further protect the holder of that transport document, UNCITRAL — as an essential part of the compromise referred to above — added the express statement condition for the application of Article 47(2) and included it in the chapeau. Consequently, the condition must be taken as a sort of caution against the possible result of Article 47(2). Any holder could see from the document itself the risks that it might run when accepting the transport document if it fails to protect its interests.[163]

---

[158] *See* above VI.3.
[159] *See* above VII.2.
[160] *See* also above notes 69-61 and accompanying text.
[161] "Expressly" means, amongst others, that an incorporation by reference to this statement, for instance, when it is included in a charterparty, is insufficient for Article 47(2) to apply. *See* also above note 151; 2008 Commission Report, paras 160-161,165.
[162] *See* above VIII.
[163] Knowing the risks, the holder can protect its interests in several ways. *See, e.g.,* below at note 168 and accompanying text.

In conclusion, Article 47(2) may apply as an alternative to Article 48, but only if the transport document or electronic transport record includes wording to the effect that the goods may be delivered without surrender of the document or record. [164]

4. Delivery on Instruction of the Shipper or Documentary Shipper

Subsections (a), (b), and (c) of Article 47(2) address deliveries on the shipper's or documentary shipper's instructions. When the goods are undeliverable under Article 47(1), the carrier may seek delivery instructions from the shipper or the documentary shipper. When the carrier delivers the goods according to those instructions, it is discharged from its delivery obligation under the contract of carriage.

Article 47(2)(a)-(b) follows the same principle for negotiable documents and records as Article 45(c)-(d) does in the context of non-negotiable documents and records.[165] Indeed, the wording of the respective subsections is similar. The language is adjusted only to the extent necessary to apply to a negotiable document or record. Thus our analysis of Article 45(c)-(d)[166] applies, *mutatis mutandis*, to Article 47(2)(a)-(b).

Carriers commonly seek delivery instructions from the shipper. It is the long-standing practice in many commodity trades in which often no transport document is available when the goods arrive at their destination. Many charterparties require the carrier to apply to the charterer for delivery instructions when no transport document is available and to deliver the goods, without surrender of the transport document, to the person designated by the charterer.[167] In some trades, the ship customarily carries on board an original transport document, which the captain hands over at the destination to the person designated by the shipper/charterer. That custom is essentially a delivery of the goods on the instruction of the shipper/charterer, and the transport document does not properly serve any legitimation function.

While the practice of seeking delivery instructions from a shipper/charterer is far from new, the legal consequence under the Rotterdam Rules when a carrier follows those instructions represents an important innovation. The carrier's discharge from its delivery

---

[164] The following clause may serve as an example that fully complies with the intention of Article 47 as a whole:
"One original transport document must be surrendered, duly endorsed, in exchange of the goods. When no original is presented at the place of destination, the carrier has the option to invoke Article 47(2) of the Rotterdam Rules with the result that the goods may be delivered without surrender of this transport document."
[165] *See* above VI.3.
[166] *See* above VI.3.
[167] *See* also below note 180 and accompanying text.

obligation, regardless of whether the transport document has been surrendered, is a novelty.

The carrier's potential discharge requires holders of transport documents to be alert to the possible arrival date of the goods. In their trade financing arrangements, banks should require their clients to list them as notify parties on the transport documents. When a holder or a prospective holder of a transport document is in doubt whether a cargo may already have been delivered, it should make contact with the carrier, preferably immediately prior to becoming a holder, and request advice on the whereabouts of the cargo. A bank that is not already a notify party should contact the carrier to become one. In this age of electronic communication, making contact is relatively easy, particularly since Article 36 requires the transport document to contain the carrier's name and address. Having due regard to the essential legitimation function of the transport document, the requirement of alertness relating to the arrival date of the goods should not overburden a holder. On the contrary, the requirement is fully in line with the traditional system.[168] Indeed, holders must be vigilant to avoid the risks of letter of indemnity practice even without Article 47(2).

The discharge of the carrier's delivery obligation under Article 47(2)(b) is subject to Article 47(2)(e).[169] Because the carrier runs the risk under subsection (e) that it might be liable in damages to a bona fide holder when it delivers the goods without the surrender of the transport document, subsection (c) provides for a statutory indemnity by the shipper to the carrier against the risk. Furthermore, in some circumstances it may be reasonable for the shipper, in addition to the indemnification, to provide security to the carrier.[170] As an additional benefit, the statutory indemnity and possible security obligation may deter shippers from giving incorrect or frivolous instructions to a carrier.

In most cases, subsection (b) and (c), taken together, should supersede the current practice of issuing letters of indemnity or other contractual indemnities.

5. The Status of Persons Who Become Holders after Delivery

The question arises whether, after the delivery of the goods under Article 47(2)(a) and (b), a transport document that has not been surrendered still has any value. We must consider two different cases.

(1) Genuine Delay

The first case involves a genuine delay in transferring of the transport document, with the

---

[168] *See* above VIII.
[169] *See* above XI.5(2).
[170] *See* second sentence of Article 47(2)(c).

result that the goods themselves move more quickly than the transport document.[171] Then it may happen that a person buying the goods before they are delivered becomes the holder of the transport document only after a delivery without surrender of the transport document. In other words, the transport document is still going through the chain of sellers and buyers after delivery has already taken place. In that case, the transport document, after delivery of the goods, no longer incorporates the right to obtain delivery, but may still incorporate other rights. Article 47(2)(d) does not specify those other rights because they will depend on the terms of the transport document and other circumstances. For example, if the goods arrive in damaged condition, then the holder may still assert a claim for damages unless the amount of the damages was already deducted from the purchase price as between buyer and seller in the chain of sales. If the purchase price was already adjusted, then the claim for damages will belong to the party that paid the full purchase price to its seller but received the discounted purchase price from its buyer.

The effect of subsection (d) is not restricted to buyers after delivery has taken place.

Its wording is more general. It refers to rights under the transport document that still may exist for persons that become the holder after delivery but "pursuant to contractual or other arrangements made before such delivery." Those "contractual or other arrangements" do not necessarily refer only to sales, but may, for instance, include any arrangement between banks relating to a documentary credit process.[172]

Because there is no form requirement, the "contractual or other arrangements" may be verbal.[173] This may be concluded from the fact that Article 3 (dealing with form requirements) does not mention Article 47(2).

(2) Lack of Knowledge.

In the second case, a person becomes holder of a transport document after delivery and "did not have and could not reasonably have had knowledge of such delivery at the time that it became a holder."[174] Then, notwithstanding that the carrier would otherwise have been discharged of its delivery obligation under subsections (b) or (d), the holder "acquires the rights incorporated in the negotiable transport document." Again, the subsection does not specify which rights are incorporated, but in view of the intention of this provision, those rights must include the right to obtain delivery of the goods from the carrier. Thus subsec-

---

[171] *See* Article 47(2)(d). This provision is inspired by UK COGSA 1992, Article 2(2)(a); *see* The Law Commission, *Rights of suit in respect of carriage of goods by sea*, LAW COM. No. 196, London: HMSO, paras 2.42-2.44.
[172] *See*, specifically, 17th Session Report para. 88.
[173] *See* 2008 Commission Report para. 163.
[174] Article 47(2)(e).

tion (e) protects the bona fide holder. That person is entitled to rely on the certainty that the system is designed to provide.

Subsection (e) includes a presumption that the holder at the time that it became a holder had or could reasonably have had knowledge of the delivery of the goods when the transport document includes the expected time of arrival of the goods, or indicates how to obtain information as to whether the goods have been delivered.[175] For the carrier, the presumption should be an inducement to state the relevant cargo information data on the transport document.[176] UNCITRAL expected both carriers and cargo interests to optimally use the modern means of communication available.[177]

6. The Standard for the Shipper's "Reasonable Effort"

In Draft Convention WP.101 and earlier texts, the shipper had an obligation to provide the carrier with adequate delivery instructions when the carrier requested them under the provisions that ultimately became Articles 45(c), 46(b), or 47(2)(a).[178] In the final text of the Convention, those articles no longer impose an obligation on the shipper.[179] UNCITRAL made the change because as a practical matter the shipper may not be in a position to provide adequate delivery instructions to the carrier.[180]

In several commodity trades in which transport documents are not customarily available at the place of destination when the goods arrive, the charterer/shipper usually keeps track of the sales of the goods during carriage. It is thus perfectly aware of the identity of the final buyer. In those trades, all parties involved in the transactions (including the financing banks) are or should be aware of the typical practice of delivering the goods without the surrender of the transport document. In that context, the shipper may safely give the carrier the requested instructions to deliver the goods to the final buyer. In most cases, the trans-

---

[175] The presumption assumes that the prospective holder is alert when it accepts the transport document. Because UNCITRAL introduced the cautionary statement that the goods may be delivered without presentation of the transport document only at the very last stage of discussion, the effect of the statement on the provision of subsection (e) was not discussed any further.

[176] It might be advisable that carriers not only include its name, address and telephone number in the transport document, but also print wording therein along the following line:

"For information on delivery, apply to customer.service@carrier.com or to Carrier's agent at the place of destination. For contact details, see www.carrier.com."

[177] See also Article 28.

[178] See, e.g., Draft Convention WP.101 Articles 47(c), 48(b), 50(d).

[179] This was one of the essential practical corrections that were made at the final stage of discussions. See above notes 154-157 and accompanying text.

[180] See also Article 55(1). In view of the intentions of, on the one hand, Articles 45(c), 46(b), and 47(2)(a), and, on the other, Article 55(1), it may be concluded that, when the controlling party or the shipper is in a position to provide adequate delivery instructions, it must do so.

port document ultimately arrives and is surrendered to the carrier. In those trades, Article 47(2) will work well.

Sometimes, the shipper may have information about the identity of the final buyer (or its financing bank), or may be in a position to discover the identity relatively easily. In those cases it also makes sense for the carrier to seek instructions from the shipper because the shipper should be able to assist the carrier in locating the holder, thereby promoting a proper delivery.

In some cases, however, the shipper may have no idea who is the holder or the final buyer of the goods. For example, if the shipper sells the goods and transfers the transport document upon payment, but then further sales take place, the shipper may be unable to trace the ultimate buyer or the holder. In that context, the shipper is not able to give the carrier adequate delivery instructions.[181]

Because the shipper's ability to provide instructions varies widely depending on the context, a number of questions arise. What is the proper standard for the shipper to cooperate with the carrier in locating the controlling party,[182] the consignee,[183] or the holder?[184] To what extent should the shipper itself attempt to provide the carrier with adequate delivery instructions?

For a proper answer to these questions, we may begin with the chapter on the shipper's general obligations.[185] Article 28 establishes the obligation of the shipper and the carrier to cooperate in providing information and instructions to each other for the proper handling and carriage of the goods. Under that article, the parties must conform to a fairly undemanding standard. The information must be in the possession of the other party and that party must be reasonably able to provide the necessary instructions. Should the same standard be applied in relation to the level of cooperation between the parties on the matter of delivery?

In our view, the standard for the level of cooperation should be set somewhat higher for delivery matters. The carrier has an obligation to deliver the goods and the consignee, because of the transport document's "legitimation" function, has a systematic duty to make

---

[181] It must be noted that under the Article 45(c) and (d), 46(b) and (c), and 47(2)(a) and (b), the carrier has no obligation to comply with the instructions from a shipper. If a carrier knows or reasonably ought to know that the shipper's instructions are wrong or frivolously given, its general duty of bona fide implementation of contractual obligations would prevail that it carries out such instructions. This general duty is referred to in Article 2 as "the observance of good faith in international trade."
[182] *See* Article 45(c); above notes 52-55 and accompanying text.
[183] *See* Article 46(b); above VII.2.
[184] *See* Article 47(2)(a); above notes 165-167 and accompanying text.
[185] *See* Articles 27-29.

itself known to the carrier.[186] When the consignee cannot be located, the carrier must exercise "reasonable effort" to locate that person.

The same standard of "reasonable effort" should apply to the shipper. The deliverability of the goods is, generally, the responsibility of the cargo side.[187] When a consignee or holder fails to comply with its duty to make itself known to the carrier, it is logical to expect the original contracting party on the cargo side, the shipper, to exercise reasonable efforts to cooperate with the carrier in locating the consignee or holder. Also conforming to the same standard of reasonable efforts, the shipper should attempt to provide the carrier with adequate delivery instructions. And when it is in a position to provide such instructions, it must do so.[188]

7. The Effectiveness of Article 47(2)

The practical effectiveness of Article 47(2) is likely to vary depending on the context. If the transport document includes the express statement that the goods may be delivered without surrender, our discussion above[189] explains how Article 47(2) should work well when the transaction has been structured in a way that reduces or ignores the transport document's legitimation function. In other cases, the carrier's and the shipper's reasonable efforts under Article 47(2) may identify the holder or otherwise enable the carrier to receive adequate delivery instructions, with the result that a proper delivery is possible. When despite the carrier's and the shipper's reasonable efforts, however, proper delivery of the goods cannot be arranged, the carrier has no option but to invoke Article 48.[190]

---

[186] *See* above note 93 and accompanying text.
[187] *See* above III.(ii) and also Article 45(b), above VI.2, that obliges the controlling party to provide to the carrier the name and address of the consignee. Under Article 46, above VII.2, this name and address is assumed to be stated on the document. But this obligation to provide the consignee's name and address in itself does not guarantee that the consignee can be located and/or that delivery can take place.
[188] Our analysis of the proper standard for the shipper's "reasonable effort" is included in our discussion of Article 47(2) because that is the context in which the issue most commonly arises in practice. But the analysis applies equally to cases under Articles 45 and 46. *See* also above note 180.
[189] *See* above XI.4 and 5.
[190] *See* above V; notes 158-160 and accompanying text.

XII. Some personal Conclusions and Recommendations

1. First Conclusion: The Delivery Rules Are Complex and Difficult to Understand

The assertion that the delivery rules of the Rotterdam Rules are complex and difficult to understand is right. This is caused by a combination of the following reasons:
(i) the rules had to make distinction between the type of transport document issued, while the actual situation of documentation in maritime transport is complex and difficult to understand, even for the practitioners;
(ii) some actual documentary practices have turned into malpractices, particularly the custom of delivery without production of the bill of lading;
(iii) the starting point of the Convention was trying to provide certainty to existing practices and not trying to change these practices.

2. Second Conclusion: Though, They Enhance Legal Certainty

The Articles 43 - 48[191] follow as close as possible the nature of the contract of carriage[192] as well as the roots of the bill of lading system (i.e. legitimation function of the document)[193] and, by doing so, aim to enhance legal certainty for the practitioners.

3. Third Conclusion: Third Party Holder Must Be Active When the Goods Arrive at Destination

Doing nothing when the goods arrive at destination, if ever, is no reasonable option anymore for a third party holder of a negotiable transport document or record.
It has been set out that a holder has no legal duty to take delivery of the goods at destination, but has a systematical duty to take care that a carrier may dispose of the goods.[194] The fact that, instead, under Article 47(2), provided the document states the caution mentioned in the chapeau of this provision, a shipper may fulfil that role is indicated in this paper as an

---

[191] *See* above IV, VI, VII, IX-XI.
[192] *See* above III.
[193] *See* above VIII.
[194] *See* above note 93 and accompanying text.

incentive for the holder to take action.[195]

It has to be realised however that there is another incentive that may even be stronger. If the holder doesn't do anything when the goods have arrived at destination, i.e. does not produce the bill of lading, the goods are undeliverable and Article 48 applies.[196] Under Article 48 the carrier has no responsibility under the contract of carriage anymore, with the consequence that also its obligation to deliver the goods to the consignee[197] has gone. In other words, when under Article 48 a carrier disposes of the goods "as circumstances reasonably require", it cannot be sued for misdelivery.[198] This may lead to the following conclusion:

4. Fourth Conclusion: When No Bill of Lading Can Be Presented, the Cargo Side Might Give Article 47(2) Preference over Article 48

The (in UNCITRAL contentious) Article 47(2), though it provides for the authority of another person than the holder to instruct the carrier on delivery, may provide more legal certainty for bill of lading holders than the alternative (in UNCITRAL non-contentious) Article 48. Both articles apply to the situation that a bill of lading holder does not present the bill of lading and, consequently, the goods are undeliverable.

Under Article 48 a bill of lading holder, after the carrier has disposed of the goods by, for example, delivering them against a letter of indemnity, has no claim on the carrier for misdelivery. He may only have a claim 'for failure to take steps that would have been reasonable in the circumstances to preserve the goods and the carrier knew or ought to have known that the loss or damage to the goods would result from its failure to take such steps.'[199]

Under Article 47(2), specifically written for the delivery against a letter of indemnity situation,[200] a bill of lading holder has no claim for misdelivery either (unless Article 47(2)(e) applies), but a carrier is assumed to first exercise reasonable efforts to locate this holder and to ask for delivery instructions. Furthermore, when carrier has delivered the goods under Article 47(2)(a) a holder to whom a 'late' bill of lading is transferred may, nevertheless, acquire rights[201] and the innocent holder that did not know and could not either that deliv-

---

[195] *See* above III.(iii), VI.4 and notes 165-166 and accompanying text.
[196] *See* Article 48(1)(c); above notes 117-123 and accompanying text.
[197] *See* Articles 11, 47.1(a); above IX.2.
[198] For English law cases in which the carrier delivered the goods without production of the bill of lading and, nevertheless, the holder had no claim on the carrier anymore, *see* '*The Delfini*' [1990] 1 Lloyd's Rep. 252; '*The Future Express*' [1992] 2 Lloyd's Rep. 79, [1993] 2 Lloyd's Rep. 542 (C.A.).
[199] *See* Article 48(5); above notes 139-144 and accompanying text.
[200] *See* above XI.1 and 2.
[201] *See* Article 47(2)(d); above XI.5(1).

ery had taken place, is protected.[202]

5. Recommendations for Carriers

A carrier, generally, can do much in making the Articles 45 - 47 better understandable for its users when they follow the recommendations below.

(a) Make always a clear statement in the (heading of the) transport document whether it is negotiable or not. This draws the line between the application of (i) Article 47 and (ii) any of the Articles 45 or 46.

(b) Make always a clear statement in the transport document whether it has to be surrendered for obtaining delivery of the goods or not. This draws the line between the application of the Articles 45 and 46. In this regard, it may be noted that, amongst the main trading countries, US is the only jurisdiction where it is not needed that a straight bill of lading is surrendered in order to obtain delivery of the goods. Once the US has ratified the Rotterdam Rules, there is hardly any specific practical need anymore to be vague on the requirement of surrender of transport documents.

(c) In case of a negotiable transport document, state clearly the option to follow the procedures of Article 47(2);[203] Even with this option, which may create advantages for all parties, the alternative of applying Article 48 remains.[204]

(d) State always clearly the carrier's name and contact details in the transport document and provide to prospective holders access to cargo information data, including data on delivery; The first part is in line with the obligation under Article 36(2)(b) and the second part triggers the presumption in Article 47(2)(e).[205] The whole recommendation (d) may foster smooth relations between carriers and consignees generally.

(e) In the long run, agree with customers on e-commerce systems based on a transfer of the right of control, thereby eliminating to a large extent the current difficulties with documentary processes.[206] E-commerce systems on the basis of electronic documents are no genuine solution for most documentary problems, because these are equally applicable to paper document as to their electronic equivalents.

---

[202] *See* Article 47(2)(e); above XI.5(2).
[203] For an example clause, *see* note 164.
[204] *See* above V and notes 158-160 and accompanying text.
[205] *See* above notes 175-177 and accompanying text.
[206] *See* Michael F. Sturley, *et al*. cited above at note 1, Ch III; Gertjan van der Ziel, *Delivery of the goods, rights of the controlling party and transfer of rights*, 14 JIML 606-607 (2008); Gertjan van der Ziel, *Chapter 10 of the Rotterdam Rules:Control of Goods in Transit*, 44Texas Int'l LJ 383-386 (2009-3).

6. Recommendations for Banks

Banks, generally, may reduce their risks under trade finance operations when they follow the recommendations below.

(a) Require always to be named as notify party in the transport document that the bank holds as security, or otherwise be vigilant on the date of delivery of the goods.[207] After a carrier has lost custody of the goods, the negotiable document may, at best, still represent a claim on the carrier,[208] but any proprietary rights in the goods to be exercised against the carrier may have been lost by the holder under the law otherwise applicable to the right.

(b) Don't agree to accept stale negotiable documents. Under circumstances, such documents may even not represent a claim against the carrier anymore.[209]

(c) Don't co-sign marine letter of indemnities when the bank isn't an advising bank itself (or without a counter indemnity from the advising bank). In such case the indemnifying bank would take over the credit risk from the advising bank without possibly knowing the eventual debtor's solvency or payment morale. Does a possible fee outweigh this risk?

---

[207] *See* above note 168 and accompanying text.
[208] Not always, *see* above note 198.
[209] *See* "The Future Express", cited in above note 198.

Part I, Chapter 4

Rotterdam Rules and Industries

11

The Rotterdam Rules: The Carriers' Perspective

Tsuyoshi Hayasaka

I Introduction

Thank you very much for giving me the opportunity to talk in front all of you. Although I'm privileged to discuss from the carriers' perspective, I'm not in the position to represent the whole industry. Therefore, what I am about to say is exclusively my own opinion.

II General Remarks

Let me start with something general. I'd like to make an observation on the Rotterdam Rules from my long experience in taking charge of the legal affairs of shipping companies.

1. The Current Legal Schemes Are Considerably Lagging Behind the Actual Business Practice

The legal regulations that are based on the current international convention regulate only the bills of lading (B/L), although Japanese legislation is somewhat different. Moreover, the regulations only cover part of the issues that might happen during the period from "tackle to tackle." Therefore, those regulations are far from comprehensive and do not reflect the actual business practice of shipping companies at all. As a result, even experienced employees of shipping companies have so much trouble explaining about the mechanism of the legal regulations to their less experienced colleagues. Looking at this status quo, I believe that something must be done.

Because of such situations concerning legal regulations as above, we have seen more and more diversities in the items that have to be covered on the back side of a B/L. These diversities have become particularly noticeable since the advent of containerization. When making terms on the back side of a B/L form, a shipping company often tries to draw a draft which covers important matters as much as possible; however, due to the limitations in space and letter size, they unfortunately have to give up covering all those items on the back side.

There is another problem although it might be a peculiar phenomenon in Japan , the law of which covers a contract of carriage under waybills as well while the convention exclusively regulates bills of lading. A Japanese shipping company that is not accustomed in the difference between a bill of lading and a waybill , on subcontracting a leg of the transport covered by its B/L to a subcontracor , unguardedly agreed with the subcontractor about issuing a waybill , then when cargo's total loss had occurred during the subcontracted leg , it turned out that the waybill included an peculiar exemption clause. Eventually, while the Japanese shipping company was held responsible for all the loss of the cargo, it could not recover the damages from the responsible subcontractor. That was no laughing matter.

2. Concerns about the possible Predominance of Regionalism

Recently, the creation of regional legal regulations for the international carriage of goods has took on a reality in the United States and Europe. Unless proper measures are taken, different legal regimes might appear in each region, making the total legal schemes more and more complicated. In addition, given the trend of the legal discussions so far, I don't believe that these regional legal regulations will be more tolerant to shipping companies than the Rotterdam Rules. Shipping companies would be in a catch-22 situation, so to speak. (In fact, the differences in how they perceive this situation reflect the differences in attitude towards how they evaluate the Rotterdam Rules.) Therefore, although The Rotterdam Rules have some concerns which I refer to later and it would inevitable to see the increased number of several legal dispute for a while if they come into force. Personally, I hope that Rotterdam Rules will take effect.

III. Concerns from the Carriers' Perspective and What Have To Be Done

Here are some of my thoughts on the Rotterdam Rules. Please allow me not to touch upon all concerns, given the length of the treaty.

1. Abolition of Nautical Fault Defense and Extension of Seaworthiness Obligation

The abolition of the exemption of the fault of navigation and the extension of the due diligence to keep the ship seaworthy during the entire navigation will change the conventional system dramatically, making a significant impact. In particular, the cases such as where a ship loses its seaworthiness due to exonerated causes would be a difficult one in judging the due diligence. Therefore, taking responsibility for delay, as stipulated in Article 21, might become difficult.

2. Documentation

The Rotterdam Rules include a total of five types of contracts for the transport document and the electronic transport record as well as other matters, such as volume contract and the "right of control." Etc. These include many concepts that ordinary employees of a shipping company may have never heard of before. Apart from this, the whole mechanism is complicated. Explanation on how the qualification of the contract particulars work is very detailed. Therefore, carriers need to rebuild a new procedure to respond to these complex systems. They also need to spend more resources for their employees' education.

a) It is true that many of these seemingly new concepts are either those already known or those similar to the concepts already known in academic world. However, in the real business world, people are usually even unaware of the difference between a "shipper" and a "documentary shipper." Under the new system, they will probably be perplexed from the very beginning such as about how to ensure "accept to be named," which is a requirement for a documentary shipper. The new procedure also needs to be improved in terms of the management of transport documents and electronic transport records as well as on the management of the transfer of the right of control.

b) A new procedure needs to be rebuilt for the sake of the qualifications stipulated in Article 40. The procedure should also be easy to understand for those actually working on the shipping paperwork.

c) In many cases, they need to identify the party even in the case of negotiable documents, which did not usually need to be identified before. Therefore, they need to establish a secure way of identification.

d) The right of control is supposed to be valid until the completion of delivery. Therefore, they might need to consider using the freedom of contract stipulated in Article 56 to avoid possible trouble at the time of delivery.

e) They also have to be careful about "prepaid" freight. Even when freights have not yet been collected, "prepaid" bills of lading or waybills are often issued on credit base. However, because of Article 42, it becomes impossible for carriers to claim uncollected freights on account of "listed on a waybill." The end of this Article say, "This Article does not apply if the holder or the consignee is also the shipper." This sentence may not sound so special, but from my personal experience, I believe it would be helpful. I have relevant experience as below. Right after prepaid bills of lading were issued on credit base for a Pure Car Carrier, even though the freights on all the cargoes have not yet been collected, the "documentary shipper" on the bill of lading went bankrupt, causing a huge amount of uncollected freights. I checked the sales contract and found it was a FOB contract. So I exercised a lien on all the cargos at the area of unloading, but it took some time and trouble. I remember thinking, "If there was an explicit provision about this kind of situation, that'd be of great help."

f) Carriers may have to compete how quickly they can establish the kind of system of negotiable electronic transport records that can meet the conditions of Article 9(1). To adopt such a system, approval from the P & I Insurance is needed.

3. Dangerous Goods

The risk of dealing with dangerous goods is huge for shipping companies. Those items can pose a serious threat to them. Article 15 and 32 include the new concept of "reasonably appearing likely to become dangerous." This, conversely, can cause the argument, "What goods do not reasonably appear likely to become dangerous?" Therefore, my concern is that these new articles might slightly change the conventional way of thinking about dangerous goods. I am especially concerned about the possible influence of the countries that take the responsibility of the owner of dangerous goods as absolute liability.

What's more, whether something "reasonably appears likely to become dangerous" or not is likely to depend on interpretation. Article 15 stipulates that the rights to "decline to receive, or to load, ...unloading, destroying, or rendering harmless" belong to a performing party. I am afraid that the conflict of opinions is not uncommon between a carrier and a performing party, or, rather, a ship owner over dangerous goods, and the Rules might encourage such conflict.

4. Jurisdiction

In my time, I handled a total of more than 250 cases of lawsuits and arbitrations in various countries, where exclusive jurisdiction agreement was often approved. The Rotterdam

Rules do not, in principle, approve exclusive jurisdiction agreement. For cargo owners to have broad options, as stipulated in Article 66, carrier might have to be exposed to the law suits that are less dependable and/or more time-consuming than they used to. As a result, I am afraid that carrier might be compelled to agree to compromise.

5. Volume Contract

This is one of the most debatable subjects. I would like to start with my experience in service contract in the United States.

Checking the contract draft of the service contract took me more trouble than checking the charter party. That was because a shippers, who had no experience in shipping came out of nowhere and presented their particular drafts of service contract. The drafts were often based on contracts usually used by retailers or manufacturers only with some minor changes. As a result, some stipulations that were not appropriate for shipping were incorporated, such as those of sales contract and patent. In addition, since shippers usually have more bargaining power than carriers, they often claimed liability limitation to be removed and that consequential damages be included among the objects of indemnity liability. The draft even included something equivalent to product liability. I have experienced so many things that people usually don't come across in the business practice of maritime law. The contract is naturally less advantageous to carriers than a contract created under the Hague-Visby Rules, so conventional P&I insurances cannot cover all the risks. Therefore, you need to arrange additional insurances every time you conclude a contract.

Volume contract is different from service contract. However, since I believe that shipping companies have to agree to volume contract for the time being because of the difference in bargaining power, I am afraid that the same things that happened to service contract might happen. Anyway, the companies will face severe open competition. I think that supply and demand will be a decisive factor after all.

Many arguments over volume contract focus on the possibility of carriers abusing volume contract. For example, one argument, assuming that the carriers will recover the exemption of the fault of navigation that they have lost, claims that "Lower freight rate could be negotiated in exchange for the assumption by the carrier of lower level of risk." However, I think that in reality things would be more different from this argument, given the reality of supply and demand. In the first place, the merits of the contractual conditions of the exemption of navigational faults are difficult to assess in advance. For example, if a person in charge of the contract report to his or her company, "I was able to lower the freight charge because I decided on the term that exempts navigational faults," and is asked as, "Would that be really worth it?" The person would have a hard time answering the question.

In addition, I am concerned over one thing about the effect of volume contract against the third party. I think that in service contract, there is an example of the method where a consignee is listed as the contractor of the service contract; that is, a shipper, in the first place, so that many consignees can enjoy the benefit of the service contract.

6. Maritime Performing Party

Maritime performing party is a rather difficult issue for the shipping-related industries. A maritime performing party assumes the same duties and responsibilities as the carrier as stipulated in Article 19. This means that those who used to assume responsibilities only in torts and as a result are rarely directly claimed, such as charterers, port operators, and slot providers etc., will be directly claimed as under the mandatory regulations under the Rotterdam Rules. That means they will be directly claimed as under the contract and will be liable as under the contract on presumed fault basis, not under torts. Therefore, it will be inevitable to review conventional contracts and agreements that do not assume such situations, including terminal contracts and space charter agreements. What's more, since there is no commercial relationship between a cargo owner and a maritime performing party, claim negotiations will be very businesslike.

Moreover, a maritime performing party is not necessarily a carrier's direct subcontractor. For example, a maritime performing party of NVOC ,such as the owner of a vessel, its charterer and terminal facilities can all be maritime performing parties of NVOC. Therefore, this cumulative structure of maritime performing companies needs to establish a mutual communication system to prevent the double or triple request of the same claim.

Some people might say that by introducing volume contract, a shipping company can enjoy several benefits, and that NVOC, which issues bills of lading to individual cargo owners, may assume responsibility as a carrier according to the general principles of the Rotterdam Rules. However, a shipping company conventionally is directly claimed by reason of the bills of lading issued by NVOC. In the future, it will become much easier for cargo owners to make a direct claim against shipping companies that become maritime performing parties of NVOC.

Because of Article 20, a maritime performing party and a carrier assume joint and several liabilities. Therefore, they are more likely to become defendants side by side compared to before.

In case of volume contract, shipping companies need to arrange the take-over of lawsuits and indemnity properly. Otherwise, they might face the same risk and trouble they would have faced when they make direct contract with individual cargo owners.

IV. Benefits from the Carriers' Perspective

So far, I've only discussed concerns, which is not fair. Therefore, I'd like to talk about benefits as well.

1. The Rules Specifies the Shippers' Duties

These duties have conventionally been covered by applicable laws or by the adhesive terms and conditions of bills of lading. The Rotterdam Rules specify these duties, which I think deserves appreciation.

2. Article 12(2) (b)

It is not uncommon that after a carrier's cargo delivery to the authorities according to the system of "custom delivery", the authorities deliver the cargo without a bill of lading and, eventually, the carrier is taken to court at the place of loading. Therefore, I appreciate Item 2 (b) of Article 12 for its stipulation. However, it is possible that a court at the place of loading may take an extremely severe stance against a carrier concerning the verification of the system at the place of unloading and this stipulation may fail to be as effective as it is supposed to be.

3. The Rules Specifies the Measure to Be Taken for the Undeliverable Goods

The problem of unclaimed cargos occurs fairly often. I have seen even cases where cargoes were taken to the auction. Examples include frozen cargos that were left unclaimed due to the bankruptcy of the cargo owners, containers that were left with industrial waste and medical waste in them, and unclaimed used cars at the places of unloading.

4. Article 24 Clarifies the Concept of Deviation

12

The Rotterdam Rules: The Cargo Interests' Perspective

Ohki Hirata

I. Introduction

The Rotterdam Rules (hereinafter simply called "the Rules") set forth provisions related to the relationship of rights and obligations in a contract of carriage of goods by sea between carriers and cargo owners, which were set forth in the Act on International Carriage of Goods by Sea. The Rules further include provisions concerning the liabilities of a carrier during multimodal transportation on land and sea as well as the liabilities of a cargo owner for his receipt of goods. This paper focuses on a comparison between the Act on International Carriage of Goods by Sea derived from the Hague-Visby Rules to the Rules in relation to a cargo owner's claim for damages against a contracting carrier for any damage to the cargo arising during maritime transportation (the so-called Cargo Claim). This paper further examines how the Rules function in maritime transportation by examining the application of the Rules to hypothetical cases.

II. Cargo Claim

With respect to the loss or damage to the cargo that occurs during its maritime transportation, a cargo owner (an insurer of the cargo) makes a claim for damages against a carrier or his subcontracting carrier based on breach of the contract or in tort. Although the Rules cover not only the period of maritime transportation but also the period of land transportation, the paper will discuss only the loss or damage to the cargo during its maritime transportation.

Generally, problems that arise in matters of Cargo Claim include the following.[1]

1. International Jurisdiction

First is the problem of international jurisdiction. A premise of the present paper is that a Japanese court has jurisdiction. Chapter 14 and Chapter 15 of the Rules have provisions concerning jurisdiction and arbitration. However, Article 91 of the Rules sets forth that Chapter 14 and Chapter 15 of the Rules have binding power only over member countries of the Rules who have declared to be bound by them. Hence, judgments concerning the existence or non-existence of jurisdiction vary according to the existence or non-existence of the declaration set forth in Article 91 of the Rules.

2. Title to Sue

Second is the problem of under whose name a claim for damages may be made. This problem concerns "a title to sue" in laws in the United Kingdom and "a right for suit" in preparatory work of enactment of the Rules. For instance, the Carriage of Goods by Sea Act of 1992 (COGSA 1992) in the United Kingdom admits the title to sue is held by a lawful holder of a bill of lading. As there is no provision for the title to sue in the Rules, the title to sue should be judged by a governing law of contracts for the carriage of goods or by a governing law of tort.

3. Whom to Claim

A third problem concerns against to whom and by what ground a claim for damages may be made.

(1) A claim for Damages against a Contracting Carrier
This is a claim for damages against a carrier who is a party to a contract of carriage of

---

[1] To discuss the facts to prove as cause of claim, we first need to determine a governing law or a treaty that is applied to a claim. The governing law for delay interest is governed by a governing law for the main claim. When a Japanese law is designated as the governing law for a main claim, with respect to a claim for damages based on breach of the contract of carriage of goods, a claimant will claim for delay interest of a commercial statutory interest of six (6) percent per annum. On the other hand, in the case of claim for damages based on tort, a claimant will claim for delay interest of five (5) percent per annum based on the Civil Code of Japan. With respect to title to sue, when an insurer of the cargo has paid insurance money, there is a problem regarding whether the insurer obtains the title to sue in connection with the insurance subrogation.

goods by reason of his breach of contract. The Act on International Carriage of Goods by Sea sets forth a carrier's liabilities for breach of contract (and the liabilities for tort).

(2) *A Claim for Damages against a Shipowner or a Bareboat Charterer*

This is a claim for damages by reason of tort against a shipowner or a bareboat charterer who actually carries goods.

(3) *Claims for Damages against Others Who Were Engaged in the Transportation*

These are claims for damages by reason of tort against Non-Vessel Operating Common Carriers (NVOCC), such as terminal operators, stevedores, time charterers, and subcontracting carriers.

With respect to a claim or claims as stated in (b) or (c) above, the Rules newly established the concept of "Maritime Performing Party" in an attempt to solve the problems related to these claims, which is one of the characteristics of the Rules. In reality, multiple parties are engaged in single transportation, and therefore, claims for damages against those who are not a carrier are made. Hence, from the point of fairness it is desirable to establish the same relationship of rights and obligations between a cargo owner and such parties as that between a cargo owner and a carrier in the attempt to equitably solve the problems related to claims for damages.

4. Carrier's Liabilities

Although the Act on International Carriage of Goods by Sea is a domestic law of Japan derived from the Hague-Visby Rules, the Act is not a direct translation of the latter. The system of liabilities of a carrier in the Act has specific characteristics, such as the principle of negligence liability of a carrier, exemption from liability of a carrier with regard to error in navigation or management (exemption from liability of a carrier for damage to a cargo caused by a captain or a crew's negligence in navigating and managing their ship), exemption from liability for a fire (unless caused by the actual fault or privity of the carrier) and the obligation to make a ship seaworthy before and the beginning of the voyage.

It is significant that although the negligence liability of a carrier is maintained, the Rules do not provide an exemption from error in navigation or management . With respect to the exemption from liability for a fire set forth in the Rules, since a carrier is liable when his employee commits negligence, its meaning differs from exemption from liability for a fire that is set forth in the Act on International Carriage of Goods by Sea. Furthermore, the obligation for making a ship seaworthy differs from the provision in the Act on International

Carriage of Goods by Sea in that the Rules sets out an the obligation to keep such seaworthiness not only at the beginning of the voyage but also during voyage (a continuous obligation). Thus, important changes were added to the Rules regarding the liabilities and obligation of a carrier.

It is necessary to take a cargo owner's standpoint and examine the carrier's liabilities concerning the so-called Cargo Claim the following points: What principles does the Rules have for this matter? How do the Rules differ from the Act on International Carriage of Goods by Sea? Furthermore, for problems not covered by the Rules, the laws of a country agreed in a contract of carriage of goods is applied as the governing law. In these cases, what kind of problems will the governing law be applied?

III. Claims against a Carrier and a Ship Owner

Case #1 A shipper entered a contract with a carrier to the effect that the latter will carry goods by sea and that the carrier received the goods from the shipper, loaded them onto a ship and issued a bill of lading to the shipper. The bill of lading contained a clause to stipulate that the contract will be governed by Japanese law and that the Himalaya Clause to the effect that a subcontracting carrier may also invoke the provisions for exemption from liabilities enjoyed by the carrier. The bill of lading was endorsed and a consignee received it. Immediately before the arrival at a discharge port, the ship encountered heavy weather and, partly due to an error in the navigation of the ship by a captain and engine trouble (unseaworthiness of the vessel), the ship ran aground and the goods on board the ship suffered a total loss. The carrier time chartered the ship from a shipowner.

1. Application of the Act on International Carriage of Goods by Sea

(1) Claim for Damages against the Carrier

   a. Cause of Claim

The cause of claim is a claim for damages for breach of the contract of goods evidenced by the bill of lading.

The facts to prove the cause of claim are as follows:[2]

(a) The contract between the shipper and the carrier for the carriage of goods; (b) the delivery of the goods to the carrier based on the contract; (c) the occurrence of loss or damages to the goods during the custody of the carrier; (d) whether the consignee is a lawful holder of the bill of lading.

However, as we will later see, if the cause of the damage is the unseaworthiness of the vessel at the beginning of the voyage, there is an opinion that the unseaworthiness of the ship should be proved by the claimant as the cause of claim (*See* the case of the ship, *Giant Step*, which was judged by the Tokyo District Court on February 16, 2010).[3]

---

[2] Tomotaka Fujita "Acceptance of Uniformed Treaty and Domestic Changes-Example of the Act on International Carriage of Goods by Sea" in BUSINESS LAWS AT THE AGE OF RECONSTRUCTION" IN COMMEMORATION OF PROFESSOR TOSHIHIKO SEKI'S 70TH BIRTHDAY, Shoji-homu, 2011, p.381, fn. (12) states "As for the cause of claim for liabilities of a carrier concerning loss or damage to a carried good, there is no provision for it in the Act on International Carriage of Goods by Sea. So, we should consider it is almost equivalent to the cause of claim of the contract of carriage to which the Act on International Carriage of Goods by Sea does not apply." The author discusses the following requirements: It is enough for a consignee who is the holder of a bill of lading as a plaintiff to assert and establish (i) the existence of a contract of carriage of goods and that (ii) goods were lost or damaged during the period from the receipt of it by a carrier until its delivery to a consignee (or a cause of such loss or damage happened). Against this, the side of a carrier who is a debtor asserts and establishes as his defense that he exercise the due diligence to take care of the goods. On this point, there is no opposing opinion in foreign countries and the point is set forth in express terms in the treaties for carriage of goods by sea after then.

[3] 1237 Hanrei Times 232 et seq. As a comment on the judgment, Manami Sasaoka, *"Significance of Consignee" set forth in Article 20 bis 2(1) of the Act on International Carriage of Goods by Sea—the Case of the Giant Step*, 84(8) Hogaku Kenkyu 103 (2011).

In the above case, in an accident of the *Giant Step*, which ran aground and sank, all iron ore loaded on the ship also went down with the ship, resulting in a total loss of the goods. The claimant made a claim for damages against the carrier and the shipowner, asserting that the cause of the accident was the ship's unseaworthiness at the beginning of the voyage. With respect to the cause of the accident, the court held that the damage occurred because the captain failed to take proper measures at the time of the ship's encounter with the heavy weather and that the ship was in the seaworthy condition at the beginning of the voyage. The court held that "As for a claim for damages due to the breach of the obligation of make a ship seaworthy set forth in Article 5(1) of the Act on International Carriage of Goods by Sea, considering the theories of Article 5 (1) and (2) of the Act, it is reasonable to interpret that a party who claims for damages against a carrier bears the burden of proof that damage to carried goods arose by any of events listed in Items in Paragraph 1of the same Article, including unseaworthiness of a ship." Concerning this judgment, academic disputes on the issue were shown in the sentence, on which courts had not given clear judgments until then. Accordingly, this judgment is a new judgment concerning the obligation to make a ship seaworthy.

Furthermore, the above judgment held that, with respect to a claim for damages based on failure to exercise to take car of the goods as set forth in Article 3(1) of the Act, as stated above, the accident in question was caused by the delayed measures taken by the captain at the time of the ship's encounter with the heavy weather, and that because the captain's measures against the heavy weather are acts of a captain related to a ship's navigation, to which the so-called the provision for exemption from error in navigation during voyage set forth in Article 3(2) of the Act applies, thereby the carrier was exempted from his liability for damages. We think that this is the first case

b. Exemption from Error in Navigation or Management and Due Diligence

The issue concerning the fact finding in Case No. 1, is what the cause of the damage was. Depending on the cause, the existence or non-existence of the liability of the carrier is decided. Therefore, we will first examine the provisions that set forth the liabilities of a carrier in the Act on International Carriage of Goods by Sea.

Article 3(1) of the Act sets forth a care duty by a carrier for the cargo. On the other hand, Article 3(2) sets forth to the effect that, in the event of damage to the cargo due to error in navigation or management by a captain or a crew, a carrier is exempt from his liabilities. With respect to damage caused by a fire, a carrier is exempt from his liabilities in principle. However, if a fire is caused by the actual fault or privity of the carrier, the carrier is liable for the damage.

By listing events of exemption from liabilities, Article 4 of the Act includes a provision that facilitates the presentation of evidence of non-negligence by a carrier. In Case No. 1, the carrier can claim that the heavy weather the ship encoursed is an event to be exemption from liabilities, and is one that is most frequently asserted by carriers.

Article 5 of the Act sets forth an obligation for a carrier to make a ship seaworthy before and at the beginning of the voyage. The burden of proof concerning seaworthiness can be interpreted as to be held by a claimant. According to a judgment by the Tokyo District Court on February 16, 2010 (in the case of the ship, *Giant Step*), a plaintiff must present evidence that shows that the damage is caused by unseaworthiness of the vessel at the beginning of the voyage.

c. Application to Case #1

Claim for damages against the carrier

As the lawful holder of the bill of lading, the consignee has a right to claim for damages (this is a problem of a title to sue). The delay interest is six (6) percent per annum according to the Commercial Code of Japan.

First, when the cause of the accident in question is an error in navigation by the captain (Article 3(2) of the Act), the carrier is exempt from liabilities. Next, when the cause of the accident in question is unseaworthiness of the vessel at the beginning of the voyage with negligence to such unseaworthiness by the carrier, the carrier becomes liable. However, the

---

where the exemption from error in navigation during voyage was admitted in the history of such cases in Japan.

burden of proof of non-negligence of the unseaworthiness of the vessel at the beginning of the voyage is held by the carrier.

(2) Claim for Damages against the Shipowner

a. Cause of Claim

This is a claim for damages based on tort set forth in a governing law.

The facts to prove as cause of claim are as follows: (a) a negligent act by the shipowner while the goods were is in his custody; (b) loss or damage to the goods due to the negligence in (a); (c) infringement of the cargo owner's of rights of ownership in the goods or occurrence of an economic loss for the cargo owner (a title to sue).[4]

The delay interest is five (5) percent per annum.

When the cause of the accident in question is the negligence of the captain in his operation of the ship, because a captain is the legal representative of a shipowner, the liability for damages belongs to the shipowner in accordance with Article 690 of the Commercial Code.

b. The Himalaya Clause

However, as a defense, the shipowner will assert his exemption from liabilities by invoking the Himalaya Clause in the contract of carriage of goods. Under the statutory Himalaya Clause set forth in Article 20bis (2) of the Act on International Carriage of Goods by Sea, only employees of the carrier may invoke the provision for exemption from liabilities set forth in the Act. Accordingly, to admit the invocation of a provision for exemption from liabilities by an independent subcontracting carrier, such as the shipowner, the Himalaya Clause contained in the bill of lading becomes necessary. However, there is an issue regarding the validity of whether the Himalaya Clause in a bill of lading is valid or not.[5]

When the invocation of the provision for exemption from liabilities is admitted based on the Himalaya Clause, the shipowner is exempted from his liability for damages based on tort.

---

[4] In the English law, in the case of a claim for damages based on tort, the infringement of ownership of goods is its requirement. See the judgment of "Aliakmon" by the House of Lords in the United Kingdom, [1986] 2 Lloyd's Rep. 1.
[5] The judgment by the Tokyo District Court on May 24, 1994 (1400 Kinyu Homu Jijo 104)

c. Application to Case #1

In Case #1, in practice, there are many cases where a cargo owner claims damages not only against a carrier but also against a shipowner. In such cases, the shipowner relies on the Himalaya Clause contained in a bill of lading. On the other hand, because his claim is a claim for damages based on the breach of the contract by the carrier, a consignee does not need to establish the negligence of a carrier. However, the consignee has a burden of a ship owner's negligent act in his claim against the shipowner because the claim is based on tort. Furthermore, the shipowner can invoke the provision for exemption from liabilities because the Himalaya Clause is referred to in the original contract of carriage of goods.

The burden of proof in the case of a claim by a cargo owner against a shipowner based on tort should be treated the same as the burden of proof in the case of a claim based on contract against a carrier. In addition, in principle, the scope of liabilities of a shipowner should be the same scope of liabilities of a carrier. For this purpose, we think that it is desirable from the viewpoint of fairness that the statutory Himalaya Clause in the Rules is set forth rather than the Himalaya Clause in a contract.

2. Application of the Rotterdam Rules

(1) Claim for Damages against the Carrier

a. Cause of Claim (in a Suit)

With respect to a claim against the carrier, it is a right to claim for damages based on breach of the contract of carriage of goods made between the shipper and the carrier.

The facts to prove the cause of the claim are as follows:

(a) The contract between the shipper and the carrier for carriage of goods; (b) the delivery of the goods to the carrier based on the contract; (c) the occurrence of loss or damage to the goods under the custody of the carrier; (d) whether the consignee is a lawful holder of the bill of lading.

With respect to the cause of liabilities of a carrier and the burden of proof, the Rules set forth provisions that are different from the Act on International Carriage of Goods by Sea. The Rules clearly set forth the liabilities of a carrier, the duration of his liabilities, specific obligations applied to voyage, cause of liabilities of a carrier and the burden of proof (*See* Article 11 to Article 14 of the Rules).

b. Obligation to make and keep the ship seaworthy

Attention should be paid to Article 14 of the Rules, which differs from the provision of the Act on International Carriage of Goods by Sea.

Article 14 sets forth specific obligations applied to navigation. Article 5 of the Act on International Carriage of Goods by Sea sets forth an obligation to make the ship seaworthy at the beginning of the voyage. The Rules adds a important change to the conventional obligations set forth in the Act on International Carriage of Goods by Sea by imposing this obligation not only at the time of the beginning of the voyage but also during the time of voyage at sea., Conventionally, for instance, in cases where it is argued whether a ship was unseaworthy when an accident occurred or at the beginning of the voyage, with regard to an ingress of water from hatch coamings, only when the court found that the exact cause of the accident was unseaworthiness of the ship at the beginning of the voyage, a claim against the carrier should be admitted. Instead, according to the Rules, when a ship is not seaworthy at the time an accident occurs during the voyage, and such unseaworthiness is the cause of the accident, the liabilities of the carrier are recognized. Attention should be paid, however, to the following points. With respect to unseaworthiness, when a carrier is not negligent, his liabilities are not recognized. Furthermore, the time of establishing the proposition of non-negligence differs between unseaworthiness at the beginning of the voyage and at the time of an accident.

c. Cause of Liabilities of a Carrier and Burden of Proof

Article 17(1) sets forth in detail the cause of liabilities of a carrier and his burden of proof. It is one of the most important provisions in the Rules.

(a) Article 17(1)

Article 17 Paragraph 1 sets forth that a carrier's liabilities arise when a claimant proves that the loss or damage to the goods occurred when the goods were under the care of the carrier. Namely, the Paragraph sets forth the cause of claim and the burden of proof for a claim.

(b) On Article 17(2) (the Carrier's burden to prove Absence of Fault)

Article 17(2) sets forth that when the cause, or one of the causes, for the loss, damage, or delay, are proved to be not attributable to a carrier or to any persons set forth in Article 18, the carrier is exempt from all or a part of the liabilities set forth in Paragraph 1 of this Article.

This provision requires a carrier to bear the burden of proof for his non-negligence. In the Act on International Carriage of Goods by Sea, when a claim for damages is based on the breach of the contract of carriage of goods, the burden of proof for non-negligence is imposed on a carrier. We find that this provision has the same basis as a law of Japan. Under Japanese law, with respect to a claim for damages based on tort, the burden of proof for negligence of a tortfeasor lays on the claimant. In regards to a claim against a maritime performing party, which is later described, the burden of proof was converted by 180 degrees for a claim against a maritime performer as Article 17(1) is applied in accordance with Article 19.

It is noteworthy that a carrier must prove the "causes or one of the causes of loss, damage, or delay" as a requirement of Article 17(2). Namely, in specifying a cause of damage, a carrier must prove his non-negligence, in other words, that he exercises due diligence to take care of the goods.

(c) On Article 17(3) (Events of Presumption of Absence Fault of Carrier)
The fact that the events of liability exemption (force majeure),that have been accepted globally for many years, are set forth as a list is useful because it provides guidance to those who are engaged in relevant maritime and insurance industries. Paragraph 3 sets forth that when a carrier, instead of the proving the cause of loss or damage set forth in Paragraph 2, proves that one of 15 affairs, including Act of God, becomes the cause(s) of loss, damage, or delay or contributes to the same, the carrier is relieved from the all or part of the liabilities set forth in Paragraph 1 of this Article. Any of these affairs is an affair by itself for which a carrier is not negligent. Further, as later described later, Paragraph 4 Item (a) sets forth that the carrier is liable when a claimant proves that the negligence of a carrier is the cause of the occurrence of these events.

With respect to the events of presumption of absence fault of carrier, the following two (2) points should be noted in the comparison of the Act on International Carriage of Goods by Sea with the Rules.

Abolition of the navigational fault exception　　First, there is no provision for exception of error in navigation or management, which has been one of the strongest defense methods for carriers for many years. Considering the remarkable evolution in communication technology in recent years, such a provision no longer would be a necessary provision for exemption from liabilities., There are no provision in the same sense for truck drivers in land transportation and plane captains in air transportation, as the exemption from liability for carriers due to error in navigation or management.

Change of the exemption from liabilities for a fire　　The exemption from liabilities for a fire in the Act on International Carriage of Goods by Sea sets forth the exemption from liabilities of a carrier with regard to the occurrence of a fire due to the negligence of a captain or a crew. To this extent, the Act had a similar effect on the above exemption for an error in navigation or management. In the Act on International Carriage of Goods by Sea, when a carrier committed negligence by itself, which caused a fire to occur, the carrier was held liable. According to Article 17(4) of the Rules, if a fire is caused by the negligence of a captain or a crew, the carrier is held liable.

(d) On Article 17(4)- Contrary Evidence to Paragraph 1 and 2 against the Events of Presumption of No Fault of Carrier Set Forth in Paragraph 3.

A carrier is liable in the following cases:

(i) When a claimant proves that a carrier's negligence contributed or was the cause of an event of presumption of no fault of carrier set forth in Paragraph 3.

In this case, with respect to the causes of the events of presumption of no fault of the carrier set forth in Paragraph 3, a claimant directly proves the negligence of a carrier.

(ii) When a claimant proves that an affair other than presumption of no fault of the carrier set forth in Paragraph 3 contributed to loss, damage, or delay, except when a carrier proves his non-negligence in the affair.[6]

(e) Obligation to Make and Keep a Ship Seaworthy during the Voyage Set Forth in Article 17(5)—Contrary Evidence to Paragraph 3 against presumption of absence of fault of carrier Set Forth in Paragraph 3

There is a provision for the third contrary evidence against the assertion of presumption of no fault of carrier set forth in Paragraph 3 with respect to any damage that arises during voyage.

In this case, the claimant proved that loss, damage, or delay probably caused by ir contributed by the unseaworthness of the ship. Namely, it is contrary evidence against the carrier's assertion of a carrier's encounter with heavy weather or his assertion of a fire.

On this point, we should note that the degree of establishment differs from other provisions.

Against the assertion by a claimant on a ship's unseaworthiness, a carrier will assert and establish that (i) the ship's unseaworthiness is not the cause of the damage (non-existence of causation) or that (ii) he performed his due diligence to make and keep a ship seaworthty.

---

[6] This section refers to causes other than presumption of no fault of carrier set forth in Paragraph 3. This deals with the matter of causation. For example, ALEXANDER VON ZIEGLER, JOHAN SCHELIN AND STEFANO ZUNARELLI, THE ROTTERDAM RULES 2008, KLUWER LAW INTERNATIONAL (2010), p. 106, fn.83 states that "the proof of that the damage was not (only) caused by fire fighting measures in course of a fire, but by earlier undue exposure of the cargo to rain water".

In the meantime, when a carrier's liabilities are admitted, his liabilities are limited to the following three situations: (i) partial relief of liabilities (Article 17(6), (ii) limitation of liabilities concerning compensation (Article 22) and (iii) provisions for limitation of liabilities (Article 59 and after).

(f) On Article 17(6) (Provision for the Case of multiple Causation)
According to Article 17(6), when a carrier is partially relived from his liabilities, the carrier is liable for loss, damage or delay caused by an affair for which he is liable.

d. Application to Case #1
In Case #1, the carrier first asserts that the damage was caused by the ship's encounter with heavy weather. Namely, the carrier asserts or establishes the affairs of presumption of no fault of carrier set forth in Article 17(2) or Article 17(3)(b). When the cause of the damage is due to an error in navigation by the captain of the ship, as there is no provision in the Rules that corresponds to the Act on International Carriage of Goods by Sea's provision for the exemption from liabilities of the carrier due to an error in navigation, this means that the an error in navigation of the captain of the ship is a negligence of the carrier. When the carrier asserts the encounter of the ship with heavy weather, the claimant asserts and establishes that the damage to the cargo was caused by the ship's grounding due to the captain's negligence based on Article 17(4)(b). However, if the carrier fails to prove that the carrier and the captain were not negligent in the ship's navigation, then the carrier is liable.

If the cause of the damage is due to engine trouble, in other words, the ship's unseaworthiness at the time of accident, the claimant will establish that the ship's unseaworthiness at the time of the accident was probably the cause of the damage. However, if the carrier can prove that he exercised due diligence to make and keep the ship seaworthy during the voyage, he will not be liable.

The above is related to assertion and establishment concerning the carrier's cause of liabilities. The carrier must assert and establish that the contract of carriage of goods in question is the contract to which the Rules should apply. The claimant must assert and establish that he has a title to sue in the governing law of the contract of carriage of goods. He also must assert and establish the facts as requirements for the delay interest. The proof of loss or damage refers to a physical loss, damage to the cargo, or its delay. He also must assert and establish (Article 22) on the cargo's value at the time of its arrival at the destination. Although it is a problem in the governing law, insurance subrogation will also become a problem in relation to the title to sue.

(2) Claim for Damages against a Ship Owner (A Maritime Performing Party)

a. Cause of Claim

We interpret that a claim for damages against a shipowner is a claim for damages revised by the statutory liabilities of a Maritime Performing Party that were created in Article 19 of the Rules, based on a claim for damages on the basis of tort in a governing law.

We interpret the following matters as the causes of a claim.

(a) The contract of carriage of goods between the shipper and the carrier; (b) the Rules apply to the contract; (c) a shipowner falls within a maritime performing party; (d) a carrier received goods at a port of a member country of the Rules or delivered goods in a member country of the Rules or he performed his activities concerning goods at a port of a member country of the Rules (e) an affair which caused loss or damage that occured (i) during the period from when goods arrived at a loading port of a ship until the delivery of the good from a discharge port of the ship and either (ii) while a maritime performing party had custody of the goods, or (iii) at any time to the extent that it was participating in the performance of any of the activities contemplated by the contract of carriage; (f) the occurrence of loss or damage to the goods; (g) infringement of ownership of the goods of the cargo owner or occurrence of an economic loss for the cargo owner.

b. Summary of Article 19 of the Rules

Article 19 of the Rules requires a maritime performing party to bear the same rights and obligations as a carrier and admits the invocation of a defense right held by a carrier. It is a new provision that has not existed in treaties until now. We think that the article is a characteristic of the Rules and it will have a significant effect on the practice.[7]

Conventionally, if the Himalaya Clause in a contract of carriage of goods is applied to a claim for damages based on tort by a cargo owner against a shipowner, the cargo owner is put in an unfavorable position. As a subcontracting carrier, a shipowner may rely on a provision for the contractual exemption from liabilities and a provision for limitation of liability between a cargo owner and an original carrier without paying any money to them. Although with respect to a claim for damages based on breach of the contract of goods by a cargo owner against a carrier the carrier is liable for establishing his non-negligence, the cargo owner is liable for establishing the negligence of the shipowner in a claim for damages based on tort by a cargo owner against a shipowner, Compared to the carrier's position, if

---

[7] *See* Tomotaka Fujita, *Performing parties and Himalaya Protection*, presented at the Colloquium on the Rotterdam Rules 2009, September 21, 2009. Available on web. http://www.rotterdamrules2009.com/cms/index.php?page=text-speakers-rotterdam-rules-2009

the Himalaya Clause is effective, a shipowner as a subcontracting carrier is placed in a more favorable position by using the Himalaya Clause than the carrier.

Concerning the above, in the Rules, a claim by a claimant against a maritime performing party and a claim by a claimant against a carrier have the same contents in principle. With respect to a claim for damages by a cargo owner against a shipowner, the shipowner must establish his non-negligence. We thus can estimate that the chances for a cargo owner to claim against a shipowner based on Article 19 will increase, while the former hesitated because he had the burden of proof in the claim for damages against shipowner.

With respect to an amount of damages when a breach of an obligation set forth in the Rules is committed, Article 20 of the Rules stipulates that the amount should be the same amount if a shipper, a consignee, or another concerned party claims against a carrier, a subcontracting carrier, or another party. Considering the liabilities of those who perform the contract of carriage of goods, we think that this is a well-balanced rational provision.

c. Provisions for Cause of Liabilities of a Maritime Performing Party

Hereafter, we will check the provisions for the cause of liabilities of a maritime performing party.

(a) Eligibility of a Maritime Performing Party

With respect to "a maritime performing party," the Rules provides a definition of the term in Article 1(7). There is no dispute that a shipowner is applicable to a maritime performing party. However, there are arguments on the scope of parties that is applicable to a maritime performing party. A maritime performing party must be applicable to a performing party as set forth in Article 1(6) of the Rules.[8]

-A party other than a carrier as set forth in Article 1(6)(a)   Although a carrier himself is not included in the category of a performing party, an independent subcontracting carrier is included.

-A party who performs or undertakes to perform any of the carrier's obligation as set forth in Article 1(6)(a)   A performing party includes not only a party who actually performs the obligation of a carrier's himself but also a party who undertakes to perform a carrier's obligation and entrusts his obligation to another party. Accordingly, multiple performing parties can exist simultaneously in a single carriage.

-Any obligation of a carrier in a contract of carriage with respect to the receipt, loading,

---

[8] *See* Frank Smeele, *The Maritime Performing Party in the Rotterdam Rules 2009*, 2 European Journal of Commercial Contract Law 72–86 (2010).

handling, stowage, carriage, custody, lading unloading, or delivery of goods An independent contractor who is a performing party must undertake carrier's obligations that are directly related to the handling or carriage of the goods.

Accordingly, it is clear that both a warehouse operator and a terminal operator are applicable as a maritime performing party. Furthermore, a subcontracting carrier, a tugboat, a stevedore or a barge operator is included in the concept of a maritime performing party.

A party (such as a port pilot), who only assists the performance of carriage or the performance of the obligations concerning goods of a carrier or a maritime performing party and does not perform such obligations, should be excluded from the category of a performing party. In addition, a party who performs or undertakes to perform other obligations imposed on a carrier in a contract of carriage of goods, such as the obligation to make and keep a ship seaworthy and the obligation to issue documents, is also excluded from the category of performing party because these obligations are only indirectly related to the handling or carriage of the goods. However, it is possible that, when these parties simultaneously perform a carrier's obligations that are directly related to the handling or carriage of the goods, they are applicable to a performing party as set forth in Article 1(6) of the Rules.

(b) Relevance for Place

Article 19(1)(a) of the Rules sets forth requirements that a maritime performing party must have received goods for carriage in a member country, delivered goods in a member country and performed concerning goods at a port of a member country. These requirements differ from those set forth in Article 5(1) of the Rules. These references to places concern carriage by sea. The place of receipt of goods and the place of delivery of goods as set forth in this Article are actual places and not agreed upon places.

(c) Cause of Loss

Article 19(1)(b) of the Rules sets forth requirements concerning an affair that caused loss, damage, or delay happened (i) during the period between the arrival of the goods at the port of loading of the ship and their departure from the port of discharge from the ship, and either (ii) while the maritime performing party had custody of the goods, or (iii) at any other time to the extent that it was participating in the performance of any of the activities contemplated by the contract of carriage.

With respect to (i) above, a subcontracting carrier during carriage at sea is applicable to this requirement. With respect to (ii) above, a warehouse operator and a terminal operator are applicable to this requirement. Furthermore, a subcontracting carrier is also applicable to this requirement. With respect to (iii) above, a stevedore is applicable to this requirement.

A cargo owner must first establish that an affair that caused the damage took place during the period of liabilities borne by the maritime performing party. Next, the maritime performing party must establish that the cause of the damage is not due to the negligence of either himself or of his employee. Otherwise, the maritime performing party must establish that the affair occurred by the events of presumption of no fault of carrier set forth in Article 17(2). If the maritime performing party cannot establish the cause of the damage, he will be liable. If the maritime performing party can prove its non-negligence, the cargo owner must establish that the maritime performing party is liable under Article 17(4) and (5) of the Rules., The burden of proof that the cargo was sound at the time when the period of the liability of the maritime performing party is attached lays on the cargo owner.

d. Is the Existence of a Carrier under the Rules a Prerequisite for a Claim against a Maritime Performing Party?

Article 20 of the Rules sets forth that a carrier and a maritime performing party shall be liable jointly and separately. However, it is difficult to say that the existence of a carrier is a prerequisite for a claim against a maritime performing party based on this provision. In other words, Article 20 sets forth only normal cases.[9]

From the wording of Article 19(1) of the Rules according to which a maritime performing party may bear the liabilities and obligations imposed on a carrier by the Rules and may invoke the defense and the limitation of liability by a carrier as set forth in the Rules, we can assume that a carrier's liabilities are prerequisite to admitting the liabilities of a maritime performing party. On the contrary, in the case where a carrier does not bear his liabilities and obligations in the Rules (where there is no carrier contemplated by the Rules), because a contract of carriage of goods is not applicable to the Rules, we can interpret that Article 19 will not be applied.[10]

For instance, with respect to damage to a cargo at a loading port of a member country of the Rules due to the negligence of a stevedore, the stevedore is applicable to a maritime per-

---

[9] BAATZ DEBATTISA, LORENZON SERDY AND STAINLAND TSIMPLIS, THE ROTTERDAM RULES A PRACTICAL ANNOTATION, INFORMA LAW (2009), P.64 reads "As the maritime performing party is subject to the liability and is entitled to the carrier's exceptions and limits to liability, subject to the condition under Article19.1 it must be assumed that such liability for the carrier must be in existence."

[10] Richard Williams, *The Rotterdam Rules: Winners and Loser*, 16 Journal of International Maritime Law 196 (2010) states that "If the governing contract between the cargo interests and the carrier is a charterparty or COA then, for the reasons given above, the provisions of the Rotterdam Rules relating to the rights and duties of maritime performing parties will not apply. On the other hand, if the governing contract is not such a contract then it is necessary to consider whether the Rules will in fact have any impact on the liability of such subcontractors..."

forming party. However, does Article 19 not be applied if a governing contract is a charter party? In such a case, when a shipowner as a carrier issues a bill of lading and the bill is assigned to a third party, the holder of the bill of lading may be interpreted as able to make a claim against the shipowner based on Article 17 and a claim against a stevedore based on Article 19 (*See* Article 7 of the Rules).

e. Application to Case #1

The ship owner is a maritime performing party. If the requirements of Article 19 (1)(a) and (b) are met, the shipowner bears the same liabilities and obligations as the carrier. Unlike the general requirements for tort, the cargo owner does not need to first assert and establish the occurrence of the damage to the goods under the custody of him due to the negligence of the maritime performing party. However, the issue on title to sue is judged according to a governing law. The issue on delay interest is the same. There is no provision in the Rules for the relation of indemnity between the carrier and the maritime performing party. Article 20 of the Rules sets forth only joint and several liability of the carrier and maritime performing party.

IV. Specific Issues

1. Who is a Claimant? (Issue of Title to Sue)

This problem concerns the party that has a right to make a claim for damages against a carrier or a maritime performing party with respect to damage to the goods.

With respect to the right for a claim for damages arising from a contract of carriage of the goods, a shipper as a party to the contract must be able to exercise the right of claim against a carrier. However, when a bill of lading has been issued or when a consignee has already received the cargo, there are many cases where not a shipper but the holder of the bill of lading or a consignee has the interest in claiming for damages.

In the United Kingdom, conventionally, the Bill of Lading Act 1855 admitted a title to sue to a holder of a bill of lading with a requirement of the relevance of the bill of lading with the ownership of a cargo. Subsequently, the Carriage of Goods by Sea Act 1992 admitted a title to sue to a lawful holder of a bill of lading.

In this country too, a right to claim for damages is admitted against a carrier by a lawful holder of a bill of lading. However, when merely a waybill is issued, a title to sue is not admitted to a consignee that is described only on the waybill as the consignee because a waybill is not a negotiable instruments. According to Article 583(1) of the Commercial Code of Japan, a right to claim for damages is vested in the consignee when a cargo arrives at a port of discharge.

With respect to a claim for tort against a shipowner, when he is applicable to a maritime performing party, as stated earlier, he bears the same liabilities of a carrier and is entitled to rely on the defense and limitation of liability set forth in the Rules by virtue of Article 19 of the Rules. However, under English law, with respect to a title to sue for a tort claim, only an owner of a cargo is entitled to claim damages for loss that he suffered by reason of infringement of ownership of the goods owned by the cargo owner.[11] However, it is not admitted under English law that a consignee who suffered a simple economic loss would claim against a shipowner by reason of suffering such economic loss.

The problem of title to sue was taken up at the United Nations' Commission on International Trade Law (UNCITRAL) but was not adopted at the final stage. In the process of drafting the Rules, clauses related to the title to sue were deleted, and the problem of title to sue was left to governing law. In the meantime, Article 57 of the Rules does not include a clause that deals with the problem of title to sue.[12]

2. Claim for Damage Concerning Expense

Case #2 **A shipper made a contract with a carrier to the effect that the latter will carry goods by sea and the carrier received the goods from the shipper, loaded them on a ship and issued a bill of lading to the shipper. The bill of lading contained a clause to stipulate the governing law of the contract to be Japanese law and the Himalaya Clause to the effect that a subcontracting carrier may also invoke the provisions for exemption from liabilities enjoyed by the carrier. The bill of lading was endorsed and a consignee received it. Immediately before the arrival at a discharge port, the ship encountered heavy weather and, partly due to error in the navigation of the ship by a captain and unseaworthiness of the ship, the ship ran aground. Subsequently, a salvage company salved both the ship and the goods. The consignee paid the remuneration for of salvage to the salvage company. The carrier time chartered the ship from the shipowner. Can the consignee claim for damages against the carrier and the ship-**

---

[11] *See* the above footnote 4.
[12] At the 18th session of No. 3 Working Group for UNCITRAL (on November 6 to November 17, 2006), the problem on title to sue is described in detail in a report submitted by the Government of Japan (Report No. A/CN.9/WG.III/EP.76).

owner for an amount equivalent to the remuneration for the salvage?

Here, the problem is whether the consignee who paid remuneration for the salvage may claim for damages against the carrier for the expense.[13]

(1) The Act on International Carriage of Goods by Sea

In the Act on International Carriage of Goods by Sea, a problem arises as to whether a cargo owner who paid remuneration for the salvage to a salvage company may claim the charge against a carrier because of the latter's breach of the contract of carriage of goods.

Because Article 3 and Article 5 of the Act on International Carriage of Goods by Sea set forth that the carrier is liable for loss or damage of the carried goods , it becomes a problem determining whether the expense above is applicable to the loss or damage set forth in Article 3 and Article 5. Namely, as it is clear that there is expense suffered by the cargo owner because of a carrier's breach of contract, we can interpret that the carrier is liable. The problem concerns whether the damage concerning expense would fall within these Articles.

A judgment by the Tokyo District Court on July 15, 2011 held an expense of remuneration for salvage that the expense is applicable to damage regarding loss or damage to carried goods under Article 5 of the above Act. This is a new ruling as to this issue by a Japanese court.[14]

However, if we admit the liabilities of a carrier for the reason that the expense is applicable to damage regarding loss or damage to carried goods set forth in Article 5, another

---

[13] Originally, problems in the legal relationship between a cargo owner and a carrier concerning the carriage of goods by sea included the following three (3) points:

(1) When a physical loss or damage to the goods takes place, a cargo owner makes a claim for damages against a carrier because of the latter's breach of the contract of carriage of goods. The main purpose of the Hague-Visby Rules is to discipline the liabilities of the carrier in this circumstance.

(2) When a ship and its cargo encounter a marine casualty and a salvage company salves the ship and the cargo, a cargo owner pays remuneration to the salvage company for the salvage. If the cause of the marine casualty was due to a breach by the carrier in the contract of carriage of goods, the cargo owner will claim for damages against the carrier to recover the remuneration for salvage which the cargo owner had paid to the salvage company. This problem is dealt with in this paper. We do not think that the Hague-Visby Rules heed this problem. It seems that with regard to the Working Groups of the Rules, there is no official record showing that this problem was discussed.

(3) In the case of a general average and when a shipowner makes a claim for the general average contribution against a cargo owner, if the shipowner's negligence exists concerning the cause of maritime causality, as a defense of the cargo owner, then the cargo owner may refuse to pay general average contribution to the shipowner. This is so called as Rule D defense under York-Antwerp Rules.

[14] 1384 Hanrei Times 270

problem arises regarding whether expense would be subject to the limitation of liability set forth in the Act on International Carriage of Goods by Sea because we think that the provision for limitation of liability was set forth originally for cases of a physical loss or damage of the carried goods.

(2) The Rotterdam Rules

Article 17(1) of the Rules reads "the carrier is liable for loss of or, damage to the goods, as well as for delay in delivery, if the claimant proves that the loss, damage or the delay or the event or circumstance that caused or contributed to it took place... ."

We think that the claim in question here, against the carrier concerning an expense of remuneration for the salvage, is not applicable to Article 17(1) because of the latter's phrasing.

However, it is clear that a cargo owner is forced to pay an expense of remuneration for the salvage by the activity of the carrier who failed to exercise the due diligence to take care as set forth in Article 13 of the Rules or his specific obligation during the voyage set forth in Article 14. Accordingly, from the interpretation of the Rules, we think that a carrier's liability for compensation arises.

Article 59(1) of the Rules sets forth that with respect to the liabilities of a carrier for his breach of obligations based on the Rules, the maximum amount for the liabilities should be 875 units of account per package or other shipping unit, or 3 units of account per kilogram of the gross weight of the goods that are the subject of the claim or dispute, whichever amount is the higher. The Paragraph sets forth that "the carrier's liabilities for breaches of its obligations under this Convention," which seems to be applicable to a carrier's liabilities for his breach of obligations set forth in Article 13 or Article 14 of the Rules. This would be the matter of interpretation of Article 59(1) of the Rules.

Whether we can claim for damage for the expense against a maritime performing party is problematic. First, with respect to damage for the expense, a problem arises regarding whether a claim may be made against a shipowner by reason of tort. This is a problem not of the Rules but of the governing law. When damage for expense is admitted as damages based on tort in the governing law, a claim against a maritime performing party would be admitted.

V. Conclusion

(1) As for the rights and obligations of a carrier, the Rules has the characteristics that it

abolished the provision for the exemption from error in navigation and management of the ship during voyage that was admitted in the Act on International Carriage of Goods by Sea. With respect to the exemption from liabilities for a fire, in the event that a captain or crew is negligent, the carrier is liable. These are changes in the direction favorable to a cargo owner.

(2) Article 17 of the Rules sets forth in detail the burden of proof concerning a carrier's liabilities. While the Act on International Carriage of Goods by Sea sets forth simply the rights and obligations of a carrier, Article 17 sets forth a different matter. Because the convenience in practice has increased, the Article is significant for both carrier and cargo owner. The predictability of the same conclusion in different venues will be heightened, if the Rules have provisions related to the burden of proof. We can estimate that Article 17 shows a spirit of innovation in the Rules.

(3) It is characteristic of the Rules that it widened the scope of application of the statutory Himalaya Clause and created the liabilities of a maritime performing party. The Himalaya Clause in the Rules protects the shipowner. On the other hand, conventionally, the cargo owner had beared the burden of proof in the negligence of a shipowner in a claim for damages based on tort. However, with respect to a claim against a maritime performing party, a cargo owner now does not bear the burden of proof in the negligence of a shipowner in principle. Therefore, the burden for a cargo owner was alleviated in practice. Furthermore, from the viewpoint of fairness, we can support that the Rules established a system of liabilities under which related parties who specifically share the performance of acts of the carriage bear the same liabilities and enjoy the same rights.

(4) However, we need to distinguish clearly and strictly the scope set forth in the Rules from the scope determined by a governing law. Namely, the problem of title to sue and the problem of delay interest remain the problems of a governing law.

13

Rotterdam Rules: The Freight Forwarders' Perspective

Shuji Yamaguchi

I. Preface

Freight Forwarder is a carrier who makes a contract of carriage of goods with a shipper and uses the most suitable transportation way by sea, air or land and gives the full transportation service from collecting to delivery of goods. In multimodal transport with sea transport, a freight forwarder issues House B/L to a shipper and receives Master B/L from an actual carrier entrusted the transportation by them. Therefore, a freight forwarder is a carrier to the shipper as well as a shipper to the actual carrier.

Therefore a freight forwarder has 2 standpoints both as a carrier and as a shipper. As Rotterdam Rules provides about the liability of the carrier and the shipper, it will give a large impact to the freight forwarders' legal position.

I here explain what influence will be given to the freight forwarder as a carrier or as a shipper.

II. Freight Forwarder as a Carrier

1. Carrier's Obligation and Liability

Rotterdam Rules Article 1(5) provides "Carrier" means a person that enters into contract of carriage with a shipper.

Therefore, a freight forwarder who issues a house B/L shall be a carrier under Rotterdam

Rules. A freight forwarder shall have the carrier's obligation provides in Chapters 4, 5 and 12 of Rotterdam Rules.

The period of responsibility shall be from the receipt of the goods to the delivery (Article 12(1)). They shall properly and carefully receive, load, handle, stow, keep, carry, care for, unload and deliver the goods (Article 13(1)) and be bound before, at the beginning of and during the voyage by sea to exercise due diligence to make and keep the ship seaworthy (Article 14(1)).

They are liable for loss of or damage to the goods if the claimant proves the loss or damage took place during the period of the carrier's responsibility (Article 17(1)). They shall be relieved from the liability if the events or circumstance provided in Article 17 para3 caused or contributed the loss or damage but be still liable if the loss or damage is attributable to their fault (Article 17(1)).

Under Rotterdam Rules, the error in navigation shall not be the carrier's exemption and the carrier is liable for fire if their fault is attributable to it.

A freight forwarder shall owe much heavier liability under the Rotterdam Rules than that under Hague-Visby Rules.

The carrier's liability shall be limited to 875 SDR per package or 3 SDR per kilogram of the gross weight of the goods (Article 59(1)).

2. Reclaim to the Actual Carrier

(1) A maritime performing party who performs or undertakes to perform any of the carriers' obligation from the port of loading to the port of discharge shall be jointly and severally liable with a freight forwarder, a contractual carrier (Article 20(1)). Therefore, an actual carrier shall be liable to a shipper directly. If a shipper claims against the actual carrier, the freight forwarder may not face the claim. However, if a shipper claim against the freight forwarder, they should reclaim to the actual carrier.

(2) Time for suit is provided in Article 62.
Article 62(1) provides that "No judicial arbitral proceedings in respect of claims or disputes arising from a breach of an obligation under this Convention may be instituted after the expiration of a period of two years". But Rotterdam Rules has a special provision of the time for suit for reclaim (Article 64). Article 64 provides:

> "An action for indemnity by a person held liable may be instituted after the expiration of the period provided in article 62 if the indemnity action is instituted within the later of

(a) The time allowed by the applicable law in the jurisdiction where proceedings as instituted or

(b) 90 days commencing from the day when the person instituting the action for indemnity has either settled the claim or been served with process in action against itself whichever earlier."

Japanese Carriage of Goods by Sea Act Article 14(3) allows 3 months of time from the action is instinited. Rotterdam Rules give a longer time. Under Japan COGSA, the time shall be counted from the proceedings are instituted but the defendants do not know when the proceedings are commenced. It usually takes one or two months to serve the writ from the commencing the proceedings. Then sometimes there would not be much time remained or maybe the time would be over when the writ is served. Under Rotterdam Rules, time shall be counted from the writ is served. It becomes easier for the freight forwarder to institute the indemnity claim under the Rules.

(3) Rotterdam Rules provider articles about Jurisdiction. According to Article 66(1)

"the plaintiff has right to institute judicial proceedings against the carrier, a freight forwarder;
(a) In a competent court within the jurisdiction of which is situated one of the following places:
(i) The domicile of the carrier
(ii) The place of receipt agreed in the contract of carriage
(iii) The place of delivery agreed in the contract of carriage or
(iv) The port where the goods are initially loaded on a ship or the port where the goods are finally discharged from a ship; or
(b) In a competent court or courts designated by an agreement between the shipper and the carrier for the purpose of deciding claims against the carrier that may arise under this Convention."

The actual carrier may be litigated at their domicile, their place of receipt, their place of delivery, their loading port or their discharging port or their agreed jurisdiction.

For example, in case a freight forwarder receives the goods at Saitama, loads them at Tokyo port and discharges at Rotterdam port and delivers them at Dusseldolf, the proceedings against the forwarder may be commenced at Dusseldolf. However, the freight forwarder may commence the proceedings for an indemnity claim against the actual carrier who transported the goods from Tokyo to Rotterdam not at Dusseldolf but at Rotterdam.

Furthermore, the provisions of Chapter 14 Jurisdiction shall bind only Contracting States that declare that they will be bound by them (Article 74). Then the provisions about jurisdiction shall not be applicable to all the Contracting States. It is assumed that many of the Contracting States may not want the application of Chapter 14. If it is the case, even after

Rotterdam Rules become in effect, the jurisdiction clauses on the bill of lading shall be regarded to be valid. If the jurisdictions agreed in the House B/L and that in the Master B/L are not the same, the indemnity claim proceedings may be instituted at other pace than the place of the original proceedings.

(4) The largest problem in the indemnity claim from a freight forwarder shall be that Rotterdam Rules may not be applicable to the actual carrier even in case the Rules apply to the freight forwarder.

Rotterdam Rules apply to contracts of carriage in which the place of receipt and the place of delivery are in different States and the port of loading of a sea carriage and the port of discharge of the same sea carriage are different States if any one of the following places is located in a Contracting State: (a) The place of receipt (b) The port of loading (c) The place of delivery or (d) the port of discharge (Article 5(1)).

Let us assume that the goods were received in Country A, loaded in Country B, discharged in Country C and delivered in Country D. Then, Country D is the Contracting State of Rotterdam Rules. The freight forwarder issues the House B/L covering the place of receipt, Country A to the place of delivery, Country D. The Master B/L only covers from the port of loading, Country B to the port of discharge, Country C. In this case, as the place of the delivery of the House B/L is located in the Contracting State of the Rotterdam Rules, the Rotterdam Rules shall be applicable to the Freight forwarder B/L. However, the Master B/L only covers from Country B to Country C. Therefore the Rotterdam Rules do not apply to the Master B/L. If the Country B is Hague-Visby Contracting State, Hague-Visby Rules shall be applicable to the Mater B/L. In this case, the freight forwarder shall not be exempted from the error in navigation but the actual carrier shall be.

The Freight forwarder shall pay 877 SDR per package or 3 SDR per kg of the gross weight of the goods lost or damaged whichever higher but the actual carrier can limit its liability at 666.67 SDR per package or 2 SDR per kg of the goods whichever higher.

The time limit for lawsuit applicable to the freight forwarder shall be 2 years but one-year time limit shall be applicable to the actual carrier. Therefore, when the freight forwarder is claimed from the shipper, the indemnity claim against the actual carrier may be time barred.

Accordingly, if both the Rotterdam Rules Contracting States and the Hague-Visby Contraction States exist, the freight forwarder may be in dangerous status. In order to avoid such situation the freight forwarder should be careful and not issue the House B/L to Country D but only to Country C, non- Rotterdam Rules Country.

(5) The Rotterdam Rules Article 80(1) provides about the Volume Contract that "Notwithstanding article 79 as between the carrier and the shipper, a volume contract to which this Convention applies may provide for greater or lesser rights, obligations and liabilities than those imposed by this Convention."

"Volume Contract" means a contract of carriage that provides for the carriage of a specified quantity of goods in a series of shipments during an agreed period of time. The specification of the quantity may include a minimum, a maximum or a certain range (Article 1(2)).

When a freight forwarder undertakes to transport a large quantity of cargoes for a certain period, he may be requested to execute a Volume Contract, by which he waives or limits exemptions, limitation of liability or limitation of time. In such a case, the freight forwarder will not claim to the actual carrier the liability owed to the shipper.

When a freight forwarder is allocated a large cargo space from the actual carrier, he may be requested to execute a Volume Contract which provides the exemption of the actual carrier or lesser limitation of liability. In such a case, the freight forwarder may face the full liability in the Rotterdam Rules from the shipper's claim but he will not be able to claim to the actual carrier on the same basis. When a freight forwarder executes a Volume contract, he should be careful.

III Freight Forwarder as a Shipper

1. "Shipper"

The Convention Article 1(8) provides "Shipper" means a person that enters into a contract of carriage with a carrier. As a freight forwarder enters into a contract with an actual carrier, it is a "Shipper" under the Rotterdam Rules.

2. Dangerous Goods

Chapter 7 of the Convention stipulates Obligations of the Shipper to the Carrier.

The most important provision in the chapter is Article 32, which provides special rules on the dangerous goods.

Article 32 provides that:

"When goods by their nature or character or reasonably appear likely to become, a danger to person or property or to the environment:

(a) The shipper shall inform the carrier of the dangerous nature or character of the goods in a timely manner before they are delivered to the carrier or a performing party. If the shipper fails to do so and the carrier or performing party does not otherwise have knowledge of their dangerous nature or character, the shipper is liable to the carrier for loss or damage resulting from such failure to inform; and

(b) The shipper shall mark or label dangerous goods in accordance with any law, regulations or other requirements of public authorities that apply during any stage of the intended carriage of the goods. If the shipper fails to do so, it is liable to the carrier for loss or damage from such failure."

The shipper's liability under the article shall be strict liability (Article 30(2)). A freight forwarder does not have cargo information more than that declared by the shipper. However, if the cargo entrusted to the actual carrier is dangerous the freight forwarder shall be liable to the actual carrier, even though the forwarder does not know it is. At least the goods listed in International Maritime Dangerous Goods (IMDG) Code should be informed timely. Otherwise, the freight forwarder, as the shipper, shall be liable for the accident occurred.

For Example, in case the cargo is actually a dangerous cargo listed IMDG Code but the freight forwarder does not know nor notify it is and then the cargo explodes and gets fire and the actual carrier is suffered, The freight forwarder should indemnify the loss or damage suffered by the actual carrier. Of course, the freight forwarder shall be able to claim to the shipper of the House B/L based on the same article. However, there may be a possibility that the shipper does not have sufficient asset to indemnify the loss or damage.

In case other cargoes are damaged by explosion or fire, the freight forwarder may not be liable for the damage of other cargoes unless he acted intentionally or negligently.

In case a freight forwarder fails to inform the dangerous cargo even though the forwarder has been notified so, the forwarder shall be fully liable for the damage resulted to the actual carrier and other cargoes.

3. Liability under Article 31

Article 31 provides that

"1. The shipper shall provide to the carrier, in a timely manner, accurate information required for the complication of the contract particulars and the issuance of the transport documents or electronic transport records, including the particulars referred to in article 36 paragraph 1; the name of the party to be identified as the shipper in the contract particulars: the name of the consignee, if any: and the name of the person to whose order the transport document or electronic transport record is to be issued, if any."

"2. The shipper is deemed to have guaranteed the accuracy at the time of receipt by the carrier of the information that is provided according to paragraph 1 of this article. The shipper shall indemnify the carrier against loss or damage resulting from the inaccuracy of such information" The liability shall be strict liability (Article 30(2)).

Therefore, the freight forwarder should be very careful about the information required for the complication of the contract particulars and ask the shipper to confirm the accuracy of the information. The freight forwarder should be strictly liable for loss or damage resulted from the inaccuracy of the information.

4. Obligation under Article 27(3)

The Convention Article 27(3) provides:

"When a container is packed or vehicle is loaded by the shipper, the shipper shall properly and carefully stow, lash and secure the contents in or on the container, or vehicle and in such a way that they will not cause harm to persons or property."

The freight forwarder as shipper should deliver the container stowed, lashed and secured properly and carefully to the actual carrier.

There is a question whether the freight forwarder shall be liable for the loss or damage to the ship or other cargo resulted from the improper stowage of cargo in the container.

Article 30(1) provides that

"The shipper is liable for loss or damage sustained by the carrier, if the carrier proves that such loss or damage was caused by a breach of the shipper's obligation under the Convention"

Therefore, the carrier shall prove the shipper's breach of the obligation that the stowage in the container is not sufficient for the ocean carriage.

Article 30(2) provides that:

"Except in respect of loss or damage caused by a breach by the shipper of its obligations pursuant to article 31 paragraph 2 and 32, the shipper is relived of all or part of its liability if the cause or one of the causes of the loss or damage is not attributable to its fault or to the fault of any person referred to in article 34."

Article 34 provides that:

"The shipper is liable for the breach of its obligations under this Convention caused by the acts or omissions of any other person, including employees, agents and subcontractors to which it has entrusted the performance of any its obligations but the shipper is not liable for acts or omissions of the carrier or a performing party acting on behalf of the carrier, to which the shipper has entrusted the performance of its obligation."

If the freight forwarder does not stow the cargo into the container but received the packed container, he will not be liable for the loss or damage caused by the improper stowage in the container as he is not negligent.

If the freight forwarder or its subcontractor stowed the cargo in the container, he, as the shipper, shall be liable for the loss or damage caused by the improper stowage in the container. In case loss or damage incurred to other cargo, the freight forwarder shall be liable only if it consists of tort. When the freight forwarder's subcontractor actually stows, the freight forwarder may not be liable as there is no negligence in the part of the freight forwarder.

IV. Conclusion

As we discussed above, the freight forwarder is the shipper as well as the carrier under the Rotterdam Rules. Therefore, the freight forwarder may have heavy burden and will be in the difficult position under the Convention.

14

The Rotterdam Rules: The Insures' Perspective

Masaru Ishii

I. Introduction

As has already been discussed, under the Convention the current rules for the apportionment of liabilities between the carrier and the shipper have been reviewed and many rules have been revised and some newly introduced. Here I will report on the possible impact of the Convention on marine insurance from a practical view point.

After briefly reviewing the relationship between marine insurance and the Convention, I will set out my personal opinion on the important changes in respect of the carrier's liabilities to the shipper as well as on the possible implications for General Average and Salvage.

II. Impact on Marine Insurance

First of all, I will review the possible impact of the Convention on marine insurance.

Obviously, the Convention widens the obligations on the carrier by way of a change to the apportionment of liabilities between the carrier and the shipper under the contract of the carriage, such as the removal of the error in navigation defence and increased limits of liability.

It is no surprise that the various interested parties have different views about the changes in the carrier's liabilities to the shipper.

Loss or damage to the cargo and charges sustained or incurred by the cargo during the voyage, which may be borne by the carrier and/or the shipper are covered under different insurance policies, namely the hull insurance policy and P&I Club cover for the shipowner and the cargo insurance policy for the cargo owner. Cargo claims against the carrier responsible for cargo damage are usually pursued by the subrogated cargo underwriter after settling the insurance claim with the cargo owner.

Even if the apportionment of liability for cargo loss or damage is changed, or the carrier's limit of liability increased, the gross claim amount, which includes items such as salvage costs and port of refuge expenses will still remain at the same level.

From the marine insurance view point, theoretically, if there is a change in the amount of loss to be covered under each policy, the premium rate should change according to the increased or reduced risks. If the carrier's liability is increased, the P&I Club policy will provide wider coverage to meet the demand of their members.

Therefore as a whole, the insurance industry would appear to be in a neutral position to the Convention and the insurers are ready to provide the necessary insurance coverage under the Convention as required by the carriers, the shippers and the other parties concerned.

III. Points in Favour of Cargo Interests

The next issue to consider is the important changes in the Convention in favour of the cargo interests.

1. The Removal of the Error in Navigation Defence (Article17 and18)

A significant change to the current position is the removal of the defence of error in navigation, which is frequently to blame for collision, stranding, capture and other maritime casualties.

This means that the cargo interests can claim against the carrier for cargo loss or damage if the fault of the master or crew of the ship is proven.

This is in favour of the cargo interests and a very important change to the current position in the Convention.

The error in navigation defence is one of the most difficult and unique points to explain to people outside the maritime industry. Even many cargo owners or persons in charge of dealing with foreign trade do not seem to understand the ground of such a defence.

This is obviously different from the principle applied to the liability of an inland carrier who is liable for cargo damage caused by collision or overturning of the truck due to the driver's negligence.

As the Convention extends its scope of application to the inland leg of multi modal transportation, a common principle of liability will now apply for the sea leg and the inland leg, which is far easier to understand for the cargo owner who is not familiar with contracts of maritime transportation.

2. The Fire Defence(Article 17)

Under the current rules the carrier enjoys the benefit of exemption from liability for cargo damage caused by fire on board a vessel unless caused by his actual fault or privity.

However the Convention changes the rule as an error in navigation defence and the carrier is responsible for fire damage proved by the claimant to have been caused by the fault of the master, crew or employees.

3. Increased Limitation of Liability (Article 59)

This is also a benefit for the cargo interests.

As for Japanese law, the limitation under Japan COGSA 1992 is 666.67SDR or ¥80,000 per package but under the Convention, the limit is increased to 875SDR per package or ¥105,000.

As for weight limitation, the current 2SDR per kg limit is also increased to 3SDR so by 50%.

4. Extension of the Time Limit (Article 62)

The Convention applies a two years time limitation period for commencing proceeding for a cargo claim against the carrier, whereas the current time limitation period is only one year.

This is clearly a point in favour of a cargo claimant as practically, it often takes more than one year from the date of delivery of the cargo, until the settlement of the cargo claim. So, a cargo claimant is frequently obliged to obtain the carrier's agreement to extend the time limit or take legal action. The new rule greatly lightens the cargo claimant's burden.

5. Continuing Obligation of Seaworthiness (Article 14)

Under the current rules the carrier is required to exercise due diligence to make the ship seaworthy only before and at the beginning of the voyage, but the Convention extends this obligation of the carrier to the period of the voyage. As it extends the carrier's obligation of seaworthiness this new provision is of course more favourable to cargo interests.

IV. Points in Favour of Ship Interests

There are changes which I think practically speaking are of benefit for the ship interest.

1. Volume Contract (Article 80)

Under the Convention in principle, the obligations in the rules cannot be deviated from by the carrier, but the volume contract provision is an exception to this and in the case of a volume contract the carrier is allowed to reduce its liabilities by contract so on the face of it, this rule is in favour of the carrier.

This type of contract seems to be popular in the US, but it is not familiar to or used by those in other countries, including Japan. Some commentators have objected to the Convention because of this Article.

2. Jurisdiction (Article 66, 67 and 74)

The Convention allows a cargo claimant to chose one of several jurisdictions in which to bring their claim against the carrier, such as the place of receipt and delivery (Article 66), thus potentially restricting the enforceability of an agreement for exclusive jurisdiction in a bill of lading. As far as this stipulation is concerned, it seems to be in favour of the cargo claimant. However, Article 74 states that only Contracting States that positively declare to be bound by this Chapter of the Convention shall be subject to the rule in Article 66. As many countries may not like to declare to be bound, then on the contrary, Article 67 allows the carrier to rely on an exclusive jurisdiction clause which is a point in favour of the carrier.

3. Obligation or Liability of the Shipper (Article 32, 43, 58 etc.)

The new rules for the shipper's unlimited liability for undeclared dangerous cargo (Article 32) and the obligation to accept delivery (Article 43) and the liability of the holder of the transport document (Article 58) are all in favour of the carrier.

4. Liability of Maritime Performing Party (Article 19)

Some commentators have stated that this Article is in favour of a cargo claimant, because it allows an additional and alternative claim against a maritime performing party. Nevertheless, I think that as far as Himalaya clause is concerned it is in favour of the carrier side because there will no longer be any need for it in a bill of lading.

5. Period of Responsibility (Article 12 and 13)

The reference to FIO (free in and out) clauses in Article 12 and 13 are both in favour of the carrier. In particular, the latter type of provision is now clarified to be effective and the carrier can limit the scope of his liability.

When we see the current situation in the US, the extension of the applicable period of carriage from door to door including non sea legs of international carriage (Article 12) seems to be for the benefit of the carrier as it protects him for the inland leg of transportation.

There still seem to be some argument outstanding in the US as to whether rail carriers are protected or not by USCOGSA, for an inland leg of carriage covered by a through bill of lading, for export cargo. This is despite the US Supreme Court having delivered two opinions (the Kirby case in 2004 and the Regal-Beloit case in 2010) both disallowing application of the Carmack Amendment to the Interstate Commerce Act.

In the US, maritime and trade associations are requesting the US State Department to expedite ratification of the Convention. If the US ratifies the Convention the position would be greatly in favour of a carrier who undertakes inland transportation by rail under a through bill of lading.

The Convention states that nothing in the Convention affects the application of any international conventions governing the carriage of goods by another mode (Art.82). So for inland carriage in Europe the CMR Convention will remain applicable to inland transportation. However, the European Shipper's Council has questioned the Convention fearing that it may affect the CMR limitation of liability namely 8.33SDR per kg, which is higher than the limit under the Convention namely 3SDR per kg.

V. General Average (Article 84)

Apart from cargo damage claims, I think that general average claims will also be significantly affected by elimination of the "error in navigation defence"

As you may know, general average is a system peculiar to the marine adventure being even more ancient in origin than marine insurance.

Under the system of General Average, in the case of stranding, collision, fire or other maritime casualty, hull and cargo interests contribute to sacrifice or expenditure, such as salvage or port of refuge costs, voluntarily incurred for the safety of the common adventure.

Under the Convention, Article 84 provides "Nothing in this Convention affects the application of terms in the contract of carriage or provisions of national law regarding the adjustment of general average." So, it appears that the Convention will not affect the current general average system at all. But I am sceptical about this. Even if general average is duly adjusted and contributions claimed by the shipowners, the cargo interests may now be able to refuse to pay in many more cases.

This is because of the operation of Rule D of York Antwerp Rules, (international rules on general average), which stipulates "Right to contribution in general average shall not be affected, though the event may have been due to the fault of one of the parties," and continues " but this shall not prejudice any remedies or defences which may be open against or to that party in respect of such fault".

Lowndes and Rudolf 13ed. a well known text book on general average states as to the relationship between the Convention and general average as follows:

" under the Convention the exception will be removed so it is hardly necessary to mention that the absence of this exception would greatly increase the number of cases in which a claim for contribution can be successfully defended on the ground of actionable fault. "

So it will become difficult to maintain the principle of general average that the shipper and the shipowner shall contribute to sacrifice and expenses made or incurred for the common safety of the property involved in a common maritime adventure.

There may be the possibility that the shipowner shall declare frustration or abandonment of the voyage at the port of refuge after a casualty declining to forward the cargo to the final destination as less likely for him to recover GA contribution to the forwarding costs.

As to the future impact on general average and marine insurance of the Convention, I personally suppose that a shipowner whose claim for contribution is rejected by a cargo owner, may arrange insurance coverage with their P&I Club for non recoverable general average contribution, or alternatively under their hull insurance policy by using a special clause such as a small general average clause or by voyage expenses insurance.

VI. Salvage

In some cases salvage charges are adjusted under general average declared by the shipowner, but unless so adjusted, they are borne by the respective salved interests.

Thus the cargo owner is obliged to pay salvage charges to the salvor for his salved cargo. But, under the Convention the carrier will be liable for such loss if the casualty is caused by an error in navigation.

As a consequence the shipowner will in fact be finally responsible for the salvage costs, so the practice of cargo salvage will be changed drastically in the same way as general average.

VII. Uniformity

In the circumstances what is most important to note is that there will be more time and cost incurred because of the conflict between the Convention and the Hague Visby Rules, by arguments as to how to apportion liability for cargo damage and costs incurred between the parties.

I have mentioned the possible significant changes for general average and salvage, but the same situation will arise in connection with cargo claims to determine the applicable law and jurisdiction. So, the number of litigation cases is likely to increase.

It is rumoured that the US will ratify the Convention shortly. If the US ratifies because trade with US is very important to Japan, practically speaking this will have a big impact for Japanese interests that is which rules Japan COGSA or new US COGSA is to be applied for shipments between Japanese and US ports,.

As we have seen, the current practice will be affected significantly by the conflicting Rules. So, I think that it is necessary for Japanese interests to reach an agreement about their position towards the Convention at the earliest stage, to save cost and avert possible confusion.

Part I, Chapter 5

The Rotterdam Rules and Asia-Pacific States

15

People's Republic of China

Dihuang Song

In People's Republic of China ("China"), like other countries it is difficult to summarize its position in five minutes. Apparently, there were some controversies both in preparation process and after the adoption of the Rotterdam Rules around the international community, and it is certainly not surprising that views towards this innovative convention is also diversified in China. In particular as I mentioned part of it in my speech just now, there were some general complaints of the complexity of the rules and sometimes difficulties in understanding those articles and cross reference of each articles from back and forth and so on. So that was the general views of the people in the industry, i.e., in the shipping industry and in the cargo's industry. They have some negative thoughts about these innovative Rotterdam Rules as these Rules are far more complicated than Hague Rules or Hague Visby Rules.

As you also probably are aware that China has not acceded nor ratified any of the existing international convention, either Hague rules or Hague-Visby rules or Hamburg rules, so I think as a comparison probably it's easier for China if we decide to adopt the Rotterdam Rules. We don't have to abandon or substantively revising our existing laws and as a matter of Chinese law once we decide to adopt an international convention, we don't need to have a second legislation in order to convert it into our domestic law. So once China decide to ratify Rotterdam Rules, they will become part of Chinese law, and if there's any conflict of existing domestic law with the international convention, then the international convention will prevail.

So that's the positive side, but the sad side is that we have conducted substantive and comprehensive studies over the rules by the relevant ministries of China that is the Ministry of Transport notably representing shipping industry and on the other hand the Ministry of Commerce, perhaps representing mostly the cargo and trading companies or freight forwarders. So they have conducted a comprehensive study over these rules and sadly a decision is yet to be made and I understand they have instructed various universities like Dalian Maritime University, China University of Political Science and Law and also Beijing University and I have been able to review some of their reports, but apparently the government is still hanging around and wish to see the stance of the other countries particularly those of major trading partners like United States. Prof. Michael Sturley will explain the position of United States. Unfortunately the position of China is still unclear and we do not know what final decision is going to be taken by the Chinese government, whether to ratify it or not.

But my personal recommendation is that we should go for it. I completely agree with Professor Van der Ziel. Indeed, my conclusion is that it is true that the new rules are complicated, but that it's not the harshness of the international convention, it's not the complexity of the convention that makes people worry or express doubt, instead it is the harshness of the business, the harshness, complexity of the modern trade and transportation that require a modern international convention that could deal with it. Just like Mr. Beare mentioned, we do need a change.

16

The Rotterdam Rules in Japan

Tomotaka Fujita

I will explain the status quo of the Rotterdam Rules in Japan.

To the best of my knowledge, the government has not yet decided, or perhaps not even examined, whether Japan should join the new Convention. Japanese industry groups may have their opinion. But, unlike their counterparts in Europe or in the United States, they have not expressed, at least explicitly, their position on the Rotterdam Rules. In short, two years after the signing ceremony, nothing has happened in this country. Relevant parties still keep their "wait and see" position. This is the very reason why we organized this symposium.

I want to add one remark on the signing of the Convention. Japan has not signed the Rotterdam Rules yet. Although this is sometimes interpreted as a negative message by the Japanese government, perhaps it is not true. Japan does not usually sign conventions of this sort unless their ratification is almost certain. "Accession," rather than ratification, is often used when Japan joins an international convention. When a state uses "accession," it does not have to sign prior to finally deciding on whether or not to join the international convention. Therefore, Japan's failure to sign the Rotterdam Rules does not necessarily mean that the Japanese government has a strong complaint against them. It is more accurate to say that Japan has not yet made up its mind, or perhaps has not yet considered the issue seriously.

People in the other countries may be curious as to why both the government and industry are so passive, but this should not be surprising if you remember that Japan joined the Hague-Visby Rules in 1992, a full 24 years after their adoption. It took 28 years for Japan to join CISG, in 2008. It is not unusual for Japan to maintain an attitude of "wait and see" for decades with respect to this kind of private law conventions. I do not want to examine the reasons behind this very cautious attitude toward international conventions. It is beyond the scope of this symposium.

Nor do I want to make any comments as to whether the Rotterdam Rules are good for Japanese industry. It is beyond my role. The carriers, cargo interests, freight forwarders, and insurers will express their views during the next session. It would make more sense to hear their voices than mine.

Instead, I wish to take this opportunity to give some advice for the government or industry when they consider whether to accept or to reject the Rotterdam Rules someday.

First, we should not ask whether the Rotterdam Rules are a perfect instrument. This is not a relevant question. The real question is whether the Rules, as a whole, are better than other possible regimes.

What would these "other possible regimes" be, then? It is important to recognize that the Hague-Visby Rules are not a candidate. Imagine what would happen if the Rotterdam Rules failed. The Hague-Visby regime might remain for some time, but sooner or later they would lose their predominant position. After the fall of the Hague-Visby regime, "regionalism" may most likely prevail in the area of international carriage of goods. The revised Carriage of Goods by Sea Act has been pending in the United States Congress and seems ready to be approved once they think the Rotterdam Rules are a failure. In Europe, new regulations on multimodal transportation are about be discussed at the EU level. We should compare the Rotterdam Rules with these alternative future regimes. It is pointless to compare them with the situation under the Hague-Visby Rules.

Finally, we should note that time is limited. We may quite likely to lose an opportunity to make a meaningful decision if we keep silence too long.

I hope the industry and the government make a sensible decision in due course.

17

Korea

In Hyeon Kim

The Republic of Korea ("Korea") did not have the momentum to begin a discussion on whether Korea should ratify the Rotterdam Rules (hereinafter RR) during 2009, 2010 and 2011. However, several articles on the RR have appeared in Korean journals, and government and industry have shown interest in the ratification of the RR by other countries.

The Ministry of Justice and the Ministry of Land, Transport and Maritime Affairs are two governmental agencies in charge of the private international Convention. The Ministry of Land, Transport and Maritime Affairs is heavily influenced by the opinion of the Korean Shipowners' Association. However, the Ministry of Justice is a neutral agency.

The Korea Shipowners' Association and the Korea P & I Club are two influential private organizations that represent the interests of shipowners and carriers. They showed a tendency to oppose the early ratification of the Rules.

In response to my interview, the persons in charge of the RR in major liner shipping companies replied that they did not feel any urgent need to ratify the RR earlier than any other neighboring and competing countries, such as China and Japan.

They expressed the opinion that Korean shipping companies would be negatively affected by the deletion of the error of navigation defense under the RR, which is different from the US situation. They say that it would increase payments to the cargo interest, raise freight charges and finally, Korean shipping companies would lose in the competition with other major liner companies.

Regarding the volume contract, they felt that Korean liner companies would not have the same bargaining power as the volume cargo owners, even under the freedom of contract regime of the volume contract. Thus, the volume contract under the RR will would not be advantageous to Korean liner companies, which are regarded as medium sized as opposed to super-sized liner companies, such as the Maersk Line.

The Korean Shipper's Association is less influential than the Korean Shipowners' Association. They are in an affirmative position with regard to the Rules. They welcome the deletion of the error of navigation defense and the volume contract.

There are several opinion leaders in Korea on the maritime law. Maritime lawyers representing the shipowners' interest are reluctant to ratify the RR. However, maritime lawyers representing cargo interests welcome the RR and support its early ratification. Judges who are specialists in maritime law show a tendency towards early ratification.

In response to my interview, every interviewee (15) agreed that ratification of the RR by the US and China will affect Korea. Almost all interviewees also agreed that a regional convention for European countries or East-Asian countries is not desirable because it is against the goal of unification and predictability in the international private law convention.

In my personal view, Korea is not likely to ratify the RR within two or three years. However, if the US and China ratify the RR, and Korean industry and government start discussion on their ratification, the process of ratification will be accelerated. I hope that this seminar will provide East-Asian countries with a powerful momentum to ratify the RR.

One positive movement in Korea is that in November 2011, the Transport Law Special Committee established by the Korean Ministry of Justice decided to submit a paper requesting the Korean government to ratify the 1996 Protocol to 1976 LLMC. This is a good message in that the Korean government may forego the traditional attitude of incorporating most provisions in maritime conventions into its national law without ratifying them and go along with other major shipping country with early ratification of them, like Japan. The Committee might study whether they will recommend that the Korean government to ratify the RR soon.

18

Singapore

Stephen Girvin

Thank you, ladies and gentleman, I speak about Singapore. Although it will be self evident, to anybody looking at me, that I have no standing to represent Singapore as the locals would say I'm an 'Ang Moh' or in Cantonese I'm a 'Gweilo', a foreigner. Nevertheless, I will try to give some indication as to where I think things are going and where they have got to, so far as Singapore is concerned.

Now within Singapore, essentially there are two potential bodies looking at the Rotterdam Rules. The first of these is the government legal office, the Attorney General's Chambers (or the AGC) and, in fact, one of the senior government officers in the AGC attended pretty much all the working groups, representing Singapore. Then additionally there is the Maritime and Port Authority (the MPA). Now the MPA inevitably has a regulatory role to perform, holding the ports under its control essentially. And they also would have an interest in the Rotterdam Rules. But inevitably it would be the legal office, the Attorney General's Chambers (the AGC), who would have primary responsibility for determining whether or not Singapore should in fact ratify the Rotterdam Rules.

Singapore, like some of the other jurisdictions we have heard about today, has not traditionally been at the forefront of ratification of multilateral conventions (and that includes, of course, maritime conventions). To give a couple of illustrations. The London Limitation Convention of 1976 (LLMC), which came into force in 1986 was not in fact ratified by Singapore until 2004. The CISG of 1980, the Sale Convention, which into force in 1988 was not ratified by Singapore until 1996. So, at the moment, I think the official position in Singapore is very much one of 'sit tight' and see which way the wind blows. If Singapore's major trading partners take active steps to ratify the rules – and those trading partners would obviously be countries like the United States and China and the Europe Union – then there would be a powerful incentive for Singapore to look more carefully at the Rotterdam Rules and potentially ratify them.

Although I am representing what I believe to be the official position, this is not to say that there 's no interest within Singapore in the Rotterdam Rules. Inevitably, there have been quite a lot of high powered seminars which have been held since the completion of the Rules and the signing ceremony in Rotterdam. The Maritime Law Association (MLAS) has been quite active in holding a number of seminars on the rules. The Singapore Academy of Law (SAL) has also been responsible for holding a number of seminars and I have been responsible for one or two of those. And then there is the Singapore Shipping Association (SSA) which represents ship owners in Singapore. They have a legal and insurance committee and I sit on that committee in an advisory capacity. That committee has also been looking at the various provisions of the Rotterdam Rules, particularly in relation to advice received by the International Chamber of Shipping.

So, to conclude, I am afraid it is a 'wait and see' game at least for now. Thank you very much.

19

The United States

Michael Sturley

Good morning, everyone. I have been told that you are all waiting to hear what I am going to say about the United States, but first I need to start with the same disclaimer as Professor Girvin. I am not here in any official capacity, and I do not speak on behalf of the U.S. government. I nevertheless believe that I can accurately report on the current situation in the United States.

The U.S. situation is that the government remains committed to ratification of the Rotterdam Rules as soon as possible. The reason that the government remains committed is that the U.S. stakeholders — the U.S. commercial interests that will be governed by the new convention — remain committed to ratification. And the reason that our stakeholders remain committed is that they were involved throughout the process and fully understand what is at issue. Those of you who attended the UNCITRAL negotiations will remember that the United States regularly had the largest delegation in the room because we included so many of our commercial stakeholders in the delegation. When contentious issues came up during the sessions, we could get immediate guidance from those who would be most directly affected by the new Rules.

During the negotiation of the Rotterdam Rules, we in the U.S. delegation succeeded in meeting our objectives on some issues but not on others. If we were to compare the Rotterdam Rules to the hypothetical "perfect convention" that we would like to have achieved, therefore, we would see that the Rotterdam Rules are not "perfect" from our perspective. But as Professor Fujita has just suggested, that hypothetical perfect convention is simply not an option. In any negotiation, there must be compromise. Everyone will win on some issues and lose on other issues. On balance, however, our commercial interests are satisfied with the final result because it is better than anything else that is realistically imaginable. Indeed, the Rotterdam Rules are much better than any other option that is or might be available in the foreseeable future. The new convention represents a significant improvement over our current situation, and a very significant improvement over the very real possibility of national and regional approaches in this field in which uniformity is so important. Our commercial interests are therefore committed and thus our government is committed to U.S. ratification.

There have been a few pockets of opposition, generally from lawyers who practice in and around the area, and each of those pockets of opposition has been addressed. Most of the opposition has been based primarily on a lack of knowledge or on incomplete knowledge. I had a conversation just last evening with someone who mentioned a U.S. opponent whom he knew, but he said that the opponent now seemed to be in favor of the Rotterdam Rules. As it happens, I know the lawyer in question, and I can explain why his views changed. He had indeed opposed the Rotterdam Rules because he did not understand what they involved. He had been taking a very limited view, focusing only on his disappointments in the negotiation. Once he more fully understood what the new convention would do, he said, "Oh, is that what they do? In that case, I will support them now." Seminars such as this are a tremendous opportunity because as people better understand the Rotterdam Rules they appreciate how the Rules will be a significant improvement (and that ratification would be a good idea). The advantage that we have in the United States is that our stakeholders have been involved in the process from the beginning and therefore our major stakeholders already understand and support the Rotterdam Rules.

In view of what I have just said, certain questions naturally arise: "Why hasn't the United States ratified yet?" "Why has there been such a long delay since the signing ceremony?" The delay here, as in so many such cases, results from a combination of circumstances. The head of the U.S. Delegation throughout the negotiations retired almost immediately after the signing ceremony. Her successor is a wonderful lawyer. He is very smart and he works very hard, but he first came to the project after the signing ceremony (while he was still completing prior work and also beginning other new assignments). He obviously had a lot to learn. Those of you who have worked on learning the Rotterdam Rules yourself appreciate how much time it takes to understand them. And he had to understand them not only well enough to satisfy himself that they should be ratified but to persuade the other agencies of the government, to persuade the President, and to persuade the Senate that they should be ratified.

Addressing the pockets of opposition has also been a time-consuming enterprise. For some opponents, it was simply a matter of education. Some opponents raised new objections that had not been considered before, and the questions that they raised needed to be resolved. Some of the delay was caused not by opponents but by interested parties who simply wanted to ensure that they understood how the Rotterdam Rules will work in practice.

As will undoubtedly be the case in most countries, it has been necessary in the United States to decide how the Rotterdam Rules will interact with other legislation that is already in force. On some issues, the answer is obvious. The U.S. Carriage of Goods by Sea Act (COGSA) will be superseded for voyages in international trade that are within the scope of the Rotterdam Rules. But what about domestic shipments that are sometimes covered by COGSA today? And how should ratification of the Rotterdam Rules affect the U.S. Harter Act or Pomerene Act? Resolving those questions has inevitably been time-consuming.

In the midst of the process, it was also recognized that the final version of the Rotterdam Rules contained a technical error that could cause practical problems. Indeed, it was feared that the error could provoke serious opposition to the convention. Fortunately, the UNCITRAL secretariat also recognized the problem and began the process to correct it. But while that problem is being resolved, the U.S. ratification process is moving more slowly.

The process in the United States is also very thorough. The Rotterdam Rules have been subject to several layers of review within the State Department, and substantial documentation is associated with that review. Ultimately the State Department must prepare and approve what we call the "transmittal package." When that is complete, it goes out for what is known as interagency review, which is when other departments in the federal government have their chance to weigh in on what they think should be done. The good news is that the interagency review has already been occurring informally, since other agencies were part of the negotiation process from the beginning. But the process must still be completed formally.

After interagency review, the State Department will send the completed transmittal package to the President. It is unlikely that the President himself is going to study the transmittal package in any detail. The President has some other items on his agenda. News reports suggest that he is very concerned about U.S. jobs. In 2012, he will probably be very concerned about keeping his own job. Thus the focus in the White House will be not on the substance of the Rotterdam Rules but on the President's political advisors' evaluation of whether anything in the Rotterdam Rules might become a political issue. They will want to make sure that the U.S. ratification of the Rotterdam Rules will not become an issue in the presidential election that he will have to defend during the debates (and they may even look to see if there is anything in the convention that could help his re-election chances).

I think we all know that nothing in the Rotterdam Rules is going to excite any political interest whatsoever. It may take the President's political advisors longer to reach that conclusion than it takes us, but once they do the President should formally transmit the convention to the Senate for its approval.

As an aside, I might mention that the lack of political interest in the Rotterdam Rules means that the 2012 presidential election should be completely irrelevant to the prospects for U.S. ratification. The convention was negotiated and approved by the U.N. General Assembly during a republican administration, but the United States signed the convention during a democratic administration. Updating and modernizing commercial law will benefit U.S. commercial interests, whichever party may be in power.

Under our constitutional system, the Senate must give its advice and consent before the President can ratify a convention such as the Rotterdam Rules. This requires a two-thirds majority in the Senate, but that is not particularly relevant. When the Senate votes on the Rotterdam Rules, it will almost certainly be a unanimous. If a senator were to object, it is likely that the vote would simply be postponed until that senator's concerns could be addressed. But it is unlikely that any senator will have any concerns. Senators will want to know that U.S. commercial interests favor the convention, and because they do the convention is likely to sail through the Senate unanimously as soon as the Senate leadership is willing to devote the time to address it. So once the Rotterdam Rules go to the Senate, it will simply be a question of inertia: When will the leadership in the Senate be willing to devote five or ten minutes of Senate time to something that will get senators no significant news coverage and that will not help their re-elections at all?

My personal hope is that in the period between the election and the end of the session — when everyone is looking forward to the new session and the Senate is unable to accomplish anything controversial — they will try to complete some business that is not controversial, and thus give their advice and consent so that we can ratify quickly.

But I must also admit that once things get into the Senate it's a black hole where anything could happen. We have just heard how long it took Japan to ratify the Hague-Visby Rules, but in the United States we have waited even longer. It took us 12 years to ratify the Hague Rules. In other words, there are risks that it will be a time-consuming process simply from inertia. But inertia is not opposition. We are committed to ratification and we plan to ratify as quickly as we can overcome the inertia. As Isaac Newton has explained, however, it takes considerable force to take a large mass that is not in motion and to put it into motion. Our government is a large bureaucracy that does not always move nimbly. We nevertheless hope that it will move soon.

Part II

Workshop on the Rotterdam Rules

The Rotterdam Rules in the Asia-Pacific Region: Workshop

Q.1 Carrier's Obligation: Validity of Terms and Conditions in Standard Form Bill of Lading

(1) The Caspiana Clause

Bills of lading often contain a clause that permits the carrier to discharge the goods at a different place than the original destination under exceptional situations in which it becomes physically impossible or economically impractical for the carrier to complete the carriage. In many countries, such a clause, known as the "Caspiana Clause," has been understood as valid under the Hague-Visby Rules. Article 11 of the Rotterdam Rules stipulates that the carrier shall carry the goods to the place of destination and deliver them to the consignee. Article 79 provides that any term in a contract of carriage is void to the extent that it directly or indirectly excludes or limits the obligations of the carrier under the Rules. Is the Caspiana Clause also valid under the Rotterdam Rules?

(2) The Retla Clause

The validity of the "Retla Clause" is controversial under the Hague-Visby Rules. The clause typically provides that superficial rust or any similar condition of iron, steel, or metal products does not constitute "damage" and that acknowledgement of receipt of the goods in apparent good order and condition does not mean that the goods were free of visible rust, oxidation, or moisture. Similar type of clauses also stipulate that the phrase "apparent good order and condition" with reference to the unpacked goods does not mean that the goods when received were free from any dents, scratches, holes, cuts, and bruises that could not have been found by ordinary care and diligence. Under the Rotterdam Rules the carrier is relieved of all or part of its liability for loss of or damage to the goods, as well as for delay in delivery, if it proves that the loss or damage arose from an inherent defect, quality, or vice of the goods (Article 17(3)(j)). The Rules also provide that the contract particulars in the transport document or electronic transport record shall include a statement of the apparent order and condition of the goods at the time the carrier or a performing party received them for carriage (Article 36(2)). Do the Rotterdam Rules regulate the validity of the Retla Clause? Or is the issue left to applicable national law or court decisions?

Sample of the Caspiana Clause (Multimodel Transport Bill of Lading issued by the Japan International Freight Forwarders Association, Inc.)
10. CONTINGENCIES
(1) If at any time the performance of the Carriage hereunder is or is likely to be affected by any hindrance, danger, or disturbance of whatsoever kind which cannot be avoided by exercise of reasonable endeavors, the Carrier may, whether or not the Carriage is commenced, without notifying the Merchant, treat the Carriage as terminated and discharge, land, store, or take any other necessary means whatsoever on the Goods or any part thereof and place them at the Merchant's disposal at any place or port which the Carrier may deem safe and convenient whereupon the responsibility of the Carrier in respect of such Goods shall cease. In such a case, the discharge, landing and storing and any means whatsoever taken shall constitute complete and final delivery and full performance of the Carriage hereunder, and the Carrier shall be discharged from any further responsibility of the Goods.

(2) The situations referred to in the preceding paragraph shall include, but not limited to, those caused by the existence or apprehension of war, declared or undeclared, hostilities, warlike or belligerent acts or operations, riots, civil commotions or other disturbances; or interdict or prohibition of or restriction on commerce or trading; quarantine, sanitary or other similar regulations or restrictions; strikes, lockouts or other labor troubles whether partial or general and whether or not involving employees of the Carrier or any Actual Carrier; congestion of port, wharf, sea terminal or any other place; shortage, absence or obstacles of labor or facilities for loading, discharge, delivery or other handling of the Goods: epidemics or diseases; bad weather or any other obstacles to the Carriage of the Goods.

(3) In case of the preceding paragraphs, the Carrier shall be entitled to all freight and other charges due and the Merchant shall be liable for payment of all freight to the Port of Discharge or place of landing or for any other expenses incurred at such port or place as a result of the discharge, landing, storing or other means whatsoever taken by the Carrier in relation to the Goods.

Sample of the Retla Clause and Similar Clauses (Multimodel Transport Bill of Lading issued by the Japan International Freight Forwarders Association, Inc.)
14. AUTOMOBILE AND OTHER UNPACKED GOODS
The term apparent good order and condition with reference to any automobile, rolling stock, trac-

tor, machinery and other unpacked goods does not mean that the condition of the Goods when received were free of any dent, scratch, hole, cut and bruise that could not have been found by ordinary care and diligence. The Carrier shall in no event be liable for such conditions.

15. IRON, STEEL AND METAL PRODUCTS

Superficial rust, oxidation, moisture or any like condition of any iron, steel or metal products is not a condition of damage but is inherent to the nature of the Goods and acknowledgement of receipt of the Goods in apparent good order and condition does not mean that the Goods when received were free of visible rust, oxidation or moisture. The Carrier shall in no event be liable for loss or damage arising out of or resulting from such inherent nature of the Goods.

Amemiya: Q.1 is related to validity of terms and conditions in standard form bills of lading. In this case, I would take up two clauses, that is to say, the Caspiana Clause as a clause that has been understood as valid under the Hague-Visby Rules and the Retla Clause as a clause that is controversial under the same Rules. If the performance of the carriage is or is likely to be affected by any hindrance or danger of whatsoever kind which cannot be avoided by exercise of reasonable endeavors, the Caspiana Clause permits the carrier to discharge the goods at a different place than the original destination and to treat the carriage as terminated. In this regard, is the Caspiana Clause void under Article 79 of the Rotterdam Rules as it directly excludes the carrier's obligation to carry the goods to the place of destination and deliver them to the consignee (Article 11)?

The Retla Clause typically provides that superficial rust or any similar condition of any iron, steel, or metal products does not constitute "damage" but is inherent to the nature of the goods and that acknowledgement of receipt of the goods in apparent good order and condition does not mean that the goods when received were free of visible rust, oxidation, or moisture. Article 36(2) of the Rotterdam Rules provides that the contract particulars in the transport document or electronic transport record shall include a statement of the apparent order and condition of the goods at the time the carrier or a performing party received them for carriage. The first issue is whether the Retla Clause is void under Article 79 of the Rotterdam Rules as it directly excludes the above obligation. Article17(3)(j) provides that the carrier is relieved of all or part of its liability for loss of or damage to the goods, as well as for delay in delivery, if it proves that the loss or damage arose from an inherent defect, quality, or vice of the goods. If superficial rust of iron or steel is proved to be arisen from an inherent defect, the carrier will be relieved of liability for such rust. Therefore, is such clause unnecessary?

Q.1(1)

Fujita: This question examines what is and what is not changed under the Rotterdam Rules compared with the previous liability regime. Mr. Beare, could you give us the answer to the question because you addressed the "Need for Change" (*See*, p. 9 et seq.) in your presentation?

Beare: The short answer to Q.1(1) is yes. Article 11 refers to "the place of destination". I would say that the place of destination, prima facie, is either the port of discharge or the place of delivery as specified in the contract. But that can be modified by the terms of the contract and the incorporation of a Caspiana Clause, to my mind, modifies the place of destination. So I think that the Caspiana Clause would be valid and that Article 79 would not apply.

There is jurisprudence that distinguishes between *reasonable* Caspiana Clauses and unreasonable clauses. An example of an unreasonable clause is one that would permit a carrier that had not been paid hire under its time charter to discharge the goods at the nearest available port. But war clauses and piracy clauses, which are specifically designed to meet present day hazards of shipping, would, I think, be allowed under the Rotterdam Rules, just as they are under the Hague-Visby Rules.

Fujita: Thank you for your explanation. It sounds like a reasonable interpretation of the provision. What about the second question on the "Retla Clause"?

Q.1(2)

Beare: Sample clause 15 provides that "the Carrier shall in no event be liable for loss or damage arising out of or resulting from such inherent nature of the goods." Article 17(3)(j) refers to "the inherent defect, quality, or vice of the goods". These are precisely the same words as in Article IV(2) of the Hague Rules. So, my view is that there would be no difference in the treatment of such a Retla Clause under the Rotterdam Rules from that under the current Hague-Visby Rules.

Fujita: Professor Sturley, do you have a different view?

Sturley: I wouldn't disagree, but I would supplement that answer by noting that the Retla Clause comes in various forms. I think the answer that Mr. Beare gave for one type of Retla Clause is completely accurate. But in the U.S. trade, the case for which the Retla Clause is named — a decision of the U.S. Court of Appeals for the Ninth Circuit *(Tokio Marine & Fire Insurance Company, Ltd. v. Retla Steamship Company*, 426 F.2d 1372 (9th Cir. 1970)) — illustrates a very different sort of Retla Clause. Moreover, it has been expanded in U.S. trade to govern a number of different things, such as wood products for example. To the extent the clause excuses the carrier from liability for damages caused by "inherent vice", it is perfectly valid, but it is also perfectly unnecessary because the Rotterdam Rules, like the Hague and Hague-Visby Rules, already excuse the carrier from liability for inherent vice. To the extent that the Retla Clause in question, like many Retla Clauses, also excuses the carrier from stating the apparent order and condition of the goods, which is controversial under the Hague and Hague-Visby Rules, I think it is not controversial at all under the Rotterdam Rules. The Rotterdam Rules make it quite clear that the carrier must state the apparent order and condition of the goods and failing to do so creates the presumption that the goods were in apparent good order or condition at the time of shipment.

So the answer depends on what kind of Retla Clause we are talking about. Some clauses that have been held valid under current law will no longer be valid, but the sort of clause Mr. Beare was describing would be perfectly valid, even if it is also perfectly unnecessary under the Rotterdam Rules.

Fujita: Thank you for your supplementary remarks on the Retla Clause.

Q.2 Period of Responsibility and Liabilities

> Let us assume that the shipper is the controlling party (Article 51(1)) and the consignee, upon the arrival of the goods at the place of destination, requests the carrier to keep the goods until a certain date on which the consignee promises to ultimately (physically) collect the goods. Under this situation, does the right of control (for instance, the right to instruct the carrier to regulate the temperature of reefer containers) still vest in the shipper? Under the Rotterdam Rules, the right of control lapses when the period of responsibility of the carrier (Article 12) ends, i.e., when the goods are delivered. Can we regard the goods as having been delivered to the consignee when the carrier has informed the consignee that the goods are being held on its behalf even if the carrier still retains actual custody of the goods? In this hypothetical situation, if we assume that the goods are regarded as having been delivered to the consignee, is the carrier's responsibility for loss of or damage to the goods, caused by the carrier's (custodian's) fault after such "delivery," outside the scope of the Rotterdam Rules?

Amemiya: Q.2 is related to "delivery of goods". Article 51(1) of the Rotterdam Rules provides that except in the cases referred to in Article 51(2), (3) and (4), the shipper is the controlling party. Upon the arrival of the goods at the place of destination, at the request of the consignee the carrier manifests an intention that goods shall thenceforward be possessed on behalf of the consignee and the possessory rights is transferred to the consignee constructively. Article 50(2) of the Rotterdam Rules provides that the right of control exists during the entire period of responsibility of the carrier, as provided in article 12, and ceases when that period expires. Article 12 provides that the period of responsibility of the carrier for the goods ends when the goods are delivered. The first question is whether the shipper's right of control ends as the goods have been delivered when the possessory rights was transferred to the consignee constructively even if the carrier still retains actual custody of the goods. If so, is the carrier's responsibility for loss of or damage to the goods, caused by the carrier's (custodian's) fault after such delivery outside the scope of the Rotterdam Rules?

Fujita: May I ask Professor Van der Ziel to answer the question because it is related to your presentation: delivery of the goods?

Van der Ziel: My short answer is that the actual custody doesn't matter so much. The essence of delivery under the Rotterdam Rules is the transfer of responsibility between the carrier and the consignee.

For example, if the contract of carriage in respect of a shipment of oil says that delivery will take place when the oil passes the ship's manifold, then the ship's manifold is the location of delivery. And it doesn't matter if the oil after passing the ship's manifold would remain under the custody of the carrier in the land tank. So "delivery" doesn't depend so much on what physically happens. What matters is the transfer of responsibility between one party and the other party.

In practice, much physical handling may be carried out by agents, either agents of the carrier or agents of the consignee and it may be difficult to determine on whose behalf a certain person that physically handles the goods, acts. In such event, the agreed time and location of delivery may be decisive: the person performing the cargo handling operations acts on behalf of the carrier prior to the agreed time and location of delivery and acts on behalf of the consignee after the agreed time and location of delivery.

Returning to the matter of the right of control in this hypothetical case, the right of control of the shipper in the question terminates at the moment that the responsibility is transferred between the carrier and the consignee. So after transfer of responsibility there is no right of control in the hands of the shipper anymore, and the only person from whom the carrier may accept instructions is, in this case, the consignee.

Fujita: May I ask for the clarification with respect to your answer. You said the physical possession is not relevant for determining carrier's period of responsibility. Therefore, the period of responsibility can end even when the carrier still maintains the physical possession of the goods. Is this conclusion drawn from the text of the Rotterdam Rules itself? Or does it depend on the fact that the applicable law recognizes a delivery without a transfer of physical possession. For instance, Japanese Civil Code recognizes the "delivery" in this hypothetical case as a form of valid transfer of possession (Article 183). Is this relevant to your argument? Or your conclusion holds regardless of the rules on delivery under applicable law.

Van der Ziel: The relevant provision seems to me article 12(3), saying that for the purpose of determining the carrier's period of responsibility, parties may agree on the time and location of delivery. Let me again give an example. When a charterparty includes a clause: "delivery shall take place alongside the vessel as fast as she can deliver," then that clause determines the place of delivery, namely alongside the vessel, and also the time of delivery, namely as fast as the ship is able to unload the cargo. So, at that point of time and at that place, the consignee has to collect the cargo. Let us assume that the cargo is timber. Then, the consignee must put a lorry on the quay (alongside the vessel) on which the vessel's derrick or crane may put the bundles of timber. When the lorry is full, the consignee may drive it away to its premises and another lorry has to be put in place. When there are no (sufficient) lorries, a forklift truck may shift the bundle from alongside the vessel to a shed near the quay for (temporary) storage. In the latter case, the cargo remains under the custody of the carrier because the consignee did not (yet) collect the goods. But legally, under the Rotterdam Rules, alongside the vessel a transfer of responsibility from the carrier to the consignee takes place and the forklift driver that carries the bundle from the quay to the shed is acting on behalf of the consignee. This is why I said that the term delivery under the Rotterdam Rules effectively is a transfer of responsibility, and not so much a physical transfer of cargo.

Returning to your question, this is the interpretation of the Rotterdam Rules and it is irrelevant whether the applicable law recognizes a delivery without a transfer of physical possession.

Fujita: Thank you. If the "delivery" takes place in this hypothetical case and the carrier's period of responsibility is over, then which law applies to the loss of or damage to the goods which are physically in custody of the carrier? Is the carrier's possible liability under this situation outside the scope of the Rotterdam Rules and the national law applies? Or the Rotterdam Rules still provides for the carrier's liability?

Van der Ziel: Thank you for the opportunity to clarify this matter further. For the question whether the period of responsibility of the carrier under the contract of carriage has ended, the agreement of the parties on the time and location of delivery is decisive. In the period after the agreed time and location the carrier has no responsibility under the contract of carriage anymore and the right of control has ended as well. All this is addressed in the Rotterdam Rules and is irrespective of national law.

However, when the goods that are still in the carrier's custody after its responsibility under the contract of carriage has come to an end because delivery has taken place, in my view, national law applies to such period of continued custody. For example, national law may view the continued custody as based on an (implied) contract of storage or on *negotiorum gestio*. In view of the fact that your question relates to goods that are already delivered, article 48 doesn't apply because this provision addresses undelivered goods.

The short answer to the question is therefore that the carrier's possible liability under this situation is outside the scope of the Rotterdam Rules and that national law applies.

Fujita: Thank you for the answer. Mr. Song, do you have any comment?

Song: Thank you, Professor Fujita. I just want to make a few comments. I entirely agree with Professor Van der Ziel as to the timing of the delivery depends on the terms of the contract of carriage. It does not necessarily relate to the actual custody of the goods. So that I am not going to go on further on that, but I wish to draw your attention to the scenario in this question.

Let us assume that shipper is the controlling party. Because Q.2 specifically refers to Article 51(1), I would assume that that was a situation – a scenario where neither a negotiable nor a non-negotiable document – an electronic record is contemplated to be issued. First, I wish to clarify this point.

Second, I was a little bit confused when the question says first that the shipper is a controlling party according to Article 51, and then the consignee, upon the arrival of the goods at the place of destination, requests the carrier to keep the goods. Apparently, we have to make sure whether the shipper has transferred the right of control to the consignee at this time and if it does then certainly the right of control have been transferred to the consignee. And then the question does not arise whether the right of controls is still vested in the shipper since it has been transferred to the consignee.

Fujita: Thank you very much for your clarification. You are correct in assuming that no negotiable transport documents or negotiable electronic transport record is issued in this hypothetical case (*See* Article 51(3) and (4)). It is also assumed that no non-negotiable transport document that indicates that it shall be surrendered in order to obtain delivery of the goods has been issued (*See* Article 51(2)). If such a document or a record has been issued, the question becomes more complicated.

Second, for the sake of simplicity, Q.2 presupposes that right of control is not transferred by the shipper. Even we assume that the carrier's period of responsibility still continues and the right of still exists, the shipper cannot exercise the right of control once it is transferred to the consignee.

Q.3 Carrier's Obligations and Liabilities and the FIO Clause

(1) The carrier and the shipper sometimes agree that the loading, stowing, and unloading of the goods are performed by the shipper (FIO clause). The validity of the FIO clause has been disputed under the Hague-Visby Rules. For example, English case law has held the FIO clause valid considering that the clause determines the scope of the contract of the carriage rather than relieving the carrier of its responsibility (*Pyrene v. Scindia Navigation* [1954] 2 QB 402; *Jindal Iron and Steel Co,Ltd,and Others v. Islamic Solidarity Shipping Company (The JORDAN II")*, [2005] 1 Lloyd's Rep 57).

However, the Rotterdam Rules adopt a different approach. While they assume that the activity under the FIO clause is covered within the carrier's period of responsibility (Article 12(3)), Article 13(2) of the Rotterdam Rules explicitly permits the FIO clause, Article 17(3)(i) refers to the activity under the FIO clause as an exoneration, and Article 17(4)(a) provides that the shipper can still hold the carrier liable proving the carrier's fault.

Is there any practical difference between the solutions provided for under the Rotterdam Rules and solutions provided for in the case law referred to above? For example, the carrier might be held liable if the loading or unloading of the goods performed by the crew caused damage to the goods. However, such a claim has been thought to be based on torts rather than on the contract of carriage. Is this solution different under the Rotterdam Rules?

(2) Company A (the carrier) enters into a contract of carriage by sea with B (the shipper) and the contract contains an FIO clause. Company A has a branch that also offers the stevedore service. Company A enters into a stevedore contract with B and loads the goods onto the ship for the carriage mentioned above. The stevedore contract contains a clause that Company A is liable only for the loss of or damage to the goods caused by its gross negligence. The goods are loaded onto and stowed on the ship by Company A's employee and Company A issues a bill of lading which includes an FIO clause applicable to B. C (the consignee) obtains the bill of lading from B. However, C noticed that the goods were damaged due to improper stowage at the port of loading.

(i) C (the consignee) makes claims for Company A's liability under the bill of lading issued by Company A. Company A argues that: (a) the loading is performed under a stevedore contract and not under the contract of carriage and, therefore, Company A is not liable pursuant to Article 17 (3) (i) of the Rotterdam Rules, and (b) even if A cannot invoke Article 17(3)(i), as a maritime performing party, Company A can limit its liability under Article 59. Is Company A's argument correct?

(ii) C (the consignee) claims for Company A's liability based on torts. C argues that the stowage by Company A's employee is performed pursuant to the FIO clause on behalf of the shipper and Company A's liability as the stevedore lies outside the scope of the Rotterdam Rules. Therefore, C concludes that Company A cannot limit its liability under the Rotterdam Rules. In response, Company A invokes Article 4 (1) and asserts the liability limitation. Which argument is correct?

(iii) What if B compensates C for the damage caused before the voyage and brings a recourse action against Company A subrogating C's claim?

Tozuka: If the cargo interests is agreed with a carrier to load, handle, stow, or unload the goods under the terms so called "Free in Free out" no clear stipulation is existing in Hague or Hague-Visby Rules, There is a concept that such CARGO' interests work is expelled from the carriage contract coverage, and the contractual carrier's obligation. This concept is supported by UK jurisprudence. Rotterdam Rules however are referring to this FIO terms at the Article 13 paragraph 2 and put its exemption clause at Article 17 paragraph 3 (1). Under the Rotterdam Rules, even if the FIO terms are agreed, carrier still have a general duty to care for loading, handling, stowing or unloading the goods but not liable by the exemption clauses of Article 17. It seems to be the Rotterdam Rules scheme is little different in comparison with the concept of Hague or Hague-Visby Rules, and we have a question whether the FIO scheme and party's liability is changed by the Rotterdam Rules.

As for the question (2), when a carriage contract was made under FIO terms, and when the same entity made another contract of loading, handling, stowing or unloading the goods with the different cargo interest, under concept of Hague or Hague-Visby Rules, as there is no duty imposed on the contractual carrier by its carriage contract but by another stevedore contract. Is the scheme is changed by the Rotterdam Rules? As the Rotterdam Rules said the carrier is once liable and relieved of all or part of its liability if it proves that loading, handling, stowing or unloading the goods performed pursuant to an agreement in accordance with Article 17 paragraph 3(1). If a company is liable as the carrier together with under a separate stevedore contract, the carrier has a benefit for RR's limitation regulated by Article 59 for its stevedore contract. and whether liability of the carrier is same when a claim is coming from the stevedore contract party or when a claim is coming from a bill of lading holder where FIO contract terms are stipulated?

Q.3(1)

Fujita: I want to ask for Mr. Beare's answer to Q.3(1) because it is related to English case law.

Beare: The question refers to the recent English case of the *JORDAN II* which was decided by the House of Lords. I will read from the lead judgment of Lord Steyn: "The central issue is whether (as shippers and consignees argue) Article III,r2 of the [Hague and Hague-Visby] Rules defines the irreducible scope of the contract of service to be provided by the carrier by sea or (as the carrier argues) Article III,r2 merely stipulates the manner of performance of the functions which the carrier has undertaken by the contract of service." That was the central issue which the court had to decide in the JORDAN II. What the court did decide was to uphold the judgment of Devlin J in the earlier case of *Pyrene v. Scindia*, which is also referred to in the question. And if I may, I will read from the end of Devlin J's judgment. "But I see no reason why the Rules should not leave the parties free to determine by their own contract, the part which each has to play."

On this view the whole of contract of carriage is subject to the Rules, but the extent to which loading and discharging are brought within the carrier's obligations is left to the parties themselves to decide. Although the route, by which the Rotterdam Rules and the English case law come to the conclusion is different, I think the provision in Article 13(2) of the Rotterdam Rules makes it perfectly plain that the parties can decide that the loading, handling, storage or unloading of the goods is to be performed by the shipper. So it may be that for the practical purposes we come to the same conclusion, but, as I have said, by a different route.

Fujita: As Mr. Beare pointed out, the Rotterdam Rules provides a different route to reach the same conclusion as the English court with respect to the validity of the FIO clause. But is it just a different explanation? Or is there any difference in substance? Professor Van der Ziel, do you have any observation on this point?

Van der Ziel: Thank you. I may add that Free In and Out only means that loading, handling, stowing, or unloading of the goods is to be performed by the shipper. But if you look at the obligations of the carrier under the first paragraph of Article 13, you will see that "receive, carry, keep, care for" remain. For instance, if during loading or discharge operations the cargo is stolen due to insufficient security measures taken by the carrier or the cargo suffers water damage because the carrier omits to close the hatches during a rain period, then, even if a Free In and Out Clause applies, the carrier may remain liable because the period of loading and discharging is within the period of his responsibility. Under a Free In and Out Clause the defence of the carrier under Article 17(3)(i) only applies to loss or damage to the goods caused by improper loading, handling, stowing, or unloading of the goods. But the carrier's liability for loss or damage caused by a breach of other obligations than loading, discharging, stowing, and handling (such as 'care') is not affected by a Free In and Out Clause.

Fujita: Thank you for you explanation. Another difference with the English case law is suggested in the last paragraph of Q.3(1). If the crew is involved in the loading or unloading of the goods and its fault caused the damage, the carrier may be responsible. Under the English case law, the liability is based on torts because the loading and unloading is outside the scope of the contract of carriage. In contrast, the loading and unloading under an FIO clause is within the carrier's period of responsibility under the Rotterdam Rules. If the employee of the carrier is involved in loading and unloading, the carrier owes liability under contract of carriage rather than liability in torts (See Article 17(3)(i)).

Q.3(2)

Fujita: Professor Sturley will answer the Q.3(2).

Sturley: To my mind the first issue here is whether or not the Stevedore Company is sufficiently independent of the carrier company. Reading the question, I got the sense that they were the same company but I am not completely sure. In any event, I think that this issue is outside the scope of the Rotterdam Rules. The Rotterdam Rules do not attempt to go into company law to determine whether or not closely affiliated companies are really the same company or really two different companies.

If we assume that they are the same company — company A is the carrier and it also has a branch that performs Stevedoring services, but under applicable law it is a single company — then the answer to the question here is very straightforward. It was specifically addressed by the Working Group and I think the text is clear. If I can put in a shameless plug for our treatise (MICHAEL F. STURLEY, TOMOTAKA FUJITA AND G.J. VAN DER ZIEL, ROTTERDAM RULES: THE UN CONVENTION ON CONTRACTS FOR THE INTERNATIONAL CARRIAGE OF GOODS WHOLLY OR PARTLY BY SEA, SWEET & MAXWELL, 2010), we address this issue in ¶ 5.037. The answer is that the carrier is still liable for its own fault. Even if there is a separate stevedoring contract, the loading and unloading is still within the carrier's period of responsibility, regardless of whether there is a FIO Clause, a FIOS Clause, or some variation on the FIO Clause. The carrier can escape liability for damages caused by the shipper, but it does not escape liability for the damage that it caused. And if you look at Article 17(3)(i), which addresses loading, handling, stowing, and unloading performed under Article 13(2), it explicitly excludes the case in which "the carrier or a performing party performs such activity on behalf of the shipper, the documentary shipper or the consignee." Sometimes a FIO Clause is simply a cost clause, saying that the cost of loading and unloading is not part of the contract carriage. The carrier may still do the work, but the shipper will pay for it separately. Then the carrier is responsible for whatever damage is caused by its fault. And it cannot claim the benefit of Article 17(3)(i) by its terms. Therefore, Company A's argument in (i)(a) must be rejected.

So the answer to the first question under Q.3(2) is that the carrier is responsible for its own fault or the fault of the maritime performing party even if there is an FIO Clause. That is the bad news for the carrier. The next question is: Can the carrier claim the benefit of the limitation provisions? More specifically, can the carrier limit its liability under Article 59? This is now the good news for the carrier, because the answer is "yes"'. Although the carrier is responsible for the breach of its obligations, and is responsible for the fault of itself or of its performing parties, the limitations under Article 59 do apply.

For the next question, Q.3(2)(ii), I again start by asking whether or not the stevedore company is sufficiently independent of the carrier company. If the stevedore company is considered an independent company acting on behalf of the shipper, then the Rotterdam Rules do not apply and Company A cannot limit its liability under the Rotterdam Rules. Of course, this may be a Pyrrhic victory for the claimant if Company A can enforce its exculpatory clause in the stevedoring contract, but that would be an issue outside the scope of the Rotterdam Rules.

But if we again assume that Company A is a single company, with the result that the loading was performed by the carrier, then it does not matter if the cargo claimant says, "I am not suing you under the contract of carriage, I am suing you in tort for your negligent performance under the Stevedoring contract." The action is nevertheless an action against the carrier and Article 4 applies. The defenses and limitations of the Convention apply regardless. So the bad news for Company A is that it is liable, but the good news is that it can limit liability regardless of how the action is framed.

The answer to the next question, Q.3(2)(iii), turns largely on the law of subrogation, which is outside the scope of the Rotterdam Rules. If the applicable law governing subrogation gives B the same rights against Company A that C could have pursued, then the answers here will be the same as in Q.3(2)(i) and (ii), which addressed C's potential claims against Company A. In the absence of any subrogation rights, B might have its own claims against Company A because B was the shipper. On the other hand, it is also possible that B will have no independent rights because it has already sold the goods to C. Because UNCITRAL made an explicit decision not to address title to sue in the Convention, the answer here must also be found in otherwise applicable law. If B as shipper can pursue its own claims against Company A, however, the analysis will again be substantially the same as in Q.3(2)(i) and (ii).

Q.4 Carrier's Liability (1): Basic Questions

Company A (the carrier) and B (the shipper) enter into a contract of carriage of goods by sea from Long Beach, California, USA to Yokohama, Japan with respect to machinery that was stuffed into a container (hereinafter referred to as the "Cargo"). Company A loads the Cargo on the ocean vessel C and issues a bill of lading to B in which the consignee is described as D. The sales contract between B and D stipulates that the ownership of the Cargo shall be transferred from B to D when the Cargo is loaded on C.

During the Pacific Ocean voyage, C experiences heavy pitching partly due to rough sea waters, partly caused by a low pressure area that approached rapidly and unexpectedly, and partly due to engine trouble. The Cargo suffers damages. The combination of insufficient stuffing of the Cargo on the container, the engine trouble of the ship, and the rough sea caused by low pressure contributes to damaging the Cargo.

(1) Article 17 of the Rotterdam Rules provides for the carrier's liability for loss, damage, or delay of goods. Article 17 refers to the "claimant" but the Rules do not specify any definition of "claimant."

Does the applicable law govern who can sue and on what capacity that action can be taken? There is a related question as to the condition or conditions upon which the claimant can sue. For example, is it sufficient for the claimant to show that it is the lawful holder of the bill of lading that covers the damaged goods in question or is it necessary to show that the claimant suffers the loss of the ownership or other economic interests of the goods? Is the issue subject to the governing law of the contract?

(2) In the above hypothetical case, what is the solution under Article 17 (6)? (Please note that Article 17 (3) (b), (k) and Article 17 (5) (a) (i) are concurrently applicable). Article 17 (6) deals with the situation in which several events contributed to the loss, damage, or delay and addresses how the carrier should only be partially liable only for these occurrences; however, it does not explicitly provide for the solution when the degree of contribution of each event is not proven. Does the court have full discretion to decide the carrier's liability in this situation?

Hirata: Article 17 of the Rotterdam Rules provides for the carrier's liability for loss, damage, or delay of goods and it refers to the "claimant". However the Rules do not have any definition of "claimant". It may be worth noting that it is important to distinguish issues regulated by the Rules from those regulated by national law. It is question whether the claimant should be governed by the Rules or a national law. Furthermore, it is also question whether those who suffer merely economic loss rather than loss of ownership should be entitled to be a claimant.

So far as Q.4(2) is concerned, in the hypothetical case, there are many potential causes such as perils of the sea, insufficient packing, unseaworthiness of the vessel. Article 17 deals with the situation of multiple causation cases. How dose this article work before courts?

Q.4(1)

Fujita: Professor Honka gave the presentation on carrier's liability. So, could you kindly give us your answer to Q.4 on the basis of carrier's liability?

Honka: I was just thinking that I'm happy not to be sitting in a university exam because I'm sure I would have failed by now. Anyway, there are lots of facts in this question, but you asked fairly straightforward questions.

The question of title to sue was at some stage included in the draft Instrument, and that, of course, would have given improvement on uniformity on this particular question. Also considering that there are variations in national law in this respect. But this particular chapter was at some stage omitted, so there is nothing in the Rotterdam Rules on this issue. It means that this is something that would mainly be a question of national law. And then the question arises what national law if it is international dispute. And I would afford that at least considering my legal background, this would be rather a procedural question. The private international law rules would say that that's *lex fori*, the law of the place where the proceeding takes place. And in my part of the world we have a fairly liberal approach to who is entitled to sue. But I won't go into that because that is not on the Rotterdam Rules level.

On the other hand, I would have thought that even if it would be accepted that this is a procedural matter and there is no direct answer in the Rotterdam Rules, the Rotterdam Rules might have an indirect influence because the Convention does include a lot of parties — carrier, the maritime performing party, shipper, consignee, controlling party, holder — and of course, such substantive rules might influence any national courts' or arbitrators' decision on what the position of those parties would be. And that might verify the situation in the respect that any of those parties would be considered to have a substantive interest in the dispute and that would suffice.

Fujita: Thank you for your response. As you correctly mentioned, the Draft Instrument once contained provisions on who can sue (*See* Chapter 14 (Articles 67 and 68) contained in Transport Law: Draft convention on the carriage of goods [wholly or partly] [by sea], U.N. doc. no. A/CN.9/WG.III/WP.56 (8 September 2005)). The UNCITRAL Working Group decided to delete these provisions at its 18th Session (*See* Report of Working Group III (Transport Law) on the work of its eighteenth session (Vienna, 6-17 November 2006), U.N. doc. no. A/CN.9/616 (2006), paras.114-118). The Report of the Working Group noted that "It had, however, become apparent that the purpose of the chapter, however laudable, was overly ambitious and that it was unlikely that the Working Group could reach a consensus on the substance dealt with therein." (*ibid.*, para.116).

Q.4(2)

Fujita: Then, apart from the question of who the plaintiff can be, what is the carrier's liability under the situation in Q.4? Three causes contributed to the damage of the goods in this situation. Professor Honka, please.

Honka: Article 17(6) was a difficult paragraph to draft because I know that several efforts were made on this issue. I think it was particularly an American problem on how the drafting should be. In many other jurisdictions, the exact drafting wasn't considered so important necessarily. That's partly the explanation why this is formulated in a way that is possibly somewhat unfamiliar in other jurisdictions. But also together with Article 17(6), there was a lot of discussion on causation theories, particularly expressed by the Swiss delegation saying how it is with different types of causation if there are concurrent causes or a chain of causes or causes that need to act together to cause damage in the first place.

We don't see any that kind of separation in Article 17(6) at all, and that might of course create certain problems as well. You ask here, does the court have full discretion to decide the carriers liability in this situation when the degree or contribution of each event is not proven? I wouldn't say that any court would have full discretion because the court would have to consider evidence and what is considered to be proved and in the end perhaps evaluate the probabilities of the effect of the different causes. But, taking that into consideration, I think, in this kind of a situation, there is quite a lot of room for discretion for the court. That's all I can say.

And I also want to add that in my part of the world the issue of "contributory causes" is completely familiar, and it hasn't really ever been considered a huge problem. Discretion very often must be used. How do you mathematically calculate different faults by different persons? It is of course rather impossible.

Q.5 Carrier's Liability (2): Delay in Delivery, Loss of the Goods, and Non-performance

(1)A carrier receives 1,000 pieces of goods for carriage by sea from the shipper. The carrier fails to load 100 pieces of the goods into the container and, thus, carries only 900 pieces of the goods to the destination. The ship agent at the destination informs the carrier of the 100-piece shortage and the carrier arranges another carriage for the outstanding 100 pieces on another vessel. As a result, the delivery of 1,000 pieces of the goods, as a whole, is delayed for three weeks from the date when it was originally expected to be delivered. The consignee files a claim against the carrier for the loss caused by the decline in the market price of the goods during the three-week delay. The carrier argues that it is not liable for the loss caused by delay because it did not agree on the date of the delivery of the goods. The contract of the carriage does not contain any clause as to the date of the delivery of the goods. Before the contract was signed, the shipper had checked the shipping schedule provided by the carrier to determine when the vessel was supposed to arrive at the destination and asked if it was safe to assume that the carriage vessel would arrive on time on the expected date. Is the carrier not liable at all for the loss claimed by the consignee in above hypothetical case?

(2) Let us assume that the bill of lading contains the clause which explicitly states that the carrier shall not be liable for any loss caused by delay. Let us assume further that the consignee claims the liability for the loss of 100 pieces of the goods after the shipping agent delivers 900 pieces to the consignee. Is the carrier liable for the loss? Is the conclusion the same if the carrier delivers the outstanding 100 pieces of the goods three weeks later?

(3) To state it more generally, how can we distinguish between the cases of the loss of the goods, the delay of the delivery, and the simple non-performance of the contract of carriage of goods? Let us consider the following:
(i) Parts of the goods were missing and the cargo owner files a claim for the loss of these goods. The missing goods are finally found and delivered to the consignee. The delivery of the goods is delayed later than was originally expected. Is the carrier not liable unless there is an agreement of the date of delivery because this case involves delay of delivery rather than the loss of the goods?
(ii) While the shipper delivers the goods to the carrier for shipment, the carrier forgets about the goods and does not start loading them onto the vessel. A few day later the carrier finds the goods, starts loading them, and carries the goods to the destination. Is the carrier not liable unless there is an agreement regarding the date of delivery because this case represents a case of "delay"? Can the shipper treat the delay as a non-performance of the contract after a reasonable time and hold the carrier responsible?

Hirata: This question deals with delay of delivery of the goods, loss of the goods, and non-performance of the contract of carriage of goods. Article 21 of the Rotterdam Rules admits a liability of carrier arising from the delay of delivery of the goods if there is an agreement of the time of delivery of the goods. It is understood that an implied agreement on the time of delivery would be acceptable. If the bill of lading contains a clause that explicitly states that the carrier shall not be liable for any loss caused by delay, can we understand that the carrier will not be liable for loss of delay? So far as the partial non-delivery of goods is concerned, can we claim damages against the carrier on the basis of either loss of cargo or breach of contract?

Q.5(1)

Fujita: Q.5 is also a question on carrier's liability. Therefore, I will ask Professor Honka to answer it. The first question is whether the carrier is not liable for delay at all. There is no explicit agreement on the time of delivery in the contract of carriage.

Honka: Yes, as you rightly put the delay provision in Article 21 is very narrow, indeed, and I think it was Stuart Beare who emphasized the background to Article 21. It has partly to do also with the fact that it got involved with the matter of – the shippers' liability for the shippers delay. And they were kind of interrelated in finding a solution, but this is a solution as far as the carrier side is concerned. But thus, as said already today, that can be an implied term of the contract you don't express, you need to agree upon a time of delivery can also be implied and you hear say as facts that the shipper had asked the carrier if it was safe to assume that the carriage vessel would arrive on time, on the expected date according to the published shipping schedule. Now that is the only point where you could argue that there must, might be some implied terms here.

But if you look at practicality, so I would assert the shipping schedules very often themselves have reservations whether a shipping company or the operator states that this is just a model or a proposal. And these schedules might be changed when the need arises so any that kind of reservation. So, to combine that with some sort of implied agreement I would think that you would need more evidence or more proof to show that there really is an implied term. The schedule might tail up, but I don't think it can be in practice decisive.

Fujita: Thank you. The drafting history with respect to "kind of interrelated in finding a solution" can be found in the report of the 19th Session Report of the UNCITRAL Working Group (*See* Report of Working Group III (Transport Law) on the work of its nineteenth session (New York, 16-27 April 2007), U.N. doc. no. A/CN.9/621 (2007), paras 177–184). Article 21 provides that the delay in delivery occurs when the goods are not delivered within the agreed time. Although the article does not exclude the possibility of an "implied" agreement, the facts described in the question alone may not be enough to convince the court of the existence of such an agreement. What about Q.5(2)? In this case, the plaintiff cannot claim for delay liability because the provision in the bill of lading clearly denies the existence of an "implied" agreement. But is it possible for the plaintiff to say "I received only

900 pieces. 100 pieces are missing. So, I claim for the compensation of 100 pieces of lost goods"?

Q.5(2)

Honka: Well, this is the open question because there is no conversion rule in the Rotterdam Rules. The Hamburg Rules say that the person entitled to make a claim for the loss of goods may treat the goods as lost if they had not been delivered as required within 60 consecutive days following the expiry of the time for delivery and so on and so on. So, a conversion rule is included in the Hamburg Rules, but not here. But I would say that conversion might be a national affair. So it is not necessarily excluded, at least it's not explicitly forbidden even under the Rotterdam Rules.

And I know for example again, for my part of the world that when we apply at present the Hague-Visby Rules, they have been supplemented by those parts of the Hamburg Rules are not in contradiction with the Hague-Visby Rules. And that for example means that when the Hague and Hague-Visby Rules decide the carriers' liabilities from tackle to tackle, it has been considered by the legislator that it's completely possible to enlarge to port to port because the Hague Rules don't cover that part at all. This is a bit of a same thing. When the Convention is silent, there might be a national provision or even a principle. But of course, if that's just a principle you don't really have any exact dates like in the Hamburg Rules. So, I can't really answer that for sure either, but all I'm saying is that that conversion might be possible but that wouldn't take place on the basis of the Rotterdam Rules. And if then that kind of a conversion is considered to have taken place, then it would be obvious that you would have to return to the Rotterdam Rules as far as the loss of goods and liability, like I said.

Fujita: Thank you Professor Honka. If I understand your argument correctly, a court may find that the goods are lost even if they are not physically lost and there still remains a possibility of delivery with a substantial delay. And you think this is a matter of applicable national law rather than the regulation under the Rotterdam Rules. Although I am persuaded by your argument, I have to confess that I am not sure how the conversion occurs under Japanese law especially when the carrier does not assume any obligation to deliver the goods within certain period of time. Mr. Song, do you have a different answer to the question?

Song: Well, I'm not trying to answer the question, but certainly we have to be sure that delay in delivery under the Rotterdam Rule hardly exists when there is a specific agreement on the timing of delivery. So this is similar to the Chinese Maritime Code. So, I was wondering if the bill of lading contains such a clause, the carrier shall not be liable for any loss caused by delay. And on the other hand, if there was a specific agreement on the timing of delivery and such a clause, there is apparently a conflict of the two. Otherwise, I mean, if there is no conflict, there is no delay in delivery. So, I think that should be firstly resolved issue in these scenario.

Sturley: I'm not answering a question, but asking a question. Mr. Song and I were actually thinking on similar terms. It strikes me that if the bill of lading contains a clause saying the carrier shall not be liable for any loss caused by delay that would be invalid under Article 79, because you can't exclude that. What you will have instead — as Mr. Song was suggesting in following up on what Professor Honka just said — is a clause to ensure that no agreement as to when delivery will take place can be implied. The clause that would be included in the bill of lading will be something that defeats that implication. So the clause would not disclaim liability for delay, but would make it clear that the carrier is not assuming any obligation to deliver at a particular time. Or perhaps the carrier would assume an obligation to deliver within 17 years of the scheduled time!

Fujita: I really appreciate for the comments from both of you. First, let me clarify the intention of Q.5(2). The bill of lading contains a "no liability for delay" clause and does not contain a specific agreed time for delivery. When we drafted the question, we assumed that the wording "no liability for delay" effectively exclude the "implied agreement of time for delivery" and it does not violate Article 79. This is why the consignee seeks for carrier's liability for the loss of goods rather than for delay in delivery in Q.5(2). But after listening to your comments, there may be a danger for the carrier to use such a simple provision because it might be regarded as void by the court. A more careful carrier would choose a different term in a bill of lading such as "There is no guarantee for the time for delivery. The carrier does not assume any obligation to deliver the goods within certain period of time and it is not liable for delay in delivery." Once the carrier can effectively avoid liability for delay, then, we return to Professor Honka's analysis of possible "conversion".

Q.5(3)

Fujita: May I proceed to Q.5(3)? Once again, I ask Professor Honka to answer the question.

Honka: Thank you. Well, we can't really distinguish between cases of the loss of the goods, the delay of delivery, and the simple non-performance in all situations. Sometimes it might be clear, particularly in question 5(3)(i), i.e., when the missing goods are finally found and delivered to the consignee. If the cargo side hasn't claimed a total loss on the basis of an applicable conversion rule, and hasn't cancelled the contract (an issue that is not regulated by the Rotterdam Rules), then we are in a delay in the delivery of goods situation. And if there is no express or implied term of a time agreed, then this might just end in the carrier's not being liable.

In question (3)(ii), the carrier forgets about the goods and does not start loading them onto a vessel. A few days later, the carrier finds the goods, starts loading, and carries the goods to the destination. Actually, this is something I already answered. I can't really say it very much more except for the fact that if the shipper or the consignee finds himself in the situation where there is no delivery of course, it would be in their interest to stop finding out where the goods are. And whatever is said about delay liability in this respect, if they find that the goods are still in the same place of receipt or port of loading, the best action in that case would be to consider canceling the contract of carriage if that sounds more favorable than the alternative to receive delivery back, which is from the cargo interest side badly delayed. So you might have an option there, but it then needs activity from the cargo side to be able to reach that kind of situation.

Q.6 Carrier's Liability (3): Various Liability in Connection with the Goods and the Convention

(1) Lumber (the goods for carriage) falls into the water while being unloaded from the ship due to the fault of the stevedore. The consignee, wishing to prevent damage to the lumber, hires workers at the port and successfully collects the lumber without damages. The consignee files a claim against the carrier for the costs of the recovery. Is this claim subject to limitation (Article 59) and the time-bar (Article 62) under the Rotterdam Rules as "the carrier's liability for breaches of its obligations under this Convention"?

(2) Packages containing chemical substances fall into the water while they are being unloaded from the ship due to the fault of the stevedore. The port authority collects the packages in order to prevent possible danger and damages resulting from the chemical spill and files a claim against the carrier for the costs incurred. Is this claim subject to limitation (Article 59) and the time-bar (Article 62) under the Rotterdam Rules as "the carrier's liability for breaches of its obligations under this Convention"?

(3) The shipper enters into a contract of carriage with a carrier who offers a substantially low freight rate. Although the shipper delivers the goods to the place of receipt under the contract of carriage, the carrier does not begin loading the goods onto the ship. The shipper cancels the contract and hires another carrier and the new carrier brings the goods to the destination. The freight rate for the new carriage is significantly higher than the original rate. The shipper files a claim against the original carrier for the additional cost and economic loss it incurred due to the delay. Is this claim subject to limitation (Article 59, 60) and the time-bar (Article

> 62) under the Rotterdam Rules as "the carrier's liability for breaches of its obligations under this Convention"?

Tozuka: Under the Rotterdam Rules, the carrier is liable for loss, damage, or delay of the goods, but cargo interests will suffer damages not only loss, damage, or delay of the goods but also other types of damage. For example, when the cargo is scattered on the sea surface and the cargo consignee has to collect the cargo, such costs would be a loss for the consignee, even if no physical damage existed.

Although it seems that the Rotterdam Rules confine a carrier's liability to loss, damage, or delay of the goods, would a carrier be liable for other types of damages and would such types of damage be limited by Article 59 of the Rotterdam Rules? This is Q.6(1).

Under the Rotterdam Rules, is the carrier liable to a person who is not a party to the contract of carriage and could it make use of the liability limitation of the Rotterdam Rules? Q.6(2) asks the point.

Finally, a Carrier's omission may sometimes cause a delay in delivery of the goods. The cargo interest will suffer damages and to avoid such circumstance, the cargo interest may cancel the carriage contract and seek compensation for their economic loss.

Is such a claim regulated by the Rotterdam Rules? By which articles? And is it the same result (including limitation) when the carriage contract is cancelled by the reason of the carrier's breach of contract? This is Q.6 (3).

Fujita: At the first glance, Q.6 looks like another question on carrier's liability. But the real issue is the coverage of the Rotterdam Rules. Therefore, I wish to ask Professor Sturley to analyze the question.

Sturley: I do feel very much like I'm back in my student days answering an examination on questions like this. Actually, I think this question as it is phrased is fairly easy, although there are some much more difficult questions lurking behind that.

Q.6(1) involves dropping the lumber into the harbor rather than delivering it directly to the consignee. Despite the freedom that the parties have to define when "delivery" occurs, I think we can safely assume that they have not defined it as dropping the cargo into the water. Thus there was a breach of the carrier's obligation under Article 11 to carry the goods to the place of destination and deliver them to the consignee in accordance with the terms of the contract of carriage. The carrier has a clear obligation under the Convention to deliver the goods to the consignee rather than dropping them into the water. There has been a breach here. Article 59 limits the carrier's liability for the breach of its obligations under the Convention to the specified limitation amounts.

So, the question actually posed is whether the carrier may limit its liability and the answer seems to be clearly yes. The harder question is how we go about justifying the carrier's obligation to pay damages because the Rotterdam Rules are fairly clear on establishing liability for loss, damage, or delay. In this case, however, the goods were not lost or damaged. The consignee was able successfully to rescue them for the water without damage. And if there was a delay, it was fairly *de minimus* delay. The consignee must have rescued them from the water fairly quickly or they would not have been undamaged. So it does not seem that there is loss, damage, or delay. We are instead looking at is the money that the consignee spent in order to avoid the goods' being lost or damaged, as they presumably would have been if they had been left in the water. I think it is reasonably clear that the consignee will recover for those cost subject to the Article 59 limits. Although the cargo was misdelivered and could have been a total loss, the consignee was able to mitigate the damages and minimize its loss. The success of the mitigation efforts should not defeat recovery.

I think Q.6(2) is even easier because in this case it is not the consignee who is collecting the goods or suing the carrier, it is the port authority. And the port authority is not a party to the contract of carriage. It is important to recognize that the scope of the Rotterdam Rules, broadly speaking, is between carriers and shippers. It is slightly broader than that because the shipper's rights sometimes pass to other cargo interests with the result that the consignee or the controlling party, for example, becomes the cargo claimant. And on the carrier side, the Rotterdam Rules are somewhat broader in covering maritime performing parties. But the port authority has nothing to do with this. The port authority will not be suing the carrier for a breach of its obligations. The carrier owes no duty to the port authority to deliver the cargo. The duty that the carrier owes to the port authority is presumably one under port regulations or environmental law or something else outside the scope of the Rotterdam Rules. The port authority's ability to succeed in that action accordingly depends on the applicable law and the carrier's ability to limit its liability will be under whatever law applies, not the Rotterdam Rules. So, on the one hand I have no idea what the result will be in Q.6(2), but I do know that the carrier cannot limit its liability under the Rotterdam Rules, because the Rotterdam Rules have nothing to do with this.

Let us continue to Q.6(3). Will the carrier be able to limit its liability under the Rotterdam Rules? I think the answer is clearly, yes. The carrier has breached its obligation under the Rotterdam Rules. It was supposed to deliver the goods and it did not deliver the goods. It did not even begin the process of carrying them. So there has been a breach of obligation and the carrier can therefore limit its liability in any action based on that breach of obligation. So again, the answer is that the carrier has breached its obligation, but the carrier is generally entitled to limit. In this hypothetical, we know where the cargo is. It is being delivered by someone else. Maybe the shipper wants to bring the action for delay or maybe the analysis here will be somewhat like that in the first question, in which the carrier did not deliver the cargo where it was supposed to be delivered and the shipper had to hire somebody else to finish the delivery. The situation is similar in Q.6(3). The carrier's breach occurred a bit earlier in Q.6(3) than in Q.6(1). And of course, I assume that the carrier's action is in fact a breach. (Indeed, what we have here sounds like what we in the common-law world would be "anticipatory repudiation.") Of course the Rotterdam Rules do not provide details on what is sufficient to constitute anticipatory repudiation. The Rotterdam Rules do not try to reinvent all of contract law. So you may look need to look to otherwise applicable law to determine whether or not there has been a breach in the carrier's failure to whether or not the ship was justified in canceling the contract. You need to look outside the Rotterdam Rules for that. But in terms of limits I think the answer is clear: The carrier can limit in Q.6(1) and (3)and clearly not in Q.6(2).

Fujita: In all questions in Q6, damages are caused by "the breach of obligation under this Convention (the Rotterdam Rules)". Nevertheless, I think everyone agrees with Professor Sturley that the carrier's liability to the port authority in Q.6(2) is not subject to the Rotterdam Rules' limitation of liability or to time-bar. On the other hand, Q.6(1) and (3) seems to pose a more subtle question. Professor Sturley assumed that the carrier's possible liability under the facts in Q.6(1) and (3) are subject to the Rotterdam Rules' limitation of liability or to time-bar. Do you all agree to the conclusion? Professor, Honka, do you have a different opinion?

Honka: I don't have any views on Q.6(1) or (2) but on Q.6(3), I might suggest a totally different solution and it's a fact that the shipper cancels the contract of carriage. Therefore, it's difficult to see how the carrier would have any obligations if there is no contract left. And therefore, what is said in the Rotterdam Rules about the carrier's obligations wouldn't possibly apply. And if the counter-argument is that well, he had already breached his contract and that's why the contract was cancelled by the shipper, you could say well, the carrier might have said that, "I don't want you to cancel, I'm still going to carry, but they are going to be delayed and I'm not liable for delay because there is no time of delivery agreed." So I would rather say that this would be outside the Rotterdam Rules once the shipper cancels and completely so, which also means that if there is a national applicable law placing liability on the carrier for never having carried then that national law decides all the issues including, perhaps if there is a special rule on limitation on liability, but you could not derive it from the Rotterdam Rules. And the same would of course apply then for the time bar.

Fujita: Do you have any comment, Professor Sturley?

Sturley: I don't think that Professor Honka and I have disagreed on Q.6(3). I think we both agree that whether or not the shipper is entitled to cancel the contract is governed by otherwise applicable law. I think Professor Honka and I based our answers on different assumptions. I assume that under otherwise applicable law the cancellation was justified because there had been a breach. If it had been truly a complete cancellation then clearly the carrier would have no obligation. There would be nothing left. But suppose that it is a cancellation because of a breach and under applicable law the innocent party still gets to sue the carrier for damages, for the consequences of that breach. That would be what happens at least under U.S. law, and I suspect under many other systems as well. To the extent that the carrier is liable for damages because of a breach of the contract, then that liability would be subject to limitation when the original contract was subject to the Rotterdam Rules.

And on Q.6(1), I agree that there are difficult questions in terms of how you get to the consignee's ability to claim for damages, which is why I tried to avoid that problem. But the question asked is whether the carrier can limit liability and I think the answer is "yes". Because there has clearly been a breach of the Convention — even if it is unclear how the consignee claims for damages as a result of that breach — when the consignee makes a claim for damages under the Convention the carrier can limit liability.

Honka: In Q.6(1) if the liability doesn't arise under Rotterdam Rules, but the limitation does. But, there is no loss or damage in the conventional sense here. But I have only one little comparison point. I don't know if it's good or bad, but if you take general average, the cargo has the obligation to pay contribution in general average if it's the ship owner to receive. And then the question arises if it turns out later on that the carrier was liable for the accident even if there is a general average adjustment. Then the question arises whether the cargo side can refuse to pay contribution in spite of the adjustment or is entitled to reclaim of the contribution that is already paid. There is at least one court case in my part of the world where this has considered to be so close to the liability rules or the Hague-Visby system. They follow those rules in judging whether contribution really is to be paid or if there is to be paid back of contribution paid. And as a matter of fact, this particular clarification was included in the Hamburg Rules explicitly but then again omitted in the Rotterdam Rules. And I think it's a bit of a shame, but that's your leverage. But that's just an expression of the fact that you don't have the real loss or damage in the normal sense, but it's something which is so comparable and then you could say that these costs of recovery perhaps are something, I'm not saying that the Rotterdam Rules should be applied, but I'm only saying that we are at least could be very close to it or would have to particularly consider.

Fujita: I think we all agree that the Rotterdam Rules' limitation of liability and time-bar do not apply in Q.6(2). Even if the carrier's liability in this case can be phrased "the breach of obligation under this Convention", it has nothing to do with the contract of carriage and is outside the scope of the Rotterdam Rules.

Q.6(1) and (3) also deal with the carrier's liability under applicable law, not under the Convention itself. But even if the liability is not based on the Convention, it is subject to the Rotterdam Rules' limitation or time-bar if it results from "the breach of obligation under this Convention. In addition, unlike Q.6(2), the liability in Q.6(1) and (3) is somehow related to a contract of carriage and the plaintiff is the shipper or the consignee. Therefore, one could argue that carrier's liability under both cases is subject to the Rotterdam Rules' limitation of liability and time-bar more easily than Q.6(2). But I am not sure everyone can agree on the conclusion.

Q.7 Identity of the Carrier

> Vessel "P" (" Company A " is the registered owner) and vessel "Q" ("Company B" is the registered owner) are scheduled for the same route and both vessels are time-chartered to the same charterer "R". The charterer's agent at the port of loading has always issued bills of lading using BIMCO CONGENBILL 1994 with its signature "for the master."
>
> The agent issues a bill of lading that states the cargo was loaded onto vessel "P". However, the cargo is actually loaded onto a different vessel "Q", on the same date. The agent simply makes a mistake in writing vessel "P" instead of writing "Q". As the registered owner of vessel "P", Company A does not know that the agent has issued the bill of lading that incorrectly contains the name of vessel "P" instead of vessel "Q". During the voyage, vessel "Q" and all of its loaded cargo sinks. The cargo buyer and the cargo underwriter file a suit against "Company A", the registered owner of vessel "P" as stated on the bill of lading, for the loss of the cargo. Is "Company A", the registered owner of vessel "P", presumed to be a carrier pursuant to Article 37 (2) and held liable unless it can prove that it was not the carrier? Can "Company A" escape liability as the carrier if it can prove that the cargo was not actually loaded onto vessel "P"? If not, what does "Company A" need to do to prove it is not responsible and, thus, escape liability?

Ikeyama: This is a case related to the application of Article 37(2) of the Rotterdam Rules. The paragraph provides that, if a bill of lading without express identification of the carrier is issued, then the registered owner of the ship named on the bill is presumed to be the carrier. It is also provided, however, that such registered owner may rebut this presumption against him either by proving that the ship was under a bareboat charter or by identifying the carrier and its address.

Arguments by the cargo interests in this case are relying on the presumption set out in

Article 37(2). The question here is what facts shall be argued or proved by Company A, the registered owner of the ship P, who faced with those arguments but had had in fact nothing to do with the loss of relevant goods, in order for A to be held to have had nothing to do with the carriage of the goods and thereby held not liable at all, despite the description on the bill of lading to the contrary.

Girvin: Thank you very much. Well, this provision of the Rotterdam Rules on the identity of the carrier of course addresses a long-standing problem, which has often caused difficulties in relation to identifying whom the cargo claimant should sue. And that's obviously important for lots of reasons, not least the fact the clock is ticking and at some point the time bar will cancel out the claim. This was also one of the more controversial aspects of the rules. And in fact, if you look at the *travaux préparatoires*, you will see an account of some of those difficulties.

So, just to reiterate where we are factually, essentially what we've got is a situation where you've got two ships, which happened to be chartered out to the same time charter. The two ships are Vessel P and Vessel Q. The cargo is actually carried on Q, but by mistake the Bill of Lading actually says P. And following the relevant loss, which occurs when the vessel sinks, the cargo owner sues P. The question we've been asked is whether P is liable under Article 37.

Well, perhaps by way of a rider, let's just take perhaps an earlier situation which is not considered here. If the carrier was specifically identified in the relevant document of carriage in the contract particulars, then the situation would be covered quite simply by what Article 37(1) says. And that states specifically that if a carrier is identified by name, any other information relating to the identity of carrier shall have no effect to the extent that it's inconsistent with the identification.

But we don't have that situation here. We have a situation where the carrier is not named. But we have information relating to the name of the ship. So, as explained in the introduction, we are cast on Article 37(2). We don't have a bareboat charter here; we have a time charterparty. And in relation to the ships in question, we would have to have a look at what the second sentence of Article 37(2) says. Article 37(2) second sentence says that if no person is identified but the contract particulars indicate that the cargo is loaded on board a named ship, the registered owner is presumed to be the carrier.

So, as the bill of lading says P, one would expect it to be the registered owner of P that is the party liable. However, the second sentence, which I started with, says the alternative because we don't have a bare boat charter here. The registered owner may rebut the presumption of being the carrier by identifying the carrier and indicating its address. And again the question is here whether or not this is a situation where the owner should have to rebut the presumption which stands.

I would suggest that certainly one response would be that it rebut the presumption by identifying the carrier and by indicating its address. And I would have thought that would be relatively easy to do in this situation where a ship is in fact charted out to the same charter or where two ships were chartered to the same charter.

Fujita: May I ask for a clarification. Let us assume that X is an agent of Company B, shipowner of Ship Q and it has nothing to do with the Company A. Goods were loaded on Ship Q and carried by Company B. X wrote the name of Ship P on the bill of lading which is owned by Company A instead of Ship Q purely by mistake. Is Company A presumed to be a carrier simply because the description of "Ship P" appears on the bill of lading? Is Company A bound by the description made by X who has nothing to do with A?

Girvin: I guess one suggestion might be that you simply correct the mistake and point out that in fact the information is being wrongly recorded without actually having to go through the procedure under Article 37(2).

Van der Ziel: May I add something relating to Article 41? Article 41(b) starts with: "Proof to the contrary by a carrier in respect of any contract particulars shall not be admissible, when such contract particulars are included in a negotiable transport document".

I'd like to draw the attention that here reference is made to *any* contract particulars. According to Rule III(4) of the Hague-Visby Rules, only those contract particulars are conclusive evidence that are related to the description of the goods. Therefore, compared with the Hague-Visby Rules, the Rotterdam Rules extend the value of the bill of lading by making conclusive evidence also other contract particulars than those relating to the goods, which may include the name of the vessel.

This extension might have a bearing on this case because any rebuttal based on the argument that simply due to an administrative error the wrong name of the vessel was included in the bill of lading might be less effective under the Rotterdam Rules than it might be under the Hague-Visby Rules.

More generally, I like to bring this to your attention, because – up till now - many commentators on article 41 have overlooked this for the transport practice important extension of the value of a bill of lading.

Fujita: Professor Van der Ziel is, of course, right in saying that the information contained in contract particulars is conclusive evidence pursuant to Article 41(b). However, if someone who has nothing to do with me issued a bill of lading on behalf of me without my consent and write a description of the goods, such a document is not valid and the description does not bind me regardless of the evidence rule in Article 41. Isn't the situation in Q.7 comparable to such invalid document? Professor Honka, you have an observation?

Honka: Thank you. I'm not sure myself, but I would just like to raise the issue. Would this not be possible to solve on the basis of what we call rules and principles on general contract law? Let's say that a guy with a revolver came to Michael Sturley and said "please sign the bill of lading saying that it's P that's carrying", but they both know that it's Q. Is this really an issue to be solved on the basis of the Rotterdam Rules because that would be on the general contract law, a contract that is void or voidable? You have the matter of void or voidable contract also in relation to mistake. You have mutual mistake, unilateral mistake, that you would rather inspect this whole situation through those principles. I'm not sure, but I'm just trying to compare with the situation of use of force. And there are several grounds in existence that might make a contract void or voidable.

Song: Just another comment further to Professor Honka, I think this raises probably more of an agency issue rather than a Rotterdam Rules issue. Certainly the agent, not the principal itself, got it wrong here. If the principal itself got it wrong, perhaps it's difficult to rebut. But if it is an agent that got it wrong and then the principal says that the agent has no authority whatsoever to sign this wrong bill of lading on behalf of the master, is the registered owner bound? The owner of vessel P can certainly say, "sorry, this is not my bill of lading, and you should look to the agent who should be held liable for that loss or damage."

Fujita: I appreciate the comments by Professor Honka and Mr. Song which are relevant. Let me explain the intention of Q7. I am quite skeptical to the conclusion that shipowner A is bound by a description on the bill of lading if it was issued and signed by a person who has no authority — neither express, implied, nor apparent — to act on behalf of A. Of course, agency law is outside the scope of the Rotterdam Rules. But courts in many countries will see that a bill of lading issued by unauthorized agent is not binding.

Q.7 is, of course, more delicate. Both Ship P and Ship Q are chartered to "R" and R's agent issued the bill of lading with the signature "for the master". Therefore, we cannot say there is no relationship between agent R and A as the owner of Ship P. Therefore, we can argue that the description on the bill of lading is binding vis-à-vis A and A is presumed to be a carrier under Article 37(2). But, to my mind, the simple fact that the name of A's ship appears on the bill of lading may not always justify the application of Article 37(2).

Q.8 Parties Involved in a Contract of Carriage: Carrier, Performing Party, and Agent, etc.

A trading company ("A") that is a member of a cargo consortium, asks a NVOC ("B"), a forwarder, to make an arrangement for the carriage of voluminous project cargo to its local site. The forwarder B arranges a contract of carriage with a sea carrier ("C"), under the name of the trading company "A" and "A" was stated as the shipper on the bill of lading. The plant cargo in question is made by another consortium member and this manufacturer asks a stevedore company ("D") to stow the cargo on a flat rack container. The cargo slips from the flat rack container during the voyage and damaged the side wall of the vessel. This slip incident is caused by poorly secured cargo, an action that is performed by "D".

(1) (i) The sea carrier ("C") files a claim for the vessel's damage against "A", who is stipulated as the shipper on the bill of lading. "A" denies its liability as the shipper. "A" argues that the contract of carriage was concluded between "B" and "C", and "A" is not a party to that contract. Moreover, "A" asserts that it never accepted that its name ("A") appeared on the bill of lading and, hence, it is not a "documentary shipper." (Article 1(9)) Furthermore, "A" also argues that it was "D" that secured the plant cargo onto the flat rack container, and since "D" contracted with the manufacturer and not with "A", "D" 's fault is not attributable to "A". Are "A" 's arguments well founded?

(ii) The carrier "C" files a claim with "B" for the vessel's damage because "B" has arranged this carriage and has entered into a contract with "C". "B" argues that the contract of carriage was concluded between "A" and "C" and, as is stated on the bill of lading, "B" is only acting as an agent. Therefore, "B" argues that it is not responsible as the shipper. Is "B" 's argument well founded? Is the conclusion the same when another volume contract exits between "A" and "B" for the carriage of the project cargo?

(2) The stevedore company "D" agrees with " C" to perform the loading all of the cargo containers onto the vessel used in the carriage. The manufacturer asks "D" to stow the cargo on the flat rack container. The plant cargo, therefore, is received by "D" from the manufacturer, is secured on the flat rack container, and is carried to the port container yard by "D". Finally, the cargo is loaded onto the vessel by "D". Under these circumstances, can the stevedore company "D", as a maritime performing party, enjoy the benefit of liability limitation under Article 59 for a claim from shipper "A" or the manufacturer?

Tozuka: A documentary shipper is defined as "a person, other than the shipper, that accepts to be named as shipper in the transport document"(Article 1(9)). But if a shipper allows a carrier to make a subcontract of carriage, will it be regarded as accepting to be named as the shipper in the subcontract of carriage? Is it determined by each national law or do the Rotterdam Rules address that? These are the issues asked in Q.8(1)(i).

As Article 34 says that the shipper is liable for the breach of its obligation caused by any other person to whom the shipper entrusted the performance of any of its obligations, we would like to have an advice whether the shipper is liable for its seller's subcontractor's activity although a sales contract is not a contract entrusting the shipper's obligation performance. Q.8(1)(ii) asks the point.

Finally, when a company is also instructed by a carrier to assist its carriage or its stevedore work, is the company entitled to limit his liability against the shipper even if it was breach of a shipper's obligation? This is Q.8(2).

Q.8(1)

Fujita: May I ask Professor Sturley to answer the question?

Sturley: This is a very easy a question to answer and the answer is "I don't know." But there is a good reason I don't know. This is really a factual question. There is one issue on which everyone in the UNCITRAL Working Group agreed over and over again. That is the Rotterdam Rules do not address questions of agency law and questions of agency law are left to otherwise applicable law. If you look through the Working Group Reports, you will find many references to the conclusion that the Rotterdam Rules do not address agency.

So it is very clear that under the Rotterdam Rules, "A" could be the documentary shipper if "B", the NVOC in this case, had been acting as "A"'s agent. It is clear that an agent can bind a documentary shipper. If I am a trading company wanting to ship goods and I send my agent to the carrier and tell my agent to put my name in as the shipper, all that can clearly be done through an agent. Indeed, almost everyone we are talking about here is a corporation and one of the most basic principles of company law is that corporations can act only through their agents and their employees. So it can happen and it's simply a factual question or a question to be determined by otherwise applicable law whether or not "B" was acting as "A"'s agent. Or alternatively, if "B" acted as a carrier, for example, and "B" agreed to carry the cargo and then subcontracted that carriage with "C", that is also a possibility. But again, that would be a factual question and the agency questions are not governed by the Rotterdam Rules they'll be governed by otherwise applicable law. So, if we assume that "B" is an agent then "A" can be the documentary shipper that consented to be named as a shipper through the agency or could be even an actual shipper but this entire question turns on facts and agency and the Rotterdam Rules do not answer it.

Fujita: Well, Q.8(1)(i) is partly solved by the Rotterdam Rules and partly by the applicable national law of agency. Professor Van der Ziel, do you have something to add.

Van der Ziel: Thank you. I would like to make a supplementary remark on the basis of these facts. I doubt whether "A" is a documentary shipper. A documentary shipper is defined as a person other than the shipper, who nevertheless is mentioned as a shipper in the document and accepts to be named as such. The facts as stated don't seem to correspond with this definition. "A" asked the NVOC to make a booking and if that booking is made on his behalf, then "A" is simply the real shipper and is rightfully stated as such in the Bill of Lading. The question does not state to whom the Bill of Lading is issued, but normally in cases like this one the Bill of Lading is issued to the NVOC acting on behalf of "A". So, in my view, the facts lead to a straight-forward case, in which "A" is the shipper.

When "A" is the shipper, it assumes the shipper's obligations (in this case those of Article 27(1)). Whether the actual securing on the flat rack is done by the shipper or by somebody else doesn't matter, as long as the other person is somebody to whom the shipper has entrusted the securing on the flat rack (*see* Article 34). The reference in the question to a cargo consortium leads me to conclude that the manufacturing consortium member was authorized by the shipper to request a stevedore to do the stowage. This way, it can be said that the stevedoring company has been entrusted by the shipper to perform one of his obligations. This would be otherwise if the stevedore would have been acting on behalf of the carrier.

Fujita: Thank you for your observation. Of course, if "A" is the shipper, there is no need to examine if it is a "documentary shipper". Mr. Song, do you have another comment?

Song: Yes, thank you. Apparently the question here involves an FOB seller, and I presume that this happens a lot in China, because most of (I think a majority of) the exports from China to other parts of the world are FOB shipments. In other words, unless it is a liner shipment, the FOB seller may approach an NVOC or freight forwarder, not necessarily as a shipper in the sense that its buyer may have already approached the ocean carrier who in turn goes to its agent in the seller's country and approaches the seller. And the seller through its warehouse or factory arrange for some sort of work to be done by the freight forwarder. So, I think this may be complicated (in identifying the capacity of a seller). I just stop over.

Fujita: Professor Sturley, do you have any comment to the remarks by the previous speakers?

Sturley: I think the answer largely turns on what we assume the facts to be and what the law of agency is. I can entirely agree with what Professor Van der Ziel and Mr. Song said, i.e., that there are different ways of looking at this. Certainly one way of looking at it was that "A" was the shipper. One way of looking at it was that "A" is the documentary shipper. Both are assuming that "B" is acting as agent for "A". If "B" is not acting as agent for "A", then maybe not. Under the facts in the hypothetical case, now "B" is saying "I am only an agent. I am not responsible". That is a possibility, but maybe not. It depends on what the agency relationship is and what the facts are determined to be. And on both of those issues, the Rotterdam Rules do not provide an answer.

Fujita: Does the same apply to your answer to Q.8(1)(ii), i.e., it is mostly an agency law question and the solution depends on the applicable law?

Sturley: Yes, that is correct. "B" argues that it is only an agent, and that argument must be resolved under otherwise applicable law. The Rotterdam Rules do not address questions of agency. I think the volume contract between "A" and "B" would be evidence that "B" was not acting simply as "A"'s agent, but the Rotterdam Rules still to not answer the question.

Q.8(2)

Fujita: What about Q.8(2)?

Sturley: To the extent that the Stevedore is acting on behalf of the shipper — and again, you have the question of what are the facts here, what is the agency relationship, who has retained whom, and what are those relationships —then the shipper will be responsible to the carrier for the stevedore's fault. It will be responsible for the damage to the ship. But to the extent that the Stevedore was a maritime performing party retained by the carrier, then the shipper would not be responsible for the stevedore's fault. In any event, the carrier probably has an action against the stevedore outside the scope of the Rotterdam Rules for the stevedore's own fault, simply as a tortfeasor. But again, that would be outside the scope of the Rotterdam Rules.

So, I think that this question is not simply a Rotterdam Rules exam question, it is a question about a lot of otherwise applicable law. So, it seems that we may have enrolled in the wrong course here!

Q.9 Liability of a Maritime Performing Party

> (1) Do all persons who (i) do not have direct contract relationships with the shipper, and (ii) assume the carrier's obligations under a contract of carriage with respect to the loading, carrying, and unloading of the goods, and (iii) entrust the performance of the obligation to another person and do not perform the obligations by themselves constitute maritime performing parties? For example, can an intermediary charterer (time-charterer or voyage charterer) be directly sued by the shipper as a maritime performing party under the Rotterdam Rules?
>
> (2) When a claimant brings an action against a maritime performing party alone pursuant to Article 19, what should the claimant prove? More specifically, should the claimant (the cargo claimant) prove (i) there is a contract of carriage with the carrier who is not involved in the litigation, (ii) the contract is within the scope of the application of the Rotterdam Rules (Article 5, etc.), and (iii) the relationship between the defendant and the carrier satisfies the re-

quirements under Article 1(6) and Article 1(7) of the Rule? If the answer to these questions is affirmative, how is the conclusion supported by the text language of Article 19?

(3) Let us assume that the carrier, who is otherwise liable, is not liable due to an exoneration clause under a volume contract. Can the claimant hold a maritime performing party responsible? Or does the maritime performing party enjoy the benefit of exoneration under the volume contract?

Sasaoka: The goal of Q.9 is to concretely understand Article 19 in the Rotterdam Rules, the provision for "maritime performing party". Therefore this question might be composed of a kind of confirmation.

Q.9(1) deals with the coverage of the concept of "maritime performing party". According to Article 1(6)(a) and (7), a maritime performing party is a person who (1) has no direct relationship with a shipper and (2) assumes the carrier's obligation under a contract of carriage. What I would like to ask you is whether every person who falls into these requirements is deemed to be a maritime performing party under the Rotterdam rules even if it does not perform the obligation by itself.

Q.9(2) aims to confirm the facts to be proved by a claimant when it intends to bring a suit against a maritime performing party alone.

Q.9(3) asks whether a maritime performing party could invoke an exemption clause or a lesser limit than that of the Rotterdam Rules in a volume contract between a carrier and a shipper. Although Article 19(2) provides a rule for a case in which a carrier assumed other obligations or higher limits than that of the Rotterdam rules, we cannot find any rules for the opposite case. If an obligation or a responsibility of the maritime performing party in that case were that of the Rotterdam Rules, under Article 19(2), then the maritime performing party would bear the bigger obligation or responsibility than the carrier. Is this the result?

Q.9(1)

Fujita: Although the issue of maritime performing party is the topic of my presentation and I should be responsible to answer, I, as a moderator, should assign it to someone else. Professor Sturley, do you volunteer to answer the question? Thank you for your help.

Sturley: The answer to Q.9(1) is "yes". The intermediate parties can be maritime performing parties, depending of course on the facts. And the question is written a little bit too broadly. A person will not be a maritime performing party if it is retained by the shipper either directly or *indirectly*. So, if a shipper has an FIO clause, for example, and arranges with another company to do the loading or unloading, and that company in turn subcontracts with a third company, then that third company will not have a direct relationship with the shipper, but it will not be a maritime performing party because it was retained indirectly by the shipper. The point is that if you are not the carrier, you are not retained directly or indirectly by the shipper, and you undertake to perform some of the carrier's obligations under the carrier's umbrella, then you are a performing party, whether or not you actually do the work yourself. For example, in one of my favorite cases, which illustrates just on how bizarre this industry can sometimes be, the original shipper contracted with an NVOC to carry the cargo. The NVOC said "Yes, thank you very much, I will carry your cargo e.g., from the United States to China". The NVOC then turned around and retained a second NVOC, which said "Yes, thank you very much, I will carry this cargo from the United States to China". It then turned around and retained a third NVOC, which said, "Yes, I will carry your goods from the United States to China". And then the third NVOC contracted with the ocean carrier that actually did carry the goods from the United States to China.

The first NVOC was the original shipper's "carrier". The second and third NVOCs were maritime performing parties because they undertook the carriage by sea, even though they did not perform or intend to perform it themselves. The ocean carrier is a maritime performing party because it actually did perform the carriage. So, everyone who promises to do the work is a maritime performing party, even those that never intended to do it themselves, even if they intended to subcontract the carriage.

Fujita: I think there is no disagreement with Professor Sturley's explanation. May I proceed to Q.9(2)?

Q.9(2)

Sturley: If a cargo claimant is suing a maritime performing party under Article 19, the cargo claimant is going to have to show its entitlement. How this happens will be, to some extent, governed by the procedural law of the forum state. So, the details will be to that extent outside the scope of the Rotterdam Rules. But let me explain how it would happen in the United States. Much of the analysis is based on the Rotterdam Rules, so it should be the same to a considerable extent in most countries.

The claimant will come in and say "I am suing the defendant. Here is the basis for my suit. I am suing under Article 19 of the Rotterdam Rules. And this person is a maritime performing party who damaged my cargo." The first question that the court will ask or the first question the defendant will ask is, "Who says the Rotterdam Rules apply at all? In order for you to sue me under Article 19 of the Rotterdam Rules, you have to establish that the Rotterdam Rules themselves apply." So, you are going to have to show that there is a contract of carriage wholly or partly by sea. You are going to have to satisfy the internationality requirements and the "connection with the contracting state" requirements. You will have to show that the Rotterdam Rules apply. Just as if you sue someone based on a particular statute under Japanese law, you have to show that the statute applies. Or if you sue someone in the Japanese court under U.S. law, you have to persuade the court that U.S. Law applies. So, you will have to persuade the court that the Rotterdam Rules apply and that will require satisfying the scope of application provisions, i.e., Articles 5, 6, and 7.

And then you'll have to prove that you have the right defendant, that you are suing the person you should sue. So, if you say, you are liable as a maritime performing party, you will have to show that that person is a maritime performing party. So, we'll have to go back to the definition of performing party and show that the defendant is a performing party and then show that it is also a maritime performing party and therefore Article 19 applies.

The one caveat I would add is that the way you have asked the question, you have the cargo claimant saying I want to rely on Article 19, and thus the cargo claimant has to prove all this. But I suspect that in many cases, it will be the maritime performing party who wants to prove all of this because the cargo claimant will sue that person in tort. The cargo claimant will say, "you damaged my cargo and you must pay me my full damages". And the stevedore will say "Oh no. I am a maritime performing party and I am entitled to limit my liability under Article 59. You cannot sue me in tort, you have to sue me under the Convention". And then the stevedore will say, "here is a contract of carriage that is governed by the Rotterdam Rules, and I am a maritime performing party. So, the proof will be the same, but it will be the other party who makes the proof. But whoever wants to claim the benefit of the Rotterdam Rules will need to show that they apply and how they apply.

Fujita: Thank you. I believe that there is no disagreement in conclusion. The only question was how to reach the conclusion under the Convention's text and Professor Sturley have just given us a convincing explanation. May I proceed to Q.9(3)?

Q.9(3)

Sturley: Well, I must say, this is an excellent question. I have heard it four or five times now in different contexts. When we were discussing this in the United States, an organization of maritime performing parties asked exactly the same question.

There is a harder way and an easier way to answer this. Let me start with the easier way. The issue expressly came up during the Working Group negotiations when there was a proposal to amend the text to specify that the maritime performing party was subject to the Convention's limits, regardless of what they were. In other words, the maritime performing party would not be subject to higher limits even if the carrier agreed to higher limits in a volume contract and would not be subject to lower limits even if the carrier agreed to lower limits in a volume contract. I am particularly familiar with this proposal because the U.S. delegation made it — and we lost. *See* Report of Working Group III (Transport Law) on the Work of Its Twelfth Session, para. 163, U.N. doc. no. A/CN.9/544 (2003). The working group discussed the proposal and concluded that the maritime performing party would not be subject to higher limits unless it expressly agrees to accept them. That conclusion is stated now in Article 19(2). But if the carrier agrees to lower limits in a volume contract, then a maritime performing party will get the benefit of the lower limits. So, the maritime performing party gets the better deal whichever way it goes. The limits cannot go higher without its consent but can go lower. This is similar to the third-party beneficiary doctrine under contracts law in most countries (except England and a few other commonwealth countries).

The textual explanation is perhaps more complicated but it leads to the same result. There is a distinction between "limits of liability as provided for in this Convention", which is the language used in Article 19(1), and "the limits specified under this Convention", which is the language used in Article 19(2). The limits "specified" in the Convention are the limits of Article 59. The limits "provided for" in the Convention are whatever limits apply under the Convention, including under Article 80.

Article 20(1) similarly uses the term "the limits provided for under this Convention" instead of "the limits specified under this Convention". This also illustrates the distinction between the two usages and helps to make clear that the maritime performing party gets whatever the carrier gets, save in the exceptional case of the carrier's agreeing to a higher limit without the maritime performing party's consent.

We can also note that Article 19(2) explicitly provides for the case in which the maritime performing party has a different limit than the carrier, i.e., if the carrier agrees to higher limits and the maritime performing party does not consent. But in all other cases, the maritime performing party gets whatever the carrier gets under Article 19(1). So, the negative implication of Article 19(2) is that in the opposite situation, the general rules still apply.

Although this is a very popular question, I do not think it will be a common question in practice because I do not think that the parties will often agree to lower limits in volume contracts (for the reasons that I explained yesterday). So, this is a good question for a professor in the sense that it is more of an academic question than a question that will arise in practice.

Fujita: Thank you for your explanation. I hope everyone can follow the textual explanation that Professor Sturley gave. Like previous questions, I think, there is very little disagreement with the conclusion.

Q.10 Multimodal Transport and Limited Network Principle

> A carrier and a shipper enter into a contract for carriage from Berlin to Chicago, consisting of carriage by truck from Berlin to Rotterdam, carriage by sea from Rotterdam to New York, and carriage by rail from New York to Chicago. The contract provides for the jurisdiction of a U.S. Federal Court and U.S. law as the governing law. A portion of the cargo is lost during transit from Berlin to Rotterdam and, therefore, that portion of the cargo is not delivered. The consignee in the U.S. commences an action before a U.S. Federal Court to claim damages in respect to that loss of cargo. The limitation of liability under the Rotterdam Rules, if applicable, would be SDR43,750, while the limitation of liability under the CMR would be SDR 38,700. The consignee in the U.S. argues that the limitation under the Rotterdam Rules, rather than the limitation under the CMR, shall be applied for the following reasons:
>
> (i) The hypothetical *"separate and direct contract"* for the stage from Berlin to Rotterdam for the purpose of Article 26(a) of the Rotterdam Rules shall not be governed by the CMR but governed by the U.S. law, since one should consider that the hypothetical *"separate and direct contract"* contains the same choice of court and choice of law clauses as the actual contract. Since the U.S. law is chosen as the governing law[1], CMR does not apply. Therefore, the requirement under Article 26(a) of the Rotterdam Rules is not satisfied;
>
> (ii) Even supposing that the hypothetical "separate and direct contract" is governed by the CMR, Article 26 (chapeau) states that provisions under the Rotterdam Rules *"do not prevail over"* provisions under the CMR and does not order the court to apply provisions under the CMR whenever the hypothetical *"separate and direct contract"* is within the CMR's scope of application. Therefore, the Federal Court of the U.S., not being a Contracting State to the CMR but merely being a Contracting State to the Rotterdam Rules, is not bound to apply provisions of the CMR. Rather, it is entitled to, or even bound to, apply the Rotterdam Rules. Is the consignee's argument correct?

Ikeyama: The issue in this case is how Article 26 of the Rotterdam Rules shall apply if there was an accident during the road transport period in a typical multimodal transport composed of sea and land transport periods. Roughly speaking the said Article provides that, if loss of or damage to the goods occurred during the period before or after the sea transport, the provisions related to the carrier's responsibility in the Rotterdam Rules shall not prevail over those in the international instrument compulsorily applicable to a hypo-

---

[1] To be exact, the governing law of such a contract shall be decided by the conflict-of-laws rules in the forum, i.e., in the U.S. Federal Court. For the sake of simplicity, it is assumed that the U.S. court acknowledged the effect of the choice of law clause in the above case.

thetical separate and direct contract only for that period, if any. Such international instrument as contemplated in this case is the CMR. Then what does it mean that the Rotterdam Rules shall not prevail over the CMR? If you consider it means the CMR shall prevail over the Rotterdam Rules and it therefore applies to this case, you would conclude that, by virtue of the effect of Article 26 of the Rotterdam Rules, the limitation not under the Rotterdam Rules themselves but under the CMR shall apply to this case. The consignee in this case, however, argues that such a conclusion is wrong and limitation under the Rotterdam Rules shall apply, on the grounds set out here. The question is simply whether those arguments are correct or wrong.

The construction of this Article is a typical and crucial issue not only for the United States but also for Japan and other Asian countries. The reason becomes obvious if you replace New York and Chicago in this case with other cities in Asia. If the consignee's arguments are wrong and not the Rotterdam Rules but the CMR shall apply to such a case, it follows to mean that, if an Asian country becomes a State Party to the Rotterdam Rules, it would be obliged to apply the CMR to an accident during the road transport in Europe by virtue of the effect of the Rotterdam Rules, despite the fact that it is not a State Party to the CMR. In addition it is not because the CMR is contractually incorporated by a transport contract between the parties but because the CMR is legally incorporated by operation of Article 26 of the Rules.

We understand there already exist different views in this point. We are afraid that consideration for the adoption of the Rules may be adversely affected unless an internationally prevailing view shall be clarified, whatever such view may be. We believe this is a good opportunity to ask the views of internationally recognized persons in this area.

Fujita: Since this question involves an applicable law in a U.S. court, could Professor Sturley give us your view on the U.S. cargo interest's argument in this case.

Sturley: I will do my best to answer this interesting and most difficult question. These exams keep getting harder and harder.

First, I might add that it is not unusual for limitation under the Rotterdam Rules to exceed limitation under CMR or COTIF-CIM. Some of the delegates to UNCITRAL Working Group had real trouble understanding that principle because the CMR weight limitation is higher than the Rotterdam Rules' weight limitation. But with containerized cargo, packages are often very small. In this hypothetical, for example, the packages would weigh about 93 kilos, and at 93 kilos per package, the Rotterdam Rules package limitation is higher than the CMR weight limitation ($8.33 \times 93 = 774.69 < 875$).

In this question, we see the cargo making two different arguments in order to get the Rotterdam Rules' package limitation. The first argument says that when we look at the hypothetical separate contract, we assume that it would also include the choice-of-law clause that the head contract includes. I find it an interesting assumption that a contract includes a clause that would be unenforceable in the place it was entered or the place where it will be performed. But that may be a red herring. Perhaps it does not really matter what a choice-of-law clause in the hypothetical contract provides. If you look carefully at Article 26, you will see that there are four separate conditions that must be satisfied for Article 26 to apply.

The first condition in the chapeau, is that the loss or the event in question occurs at the right time — before loading or after discharge. That condition is satisfied here. The second condition is in Article 26(a), and I will return to that shortly. The third condition, in Article 26(b), is satisfied here because the CMR does provide that the carrier's limit of liability is 8.33 SDRs per kilo. And the fourth condition, in Article 26(c), is that the CMR provisions cannot be varied by contract. I am not expert on the CMR but I understand that by the CMR's own terms this condition has also been satisfied. So, the first, third, and fourth conditions are satisfied.

The key provision here is therefore the second condition, which is an Article 26(a). And that condition is that the CMR by its own terms would have applied under a hypothetical separate and direct contract. Even if that hypothetical separate and direct contract had included a U.S. choice-of-law clause, CMR by its own terms would say that CMR applies. CMR by its own terms would say, "ignore the U.S. choice of law clause and you apply CMR". So, the second condition is satisfied, all of the conditions are satisfied, and Article 26 should apply regardless of the hypothetical U.S. choice-of-law clause in the hypothetical contract that would have been concluded for the inland leg.

But the problem is not done yet. The exam just gets more interesting now. This brings us to the cargo claimant's second argument, which considers what happens even if Article 26 does apply. Article 26 does not say that a court must apply the terms of CMR. It instead says that the Rotterdam Rules provisions do not prevail over the CMR provisions. This is in the chapeau of Article 26. So the question now is: *Do the CMR provisions apply without regard to the Rotterdam Rules?* The Rotterdam Rules do not prevail over them. But if under U.S. choice of law principles, the CMR would not apply anyway — regardless of the Rotterdam Rules — what happens then?

The good news for my exam is that this is not a Rotterdam Rules question, and I am here to answer only Rotterdam Rules questions. This is a U.S. choice-of-law question, and I am aware of very little law on point. I know of only one reported case in the United States in which a U.S. court had to decide whether to apply CMR. The question there was whether the liability limits of the CMR or of the U.S. Carriage of Goods by Sea Act ("COGSA") applied to a shipment of bicycles stolen during the European road leg of a multimodal shipment. And, as you probably know, really expensive bicycles do not weigh very much. In fact, the more expensive they are, the less they weigh. In the reported case, the limitation of liability under CMR was solely weight-based and it was much lower than the US$500 per package limitation of liability under COGSA.

So, the carrier said, "I want to apply the CMR weight limit, which is very low because the bicycles are light." And the cargo claimant said, "I want to apply the $500 per package limit because there are many packages here, and that gives me a much higher limit." There was not a choice-of-law clause, so the reported case is not exactly the same as the question we have here. But the U.S. Court of Appeals, the court directly below the Supreme Court, applied CMR. So the carrier received the benefit of a lower limit.

Since our problem has a U.S. choice-of-law clause, it becomes more complicated. U.S. law does not have any provision on cargo damage for losses between Berlin and Rotterdam except, in this hypothetical, the Rotterdam Rules. But Article 26 specifically says the Rotterdam Rules do not prevail over the CMR provisions. So, I could easily see a U.S. court going either way on this. I think the Rotterdam Rules do not require the U.S. courts to apply CMR. It is certainly clear that the Rotterdam Rules do not require the U.S. courts to apply the limit of Article 59 of the Rotterdam Rules. If the Rotterdam Rules themselves required the U.S. courts to apply Article 59, then they would require a Dutch or a German court to do so, and that is clearly wrong. The entire point of Article 26 is to save the European courts from having to face a conflict of conventions. The German and Dutch courts would clearly be required to apply the CMR, and the Rotterdam Rules clearly permit that.

Ordinarily I would predict that a U.S. court would apply CMR as a matter of U.S. choice-of-law principles. But in this question, it is assumed that the U.S. court would give effect to the U.S. choice-of-law clause. So at the end of the day, the problem is answered by the assumption. A Japanese Court faced with a similar situation would make its decision under Japanese law, and I certainly claim no expertise on that.

Fujita: I understand that Professor Sturley agrees with the consignee's second argument while he declines the first. I have written the same conclusion in the past (Tomotaka Fujita, "The Comprehensive Coverage of the New Convention: Performing Parties and the Multimodal Implications", 44 Texas International Law Journal 349, 360-362 (2009), see also, pp. 72-73 of this volume). But I know there is a disagreement. Do you have any comment? I notice that Professor Van der Ziel has something to say.

Van der Ziel: Thank you so much. Yes, there are different views on that. And I beg to differ because in my view it has been the intention of Article 26 simply to incorporate the otherwise applicable inland conventions in the Rotterdam Rules for cases in which the damage occurs solely during the inland voyage. What the Rotterdam Rules are doing here is more or less following the system that we see in a lot of actual bills of lading in use by the container carriers, which also include the same network principle as the Rotterdam Rules, albeit with a little different wording. These bills of lading also refer to a hypothetical inland contract and then refer to the inland convention that according to its terms applies to this hypothetical contract.

In the travaux préparatoires of Article 26, you may see that the text of Article 26 has been changed many times. In the final phase, we opted for the hypothetical contract construction. And the phrase "prevails over" is left over from an earlier version of Article 26. In the final phase of discussions, the question was raised by one of the delegates whether in the newest version of Article 26, after the change to the hypothetical contract concept, the words "prevail over" were still appropriate.

This was an appropriate question because purely in terms of drafting, these words might create confusion in view of the intentions of the article. But the question was raised at the very, very end of the whole process at the moment when everybody in fact was a bit tired. Moreover, if you try changing the words "prevail over," and making a proper drafting that would have made the intention clearer, then, you may have to make a drastic redrafting of the whole article or at least of the whole chapeau, which wasn't that easily done at the time. There was hardly time and opportunity left for doing so. It was more or less for this reason said at the time by delegates, well, the intention is clear and even if the word "prevails over" might not be fully correct, we all understand what it means. This piece of history is the basis of my different view.

To summarize: the intention of the Article was to incorporate the conventions in the Rotterdam Rules, with the effect that also courts located in States that are not a Party to the CMR, may have to apply the CMR in cases when the damage solely occurs as in this example between Rotterdam and Berlin. Thank you.

Sturley: I do not disagree with anything that Professor Van der Ziel just said. The purpose of Article 26 is to incorporate the CMR provisions into the Rotterdam Rules when the CMR provisions would otherwise apply to the inland carriage considered on its own. But it was not the intention to make the CMR provisions apply more broadly than they otherwise would have. So, for example, if the cargo had gone from Berlin to Rotterdam, Rotterdam to Montreal, and Montreal to Chicago, there was certainly no intention to make the CMR apply to the Montreal-to-Chicago carriage — even though that is an international carriage by truck. But of course neither Canada nor the United States is a party to CMR, and thus the CMR would not apply to motor carriage between those countries.

I therefore think that the question we have to ask here is whether a U.S. court would apply CMR if the carriage had been only from Berlin to Rotterdam by truck. Suppose that there had been no carriage by sea at all. Suppose that we simply had a carriage by truck from Berlin to Rotterdam, and Rotterdam was the final place of delivery. For whatever reason, the cargo claimant decided to sue in the United States for damage that occurred on that carriage. Perhaps the trucking company was the subsidiary of a U.S. company, the German subsidiary was insolvent, and the claimant sued the U.S. parent company.

Would a U.S. court in that case apply CMR? Clearly a German Court would. Clearly a Dutch Court would. The U.S. court, not being bound by CMR, would decide whether to apply CMR using U.S. choice-of-law rules. Generally speaking, you would expect the court to apply either German law or Dutch law because one of those would be the law that had the closest connection with the transaction. There is no reason to think that it would be U.S. law.

But also under U.S. choice-of-law principles, a U.S. court will generally give effect to the parties' choice. So, if the parties have a U.S. choice-of-law clause, as in this hypothetical, a U.S. court might follow that. If it would — and the question here requires us to assume that it would — I do not think that the Rotterdam Rules intended to impose the CMR in situations in which the courts would not apply CMR to the inland leg standing alone. In CMR countries, the courts have to decide that issue under the terms of the CMR itself because they are bound by it. For countries outside of the CMR zone, they decide whether to apply it under the rules that they would normally use to decide whether the CMR applies to the contract for the inland leg considered in isolation. Although I think it is unlikely, that the U.S. court on the Berlin-to-Rotterdam case would choose not to apply CMR, I do not think that the Rotterdam Rules would force the court to do so, any more than CMR itself forces that choice.

As I said, in the only case in which the U.S. courts ever faced this issue, they did choose to apply CMR — albeit without a choice-of-law clause. So, I agree completely with Professor Van der Ziel that if CMR would have applied on the land-leg, then the Rotterdam Rules require courts to apply it when the damage occurs on the land leg. I am less persuaded that the Rotterdam Rules somehow require a national court to apply CMR in the multimodal carriage context if that same court would not have applied CMR in a case involving only that land leg. Now, Professor Van der Ziel is about to disagree with me.

Van der Ziel: I don't want to prolong the debate too long. But I'd like to remind you that in the earlier drafts, we had a final paragraph to what is now Article 26 that expressly said that the other paragraphs of Article 26 would apply irrespective, I repeat, irrespective of a choice of law clause. In a late stage, this paragraph was deleted for the reason that the delegates found it superfluous because they thought Article 26 is drafted now in such a way that choice of law matters do not come into the picture and, therefore, this aspect may be disregarded.

And I'm little bit surprised that now, all of a sudden, the matter of choice of law is raised again, despite that at the time, the specific provision was generally regarded as superfluous. I remember that I was one of the few delegates who liked to retain that provision, because I feared that this matter could be considered relevant again. However, from the *travaux préparatoires* you could clearly see that choice of law was finally ruled out here as being irrelevant. Thank you so much.

Fujita: I think we should check the Report of UNCITRAL Working Group (*travaux préparatoires*). By the way, to what extent should the court take travaux préparatoires into account when it interprets the text of a convention? The answer may differ in each jurisdiction.

Honka: I do not wish to interrupt, but Article 32 of the Vienna Convention on the Law of Treaties explicitly states that *travaux préparatoires* should be taken into consideration when applying a convention under certain preconditions. Further on there is an interesting English House of Lords case that debates the preconditions and how the *travaux préparatoires* are to be applied and taken into consideration in interpreting conventions (*Fothergill v Monarch Airlines Ltd* - House of Lords- [1981] AC 251; [1980] 2 All ER 696; [1980] 3 WLR 209; [1980] 2 Lloyd's Rep 295). And I think when you combine these two sources, there are some strong indications that if there is a clear statement in the Rotterdam Rules background that could clarify Article 26, that would have to be taken into consideration.

Beare: I would only add that the recent House of Lords case of the *JORDAN II*, which has been referred to earlier, entirely supports what my colleague Professor Honka has just said. Lord Steyn in his judgment said that "It is, however, equally well settled that the travaux can only assist if, as Lord Wilberforce put it in *Fothergill*, they "clearly and indisputably point to a definite legislative intention". It is interesting that this judgment followed a long exercise by counsel for the shippers who took the House through an extended tour of the relevant travaux with the aid of Professor Sturley's "The Legislative History of the Carriage of Goods by Sea Act and the *Travaux Préparatoires* of the Hague Rules".

Fujita: For your information I will cite the relevant provisions of Vienna Convention on the Law of Treaties, 1969.

"Article 31   General rule of interpretation

1. A treaty shall be interpreted in good faith in accordance with the ordinary meaning to be given to the terms of the treaty in their context and in the light of its object and purpose.

2. The context for the purpose of the interpretation of a treaty shall comprise, in addition to the text, including its preamble and annexes:

(a) any agreement relating to the treaty which was made between all the parties in connection with the conclusion of the treaty;

(b) any instrument which was made by one or more parties in connection with the conclusion of the treaty and accepted by the other parties as an instrument related to the treaty.

3. There shall be taken into account, together with the context:

(a) any subsequent agreement between the parties regarding the interpretation of the treaty or the application of its provisions;

(b) any subsequent practice in the application of the treaty which establishes the agreement of the parties regarding its interpretation;

(c) any relevant rules of international law applicable in the relations between the parties.

4. A special meaning shall be given to a term if it is established that the parties so intended.

Article 32   Supplementary means of interpretation

Recourse may be had to supplementary means of interpretation, including the preparatory work of the treaty and the circumstances of its conclusion, in order to confirm the meaning resulting from the application of article 31, or to determine the meaning when the interpretation according to article 31:

(a) leaves the meaning ambiguous or obscure; or

(b) leads to a result which is manifestly absurd or unreasonable."

Courts may sometimes rely on *travaux préparatoires*. But there are some conditions in Article 32 of the Vienna Convention. In any event, I think we should check the *travaux préparatoires* of Article 26 once again with a hope that it will conclude our discussion in one way or the other.

*A Note on the Drafting History of Article 26

Discussion in the UNCITRAL Working Group

For the discussion in the UNCITRAL Working Group referred to in the above discussion, see the following materials: Report of Working Group III (Transport Law) on the work of its eleventh session (New York, 24 March-4 April 2003), U.N. doc. no. A/CN.9/526 (2003)), paras 245–250, Report of Working Group III (Transport Law) on the work of its twelfth session (Vienna, 6-17 October 2003), U.N. doc. no. A/CN.9/544 (2003)), para.25, Report of Working Group III (Transport Law) on the work of its eighteenth session (Vienna, 6-17 November 2006), U.N. doc. no. A/CN.9/616 (2006)), paras 216–228, Report of Working Group III (Transport Law) on the work of its nineteenth session (New York, 16-27 April 2007), U.N. doc. no. A/CN.9/621 (2007)), paras 185–

193, Report of Working Group III (Transport Law) on the work of its twenty-first session (Vienna, 14-25 January 2008), U.N. doc. no. A/CN.9/645 (2008), paras 83–87, 204,

Discussion in the 41st Session of UNCITRAL (18 June 2008)

In the 41st Session of UNCITRAL (18 June 2008) where the text of the Rotterdam Rules was finalized, the delegation from Germany proposed to change the word "prevail" to "apply". (Summary record of the 870th meeting, held at Headquarters, New York, on Wednesday, 18 June 2008, at 3 p.m., A/CN.9/SR.870 and Corr.1, paras. 10 (UNCITRAL YEARBOOK Volume XXXIX (2008), pp.958)). The reason for the change, the delegation explained "was to make it clear that draft article 27 was not a conflict of conventions provision. Provided it was known where the damage had occurred and provided it had occurred where another international instrument applied, the provisions of the latter instrument would apply." (*ibid.*, para.22) Although it was supported by one delegation (Switzerland) (*ibid.*, para.18), many delegations disagreed. Norway, the Netherlands, Belarus, and Japan expressly preferred the word "prevail". Others (the U.K. France, Spain, Greece, Chile) approved the text without specific mention to the choice between "prevail" and "apply" (*ibid.*, paras. 15-21). Some delegations (Belarus and Japan) explicitly supported the word "prevail" because the court should be allowed to apply the Rotterdam Rules if there is no conflict of conventions and the court sees it should apply it (*ibid.*, paras. 20-21).

Q.11 Liability of the Shipper

Company A, a trading company, purchases pesticides (dangerous goods listed in the IMDG Code) from a chemical manufacturer and, having placed them in a dry container, delivers them to the carrier (shipowner) for carriage. During the carriage, the container bursts due to the heightened pressure caused by the rise in temperature. The pesticide seeps out and erodes the hull as well as the neighboring containers and damages the cargo therein. The bursting of the container is caused by an excessive rise in the temperature of the pesticides within the container because the container is located too close to the bunker tank and its heating pipe. It is revealed that the type of pesticide in the container differs from the kind of pesticide indicated on the transport documents and the actual pesticides in the container are less resistant to heat. The location where the container is placed is not appropriate even assuming that the pesticides were of the type that is indicated on the transport document and, therefore, the container with the pesticide as indicated in the transport document could also burst during the voyage due to the heat from the bunker tank and heating pipe. It is also found that the temperature of the bunker tank and heating pipe temporarily rises to an extraordinary degree because the heat that is required to maintain the fluidity of the bunker oil is generated by high temperature steam over a period of time that is longer than usual.

(1) Can the carrier (shipowner) claim compensation for damages to the hull against the trading company as the shipper? If it can, will the claim be admitted for the full amount of the damages to the hull?

(2) If the owner of the damaged cargo (other than Company A) claims compensation against the carrier, to what extent is the carrier (shipowner) liable?

(3) (i) Assuming that the carrier (shipowner) is held liable under Question (2), can the carrier (shipowner) make its recourse claim against Company A?

(ii) If the recourse claim by the carrier (shipowner) is accepted, will the claim be made before the carrier (shipowner) has paid the compensation, or even before the cargo owner raises the claim? What if the cargo owner makes a direct claim against Company A?

Goto. Q.11 deals with the liability of the shipper for damages to the vessel and other cargos caused by both the failure of the shipper to inform the carrier of the dangerous nature of the goods and the failure of the carrier to load the goods properly. As regards the damage to the vessel, Q.11(1) asks a question whether the shipper A can be relieved of its liability for the part caused by the carrier's fault. It seems that the answer should be in the affirmative as a matter of course, but there will be a problem how to derive that answer from the articles of the Rotterdam Rules. As regards the damage to other cargos, owners of those cargos can sue the carrier asserting that its fault has contributed to the accident and then the carrier can make the recourse claim against the shipper A, or the owners of the damaged cargos can sue the shipper A directly. The latter case will be a problem of tort law, outside of the Rotterdam Rules. In Q.11(2) and (3), we would like to ask what the situation will be in the former case.

Q.11(1)

Fujita: This is a question on shipper's liability. Naturally, I will ask Professor Kim to answer the question.

Kim: According to the facts under Q.11, Company A acted as the shipper. The actual cargo on board was different from information on the named cargo in the bill of lading furnished by the shipper A. Thus the cargo's dangerous nature was not informed correctly to the carrier. If the shipper A gave correct information on the cargo to the carrier, it might have cared for the cargo in a less heated position. Therefore, shipper A will be strictly liable for the damage to the carrier pursuant to Article 32(a).

According to the given facts, however, the carrier also contributed to the damage by stowing the pesticide in a more heated place. So, this is a case of concurrent causes. Therefore, shipper A will be liable only for the part of damages that is attributable to its failure. Which clause will be the basis of such apportionment of liability? One candidate is Article 30(3). But Article 30(3) is applicable only for a case involving the fault of the shipper. The case at issue is related to the shipper's strict liability for dangerous cargo. Therefore, Article 30(3) is not the appropriate provision to rely on. I cannot find any relevant provision under the Rotterdam Rules. So, I think that national law will provide a solution.

Fujita: Thank you. Perhaps, everyone would agree that the shipper should not be liable for all the damages when the carrier's fault also contributed to the damage. But as Professor Kim has just pointed out, Article 30(3), if read literally, does not help. I do not know how national law in other countries helps the shipper in this situation. But if Japanese law is applicable, the court can probably rely on the argument on "causation", i.e. there is only limited causation between the wrong information of the substance in the container and the damage ultimately born by the carrier because there is carrier's fault in between. We should remember that the issue of causation is left to applicable national law. Courts in other countries may have another tool that I am not familiar with in order to reach a similar conclusion.

May I proceed to the second question? Professor Kim, please give your answer to Q.11(2).

Q.11(2)

Kim: In Q.11(2), the owner of the different cargo, let us say "Cargo Owner B", claims against the carrier. So, I think this is pure contractual relationship between the carrier and Cargo Owner B. The carrier is not liable for part of the damage if it proves that the cause of part of damage is not attributable to its fault in accordance to Article 17(2). I think the carrier in this case can prove that part of damages was caused by the failure of shipper A. So this is also a case of concurring causes and Article 17(6) will give the solution. Therefore the carrier is liable only for the part which is attributable to its fault.

Fujita: This is not exactly the question of shipper's liability. Rather, it is the issue of carrier's liability under Article 17 and as Professor Kim pointed out the carrier is partly liable to the owner of the cargo other than the dangerous cargo which caused the explosion. Perhaps, there is little disagreement with the conclusion. This leads to the next question on the recourse action by the carrier. Professor Kim, could you proceed to Q.11(3)?

Q.11(3)

Kim: Yes. The carriers can make a recourse claim against the shipper. But we should study the case a little more carefully. As I explained, the carrier is liable only for the damage which is attributable to its own fault. Therefore, the carrier is not allowed to collect any amount of damages by the way of recourse claim from the shipper A because the recourse claim is based on the fault of the shipper A. In this scenario, the carrier is not liable for the part of the damages attributable to shipper A.

Fujita: So you answered the first part of Q.11(3) in negative. What about the second part of Q.11(3)?

Kim: Sorry, I did not answer the second part of the question. Although I think the carrier cannot make a recourse action, let us assume it can. Then such a recourse claim does not fall within the scope of the Rotterdam Rules. It is based on applicable national law. So the answer to the second part of Q.11(3) depends on each national law. Under Korean law, the carrier is allowed to raise a recourse claim against the shipper in order to avoid time bar defense. Under Korean tort law, the third party cargo owner is allowed to make a direct claim against shipper A based on tort.

Fujita: Thank you. Because the answer depends on applicable national law, we cannot be sure. All I can say is the solution under Japanese law seems not much different than that under Korean law as explained by Professor Kim.

Q.12 The Obligation to Accept Delivery

(1) The goods arrive at their destination and the consignee demands delivery. However, before the actual delivery of the goods, the shipper who is concerned about the financial situation of the consignee, exercises its rights of control and, without notice, changes the consignee from the originally designated consignee to another person. If the new consignee does not demand the delivery of the goods, is the former consignee obliged to accept delivery according to Article 43?

(2) The bill of lading contains the following clauses "All of the Persons coming within the definition of Merchant in this bill of lading shall be jointly and severally liable to the Carrier for the due fulfillment of all obligations undertaken by the Merchant in this bill of lading." and "The terms and conditions of the Carrier's applicable Tariff are incorporated herein." The carrier's tariff contains a provision on "demurrage charges" and the amount is extremely high irrespective of the amount of damage the carrier actually suffers as a result of the consignee's refusal to accept delivery.

After the arrival of the goods at the destination, the holder of the bill of lading demands the delivery of the goods. When the condition of the goods is examined at the warehouse in the port, the holder finds that some of the goods are rotten and are not suitable for commercial use. Furthermore, it is determined that the cost of disposal is very expensive. As a result, the holder refuses to accept delivery.

(i) Is the holder obliged to accept delivery in this case? If it is, is the holder obliged to pay the demurrage charge stipulated in the carrier's tariff (*See* Article 58 (2))?

(ii) Are there any possible measures by which the consignee could avoid the obligation either to accept delivery of the worthless goods that cannot be disposed without much cost or to incur a great measure of liability due to the refusal to accept delivery? For example, is it possible under Article 43 to take some samples of the goods or to inspect the condition of the goods without demanding delivery in order to determine whether or not to demand delivery?

(3) In the contract of carriage, the parties agree to the delivery of the goods at the port of Sendai. Unfortunately, the port of Sendai is closed due to a major earthquake that occurred just before the goods arrived. According to the Caspiana Clause (cf. Q.1) included in the contract, the carrier discharges the goods at the port of Chiba, which is the most convenient option, compared with other options (the ports of Kashima, Tokyo, and Yokohama are alternative ports) since the carrier had other goods that are supposed to be discharged at the port of Chiba. On the other hand, from a practical standpoint, the port of Chiba is inconvenient for some of the consignees.

When the consignee does not take delivery of the goods, is the carrier entitled to take actions "after their arrival at the place of destination" pursuant to Article 48? Does the place of "destination" in Article 48 include not only the place of destination agreed upon in the original contract of carriage but also the place chosen at the discretion of the carrier according to the Caspiana Clause when it is inconvenient for the consignee?

Q.12(1)

Goto: Q.12 includes three different cases regarding the obligation of the consignee to accept the goods and other related articles of the Convention or provisions of the contract of carriage. The first case deals with the relationship between the obligation to accept the goods and the right of control. According to Article 50(2) of the Rotterdam Rules, unlike Article 582(2) of Japanese Commercial Code, the right of control continues to exist after the demand for delivery. So it is possible for the shipper to exercise the right of control after the consignee has demanded delivery of the goods. The second case deals with the situation in which the consignee who has demanded delivery and examined the goods wants to reject them because they are rotten. The question is whether the consignee is obliged to accept delivery, and if so, what can it do to escape that obligation. There is a similar problem regarding the demurrage charge prescribed in the carrier's tariff, which is incorporated in the bill of lading. We would like to ask the interpretation of Article 43 regarding the obligation to accept delivery and Article 58(2) regarding the extension of obligations imposed under the contract of carriage to the holder of the bill of lading other than the shipper. The third case deals with the Caspiana Clause, which was also addressed in Q.1. When the carrier, according to the Caspiana Clause, discharged the goods at a port different from the original destination, but the consignee doesn't show up to accept the delivery, is the carrier entitled to take actions under Article 48(2)? The problem is whether the goods have remained undelivered "after their arrival at the place of destination".

Fujita: Q.12 focuses on delivery of the goods. Naturally I will ask Professor Van der Ziel to answer the question.

Van der Ziel: After the shipper has exercised its right of control to change the consignee, the first consignee isn't a consignee anymore. The second consignee now has become the right consignee. This means that the first consignee has lost its obligation to take delivery because it is no longer entitled to delivery anymore. I may remind you that "consignee" is defined as "the person entitled to delivery of the goods" and, after the change, the second consignee has become that person.

Let me explain the background of this position under the Rotterdam Rules. If the first consignee/buyer, because of insolvency, would not have paid for the goods when it claims them from the carrier, the shipper/seller must be in a position to prevent delivery of the goods to this insolvent person. For this reason the Rotterdam Rules, unlike some other transport conventions, provide that the right of control exists during the entire period of responsibility of the carrier. It follows in practice that the shipper (in possession of the right of control) may change the consignee as long as this is, from an operational point of view, reasonably possible prior to actual delivery of the goods. In other words, the Rotterdam Rules try to prevent that demanding delivery may create the possibility for a buyer to obtain the goods without having paid for them.

Fujita: Let us move on to the second question.

Q.12(2)(i)

Van der Ziel: The answer to the first part of the second question is affirmative. Once the cargo has arrived at destination and the consignee demands the cargo, it has to accept delivery. The same applies to the demurrage charge because the carrier's tariff is binding on the consignee.

Fujita: May I understand that the demurrage charge on the carrier's tariff is binding on the consignee because such liability is "ascertainable from the negotiable transport document" (Article 58(2)) and the consignee/holder who demanded delivery exercised its right?

Van der Ziel: Yes, this is the reason. Furthermore, the fact that the demurrage charge may seem unreasonably high is a commercial matter unrelated to the Rotterdam Rules. Freight and charges are deliberately not addressed in the Convention. (As a practitioner, I may add that many carriers don't set the level of demurrage charges with reference to actual damage suffered. They consider that the level must be sufficiently high that consignees will empty and return containers quickly so that carriers will regain (operational) control of the containers as soon as possible.)

Fujita: Mr. Song, do you have a comment?

Song: Just a remark. The question here is whether the holder is obliged to accept delivery in this case. I was thinking about the transfer of rights. And I think the main fact that somebody holds the original bill of lading and becomes the lawful holder of the bill does not necessarily assume the obligation to take delivery of the cargo unless it decides to do so to become a consignee. Thank you.

Fujita: Yes, you are right. Becoming a holder of the bill does not necessarily trigger the obligation to take delivery. In Q.12(2), the holder of the bill of lading demanded delivery of the goods and this triggered its obligation to take delivery under Article 46 and possible liability under Article 58(2).

May I proceed to In Q.12(2)(ii)? Professor Van der Ziel, please.

Q.12(2)(ii)

Van der Ziel: Yes, the consignee in the question should have done matters the other way around — first taking samples and, subsequently, on the basis of the result of the sampling, deciding whether to demand delivery or not. That is quite possible under Article 43. The matter of taking samples and its effect on delivery has been extensively discussed in UNCITRAL and it was generally agreed that sampling alone should not trigger the obligation to take delivery of the goods. Only demanding delivery would, which is the reason why Article 43 is drafted as it is.

Q.12(3)

Van der Ziel: Based on the facts of this (sub)question, I assume that the Caspiana Clause in this case is a valid one. Then, under this clause, the Port of Chiba has replaced the Port of Sendai as the agreed port of destination. So Chiba, instead of Sendai, now has become the new and only agreed port of destination with all the legal consequences, including those in relation to Article 48. Is this the right answer?

Fujita: Yes, please proceed on the assumption that the Caspiana Clause is valid.

Van der Ziel: Yes, I should devote some words to the matter of convenience for the carrier and inconvenience for the consignee.

In my view, the carrier must have a reasonable discretion when and in what manner to apply a Caspiana clause. It is often a contingency that gives rise to the application of a Caspiana clause and it is the duty of the carrier (and the master of the vessel) to react to the contingency in the best interest of all parties involved in the carriage. Because these interests may be conflicting, the carrier must find a reasonable balance. Often, not everybody can be satisfied and possibly, nobody will be (fully) satisfied. For these reasons, in my view, the carrier must be granted a fair discretion.

But there are limits. I referred to a *valid* Caspiana Clause but possibly we would better say that a Caspiana Clause must be validly applied. Earlier during this Workshop we heard Mr. Amemiya making reference to a clause allowing the carrier to abandon the cargo in a port of refuge. I doubt whether that is still possible under the Rotterdam Rules under all circumstances. The relevant provision is in my view Article 11 which obliges the carrier to deliver the goods "subject to this Convention" and "in accordance with the terms of the contract of carriage." The combination of these two requirements may create an area of tension. On the one hand, "subject to the Convention" includes subject to Article 79, which makes void any term in the contract of carriage that limits any obligation of the carrier, including to carry the goods to their destination and to deliver them there. On the other hand, a Caspiana Clause entitles the carrier under some circumstances to unilaterally decide to carry the goods to any other place and to deliver (in the sense of transfer of responsibility for the goods to the consignee) the goods there to the consignee. It may be argued that such delivery is allowed because the other place may be regarded as a pre-agreed place of alternative destination. In contrast, it may also be argued that such delivery limits the mandatory obligation of the carrier under Article 11 to carry the goods to their destination and to deliver these there.

As an example, let's assume that a container vessel has a fire in the engine room, the fire can be extinguished, and the vessel is towed to a port of refuge. Then, in my view, the carrier may not drop the cargo on the quay and say to the consignee: "well, it's all yours, I consider the contract of carriage as discharged." Under these circumstances, in my view, under the Rotterdam Rules the carrier is still under an obligation to deliver the cargo at the originally agreed destination. Most carriers have weekly services and it should be reasonably possible for a carrier to find alternative shipping space either on one of its own vessels or on board a competitor's vessel. The operation of a Caspiana Clause should not be a relatively easy escape from the carrier's obligation to deliver the cargo at its proper destination. The yardstick for the validity of a Caspiana Clause should be its reasonable application under the circumstances.

Q.13 Delivery of the Goods

(1) A carrier enters into a contract for carriage of goods and issues a negotiable transport document (a bill of lading), which does not expressly state that the goods may be delivered without the surrender of the transport document. The carrier delivers the goods without surrender of the transport document. Is the carrier entitled to the limitation of liability under Article 59(1) when a holder of the transport document appeared afterwards? How can Article 61 be applied in this context?

For example, are there any differences between the following situations?

(i) The carrier completely believes the explanation that the person to whom the carrier delivers the goods had a legitimate interest to claim delivery and cannot surrender the bill of lading simply because of a delay in the processing of the document.

(ii) The carrier has no information on the whereabouts of the bill of lading. However, the person to whom the carrier delivers the goods is an old customer of the carrier and, based on past trade records, the carrier believes the customer is trustworthy.

(iii) The carrier has some suspicion about the explanation that the person in question is unable to surrender the bill of lading simply due to the delay in document processing. However, the carrier delivers the goods because the person presents a letter of indemnity issued by a bank.

(2) The carrier issues a negotiable transport document that expressly states that the goods may be delivered without its surrender. Does this transport document constitute a document that "enable[s] the buyer to claim the goods from the carrier at the port of destination" required under CIF terms? *See*, INCOTERMS 2010, A8

Q.13(1)

Goto: Q.13 consists of two questions, both regarding the delivery of the goods without surrender of the transport document. The first question asks whether the carrier who delivered the goods without surrender of a bill of lading is entitled to limit liability under the Convention against the holder of the bill of lading who subsequently appears. Under the Hague-Visby Rules, this depends on whether "loss" of the goods under Article 4(5) includes such misdelivery, and some Japanese commentators assert that it doesn't. Under the Rotterdam Rules, this will depend on whether the liability of the carrier for misdelivery is a "carrier's liability for breaches of its obligations under this Convention" under Article 59(1). If this requirement is met, then Article 61(1) comes into question, since it might be said that there was an intention or recklessness of the carrier to deliver the goods without surrender of the bill of lading and the carrier should be deprived of the benefit of limitation. I think that the answer will depend on the facts, so we have three subcases, (i), (ii) and (iii), which might happen in practice.

The second question asks whether an Article 47(2) document satisfies the CIF requirements under INCOTERMS, since there will be cases in which the holder of such a document can't claim the goods from the carrier at the port of destination, when the goods have been already delivered without surrender of the document according to Article 47(2). I believe that no matter what the answer to that question is, the parties to the sales contract are able to arrange their contract on this point as they wish, but it will be desirable to have a clear view in order to make such arrangements possible.

Fujita: The first question is related to the loss of the liability limitation. Therefore, I ask Professor Honka to give us the answer.

Honka: This actually is related to the formulation in the present Hague and Hague-Visby Rules and the reference "to or in connection with the goods" (Article 4(5)), which is considered to be extremely unclear and questionable whether that would, for example, be a possibility in situations like that. Now the Rotterdam Rules to my mind are clearer on this point because in Article 47 paragraph (1)(b) it says that the carrier shall refuse delivery if the requirements mentioned above in the paragraph are not met. And one of the requirements there is "upon surrender of the negotiable transport document". So when the carrier delivers the goods without surrender in this question, it has acted in contradiction to this provision in Article 47. This means that it's a "breach of the carrier's obligations under the Convention" and according to Article 59 the carrier can limit its liability.

Then when we come to Article 61 and to the question of whether you can break the right to limit. Traditionally delivery of the goods without surrender of the bill of lading has been considered to be a serious offence as such and might even effect the loss of insurance protection. But you have to read Article 61 as it stands, and there are two serious points here. I think I'd better cite the beginning of Article 61. It reads, "Neither the carrier nor any of the persons referred to in Article 18 is entitled to the benefit of the limitation of liability as provided in Article 59, or as provided in the contract of carriage, if the claimant proves that the loss resulting from the breach of the carrier's obligation under this Convention was attributable to a personal act or omission of the person claiming a right to limit done with the intent to cause such loss or recklessly and with knowledge that such loss would probably result".

So we have the important restriction of "personal" act or omission. When you talk about a shipping company or a carrier company, what is the personal act or omission? Now I'm sure that in most jurisdictions that would be understood to be the top management of the company although you cannot draw the exact line where. So the possible application of Article 61 is dependent on further facts for each sub group that you have mentioned in (i), (ii), and (iii). But you always have to get back to the "personal" act or omission.

The other restriction is that, "recklessly and with knowledge that such loss". So it's not sufficient for the carrier to predict that some loss could arise by its behavior. It must be understood that it's just the particular loss that has taken place. So it's a bit pity that we shall say that this is "unbreakable" rule and it might just happen that the limitation right will prevail in all of your situations, but of course you can never say completely for sure because its dependent on further evidence.

Then I'm a bit unclear on what the reference to the wrong person means because to my understanding wrong delivery can take place either in the way the goods are delivered to the wrong receiver. Say that the goods are the delivered to Michael Sturley, but they should have come to me. But from my point of view the goods are lost; it's me as a consignee who suffers the loss. So you could just as well say that this is a total loss of the goods and go back to Article 17 and so on. That doesn't really affect the interpretation of Article 59 or 61 as such.

The second possibility is that this wrong delivery means that the goods are delivered and supposed to be delivered to me, but I don't have the bill of lading when they are delivered to me and then I go bankrupt and the seller at the other end hasn't received the purchase price. So in that case it's the seller who is the interested party and who suffers the loss. But that situation will not affect either the interpretation of Articles 59 or 61; you would still have to deal with these two Articles. It's just another method that might apply when you have delivered the goods to the correct receiver but at the wrong premises. It might just be that the calculation of the damage is done in a different way and in a particular way, which is not to my understanding regulated at all in the Rotterdam Rules.

Fujita: I notice Professor Van der Ziel has something to add.

Van der Ziel: Thank you. I'd like to supplement the answer. Though the question is not quite explicit on this matter, Professor Honka referred to the fact that in these cases a carrier has to refuse delivery under Article 47. I note that when a carrier refuses delivery under Article 47, the goods become undeliverable, meaning that Article 48 may apply. And under Article 48, the carrier may "take such action in respect of the goods as circumstances may reasonably require."

It might be that in all three cases referred to in the question the carrier has taken the action as reasonably required. This will fully depend on the circumstances. For example, if in case (iii) the cargo is 150,000 tons of oil, there is not much alternative than to deliver this cargo against a letter of indemnity. Further, apart from the costs involved, there are not so many ports in the world where it is possible to store 150,000 tons of oil for trading purposes. In addition, in the carriage of oil it is standing practice to deliver against a letter of indemnity and all persons involved in this trade ought to be aware of that. Under these circumstances the carrier may have done the reasonable thing. If, however, the cargo is one container loaded with non-perishable goods, in all three cases referred to in the question circumstances may reasonably require that the carrier stores the container for some time and waits for presentation of the bill of lading.

When under Article 48 the carrier acts reasonably, he is not liable at all for loss or damage to the goods. And even if he fails "to take steps that would have been reasonable in the circumstances to preserve the goods", the carrier is liable only if he "knew or ought to have known that the loss or damage to the goods would result from its failure to take such steps."

Fujita: Thank you for your comment. To be honest, we had not examined the possible application of Article 48 when we made this question. But you are right. That article might be applicable. May I proceed to the second question? I have sometimes heard an assertion that an "Article 47(2) document", i.e., a negotiable transport document with the express statement that the goods may be delivered without its surrender, does not qualify as a transport document required under CIF terms. Professor Van der Ziel, do you agree to the assertion?

Q.13(2)

Van der Ziel: No, I disagree with those people that say that a "47(2) document" would not comply with the CIF requirements. Most probably, a misunderstanding of the operation of Article 47 is involved here.

A "47(2) document" complies with the definition of "negotiable transport document" in Article 1(15) and is therefore fully subject to Article 47(1) that applies to all negotiable transport documents. Under CIF (A8) the transport document must "enable the buyer to claim the goods from the carrier at the port of destination" and under Article 47(1)(a) of the Rotterdam Rules a buyer holding a "47(2) document" "is entitled to claim delivery of the goods from the carrier after they have arrived at the place of destination". I deliberately use quotations from the INCOTERMS and the Rotterdam Rules to show that the Rotterdam Rules align to the requirement of the CIF INCOTERM.

Further, I may add that Article 47(2), as an alternative to the application of Article 48, only comes in the picture if the buyer/holder of the "47(2) document" does not claim the goods for delivery or does not surrender the "47(2) document "to the carrier when the goods have arrived at destination.

As a result, it is beyond reasonable doubt that the Rotterdam Rules are fully in compliance with the CIF INCOTERM.

Fujita: Thank you for your explanation. I, too, believe that a possible exoneration of the carrier under limited circumstances does not disqualify "a 47(2) document" as a transport document required under INCOTERMS.

Q.14 Volume Contracts

A shipping company "A", which undertakes to carry goods in a liner service, sends its employee to its customer "B", which has continually entered into a contract for carriage of goods with "A" as a shipper. The employee explains to "B" that, if "B" accepts the new contract conditions provided by "A", a freight rate, cheaper than the ordinary shipment rate, will be applied to "B"'s cargo. The conditions are as follows: (a) "B " shall ship 50 tons of cargo a year in two shipments; and (b) the shipping company's liability is based on the provisions provided for in the Hague Rules, not the Rotterdam Rules. The contract includes the following clause: "Liabilities of the carrier under this contract shall be governed by the following article in 'the International Convention for the Unification of certain rules of law relating to bills of lading, 25 August 1924' (hereinafter 'the Hague Rules')", as well as the entire text of Article 4 of the Hague Rules in red ink.

After the conclusion of the contract, the first carriage is completed properly. However, cargo damage is found at the destination after the second carriage. Although a transport document, unlike the contract, contains no provision indicating the carrier's liability, a consignee "C" is informed of that liability in advance, via an e-mail from the shipper "B".

(1) Is this contract a volume contract under the Rotterdam Rules (Article 1 (2))? What is the difference between volume contracts and other similar agreements (such as the "slot charter" and the "space charter")?

(2) Does the provision of this contract satisfy the requirements of Articles 80 (2) (a), and (b) (ii) ("prominently specifies ...") of the Rotterdam Rules? For example, would a situation meet "the individually negotiated" requirement if, after having read each provision in the volume contract that derogates from the Rotterdam Rules, the employee of "A" told "B" that "After studying this contract, please let me know if you will contract with us within one week", and "B" answered "I agree with this contract" in a week?

(3) Let us assume that the above contract is a volume contract under the Rotterdam Rules. If

the shipping company's employee strongly recommends this contract to the shipper "B" for the purpose of improving its business performance, and emphasizes that "Almost all shippers that use this vessel send their cargo under these conditions", is "B" given "an opportunity" as noted in Article 80 (2) (c)?

What if the carrier has discriminated against the shipper who enters into the contract under the Rotterdam Rules (where, for instance, the carrier gives priority to the cargo under volume contract over other cargo in the shipment)? Should the carrier provide a "notice of the opportunity" expressly and directly to the shipper? Does information posted on the shipping company's website, which offers an opportunity for such a contract, serve as a notice of this opportunity?

(4) The consignee "C" receives the e-mail information from the shipper "B", comprised of information about the carrier's liability in this contract. In this case, does "C" receive "information that prominently states..." in accordance with Article 80(5)(a)? When "C" responds to "B", saying "I accept these contract terms", does "B" give the "express consent to be bound by such derogations"?

Sasaoka: The purpose of Q.14 is to qualify the requirements of Article 80, which is on the special rules for volume contract.

In Q.14(1), I would like to ask you if an agreement that a shipper is supposed to send a small amount of cargo in only two shipments is deemed to be a volume contract under the Rotterdam rules. If you would like to send such cargo, I think you may use other agreements such as a slot charter and a space charter. So I am wondering what is the difference between volume contracts and other agreements.

Q.14(2) and (3) ask whether each situation satisfies the requirements for a derogation from the Rotterdam Rules in Article 80(2).

Q.14(4) relates to the applicability of derogations to third parties under Article 80(5). In this case, the shipper, not the carrier, provides the information on the derogation to the consignee, and then the consignee replies to the shipper, not the carrier, with an express consent to the derogation. Can the carrier invoke the applicability of the derogation to the consignee?

Fujita: Q14 focuses on the volume contract on which Professor Sturley made the presentation. Therefore, I ask Professor Sturley to answer this question.

Q.14(1)

Sturley: I can answer this question quickly. Yes, this is a volume contract. It clearly satisfies the definition of volume contracts in Article 1(2). It is different from a space charter or a slot charter. This contract does not provide for the use of space on a ship, and therefore it is not excluded from the Rotterdam Rules. The difference between the two is that the volume contract is presumptively subject to the Rotterdam Rules. So the default rule for the volume contract is that the Rotterdam Rules apply. With the space charter or the slot charter, the presumption is that the Rotterdam Rules do not apply.

Of course, by contract, the charterer can agree to the Rotterdam Rules. But absent that agreement, the presumption is that they do not apply. Since this question involves a volume contract, however, the Rotterdam Rules presumptively apply except to the extent that the parties satisfy the requirements for derogation.

Fujita: Thank you for your answer. If the contract is a "volume contract", does it satisfy the requirement under Article 80?

Q.14(2)

Sturley: Let me start with two general observations. First, on the facts given it is unimaginable that a carrier would send an employee to individually negotiate with the shipper for only 50 tons a year. What we have been told is that no carrier would individually negotiate for less than say 100 containers a year, certainly not for 50 tons. But accepting these facts, we can consider how the Rotterdam Rules would apply to that situation.

Second, you will notice when you look at Article 80 that there are a number of imprecise words that leave a court with a lot of flexibility. For example, the statement must be "prominent". Well, how "prominent" does a "prominent" statement have to be? We don't know. A derogation may have to be "individually negotiated". What does that mean? How much individual negotiation does there have to be? Then we see that the shipper has to be given "an opportunity and notice of the opportunity". How realistic does the opportunity have to be, and how clear does the notice have to be? So, there is a lot of flexibility which I confess is deliberate. When the volume contract provisions are being negotiated, some delegates wanted to have it be fairly easy to negotiate the volume contract. Some delegates wanted it to be very difficult for volume contract to be negotiated. And it was impossible to have agreement on precisely what the terms had to be. So, we're left with a situation in which courts are going to have a certain amount of flexibility.

And I suspect that the courts in some countries are going to require more prominent statements, and the courts of other countries will let carriers get away with less prominent statements. If any of this is ever litigated, which, I think, is unlikely because I don't think we will have the carriers attempting to derogate very often. But if we did, if it did go to litigation, there will be some flexibility here.

So, having said that, I will still answer the question because I think this question is very easy. It is not enough that the derogation be prominently stated. Article 80(2)(a) requires the volume contract to contain a prominent statement that the volume contract derogates from the Convention and on these facts there is no statement that this is a derogation. The shipper is told, "we are going to apply the Hague Rules instead of the Rotterdam Rules", but the shipper has to be told: "And by the way, you are enjoying fewer rights under the Hague Rules than you would have under the Rotterdam Rules". Unless the shipper is told that it is giving up rights under the Rotterdam Rules, then the statement may be prominent but it would still be the wrong prominent statement or it would not be a sufficient prominent statement.

Q.14(3)

Fujita: Let us examine another condition under Article 80. Does the carrier offer an opportunity to conclude a contract that is in compliance with the Convention under the situation described in Q.14(3)?

Sturley: Well, here my general observation applies that the Rotterdam Rules are deliberately a little bit vague on just how much is required. And some courts might say this is enough. I predict that at least a U.S. court would say that this is not enough. A carrier would have to expressly and directly give the shipper the opportunity. It would have to tell the shipper, "here is your choice". In fact, there is already a doctrine in U.S. law that is fairly similar to this under the Carmack Amendment, which is our inland carrier statute. Under that doctrine, the carrier has to offer the shipper Carmack terms for full liability. But the carrier can offer lesser liability for a different freight rate. The law developed that the carrier needs to clearly offer that choice. And if it does not clearly offer the choice, it is not enough. I do not think that offering the choice on the website is going to be enough here. Article 80(3) in a slightly different context suggests that it would not be enough to put the choice on the website. Carriers actually have to offer shippers the choice.

The way it would work in practice under our law, I think, is that the carrier would have to say, "you can have Rotterdam Rules terms and it will cost you this much, or you can have Hague Rules terms and it will cost you that much. You decide if it's worth getting the extra coverage and paying the price difference."

Q.14(4)

Fujita: Final question is the validity of the derogation vis-à-vis a third party. Is the condition under Article 80(5) satisfied under the situation in Q.14(4)?

Sturley: In answering the question, the notice to the consignee is prominent enough here, but it is still the wrong notice. The consignee still needs to receive notice that there is a derogation. The consignee needs to know, just as the shipper needs to know, that this contract reduces the carrier's liability that would otherwise apply under the Rotterdam Rules. And unless that notice is prominently given, then the notice is insufficient.

In the second part of the question, the consignee can give its consent in this fashion. It is permissible for the consignee to give the consent to the shipper for the benefit of the carrier. If the shipper then tells the carrier, the carrier can rely on that. Thus the consent is valid if it is done this way, but the carrier still needs to give the proper notice, and we do not have that on these facts.

Fujita: With respect to the first part of Q.14(4), Professor Sturley thought the information received by the consignee is not sufficient. But before we examine the contents of the notice, who should give the notice? Article 80(5)(a) does not specify who should give "information that prominently states that the volume contract derogates from this Convention" to the third party. Does this mean anyone can give the information to the third party? Or should the carrier himself give such information.

Sturley: Article 80(5) is deliberately imprecise about how the third party receives the information. The relevant factor is that the consignee does receive the information, and it does not matter who provides it. Anyone, including the shipper, could provide it. In practice, the only way that a consignee is ever likely to receive notice and give consent — other than in cases in which the consignee is also the shipper, and of course the present issue would be irrelevant in those cases — is through the shipper.

Fujita: Mr. Song, do you have additional comment?

Song: I am just going to remind everybody of the fact that there are form requirements for Article 80(2) and (5). And they are found in Article 3. The article is good to remember anyway because it refers to several other articles in the Rotterdam Rules as well. But you have certain form requirements for consent and communication. It is just a reminder. Thank you.

Fujita: Thank you for your comment. Yes, the form requirement is found in Article 3.

Part III

The Text of
United Nations Convention on
Contracts for the International
Carriage of Goods
Wholly or Partly By Sea

Corrections to the Original Text of the Rotterdam Rules

Tomotaka Fujita

On October 11, the Secretary-General of the United Nations, acting in his capacity as a depositary, circulated a depositary notification" with respect to the proposed corrections on the Rotterdam Rules text[1]. It is an established practice that the errors in the text of a convention can be corrected by a notice circulated by the depositary[2]. Since no objection was raised from a signatory State or a Contracting State within 90 days, the proposed corrections took effect on January 11, 2013 and apply to the authentic texts of the Convention and to their true copies[3]. There are two corrections:

Article 1(6)(a)   Article 1(6)(a) is the definition of a "performing party", which refers to the list of specific activities that a performing party performs on behalf of the carrier. Compared with the list of the carrier's obligations in Article 13(1), the word "keeping" is missing. This is an editorial mistake which occurred during the numerous "copying and pasting" in the drafting process, which needs to be corrected.

Article 19(1)(b)   Three conditions are enumerated with respect to the maritime performing party's liability in Article 19(1)(b). The original text read as though each one of them is stand alone because it says (i), (ii), or (iii). The intended meaning is that (i) is always necessary, and it should be combined with (ii) or (iii). Although delegations seem to have understood the meaning of the article as is just explained throughout the negotiation at UNCITRAL Working Group, the text was wrongly modified when the article was reformulated[4]. The treaty section of the United Nations thought it was another editorial mistake and

---

[1] *See* Depositary Notification C.N.563.2012.TREATIES-XI.D.8 (available at http://treaties.un.org/doc/Publication/CN/2012/CN.563.2012-Eng.pdf).
[2] *See* Article 79(2) of the Vienna Convention on the Law of Treaties.
[3] *See* Depositary Notification C.N.105.2013.TREATIES-XI.D.8 (available at http://www.comitemaritime.org/Uploads/Rotterdam%20Rules/CN.105.2013-Eng.pdf).
[4] The draft text on Feburary 13, 2007 included the following text which corresponds with Article 19(1)(b) of the final text (*See* "Transport Law: Draft convention on the carriage of goods [wholly or

decided to include it in the correction of the text.

The text included in this volume reflects the above corrections. The depositary notice from the secretariat (Depositary Notification C.N.563.2012.TREATIES-XI.D.8) is also cited in the next page.

---

partly] [by sea] ", U.N. doc. no. A/CN.9/WG.III/WP.81).

"1. A maritime performing party [that initially received the goods for carriage in a Contracting State, or finally delivered them in a Contracting State, or performed its activities with respect to the goods in a port in a Contracting State]:
(a) Is subject to the obligations and liabilities imposed on the carrier under this Convention and is entitled to the carrier's rights and immunities provided by this Convention *if the occurrence that caused the loss, damage or delay took place during the period between the arrival of the goods at the port of loading of a ship and their departure from the port of discharge from a ship, when it has custody of the goods or at any other time to the extent that it is participating in the performance of any of the activities contemplated by the contract of carriage,* and ....." (Emphasis added)

The text was amended by the draft on November 14, 2007 which are almost identical to the final text (*See* "Transport Law: Draft convention on the carriage of goods [wholly or partly] [by sea] ", U.N. doc. no. A/CN.9/WG.III/WP.101). The amendent includes several substantive changes following the discussion at 19th Session of the UNCITRAL Working Group III (New York, April 2007) which is irrelevant to the issue in question and reformulation of the article. The Secretariat explained the draft "as slightly revised and reordered by the Secretariat for improved drafting" (*See* id. footnote 40). As a result of the reformulation, the substance of Article 19(1)(b) was changed and it was, unfortunately, overlooked until the adoption of the Convention.

CN.563.2012.TREATIES-XI-D-8 (Annex/Annexe)

	Current text	Proposed corrections
1.	**Article 1(6) (*a*)** "Performing party" means a person other than the carrier that performs or undertakes to perform any of the carrier's obligations under a contract of carriage with respect to the receipt, loading, handling, stowage, carriage, care, unloading or delivery of the goods, to the extent that such person acts, either directly or indirectly, at the carrier's request or under the carrier's supervision or control.	INSERT THE WORD "KEEPING" "Performing party" means a person other than the carrier that performs or undertakes to perform any of the carrier's obligations under a contract of carriage with respect to the receipt, loading, handling, stowage, carriage, **keeping**, care, unloading or delivery of the goods, to the extent that such person acts, either directly or indirectly, at the carrier's request or under the carrier's supervision or control
2.	**Article 19 1(b)** 1. A maritime performing party is subject to the obligations and liabilities imposed on the carrier under this Convention and is entitled to the carrier's defences and limits of liability as provided for in this Convention if: * * * (b) The occurrence that caused the loss, damage or delay took place: (i) during the period between the arrival of the goods at the port of loading of the ship and their departure from the port of discharge from the ship; (ii) while the maritime performing party had custody of the goods; or (iii) at any other time to the extent that it was participating in the performance of any of the activities contemplated by the contract of carriage.	INSERT THE WORDS "AND EITHER" AFTER REQUIREMENT (i) IN SUBPARAGRAPH (b). (b) The occurrence that caused the loss, damage or delay took place: (i) during the period between the arrival of the goods at the port of loading of the ship and their departure from the port of discharge from the ship; **and either** (ii) while it had custody of the goods; or (iii) at any other time to the extent that it was participating in the performance of any of the activities contemplated by the contract of carriage.

United Nations Convention on Contracts for the International Carriage of Goods Wholly or Partly by Sea

The States Parties to this Convention,

Reaffirming their belief that international trade on the basis of equality and mutual benefit is an important element in promoting friendly relations among States,

Convinced that the progressive harmonization and unification of international trade law, in reducing or removing legal obstacles to the flow of international trade, significantly contributes to universal economic cooperation among all States on a basis of equality, equity and common interest, and to the well-being of all peoples,

Recognizing the significant contribution of the International Convention for the Unification of Certain Rules of Law relating to Bills of Lading, signed in Brussels on 25 August 1924, and its Protocols, and of the United Nations Convention on the Carriage of Goods by Sea, signed in Hamburg on 31 March 1978, to the harmonization of the law governing the carriage of goods by sea,

Mindful of the technological and commercial developments that have taken place since the adoption of those conventions and of the need to consolidate and modernize them,

Noting that shippers and carriers do not have the benefit of a binding universal regime to support the operation of contracts of maritime carriage involving other modes of transport,

Believing that the adoption of uniform rules to govern international contracts of carriage wholly or partly by sea will promote legal certainty, improve the efficiency of international carriage of goods and facilitate new access opportunities for previously remote parties and markets, thus playing a fundamental role in promoting trade and economic development, both domestically and internationally,

Have agreed as follows:

CHAPTER 1. GENERAL PROVISIONS

Article 1. Definitions

For the purposes of this Convention:

1. "Contract of carriage" means a contract in which a carrier, against the payment of freight, undertakes to carry goods from one place to another. The contract shall provide for carriage by sea and may provide for carriage by other modes of transport in addition to the sea carriage.

2. "Volume contract" means a contract of carriage that provides for the carriage

of a specified quantity of goods in a series of shipments during an agreed period of time. The specification of the quantity may include a minimum, a maximum or a certain range.

3. "Liner transportation" means a transportation service that is offered to the public through publication or similar means and includes transportation by ships operating on a regular schedule between specified ports in accordance with publicly available timetables of sailing dates.

4. "Non-liner transportation" means any transportation that is not liner transportation.

5. "Carrier" means a person that enters into a contract of carriage with a shipper.

6. (a) "Performing party" means a person other than the carrier that performs or undertakes to perform any of the carrier's obligations under a contract of carriage with respect to the receipt, loading, handling, stowage, carriage, keeping, care, unloading or delivery of the goods, to the extent that such person acts, either directly or indirectly, at the carrier's request or under the carrier's supervision or control.

(b) "Performing party" does not include any person that is retained, directly or indirectly, by a shipper, by a documentary shipper, by the controlling party or by the consignee instead of by the carrier.

7. "Maritime performing party" means a performing party to the extent that it performs or undertakes to perform any of the carrier's obligations during the period between the arrival of the goods at the port of loading of a ship and their departure from the port of discharge of a ship. An inland carrier is a maritime performing party only if it performs or undertakes to perform its services exclusively within a port area.

8. "Shipper" means a person that enters into a contract of carriage with a carrier.

9. "Documentary shipper" means a person, other than the shipper, that accepts to be named as "shipper" in the transport document or electronic transport record.

10. "Holder" means:

(a) A person that is in possession of a negotiable transport document; and (i) if the document is an order document, is identified in it as the shipper or the consignee, or is the person to which the document is duly endorsed; or (ii) if the document is a blank endorsed order document or bearer document, is the bearer thereof; or

(b) The person to which a negotiable electronic transport record has been issued or transferred in accordance with the procedures referred to in article 9, paragraph 1.

11. "Consignee" means a person entitled to delivery of the goods under a contract of carriage or a transport document or electronic transport record.

12. "Right of control" of the goods means the right under the contract of carriage to give the carrier instructions in respect of the goods in accordance with chapter 10.

13. "Controlling party" means the person that pursuant to article 51 is entitled to exercise the right of control.

14. "Transport document" means a document issued under a contract of carriage by the carrier that:

(a) Evidences the carrier's or a performing party's receipt of goods under a contract of carriage; and

(b) Evidences or contains a contract of carriage.

15. "Negotiable transport document" means a transport document that indicates, by wording such as "to order" or "negotiable" or other appropriate wording recognized as having the same effect by the law applicable to the document, that the goods have been consigned to the order of the shipper, to the order of the consignee, or to bearer, and is not explicitly stated as being "non-negotiable" or "not negotiable".

16. "Non-negotiable transport document" means a transport document that is not a negotiable transport document.

17. "Electronic communication" means information generated, sent, received or stored by electronic, optical, digital or similar means with the result that the information communicated is accessible so as to be usable for subsequent reference.

18. "Electronic transport record" means information in one or more messages issued by electronic communication under a contract of carriage by a carrier, including information logically associated with the electronic transport record by attachments or otherwise linked to the electronic transport record contemporaneously with or subsequent to its issue by the carrier, so as to become part of the electronic transport record, that:

(a) Evidences the carrier's or a performing party's receipt of goods under a contract of carriage; and

(b) Evidences or contains a contract of carriage.

19. "Negotiable electronic transport record" means an electronic transport record:

(a) That indicates, by wording such as "to order", or "negotiable", or other appropriate wording recognized as having the same effect by the law applicable to the record, that the goods have been consigned to the order of the shipper or to the order of the consignee, and is not explicitly stated as being "non-negotiable" or "not negotiable"; and

(b) The use of which meets the requirements of article 9, paragraph 1.

20. "Non-negotiable electronic transport record" means an electronic transport record that is not a negotiable electronic transport record.

21. The "issuance" of a negotiable electronic transport record means the issuance of the record in accordance with procedures that ensure that the record is subject to exclusive control from its creation until it ceases to have any effect or validity.

22. The "transfer" of a negotiable electronic transport record means the transfer of exclusive control over the record.

23. "Contract particulars" means any information relating to the contract of carriage or to the goods (including terms, notations, signatures and endorsements) that is in a transport document or an electronic transport record.

24. "Goods" means the wares, merchandise, and articles of every kind whatsoever that a carrier undertakes to carry under a contract of carriage and includes the packing and any equipment and container not supplied by or on behalf of the carrier.

25. "Ship" means any vessel used to carry goods by sea.

26. "Container" means any type of container, transportable tank or flat, swapbody, or any similar unit load used to consolidate goods, and any equipment ancillary to such unit load.

27. "Vehicle" means a road or railroad cargo vehicle.

28. "Freight" means the remuneration payable to the carrier for the carriage of goods under a contract of carriage.

29. "Domicile" means (a) a place where a company or other legal person or association of natural or legal persons has its (i) statutory seat or place of incorporation or central registered office, whichever is applicable, (ii) central administration or (iii) principal place of business, and (b) the habitual residence of a natural person.

30. "Competent court" means a court in a Contracting State that, according to the rules on the internal allocation of jurisdiction among the courts of that State, may exercise jurisdiction over the dispute.

Article 2. Interpretation of this Convention

In the interpretation of this Convention, regard is to be had to its international character and to the need to promote uniformity in its application and the observance of good faith in international trade.

Article 3. Form requirements

The notices, confirmation, consent, agreement, declaration and other communications referred to in articles 19, paragraph 2; 23, paragraphs 1 to 4; 36, subparagraphs 1 (b), (c) and (d); 40, subparagraph 4 (b); 44; 48, paragraph 3; 51, subparagraph 1 (b); 59, paragraph 1; 63; 66; 67, paragraph 2; 75, paragraph 4; and 80, paragraphs 2 and 5, shall be in writing. Electronic communications may be used for these purposes, provided that the use of such means is with the consent of the person by which it is communicated and of the person to which it is communicated.

Article 4. Applicability of defences and limits of liability

1. Any provision of this Convention that may provide a defence for, or limit the liability of, the carrier applies in any judicial or arbitral proceeding, whether founded in contract, in tort, or otherwise, that is instituted in respect of loss of, damage to, or delay in delivery of goods covered by a contract of carriage or for the breach of any other obligation under this Convention against:

    (a) The carrier or a maritime performing party;
    (b) The master, crew or any other person that performs services on board the ship; or
    (c) Employees of the carrier or a maritime performing party.

2. Any provision of this Convention that may provide a defence for the shipper or the documentary shipper applies in any judicial or arbitral proceeding, whether founded in contract, in tort, or otherwise, that is instituted against the shipper, the documentary shipper, or their subcontractors, agents or employees.

CHAPTER 2. SCOPE OF APPLICATION

Article 5. General scope of application

1. Subject to article 6, this Convention applies to contracts of carriage in which the place of receipt and the place of delivery are in different States, and the port of loading of a sea carriage and the port of discharge of the same sea carriage are in different States, if, according to the contract of carriage, any one of the following places is located in a Contracting State:

    (a) The place of receipt;
    (b) The port of loading;
    (c) The place of delivery; or
    (d) The port of discharge.

2. This Convention applies without regard to the nationality of the vessel, the carrier, the performing parties, the shipper, the consignee, or any other interested parties.

Article 6. Specific exclusions

1. This Convention does not apply to the following contracts in liner transporta-

tion:

    (a)   Charterparties; and

    (b)   Other contracts for the use of a ship or of any space thereon.

    2.   This Convention does not apply to contracts of carriage in non-liner transportation except when:

    (a)   There is no charterparty or other contract between the parties for the use of a ship or of any space thereon; and

    (b)   A transport document or an electronic transport record is issued.

Article 7. Application to certain parties

Notwithstanding article 6, this Convention applies as between the carrier and the consignee, controlling party or holder that is not an original party to the charterparty or other contract of carriage excluded from the application of this Convention. However, this Convention does not apply as between the original parties to a contract of carriage excluded pursuant to article 6.

CHAPTER 3. ELECTRONIC TRANSPORT RECORDS

Article 8. Use and effect of electronic transport records

Subject to the requirements set out in this Convention:

    (a)   Anything that is to be in or on a transport document under this Convention may be recorded in an electronic transport record, provided the issuance and subsequent use of an electronic transport record is with the consent of the carrier and the shipper; and

    (b)   The issuance, exclusive control, or transfer of an electronic transport record has the same effect as the issuance, possession, or transfer of a transport document.

Article 9. Procedures for use of negotiable electronic transport records

    1.   The use of a negotiable electronic transport record shall be subject to procedures that provide for:

    (a)   The method for the issuance and the transfer of that record to an intended holder;

    (b)   An assurance that the negotiable electronic transport record retains its integrity;

    (c)   The manner in which the holder is able to demonstrate that it is the holder; and

    (d)   The manner of providing confirmation that delivery to the holder has been effected, or that, pursuant to articles 10, paragraph 2, or 47, subparagraphs 1 (a)(ii) and (c), the electronic transport record has ceased to have any effect or validity.

2. The procedures in paragraph 1 of this article shall be referred to in the contract particulars and be readily ascertainable.

Article 10. Replacement of negotiable transport document or negotiable electronic transport record

1. If a negotiable transport document has been issued and the carrier and the holder agree to replace that document by a negotiable electronic transport record:

(a) The holder shall surrender the negotiable transport document, or all of them if more than one has been issued, to the carrier;

(b) The carrier shall issue to the holder a negotiable electronic transport record that includes a statement that it replaces the negotiable transport document; and

(c) The negotiable transport document ceases thereafter to have any effect or validity.

2. If a negotiable electronic transport record has been issued and the carrier and the holder agree to replace that electronic transport record by a negotiable transport document:

(a) The carrier shall issue to the holder, in place of the electronic transport record, a negotiable transport document that includes a statement that it replaces the negotiable electronic transport record; and

(b) The electronic transport record ceases thereafter to have any effect or validity.

CHAPTER 4. OBLIGATIONS OF THE CARRIER

Article 11. Carriage and delivery of the goods

The carrier shall, subject to this Convention and in accordance with the terms of the contract of carriage, carry the goods to the place of destination and deliver them to the consignee.

Article 12. Period of responsibility of the carrier

1. The period of responsibility of the carrier for the goods under this Convention begins when the carrier or a performing party receives the goods for carriage and ends when the goods are delivered.

2. (a) If the law or regulations of the place of receipt require the goods to be handed over to an authority or other third party from which the carrier may collect them,

the period of responsibility of the carrier begins when the carrier collects the goods from the authority or other third party.

(b) If the law or regulations of the place of delivery require the carrier to hand over the goods to an authority or other third party from which the consignee may collect them, the period of responsibility of the carrier ends when the carrier hands the goods over to the authority or other third party.

3. For the purpose of determining the carrier's period of responsibility, the parties may agree on the time and location of receipt and delivery of the goods, but a provision in a contract of carriage is void to the extent that it provides that:

(a) The time of receipt of the goods is subsequent to the beginning of their initial loading under the contract of carriage; or

(b) The time of delivery of the goods is prior to the completion of their final unloading under the contract of carriage.

Article 13. Specific obligations

1. The carrier shall during the period of its responsibility as defined in article 12, and subject to article 26, properly and carefully receive, load, handle, stow, carry, keep, care for, unload and deliver the goods.

2. Notwithstanding paragraph 1 of this article, and without prejudice to the other provisions in chapter 4 and to chapters 5 to 7, the carrier and the shipper may agree that the loading, handling, stowing or unloading of the goods is to be performed by the shipper, the documentary shipper or the consignee. Such an agreement shall be referred to in the contract particulars.

Article 14. Specific obligations applicable to the voyage by sea

The carrier is bound before, at the beginning of, and during the voyage by sea to exercise due diligence to:

(a) Make and keep the ship seaworthy;

(b) Properly crew, equip and supply the ship and keep the ship so crewed, equipped and supplied throughout the voyage; and

(c) Make and keep the holds and all other parts of the ship in which the goods are carried, and any containers supplied by the carrier in or upon which the goods are carried, fit and safe for their reception, carriage and preservation.

Article 15. Goods that may become a danger

Notwithstanding articles 11 and 13, the carrier or a performing party may decline to receive or to load, and may take such other measures as are reasonable, including unloading, destroying, or rendering goods harmless, if the goods are, or reasonably appear likely to become during the carrier's period of responsibility, an actual danger to persons, property or the environment.

Article 16. Sacrifice of the goods during the voyage by sea

Notwithstanding articles 11, 13, and 14, the carrier or a performing party may sacrifice goods at sea when the sacrifice is reasonably made for the common safety or for the purpose of preserving from peril human life or other property involved in the common adventure.

CHAPTER 5. LIABILITY OF THE CARRIER FOR LOSS, DAMAGE OR DELAY

Article 17. Basis of liability

1. The carrier is liable for loss of or damage to the goods, as well as for delay in delivery, if the claimant proves that the loss, damage, or delay, or the event or circumstance that caused or contributed to it took place during the period of the carrier's responsibility as defined in chapter 4.

2. The carrier is relieved of all or part of its liability pursuant to paragraph 1 of this article if it proves that the cause or one of the causes of the loss, damage, or delay is not attributable to its fault or to the fault of any person referred to in article 18.

3. The carrier is also relieved of all or part of its liability pursuant to paragraph 1 of this article if, alternatively to proving the absence of fault as provided in paragraph 2 of this article, it proves that one or more of the following events or circumstances caused or contributed to the loss, damage, or delay:

(a) Act of God;

(b) Perils, dangers, and accidents of the sea or other navigable waters;

(c) War, hostilities, armed conflict, piracy, terrorism, riots, and civil commotions;

(d) Quarantine restrictions; interference by or impediments created by governments, public authorities, rulers, or people including detention, arrest, or seizure not attributable to the carrier or any person referred to in article 18;

(e) Strikes, lockouts, stoppages, or restraints of labour;

(f) Fire on the ship;

(g) Latent defects not discoverable by due diligence;

(h) Act or omission of the shipper, the documentary shipper, the controlling party, or any other person for whose acts the shipper or the documentary shipper is liable pursuant to article 33 or 34;

(i) Loading, handling, stowing, or unloading of the goods performed pursuant to an agreement in accordance with article 13, paragraph 2, unless the carrier or a performing party performs such activity on behalf of the shipper, the documentary shipper or the consignee;

(j) Wastage in bulk or weight or any other loss or damage arising from inherent defect, quality, or vice of the goods;

(k) Insufficiency or defective condition of packing or marking not performed by or on behalf of the carrier;

(l) Saving or attempting to save life at sea;

(m) Reasonable measures to save or attempt to save property at sea;

(n) Reasonable measures to avoid or attempt to avoid damage to the environment; or

(o) Acts of the carrier in pursuance of the powers conferred by articles 15 and 16.

4. Notwithstanding paragraph 3 of this article, the carrier is liable for all or part of the loss, damage, or delay:

(a) If the claimant proves that the fault of the carrier or of a person referred to in article 18 caused or contributed to the event or circumstance on which the carrier relies; or

(b) If the claimant proves that an event or circumstance not listed in paragraph 3 of this article contributed to the loss, damage, or delay, and the carrier cannot prove that this event or circumstance is not attributable to its fault or to the fault of any person referred to in article 18.

5. The carrier is also liable, notwithstanding paragraph 3 of this article, for all or part of the loss, damage, or delay if:

(a) The claimant proves that the loss, damage, or delay was or was probably caused by or contributed to by (i) the unseaworthiness of the ship; (ii) the improper crewing, equipping, and supplying of the ship; or (iii) the fact that the holds or other parts of the ship in which the goods are carried, or any containers supplied by the carrier in or upon which the goods are carried, were not fit and safe for reception, carriage, and preservation of the goods; and

(b) The carrier is unable to prove either that: (i) none of the events or circumstances referred to in subparagraph 5 (a) of this article caused the loss, damage, or delay; or (ii) that it complied with its obligation to exercise due diligence pursuant to article 14.

6. When the carrier is relieved of part of its liability pursuant to this article, the carrier is liable only for that part of the loss, damage or delay that is attributable to the event

or circumstance for which it is liable pursuant to this article.

Article 18. Liability of the carrier for other persons

The carrier is liable for the breach of its obligations under this Convention caused by the acts or omissions of:

(a) Any performing party;

(b) The master or crew of the ship;

(c) Employees of the carrier or a performing party; or

(d) Any other person that performs or undertakes to perform any of the carrier's obligations under the contract of carriage, to the extent that the person acts, either directly or indirectly, at the carrier's request or under the carrier's supervision or control.

Article 19. Liability of maritime performing parties

1. A maritime performing party is subject to the obligations and liabilities imposed on the carrier under this Convention and is entitled to the carrier's defences and limits of liability as provided for in this Convention if:

(a) The maritime performing party received the goods for carriage in a Contracting State, or delivered them in a Contracting State, or performed its activities with respect to the goods in a port in a Contracting State; and

(b) The occurrence that caused the loss, damage or delay took place: (i) during the period between the arrival of the goods at the port of loading of the ship and their departure from the port of discharge from the ship and either (ii) while the maritime performing party had custody of the goods; or (iii) at any other time to the extent that it was participating in the performance of any of the activities contemplated by the contract of carriage.

2. If the carrier agrees to assume obligations other than those imposed on the carrier under this Convention, or agrees that the limits of its liability are higher than the limits specified under this Convention, a maritime performing party is not bound by this agreement unless it expressly agrees to accept such obligations or such higher limits.

3. A maritime performing party is liable for the breach of its obligations under this Convention caused by the acts or omissions of any person to which it has entrusted the performance of any of the carrier's obligations under the contract of carriage under the conditions set out in paragraph 1 of this article.

4. Nothing in this Convention imposes liability on the master or crew of the ship or on an employee of the carrier or of a maritime performing party.

Article 20. Joint and several liability

1. If the carrier and one or more maritime performing parties are liable for the loss of, damage to, or delay in delivery of the goods, their liability is joint and several but only up to the limits provided for under this Convention.

2. Without prejudice to article 61, the aggregate liability of all such persons shall not exceed the overall limits of liability under this Convention.

Article 21. Delay

Delay in delivery occurs when the goods are not delivered at the place of destination provided for in the contract of carriage within the time agreed.

Article 22. Calculation of compensation

1. Subject to article 59, the compensation payable by the carrier for loss of or damage to the goods is calculated by reference to the value of such goods at the place and time of delivery established in accordance with article 43.

2. The value of the goods is fixed according to the commodity exchange price or, if there is no such price, according to their market price or, if there is no commodity exchange price or market price, by reference to the normal value of the goods of the same kind and quality at the place of delivery.

3. In case of loss of or damage to the goods, the carrier is not liable for payment of any compensation beyond what is provided for in paragraphs 1 and 2 of this article except when the carrier and the shipper have agreed to calculate compensation in a different manner within the limits of chapter 16.

Article 23. Notice in case of loss, damage or delay

1. The carrier is presumed, in absence of proof to the contrary, to have delivered the goods according to their description in the contract particulars unless notice of loss of or damage to the goods, indicating the general nature of such loss or damage, was given to the carrier or the performing party that delivered the goods before or at the time of the delivery, or, if the loss or damage is not apparent, within seven working days at the place of delivery after the delivery of the goods.

2. Failure to provide the notice referred to in this article to the carrier or the performing party shall not affect the right to claim compensation for loss of or damage to the goods under this Convention, nor shall it affect the allocation of the burden of proof set out in article 17.

3. The notice referred to in this article is not required in respect of loss or dam-

age that is ascertained in a joint inspection of the goods by the person to which they have been delivered and the carrier or the maritime performing party against which liability is being asserted.

4.   No compensation in respect of delay is payable unless notice of loss due to delay was given to the carrier within twenty-one consecutive days of delivery of the goods.

5.   When the notice referred to in this article is given to the performing party that delivered the goods, it has the same effect as if that notice was given to the carrier, and notice given to the carrier has the same effect as a notice given to a maritime performing party.

6.   In the case of any actual or apprehended loss or damage, the parties to the dispute shall give all reasonable facilities to each other for inspecting and tallying the goods and shall provide access to records and documents relevant to the carriage of the goods.

CHAPTER 6. ADDITIONAL PROVISIONS RELATING TO PARTICULAR STAGES OF CARRIAGE

Article 24. Deviation

When pursuant to applicable law a deviation constitutes a breach of the carrier's obligations, such deviation of itself shall not deprive the carrier or a maritime performing party of any defence or limitation of this Convention, except to the extent provided in article 61.

Article 25. Deck cargo on ships

1.   Goods may be carried on the deck of a ship only if:

(a)   Such carriage is required by law;

(b)   They are carried in or on containers or vehicles that are fit for deck carriage, and the decks are specially fitted to carry such containers or vehicles; or

(c)   The carriage on deck is in accordance with the contract of carriage, or the customs, usages or practices of the trade in question.

2.   The provisions of this Convention relating to the liability of the carrier apply to the loss of, damage to or delay in the delivery of goods carried on deck pursuant to paragraph 1 of this article, but the carrier is not liable for loss of or damage to such goods, or delay in their delivery, caused by the special risks involved in their carriage on deck when the goods are carried in accordance with subparagraphs 1 (a) or (c) of this article.

3.   If the goods have been carried on deck in cases other than those permitted pursuant to paragraph 1 of this article, the carrier is liable for loss of or damage to the goods or delay in their delivery that is exclusively caused by their carriage on deck, and is

not entitled to the defences provided for in article 17.

4. The carrier is not entitled to invoke subparagraph 1 (c) of this article against a third party that has acquired a negotiable transport document or a negotiable electronic transport record in good faith, unless the contract particulars state that the goods may be carried on deck.

5. If the carrier and shipper expressly agreed that the goods would be carried under deck, the carrier is not entitled to the benefit of the limitation of liability for any loss of, damage to or delay in the delivery of the goods to the extent that such loss, damage, or delay resulted from their carriage on deck.

Article 26. Carriage preceding or subsequent to sea carriage

When loss of or damage to goods, or an event or circumstance causing a delay in their delivery, occurs during the carrier's period of responsibility but solely before their loading onto the ship or solely after their discharge from the ship, the provisions of this Convention do not prevail over those provisions of another international instrument that, at the time of such loss, damage or event or circumstance causing delay:

(a) Pursuant to the provisions of such international instrument would have applied to all or any of the carrier's activities if the shipper had made a separate and direct contract with the carrier in respect of the particular stage of carriage where the loss of, or damage to goods, or an event or circumstance causing delay in their delivery occurred;

(b) Specifically provide for the carrier's liability, limitation of liability, or time for suit; and

(c) Cannot be departed from by contract either at all or to the detriment of the shipper under that instrument.

CHAPTER 7. OBLIGATIONS OF THE SHIPPER TO THE CARRIER

Article 27. Delivery for carriage

1. Unless otherwise agreed in the contract of carriage, the shipper shall deliver the goods ready for carriage. In any event, the shipper shall deliver the goods in such condition that they will withstand the intended carriage, including their loading, handling, stowing, lashing and securing, and unloading, and that they will not cause harm to persons or property.

2. The shipper shall properly and carefully perform any obligation assumed under an agreement made pursuant to article 13, paragraph 2.

3. When a container is packed or a vehicle is loaded by the shipper, the shipper

shall properly and carefully stow, lash and secure the contents in or on the container or vehicle, and in such a way that they will not cause harm to persons or property.

Article 28. Cooperation of the shipper and the carrier in providing information and instructions

The carrier and the shipper shall respond to requests from each other to provide information and instructions required for the proper handling and carriage of the goods if the information is in the requested party's possession or the instructions are within the requested party's reasonable ability to provide and they are not otherwise reasonably available to the requesting party.

Article 29. Shipper's obligation to provide information, instructions and documents

1. The shipper shall provide to the carrier in a timely manner such information, instructions and documents relating to the goods that are not otherwise reasonably available to the carrier, and that are reasonably necessary:

(a) For the proper handling and carriage of the goods, including precautions to be taken by the carrier or a performing party; and

(b) For the carrier to comply with law, regulations or other requirements of public authorities in connection with the intended carriage, provided that the carrier notifies the shipper in a timely manner of the information, instructions and documents it requires.

2. Nothing in this article affects any specific obligation to provide certain information, instructions and documents related to the goods pursuant to law, regulations or other requirements of public authorities in connection with the intended carriage.

Article 30. Basis of shipper's liability to the carrier

1. The shipper is liable for loss or damage sustained by the carrier if the carrier proves that such loss or damage was caused by a breach of the shipper's obligations under this Convention.

2. Except in respect of loss or damage caused by a breach by the shipper of its obligations pursuant to articles 31, paragraph 2, and 32, the shipper is relieved of all or part of its liability if the cause or one of the causes of the loss or damage is not attributable to its fault or to the fault of any person referred to in article 34.

3. When the shipper is relieved of part of its liability pursuant to this article, the shipper is liable only for that part of the loss or damage that is attributable to its fault or to the fault of any person referred to in article 34.

Article 31. Information for compilation of contract particulars

1.   The shipper shall provide to the carrier, in a timely manner, accurate information required for the compilation of the contract particulars and the issuance of the transport documents or electronic transport records, including the particulars referred to in article 36, paragraph 1; the name of the party to be identified as the shipper in the contract particulars; the name of the consignee, if any; and the name of the person to whose order the transport document or electronic transport record is to be issued, if any.

2.   The shipper is deemed to have guaranteed the accuracy at the time of receipt by the carrier of the information that is provided according to paragraph 1 of this article. The shipper shall indemnify the carrier against loss or damage resulting from the inaccuracy of such information.

Article 32. Special rules on dangerous goods

When goods by their nature or character are, or reasonably appear likely to become, a danger to persons, property or the environment:

(a)   The shipper shall in-form the carrier of the dangerous nature or character of the goods in a timely manner before they are delivered to the carrier or a performing party. If the shipper fails to do so and the carrier or performing party does not otherwise have knowledge of their dangerous nature or character, the shipper is liable to the carrier for loss or damage resulting from such failure to inform; and

(b)   The shipper shall mark or label dangerous goods in accordance with any law, regulations or other requirements of public authorities that apply during any stage of the intended carriage of the goods. If the shipper fails to do so, it is liable to the carrier for loss or damage resulting from such failure.

Article 33. Assumption of shipper's rights and obligations by the documentary shipper

1.   A documentary shipper is subject to the obligations and liabilities imposed on the shipper pursuant to this chapter and pursuant to article 55, and is entitled to the shipper's rights and defences provided by this chapter and by chapter 13.

2.   Paragraph 1 of this article does not affect the obligations, liabilities, rights or defences of the shipper.

Article 34. Liability of the shipper for other persons

The shipper is liable for the breach of its obligations under this Convention caused by the acts or omissions of any person, including employees, agents and subcontractors, to which it has entrusted the performance of any of its obligations, but the shipper is not liable for acts or omissions of the carrier or a performing party acting on behalf of the carrier, to which the shipper has entrusted the performance of its obligations.

CHAPTER 8. TRANSPORT DOCUMENTS AND ELECTRONIC TRANSPORT RECORDS

Article 35. Issuance of the transport document or the electronic transport record

Unless the shipper and the carrier have agreed not to use a transport document or an electronic transport record, or it is the custom, usage or practice of the trade not to use one, upon delivery of the goods for carriage to the carrier or performing party, the shipper or, if the shipper consents, the documentary shipper, is entitled to obtain from the carrier, at the shipper's option:

(a) A non-negotiable transport document or, subject to article 8, subparagraph (a), a non-negotiable electronic transport record; or

(b) An appropriate negotiable transport document or, subject to article 8, subparagraph (a), a negotiable electronic transport record, unless the shipper and the carrier have agreed not to use a negotiable transport document or negotiable electronic transport record, or it is the custom, usage or practice of the trade not to use one.

Article 36. Contract particulars

1. The contract particulars in the transport document or electronic transport record referred to in article 35 shall include the following information, as furnished by the shipper:

(a) A description of the goods as appropriate for the transport;
(b) The leading marks necessary for identification of the goods;
(c) The number of packages or pieces, or the quantity of goods; and
(d) The weight of the goods, if furnished by the shipper.

2. The contract particulars in the transport document or electronic transport record referred to in article 35 shall also include:

(a) A statement of the apparent order and condition of the goods at the time the carrier or a performing party receives them for carriage;
(b) The name and address of the carrier;
(c) The date on which the carrier or a performing party received the goods, or on which the goods were loaded on board the ship, or on which the transport document or electronic transport record was issued; and
(d) If the transport document is negotiable, the number of originals of the negotiable transport document, when more than one original is issued.

3. The contract particulars in the transport document or electronic transport record referred to in article 35 shall further include:
   (a) The name and address of the consignee, if named by the shipper;
   (b) The name of a ship, if specified in the contract of carriage;
   (c) The place of receipt and, if known to the carrier, the place of delivery; and
   (d) The port of loading and the port of discharge, if specified in the contract of carriage.

4. For the purposes of this article, the phrase "apparent order and condition of the goods" in subparagraph 2 (a) of this article refers to the order and condition of the goods based on:
   (a) A reasonable external inspection of the goods as packaged at the time the shipper delivers them to the carrier or a performing party; and
   (b) Any additional inspection that the carrier or a performing party actually performs before issuing the transport document or electronic transport record.

Article 37. Identity of the carrier

1. If a carrier is identified by name in the contract particulars, any other information in the transport document or electronic transport record relating to the identity of the carrier shall have no effect to the extent that it is inconsistent with that identification.

2. If no person is identified in the contract particulars as the carrier as required pursuant to article 36, subparagraph 2 (b), but the contract particulars indicate that the goods have been loaded on board a named ship, the registered owner of that ship is presumed to be the carrier, unless it proves that the ship was under a bareboat charter at the time of the carriage and it identifies this bareboat charterer and indicates its address, in which case this bareboat charterer is presumed to be the carrier. Alternatively, the registered owner may rebut the presumption of being the carrier by identifying the carrier and indicating its address. The bareboat charterer may rebut any presumption of being the carrier in the same manner.

3. Nothing in this article prevents the claimant from proving that any person other than a person identified in the contract particulars or pursuant to paragraph 2 of this article is the carrier.

Article 38. Signature

1. A transport document shall be signed by the carrier or a person acting on its behalf.

2. An electronic transport record shall include the electronic signature of the

carrier or a person acting on its behalf. Such electronic signature shall identify the signatory in relation to the electronic transport record and indicate the carrier's authorization of the electronic transport record.

Article 39. Deficiencies in the contract particulars

1. The absence or inaccuracy of one or more of the contract particulars referred to in article 36, paragraphs 1, 2 or 3, does not of itself affect the legal character or validity of the transport document or of the electronic transport record.

2. If the contract particulars include the date but fail to indicate its significance, the date is deemed to be:

(a) The date on which all of the goods indicated in the transport document or electronic transport record were loaded on board the ship, if the contract particulars indicate that the goods have been loaded on board a ship; or

(b) The date on which the carrier or a performing party received the goods, if the contract particulars do not indicate that the goods have been loaded on board a ship.

3. If the contract particulars fail to state the apparent order and condition of the goods at the time the carrier or a performing party receives them, the contract particulars are deemed to have stated that the goods were in apparent good order and condition at the time the carrier or a performing party received them.

Article 40. Qualifying the information relating to the goods in the contract particulars

1. The carrier shall qualify the information referred to in article 36, paragraph 1, to indicate that the carrier does not assume responsibility for the accuracy of the information furnished by the shipper if:

(a) The carrier has actual knowledge that any material statement in the transport document or electronic transport record is false or misleading; or

(b) The carrier has reasonable grounds to believe that a material statement in the transport document or electronic transport record is false or misleading.

2. Without prejudice to paragraph 1 of this article, the carrier may qualify the information referred to in article 36, paragraph 1, in the circumstances and in the manner set out in paragraphs 3 and 4 of this article to indicate that the carrier does not assume responsibility for the accuracy of the information furnished by the shipper.

3. When the goods are not delivered for carriage to the carrier or a performing party in a closed container or vehicle, or when they are delivered in a closed container or vehicle and the carrier or a performing party actually inspects them, the carrier may qualify the information referred to in article 36, paragraph 1, if:

CHAPTER 8. TRANSPORT DOCUMENTS AND ELECTRONIC TRANSPORT RECORDS

(a) The carrier had no physically practicable or commercially reasonable means of checking the information furnished by the shipper, in which case it may indicate which information it was unable to check; or

(b) The carrier has reasonable grounds to believe the information furnished by the shipper to be inaccurate, in which case it may include a clause providing what it reasonably considers accurate information.

4. When the goods are delivered for carriage to the carrier or a performing party in a closed container or vehicle, the carrier may qualify the information referred to in:

(a) Article 36, subparagraphs 1 (a), (b), or (c), if:

(i) The goods inside the container or vehicle have not actually been inspected by the carrier or a performing party; and

(ii) Neither the carrier nor performing party otherwise has actual knowledge of its contents before issuing the transport document or the electronic transport record; and

(b) Article 36, subparagraph 1 (d), if:

(i) Neither the carrier nor performing party weighed the container or vehicle, and the shipper and the carrier had not agreed prior to the shipment that the container or vehicle would be weighed and the weight would be included in the contract particulars; or

(ii) There was no physically practicable or commercially reasonable means of checking the weight of the container or vehicle.

Article 41. Evidentiary effect of the contract particulars

Except to the extent that the contract particulars have been qualified in the circumstances and in the manner set out in article

40:

(a) A transport document or an electronic transport record is prima facie evidence of the carrier's receipt of the goods as stated in the contract particulars;

(b) Proof to the contrary by the carrier in respect of any contract particulars shall not be admissible, when such contract particulars are included in:

(i) A negotiable transport document or a negotiable electronic transport record that is transferred to a third party acting in good faith; or

(ii) A non-negotiable transport document that indicates that it must be surrendered in order to obtain delivery of the goods and is transferred to the consignee acting in good faith;

(c) Proof to the contrary by the carrier shall not be admissible against a consignee that in good faith has acted in reliance on any of the following contract particulars included in a non-negotiable transport document or a non-negotiable electronic transport record:

    (i)   The contract particulars referred to in article 36, paragraph 1, when such contract particulars are furnished by the carrier;

    (ii)   The number, type and identifying numbers of the containers, but not the identifying numbers of the container seals; and

    (iii)   The contract particulars referred to in article 36, paragraph 2.

Article 42. "Freight prepaid"

If the contract particulars contain the statement "freight prepaid" or a statement of a similar nature, the carrier cannot assert against the holder or the consignee the fact that the freight has not been paid. This article does not apply if the holder or the consignee is also the shipper.

CHAPTER 9. DELIVERY OF THE GOODS

Article 43. Obligation to accept delivery

When the goods have arrived at their destination, the consignee that demands delivery of the goods under the contract of carriage shall accept delivery of the goods at the time or within the time period and at the location agreed in the contract of carriage or, failing such agreement, at the time and location at which, having regard to the terms of the contract, the customs, usages or practices of the trade and the circumstances of the carriage, delivery could reasonably be expected.

Article 44. Obligation to acknowledge receipt

On request of the carrier or the performing party that delivers the goods, the consignee shall acknowledge receipt of the goods from the carrier or the performing party in the manner that is customary at the place of delivery. The carrier may refuse delivery if the consignee refuses to acknowledge such receipt.

Article 45. Delivery when no negotiable transport document or negotiable electronic transport record is issued

When neither a negotiable transport document nor a negotiable electronic transport record has been issued:

    (a)   The carrier shall deliver the goods to the consignee at the time and location referred to in article 43. The carrier may refuse delivery if the person claiming to be the consignee does not properly identify itself as the consignee on the request of the carrier;

(b) If the name and address of the consignee are not referred to in the contract particulars, the controlling party shall prior to or upon the arrival of the goods at the place of destination advise the carrier of such name and address;

(c) Without prejudice to article 48, paragraph 1, if the goods are not deliverable because (i) the consignee, after having received a notice of arrival, does not, at the time or within the time period referred to in article 43, claim delivery of the goods from the carrier after their arrival at the place of destination, (ii) the carrier refuses delivery because the person claiming to be the consignee does not properly identify itself as the consignee, or (iii) the carrier is, after reasonable effort, unable to locate the consignee in order to request delivery instructions, the carrier may so advise the controlling party and request instructions in respect of the delivery of the goods. If, after reasonable effort, the carrier is unable to locate the controlling party, the carrier may so advise the shipper and request instructions in respect of the delivery of the goods. If, after reasonable effort, the carrier is unable to locate the shipper, the carrier may so advise the documentary shipper and request instructions in respect of the delivery of the goods;

(d) The carrier that delivers the goods upon instruction of the controlling party, the shipper or the documentary shipper pursuant to subparagraph (c) of this article is discharged from its obligations to deliver the goods under the contract of carriage.

Article 46. Delivery when a non-negotiable transport document that requires surrender is issued

When a non-negotiable transport document has been issued that indicates that it shall be surrendered in order to obtain delivery of the goods:

(a) The carrier shall deliver the goods at the time and location referred to in article 43 to the consignee upon the consignee properly identifying itself on the request of the carrier and surrender of the non-negotiable document. The carrier may refuse delivery if the person claiming to be the consignee fails to properly identify itself on the request of the carrier, and shall refuse delivery if the non negotiable document is not surrendered. If more than one original of the non negotiable document has been issued, the surrender of one original will suffice and the other originals cease to have any effect or validity;

(b) Without prejudice to article 48, paragraph 1, if the goods are not deliverable because (i) the consignee, after having received a notice of arrival, does not, at the time or within the time period referred to in article 43, claim delivery of the goods from the carrier after their arrival at the place of destination, (ii) the carrier refuses delivery because the person claiming to be the consignee does not properly identify itself as the consignee or does not surrender the document, or (iii) the carrier is, after reasonable effort, unable to locate the consignee in order to request delivery instructions, the carrier may so advise the shipper and request instructions in respect of the delivery of the goods. If, after reasonable effort, the carrier is unable to locate the shipper, the carrier may so advise the documentary shipper and request instructions in respect of the delivery of the goods;

(c) The carrier that delivers the goods upon instruction of the shipper or the documentary shipper pursuant to subparagraph (b) of this article is discharged from its obligation to deliver the goods under the contract of carriage, irrespective of whether the non-negotiable transport document has been surrendered to it.

Article 47. Delivery when a negotiable transport document or negotiable electronic transport record is issued

1. When a negotiable transport document or a negotiable electronic transport record has been issued:

(a) The holder of the negotiable transport document or negotiable electronic transport record is entitled to claim delivery of the goods from the carrier after they have arrived at the place of destination, in which event the carrier shall deliver the goods at the time and location referred to in article 43 to the holder:

(i) Upon surrender of the negotiable transport document and, if the holder is one of the persons referred to in article 1, subparagraph 10 (a)(i), upon the holder properly identifying itself; or

(ii) Upon demonstration by the holder, in accordance with the procedures referred to in article 9, paragraph 1, that it is the holder of the negotiable electronic transport record;

(b) The carrier shall refuse delivery if the requirements of subparagraph (a)(i) or (a)(ii) of this paragraph are not met;

(c) If more than one original of the negotiable transport document has been issued, and the number of originals is stated in that document, the surrender of one original will suffice and the other originals cease to have any effect or validity. When a negotiable electronic transport record has been used, such electronic transport record ceases to have any effect or validity upon delivery to the holder in accordance with the procedures required by article 9, paragraph 1.

2. Without prejudice to article 48, paragraph 1, if the negotiable transport document or the negotiable electronic transport record expressly states that the goods may be delivered without the surrender of the transport document or the electronic transport record, the following rules apply:

(a) If the goods are not deliverable because (i) the holder, after having received a notice of arrival, does not, at the time or within the time period referred to in article 43, claim delivery of the goods from the carrier after their arrival at the place of destination, (ii) the carrier refuses delivery because the person claiming to be a holder does not properly identify itself as one of the persons referred to in article 1, subparagraph 10 (a)(i), or (iii) the carrier is, after reasonable effort, unable to locate the holder in order to request delivery instructions, the carrier may so advise the shipper and request instructions in respect of the delivery of the goods. If, after reasonable effort, the carrier is unable to locate the shipper, the carrier may so advise the documentary shipper and request instructions in respect of the delivery of the goods;

(b) The carrier that delivers the goods upon instruction of the shipper or the documentary shipper in accordance with subparagraph 2 (a) of this article is discharged from its obligation to deliver the goods under the contract of carriage to the holder, irrespective of whether the negotiable transport document has been surrendered to it, or the person claiming delivery under a negotiable electronic transport record has demonstrated, in accordance with the procedures referred to in article 9, paragraph 1, that it is the holder;

(c) The person giving instructions under subparagraph 2 (a) of this article shall indemnify the carrier against loss arising from its being held liable to the holder under subparagraph 2 (e) of this article. The carrier may refuse to follow those instructions if the person fails to provide adequate security as the carrier may reasonably request;

(d) A person that becomes a holder of the negotiable transport document or the negotiable electronic transport record after the carrier has delivered the goods pursuant to subparagraph 2 (b) of this article, but pursuant to contractual or other arrangements made before such delivery acquires rights against the carrier under the contract of carriage, other than the right to claim delivery of the goods;

(e) Notwithstanding subparagraphs 2 (b) and 2 (d) of this article, a holder that becomes a holder after such delivery, and that did not have and could not reasonably have had knowledge of such delivery at the time it became a holder, acquires the rights incorporated in the negotiable transport document or negotiable electronic transport record. When the contract particulars state the expected time of arrival of the goods, or indicate how to obtain information as to whether the goods have been delivered, it is presumed that the holder at the time that it became a holder had or could reasonably have had knowledge of the delivery of the goods.

Article 48. Goods remaining undelivered

1. For the purposes of this article, goods shall be deemed to have remained undelivered only if, after their arrival at the place of destination:

(a) The consignee does not accept delivery of the goods pursuant to this chapter at the time and location referred to in article 43;

(b) The controlling party, the holder, the shipper or the documentary shipper cannot be found or does not give the carrier adequate instructions pursuant to articles 45, 46 and 47;

(c) The carrier is entitled or required to refuse delivery pursuant to articles 44, 45, 46 and 47;

(d) The carrier is not allowed to deliver the goods to the consignee pursuant to the law or regulations of the place at which delivery is requested; or

(e) The goods are otherwise undeliverable by the carrier.

2. Without prejudice to any other rights that the carrier may have against the shipper, controlling party or consignee, if the goods have remained undelivered, the carrier may, at the risk and expense of the person entitled to the goods, take such action in respect of the goods as circumstances may reasonably require, including:

(a) To store the goods at any suitable place;

(b) To unpack the goods if they are packed in containers or vehicles, or to act otherwise in respect of the goods, including by moving them; and

(c) To cause the goods to be sold or destroyed in accordance with the practices or pursuant to the law or regulations of the place where the goods are located at the time.

3. The carrier may exercise the rights under paragraph 2 of this article only after it has given reasonable notice of the intended action under paragraph 2 of this article to the person stated in the contract particulars as the person, if any, to be notified of the arrival of the goods at the place of destination, and to one of the following persons in the order indicated, if known to the carrier: the consignee, the controlling party or the shipper.

4. If the goods are sold pursuant to subparagraph 2 (c) of this article, the carrier shall hold the proceeds of the sale for the benefit of the person entitled to the goods, subject to the deduction of any costs incurred by the carrier and any other amounts that are due to the carrier in connection with the carriage of those goods.

5. The carrier shall not be liable for loss of or damage to goods that occurs during the time that they remain undelivered pursuant to this article unless the claimant proves that such loss or damage resulted from the failure by the carrier to take steps that would have been reasonable in the circumstances to preserve the goods and that the carrier knew or ought to have known that the loss or damage to the goods would result from its failure to take such steps.

Article 49. Retention of goods

Nothing in this Convention affects a right of the carrier or a performing party that may exist pursuant to the contract of carriage or the applicable law to retain the goods to secure the payment of sums due.

CHAPTER 10. RIGHTS OF THE CONTROLLING PARTY

Article 50. Exercise and extent of right of control

1. The right of control may be exercised only by the controlling party and is limited to:

    (a) The right to give or modify instructions in respect of the goods that do not constitute a variation of the contract of carriage;

    (b) The right to obtain delivery of the goods at a scheduled port of call or, in respect of inland carriage, any place en route; and

    (c) The right to replace the consignee by any other person including the controlling party.

2. The right of control exists during the entire period of responsibility of the carrier, as provided in article 12, and ceases when that period expires.

Article 51. Identity of the controlling party and transfer of the right of control

1. Except in the cases referred to in paragraphs 2, 3 and 4 of this article:

    (a) The shipper is the controlling party unless the shipper, when the contract of carriage is concluded, designates the consignee, the documentary shipper or another person as the controlling party;

    (b) The controlling party is entitled to transfer the right of control to another person. The transfer becomes effective with respect to the carrier upon its notification of the transfer by the transferor, and the transferee becomes the controlling party; and

    (c) The controlling party shall properly identify itself when it exercises the right of control.

2. When a non-negotiable transport document has been issued that indicates that it shall be surrendered in order to obtain delivery of the goods:

    (a) The shipper is the controlling party and may transfer the right of control to the consignee named in the transport document by transferring the document to that person without endorsement. If more than one original of the document was issued, all originals shall be transferred in order to effect a transfer of the right of control; and

    (b) In order to exercise its right of control, the controlling party shall produce the document and properly identify itself. If more than one original of the document was issued, all originals shall be produced, failing which the right of control cannot be exercised.

3. When a negotiable transport document is issued:

(a) The holder or, if more than one original of the negotiable transport document is issued, the holder of all originals is the controlling party;

(b) The holder may transfer the right of control by transferring the negotiable transport document to another person in accordance with article 57. If more than one original of that document was issued, all originals shall be transferred to that person in order to effect a transfer of the right of control; and

(c) In order to exercise the right of control, the holder shall produce the negotiable transport document to the carrier, and if the holder is one of the persons referred to in article 1, subparagraph 10 (a)(i), the holder shall properly identify itself. If more than one original of the document was issued, all originals shall be produced, failing which the right of control cannot be exercised.

4. When a negotiable electronic transport record is issued:

(a) The holder is the controlling party;

(b) The holder may transfer the right of control to another person by transferring the negotiable electronic transport record in accordance with the procedures referred to in article 9, paragraph 1; and

(c) In order to exercise the right of control, the holder shall demonstrate, in accordance with the procedures referred to in article 9, paragraph 1, that it is the holder.

Article 52. Carrier's execution of instructions

1. Subject to paragraphs 2 and 3 of this article, the carrier shall execute the instructions referred to in article 50 if:

(a) The person giving such instructions is entitled to exercise the right of control;

(b) The instructions can reasonably be executed according to their terms at the moment that they reach the carrier; and

(c) The instructions will not interfere with the normal operations of the carrier, including its delivery practices.

2. In any event, the controlling party shall reimburse the carrier for any reasonable additional expense that the carrier may incur and shall indemnify the carrier against loss or damage that the carrier may suffer as a result of diligently executing any instruction pursuant to this article, including compensation that the carrier may become liable to pay for loss of or damage to other goods being carried.

3. The carrier is entitled to obtain security from the controlling party for the amount of additional expense, loss or damage that the carrier reasonably expects will arise in connection with the execution of an instruction pursuant to this article. The carrier may refuse to carry out the instructions if no such security is provided.

4. The carrier's liability for loss of or damage to the goods or for delay in delivery resulting from its failure to comply with the instructions of the controlling party in breach of its obligation pursuant to paragraph 1 of this article shall be subject to articles 17 to 23, and the amount of the compensation payable by the carrier shall be subject to articles 59 to 61.

Article 53. Deemed delivery

Goods that are delivered pursuant to an instruction in accordance with article 52, paragraph 1, are deemed to be delivered at the place of destination, and the provisions of chapter 9 relating to such delivery apply to such goods.

Article 54. Variations to the contract of carriage

1. The controlling party is the only person that may agree with the carrier to variations to the contract of carriage other than those referred to in article 50, subparagraphs 1 (b) and (c).

2. Variations to the contract of carriage, including those referred to in article 50, subparagraphs 1 (b) and (c), shall be stated in a negotiable transport document or in a non-negotiable transport document that requires surrender, or incorporated in a negotiable electronic transport record, or, upon the request of the controlling party, shall be stated in a non-negotiable transport document or incorporated in a non-negotiable electronic transport record. If so stated or incorporated, such variations shall be signed in accordance with article 38.

Article 55. Providing additional information, instructions or documents to carrier

1. The controlling party, on request of the carrier or a performing party, shall provide in a timely manner information, instructions or documents relating to the goods not yet provided by the shipper and not otherwise reasonably available to the carrier that the carrier may reasonably need to perform its obligations under the contract of carriage.

2. If the carrier, after reasonable effort, is unable to locate the controlling party or the controlling party is unable to provide adequate information, instructions or documents to the carrier, the shipper shall provide them. If the carrier, after reasonable effort, is unable to locate the shipper, the documentary shipper shall provide such information, in-

structions or documents.

Article 56. Variation by agreement

The parties to the contract of carriage may vary the effect of articles 50, subparagraphs 1 (b) and (c), 50, paragraph 2, and 52. The parties may also restrict or exclude the transferability of the right of control referred to in article 51, subparagraph 1 (b).

CHAPTER 11. TRANSFER OF RIGHTS

Article 57. When a negotiable transport document or negotiable electronic transport record is issued

1. When a negotiable transport document is issued, the holder may transfer the rights incorporated in the document by transferring it to another person:

    (a) Duly endorsed either to such other person or in blank, if an order document; or

    (b) Without endorsement, if: (i) a bearer document or a blank endorsed document; or (ii) a document made out to the order of a named person and the transfer is between the first holder and the named person.

2. When a negotiable electronic transport record is issued, its holder may transfer the rights incorporated in it, whether it be made out to order or to the order of a named person, by transferring the electronic transport record in accordance with the procedures referred to in article 9, paragraph 1.

Article 58. Liability of holder

1. Without prejudice to article 55, a holder that is not the shipper and that does not exercise any right under the contract of carriage does not assume any liability under the contract of carriage solely by reason of being a holder.

2. A holder that is not the shipper and that exercises any right under the contract of carriage assumes any liabilities imposed on it under the contract of carriage to the extent that such liabilities are incorporated in or ascertainable from the negotiable transport document or the negotiable electronic transport record.

3. For the purposes of paragraphs 1 and 2 of this article, a holder that is not the shipper does not exercise any right under the contract of carriage solely because:

    (a) It agrees with the carrier, pursuant to article 10, to replace a negotiable transport document by a negotiable electronic transport record or to replace a negotiable electronic transport record by a negotiable transport document; or

(b) It transfers its rights pursuant to article 57.

CHAPTER 12. LIMITS OF LIABILITY

Article 59. Limits of liability

1. Subject to articles 60 and 61, paragraph 1, the carrier's liability for breaches of its obligations under this Convention is limited to 875 units of account per package or other shipping unit, or 3 units of account per kilogram of the gross weight of the goods that are the subject of the claim or dispute, whichever amount is the higher, except when the value of the goods has been declared by the shipper and included in the contract particulars, or when a higher amount than the amount of limitation of liability set out in this article has been agreed upon between the carrier and the shipper.

2. When goods are carried in or on a container, pallet or similar article of transport used to consolidate goods, or in or on a vehicle, the packages or shipping units enumerated in the contract particulars as packed in or on such article of transport or vehicle are deemed packages or shipping units. If not so enumerated, the goods in or on such article of transport or vehicle are deemed one shipping unit.

3. The unit of account referred to in this article is the Special Drawing Right as defined by the International Monetary Fund. The amounts referred to in this article are to be converted into the national currency of a State according to the value of such currency at the date of judgement or award or the date agreed upon by the parties. The value of a national currency, in terms of the Special Drawing Right, of a Contracting State that is a member of the International Monetary Fund is to be calculated in accordance with the method of valuation applied by the International Monetary Fund in effect at the date in question for its operations and transactions. The value of a national currency, in terms of the Special Drawing Right, of a Contracting State that is not a member of the International Monetary Fund is to be calculated in a manner to be determined by that State.

Article 60. Limits of liability for loss caused by delay

Subject to article 61, paragraph 2, compensation for loss of or damage to the goods due to delay shall be calculated in accordance with article 22 and liability for economic loss due to delay is limited to an amount equivalent to two and one-half times the freight payable on the goods delayed. The total amount payable pursuant to this article and article 59, paragraph 1, may not exceed the limit that would be established pursuant to article 59, paragraph 1, in respect of the total loss of the goods concerned.

Article 61. Loss of the benefit of limitation of liability

1.   Neither the carrier nor any of the persons referred to in article 18 is entitled to the benefit of the limitation of liability as provided in article 59, or as provided in the contract of carriage, if the claimant proves that the loss resulting from the breach of the carrier's obligation under this Convention was attributable to a personal act or omission of the person claiming a right to limit done with the intent to cause such loss or recklessly and with knowledge that such loss would probably result.

2.   Neither the carrier nor any of the persons mentioned in article 18 is entitled to the benefit of the limitation of liability as provided in article 60 if the claimant proves that the delay in delivery resulted from a personal act or omission of the person claiming a right to limit done with the intent to cause the loss due to delay or recklessly and with knowledge that such loss would probably result.

CHAPTER 13. TIME FOR SUIT

Article 62. Period of time for suit

1.   No judicial or arbitral proceedings in respect of claims or disputes arising from a breach of an obligation under this Convention may be instituted after the expiration of a period of two years.

2.   The period referred to in paragraph 1 of this article commences on the day on which the carrier has delivered the goods or, in cases in which no goods have been delivered or only part of the goods have been delivered, on the last day on which the goods should have been delivered. The day on which the period commences is not included in the period.

3.   Notwithstanding the expiration of the period set out in paragraph 1 of this article, one party may rely on its claim as a defence or for the purpose of set-off against a claim asserted by the other party.

Article 63. Extension of time for suit

The period provided in article 62 shall not be subject to suspension or interruption, but the person against which a claim is made may at any time during the running of the period extend that period by a declaration to the claimant. This period may be further extended by another declaration or declarations.

Article 64. Action for indemnity

An action for indemnity by a person held liable may be instituted after the expiration of the period provided in article 62 if the indemnity action is instituted within the later of:

(a) The time allowed by the applicable law in the jurisdiction where proceedings are instituted; or

(b) Ninety days commencing from the day when the person instituting the action for indemnity has either settled the claim or been served with process in the action against itself, whichever is earlier.

Article 65. Actions against the person identified as the carrier

An action against the bareboat charterer or the person identified as the carrier pursuant to article 37, paragraph 2, may be instituted after the expiration of the period provided in article 62 if the action is instituted within the later of:

(a) The time allowed by the applicable law in the jurisdiction where proceedings are instituted; or

(b) Ninety days commencing from the day when the carrier has been identified, or the registered owner or bareboat charterer has rebutted the presumption that it is the carrier, pursuant to article 37, paragraph 2.

CHAPTER 14. JURISDICTION

Article 66. Actions against the carrier

Unless the contract of carriage contains an exclusive choice of court agreement that complies with article 67 or 72, the plaintiff has the right to institute judicial proceedings under this Convention against the carrier:

(a) In a competent court within the jurisdiction of which is situated one of the following places:

(i) The domicile of the carrier;

(ii) The place of receipt agreed in the contract of carriage;

(iii) The place of delivery agreed in the contract of carriage; or

(iv) The port where the goods are initially loaded on a ship or the port where the goods are finally discharged from a ship; or

(b) In a competent court or courts designated by an agreement between the shipper and the carrier for the purpose of deciding claims against the carrier that may arise under this Convention.

Article 67. Choice of court agreements

1. The jurisdiction of a court chosen in accordance with article 66, paragraph (b), is exclusive for disputes between the parties to the contract only if the parties so agree and the agreement conferring jurisdiction:

(a) Is contained in a volume contract that clearly states the names and addresses of the parties and either (i) is individually negotiated or (ii) contains a prominent statement that there is an exclusive choice of court agreement and specifies the sections of the volume contract containing that agreement; and

(b) Clearly designates the courts of one Contracting State or one or more specific courts of one Contracting State.

2. A person that is not a party to the volume contract is bound by an exclusive choice of court agreement concluded in accordance with paragraph 1 of this article only if:

(a) The court is in one of the places designated in article 66, paragraph (a);

(b) That agreement is contained in the transport document or electronic transport record;

(c) That person is given timely and adequate notice of the court where the action shall be brought and that the jurisdiction of that court is exclusive; and

(d) The law of the court seized recognizes that that person may be bound by the exclusive choice of court agreement.

Article 68. Actions against the maritime performing party

The plaintiff has the right to institute judicial proceedings under this Convention against the maritime performing party in a competent court within the jurisdiction of which is situated one of the following places:

(a) The domicile of the maritime performing party; or

(b) The port where the goods are received by the maritime performing party, the port where the goods are delivered by the maritime performing party or the port in which the maritime performing party performs its activities with respect to the goods.

Article 69. No additional bases of jurisdiction

Subject to articles 71 and 72, no judicial proceedings under this Convention against the carrier or a maritime performing party may be instituted in a court not designated pursuant to articles 66 or 68.

Article 70. Arrest and provisional or protective measures

Nothing in this Convention affects jurisdiction with regard to provisional or protective measures, including arrest. A court in a State in which a provisional or protective measure was taken does not have jurisdiction to determine the case upon its merits unless:

(a) The requirements of this chapter are fulfilled; or
(b) An international convention that applies in that State so provides.

Article 71. Consolidation and removal of actions

1. Except when there is an exclusive choice of court agreement that is binding pursuant to articles 67 or 72, if a single action is brought against both the carrier and the maritime performing party arising out of a single occurrence, the action may be instituted only in a court designated pursuant to both article 66 and article 68. If there is no such court, such action may be instituted in a court designated pursuant to article 68, subparagraph (b), if there is such a court.

2. Except when there is an exclusive choice of court agreement that is binding pursuant to articles 67 or 72, a carrier or a maritime performing party that institutes an action seeking a declaration of non-liability or any other action that would deprive a person of its right to select the forum pursuant to article 66 or 68 shall, at the request of the defendant, withdraw that action once the defendant has chosen a court designated pursuant to article 66 or 68, whichever is applicable, where the action may be recommenced.

Article 72. Agreement after a dispute has arisen and jurisdiction when the defendant has entered an appearance

1. After a dispute has arisen, the parties to the dispute may agree to resolve it in any competent court.

2. A competent court before which a defendant appears, without contesting jurisdiction in accordance with the rules of that court, has jurisdiction.

Article 73. Recognition and enforcement

1. A decision made in one Contracting State by a court having jurisdiction under this Convention shall be recognized and enforced in another Contracting State in accordance with the law of such latter Contracting State when both States have made a declaration in accordance with article 74.

2. A court may refuse recognition and enforcement based on the grounds for the refusal of recognition and enforcement available pursuant to its law.

3. This chapter shall not affect the application of the rules of a regional economic integration organization that is a party to this Convention, as concerns the recognition or enforcement of judgements as between member States of the regional economic inte-

gration organization, whether adopted before or after this Convention.

Article 74. Application of chapter 14

The provisions of this chapter shall bind only Contracting States that declare in accordance with article 91 that they will be bound by them.

CHAPTER 15. ARBITRATION

Article 75. Arbitration agreements

1. Subject to this chapter, parties may agree that any dispute that may arise relating to the carriage of goods under this Convention shall be referred to arbitration.

2. The arbitration proceedings shall, at the option of the person asserting a claim against the carrier, take place at:

(a) Any place designated for that purpose in the arbitration agreement; or

(b) Any other place situated in a State where any of the following places is located:

(i) The domicile of the carrier;

(ii) The place of receipt agreed in the contract of carriage;

(iii) The place of delivery agreed in the contract of carriage; or

(iv) The port where the goods are initially loaded on a ship or the port where the goods are finally discharged from a ship.

3. The designation of the place of arbitration in the agreement is binding for disputes between the parties to the agreement if the agreement is contained in a volume contract that clearly states the names and addresses of the parties and either:

(a) Is individually negotiated; or

(b) Contains a prominent statement that there is an arbitration agreement and specifies the sections of the volume contract containing the arbitration agreement.

4. When an arbitration agreement has been concluded in accordance with paragraph 3 of this article, a person that is not a party to the volume contract is bound by the designation of the place of arbitration in that agreement only if:

(a) The place of arbitration designated in the agreement is situated in one of the places referred to in subparagraph 2 (b) of this article;

(b) The agreement is contained in the transport document or electronic transport record;

(c) The person to be bound is given timely and adequate notice of the place of arbitration; and

(d) Applicable law permits that person to be bound by the arbitration agreement.

5. The provisions of paragraphs 1, 2, 3 and 4 of this article are deemed to be part of every arbitration clause or agreement, and any term of such clause or agreement to the extent that it is inconsistent therewith is void.

Article 76. Arbitration agreement in non-linertransportation

1. Nothing in this Convention affects the enforceability of an arbitration agreement in a contract of carriage in non-liner transportation to which this Convention or the provisions of this Convention apply by reason of:

(a) The application of article 7; or

(b) The parties' voluntary incorporation of this Convention in a contract of carriage that would not otherwise be subject to this Convention.

2. Notwithstanding paragraph 1 of this article, an arbitration agreement in a transport document or electronic transport record to which this Convention applies by reason of the application of article 7 is subject to this chapter unless such a transport document or electronic transport record:

(a) Identifies the parties to and the date of the charterparty or other contract excluded from the application of this Convention by reason of the application of article 6; and

(b) Incorporates by specific reference the clause in the charterparty or other contract that contains the terms of the arbitration agreement.

Article 77. Agreement to arbitrate after a dispute has arisen

Notwithstanding the provisions of this chapter and chapter 14, after a dispute has arisen the parties to the dispute may agree to resolve it by arbitration in any place.

Article 78. Application of chapter 15

The provisions of this chapter shall bind only Contracting States that declare in accordance with article 91 that they will be bound by them.

CHAPTER 16. VALIDITY OF CONTRACTUAL TERMS

Article 79. General provisions

1. Unless otherwise provided in this Convention, any term in a contract of carriage is void to the extent that it:

(a) Directly or indirectly excludes or limits the obligations of the carrier or a maritime performing party under this Convention;

(b) Directly or indirectly excludes or limits the liability of the carrier or a maritime performing party for breach of an obligation under this Convention; or

(c) Assigns a benefit of insurance of the goods in favour of the carrier or a person referred to in article 18.

2. Unless otherwise provided in this Convention, any term in a contract of carriage is void to the extent that it:

(a) Directly or indirectly excludes, limits or increases the obligations under this Convention of the shipper, consignee, controlling party, holder or documentary shipper; or

(b) Directly or indirectly excludes, limits or increases the liability of the shipper, consignee, controlling party, holder or documentary shipper for breach of any of its obligations under this Convention.

Article 80. Special rules for volume contracts

1. Notwithstanding article 79, as between the carrier and the shipper, a volume contract to which this Convention applies may provide for greater or lesser rights, obligations and liabilities than those imposed by this Convention.

2. A derogation pursuant to paragraph 1 of this article is binding only when:

(a) The volume contract contains a prominent statement that it derogates from this Convention;

(b) The volume contract is (i) individually negotiated or (ii) prominently specifies the sections of the volume contract containing the derogations;

(c) The shipper is given an opportunity and notice of the opportunity to conclude a contract of carriage on terms and conditions that comply with this Convention without any derogation under this article; and

(d) The derogation is neither (i) incorporated by reference from another document nor (ii) included in a contract of adhesion that is not subject to negotiation.

3. A carrier's public schedule of prices and services, transport document, electronic transport record or similar document is not a volume contract pursuant to paragraph 1 of this article, but a volume contract may incorporate such documents by reference as terms of the contract.

4. Paragraph 1 of this article does not apply to rights and obligations provided in articles 14, subparagraphs (a) and (b), 29 and 32 or to liability arising from the breach thereof, nor does it apply to any liability arising from an act or omission referred to in article 61.

5. The terms of the volume contract that derogate from this Convention, if the volume contract satisfies the requirements of paragraph 2 of this article, apply between the carrier and any person other than the shipper provided that:

(a) Such person received information that prominently states that the volume contract derogates from this Convention and gave its express consent to be bound by such derogations; and

(b) Such consent is not solely set forth in a carrier's public schedule of prices and services, transport document or electronic transport record.

6. The party claiming the benefit of the derogation bears the burden of proof that the conditions for derogation have been fulfilled.

Article 81. Special rules for live animals and certain other goods

Notwithstanding article 79 and without prejudice to article 80, the contract of carriage may exclude or limit the obligations or the liability of both the carrier and a maritime performing party if:

(a) The goods are live animals, but any such exclusion or limitation will not be effective if the claimant proves that the loss of or damage to the goods, or delay in delivery, resulted from an act or omission of the carrier or of a person referred to in article 18, done with the intent to cause such loss of or damage to the goods or such loss due to delay or done recklessly and with knowledge that such loss or damage or such loss due to delay would probably result; or

(b) The character or condition of the goods or the circumstances and terms and conditions under which the carriage is to be performed are such as reasonably to justify a special agreement, provided that such contract of carriage is not related to ordinary commercial shipments made in the ordinary course of trade and that no negotiable transport document or negotiable electronic transport record is issued for the carriage of the goods.

CHAPTER 17. MATTERS NOT GOVERNED BY THIS CONVENTION

Article 82. International conventions governing the carriage of goods by other modes of transport

Nothing in this Convention affects the application of any of the following international conventions in force at the time this Convention enters into force, including any future amendment to such conventions, that regulate the liability of the carrier for loss of or damage to the goods:

(a) Any convention governing the carriage of goods by air to the extent that such convention according to its provisions applies to any part of the contract of carriage;

(b) Any convention governing the carriage of goods by road to the extent that such convention according to its provisions applies to the carriage of goods that remain loaded on a road cargo vehicle carried on board a ship;

(c) Any convention governing the carriage of goods by rail to the extent that such convention according to its provisions applies to carriage of goods by sea as a supplement to the carriage by rail; or

(d) Any convention governing the carriage of goods by inland waterways to the extent that such convention according to its provisions applies to a carriage of goods without trans-shipment both by inland waterways and sea.

Article 83. Global limitation of liability

Nothing in this Convention affects the application of any international convention or national law regulating the global limitation of liability of vessel owners.

Article 84. General average

Nothing in this Convention affects the application of terms in the contract of carriage or provisions of national law regarding the adjustment of general average.

Article 85. Passengers and luggage

This Convention does not apply to a contract of carriage for passengers and their luggage.

Article 86. Damage caused by nuclear incident

No liability arises under this Convention for damage caused by a nuclear incident if the operator of a nuclear installation is liable for such damage

(a) Under the Paris Convention on Third Party Liability in the Field of Nuclear Energy of 29 July 1960 as amended by the Additional Protocol of 28 January 1964 and by the Protocols of 16 November 1982 and 12 February 2004, the Vienna Convention on Civil Liability for Nuclear Damage of 21 May 1963 as amended by the Joint Protocol Relating to the Application of the Vienna Convention and the Paris Convention of 21 September 1988 and as amended by the Protocol to Amend the 1963 Vienna Convention on Civil Liability for Nuclear Damage of 12 September 1997, or the Convention on Supplementary Compensation for Nuclear Damage of 12 September 1997, including any amendment to these conventions and any future convention in respect of the liability of the operator of a nuclear installation for damage caused by a nuclear incident; or

(b) Under national law applicable to the liability for such damage, provided that such law is in all respects as favourable to persons that may suffer damage as either the Paris or Vienna Conventions or the Convention on Supplementary Compensation for Nuclear Damage.

CHAPTER 18. FINAL CLAUSES

Article 87. Depositary

The Secretary-General of the United Nations is hereby designated as the depositary of this Convention.

Article 88. Signature, ratification, acceptance, approval or accession

1. This Convention is open for signature by all States at Rotterdam, the Netherlands, on 23 September 2009, and thereafter at the Headquarters of the United Nations in New York.

2. This Convention is subject to ratification, acceptance or approval by the signatory States.

3. This Convention is open for accession by all States that are not signatory States as from the date it is open for signature.

4. Instruments of ratification, acceptance, approval and accession are to be deposited with the Secretary-General of the United Nations.

Article 89. Denunciation of other conventions

1. A State that ratifies, accepts, approves or accedes to this Convention and is a party to the International Convention for the Unification of certain Rules relating to Bills of Lading signed at Brussels on 25 August 1924; to the Protocol signed on 23 February 1968 to amend the International Convention for the Unification of certain Rules relating to Bills of Lading signed at Brussels on 25 August 1924; or to the Protocol to amend the International Convention for the Unification of certain Rules relating to Bills of Lading as Modified by the Amending Protocol of 23 February 1968, signed at Brussels on 21 December 1979 shall at the same time denounce that Convention and the protocol or protocols thereto to which it is a party by notifying the Government of Belgium to that effect, with a declaration that the denunciation is to take effect as from the date when this Convention enters into force in respect of that State.

2. A State that ratifies, accepts, approves or accedes to this Convention and is a party to the United Nations Convention on the Carriage of Goods by Sea concluded at Hamburg on 31 March 1978 shall at the same time denounce that Convention by notifying the Secretary-General of the United Nations to that effect, with a declaration that the denunciation is to take effect as from the date when this Convention enters into force in re-

spect of that State.

3. For the purposes of this article, ratifications, acceptances, approvals and accessions in respect of this Convention by States parties to the instruments listed in paragraphs 1 and 2 of this article that are notified to the depositary after this Convention has entered into force are not effective until such denunciations as may be required on the part of those States in respect of these instruments have become effective. The depositary of this Convention shall consult with the Government of Belgium, as the depositary of the instruments referred to in paragraph 1 of this article, so as to ensure necessary coordination in this respect.

Article 90. Reservations

No reservation is permitted to this Convention.

Article 91. Procedure and effect of declarations

1. The declarations permitted by articles 74 and 78 may be made at any time. The initial declarations permitted by article 92, paragraph 1, and article 93, paragraph 2, shall be made at the time of signature, ratification, acceptance, approval or accession. No other declaration is permitted under this Convention.

2. Declarations made at the time of signature are subject to confirmation upon ratification, acceptance or approval.

3. Declarations and their confirmations are to be in writing and to be formally notified to the depositary.

4. A declaration takes effect simultaneously with the entry into force of this Convention in respect of the State concerned. However, a declaration of which the depositary receives formal notification after such entry into force takes effect on the first day of the month following the expiration of six months after the date of its receipt by the depositary.

5. Any State that makes a declaration under this Convention may withdraw it at any time by a formal notification in writing addressed to the depositary. The withdrawal of a declaration, or its modification where permitted by this Convention, takes effect on the first day of the month following the expiration of six months after the date of the receipt of the notification by the depositary.

Article 92. Effect in domestic territorial units

1. If a Contracting State has two or more territorial units in which different systems of law are applicable in relation to the matters dealt with in this Convention, it may,

at the time of signature, ratification, acceptance, approval or accession, declare that this Convention is to extend to all its territorial units or only to one or more of them, and may amend its declaration by submitting another declaration at any time.

2. These declarations are to be notified to the depositary and are to state expressly the territorial units to which the Convention extends.

3. When a Contracting State has declared pursuant to this article that this Convention extends to one or more but not all of its territorial units, a place located in a territorial unit to which this Convention does not extend is not considered to be in a Contracting State for the purposes of this Convention.

4. If a Contracting State makes no declaration pursuant to paragraph 1 of this article, the Convention is to extend to all territorial units of that State.

Article 93. Participation by regional economic integration organizations

1. A regional economic integration organization that is constituted by sovereign States and has competence over certain matters governed by this Convention may similarly sign, ratify, accept, approve or accede to this Convention. The regional economic integration organization shall in that case have the rights and obligations of a Contracting State, to the extent that that organization has competence over matters governed by this Convention. When the number of Contracting States is relevant in this Convention, the regional economic integration organization does not count as a Contracting State in addition to its member States which are Contracting States.

2. The regional economic integration organization shall, at the time of signature, ratification, acceptance, approval or accession, make a declaration to the depositary specifying the matters governed by this Convention in respect of which competence has been transferred to that organization by its member States. The regional economic integration organization shall promptly notify the depositary of any changes to the distribution of competence, including new transfers of competence, specified in the declaration pursuant to this paragraph.

3. Any reference to a "Contracting State" or "Contracting States" in this Convention applies equally to a regional economic integration organization when the context so requires.

Article 94. Entry into force

1. This Convention enters into force on the first day of the month following the expiration of one year after the date of deposit of the twentieth instrument of ratification, acceptance, approval or accession.

2. For each State that becomes a Contracting State to this Convention after the date of the deposit of the twentieth instrument of ratification, acceptance, approval or accession, this Convention enters into force on the first day of the month following the expiration of one year after the deposit of the appropriate instrument on behalf of that State.

3. Each Contracting State shall apply this Convention to contracts of carriage concluded on or after the date of the entry into force of this Convention in respect of that State.

Article 95. Revision and amendment

1. At the request of not less than one third of the Contracting States to this Convention, the depositary shall convene a conference of the Contracting States for revising or amending it.

2. Any instrument of ratification, acceptance, approval or accession deposited after the entry into force of an amendment to this Convention is deemed to apply to the Convention as amended.

Article 96. Denunciation of this Convention

1. A Contracting State may denounce this Convention at any time by means of a notification in writing addressed to the depositary.

2. The denunciation takes effect on the first day of the month following the expiration of one year after the notification is received by the depositary. If a longer period is specified in the notification, the denunciation takes effect upon the expiration of such longer period after the notification is received by the depositary.

DONE at New York, this eleventh day of December two thousand and eight, in a single original, of which the Arabic, Chinese, English, French, Russian and Spanish texts are equally authentic.

IN WITNESS WHEREOF the undersigned plenipotentiaries, being duly authorized by their respective Governments, have signed this Convention.

The Rotterdam Rules in the
Asia-Pacific Region

(英語版 アジア太平洋地域における
ロッテルダム・ルールズ)

2014年11月21日　初版第1刷発行

編著者　藤　田　友　敬

発行者　塚　原　秀　夫

発行所　株式会社　商事法務
〒103-0025 東京都中央区日本橋茅場町 3-9-10
TEL 03-5614-5643・FAX 03-3664-8844〔営業部〕
TEL 03-5614-5649〔書籍出版部〕
http://www.shojihomu.co.jp/

落丁・乱丁本はお取り替えいたします。　　印刷／(有)シンカイシャ
© 2014 Tomotaka Fujita　　　　　　　　　　Printed in Japan
Shojihomu Co., Ltd.
ISBN978-4-7857-2222-7
＊定価はカバーに表示してあります。